THE HISTORY AND THEORY
OF INTERNATIONAL LAW

Crafting the International Order

THE HISTORY AND THEORY OF INTERNATIONAL LAW

General Editors

In the past few decades the understanding of the relationship between nations has undergone a radical transformation. The role of the traditional nation-state is diminishing, along with many of the traditional vocabularies which were once used to describe what has been called, ever since Jeremy Bentham coined the phrase in 1780, 'international law'. The older boundaries between states are growing ever more fluid, new conceptions and new languages have emerged which are slowly coming to replace the image of a world of sovereign independent nation states which has dominated the study of international relations since the early nineteenth century. This redefinition of the international arena demands a new understanding of classical and contemporary questions in international and legal theory. It is the editors' conviction that the best way to achieve this is by bridging the traditional divide between international legal theory, intellectual history, and legal and political history. The aim of the series, therefore, is to provide a forum for historical studies, from classical antiquity to the twenty-first century, that are theoretically informed and for philosophical work that is historically conscious, in the hope that a new vision of the rapidly evolving international world, its past and its possible future, may emerge.

PREVIOUSLY PUBLISHED IN THIS SERIES

The Justification of War and International Order
From Past to Present
Edited by Lothar Brock and Hendrik Simon

Remaking Central Europe
The League of Nations and the Former Habsburg Lands
Edited by Peter Becker and Natasha Wheatley

Crafting the International Order

Practitioners and Practices of International Law since c. 1800

Edited by

MARCUS M. PAYK

and

KIM CHRISTIAN PRIEMEL

OXFORD
UNIVERSITY PRESS

OXFORD
UNIVERSITY PRESS

Great Clarendon Street, Oxford, OX2 6DP,
United Kingdom

Oxford University Press is a department of the University of Oxford. It furthers the University's objective of excellence in research, scholarship, and education by publishing worldwide. Oxford is a registered trade mark of Oxford University Press in the UK and in certain other countries

First Edition published in 2021

Impression: 1

Published in the United States of America by Oxford University Press
198 Madison Avenue, New York, NY 10016, United States of America

British Library Cataloguing in Publication Data

Data available

Library of Congress Control Number: 2020948166

ISBN 978–0–19–886383–0

DOI: 10.1093/oso/9780198863830.001.0001

Printed and bound by
CPI Group (UK) Ltd, Croydon, CR0 4YY

Series Editor's Preface: In Search of Normative Dark Matter

The relationship between politics and law has often been conceived as a dichotomy, as the relationship between two mutually exclusive domains characterized, respectively, by the exercise of raw power and the pull of normative reason. There is certainly a time-honoured sense in which what is law has ceased to be part of politics, and what is politically alive cannot acquire the dignity of law. Politics on this view never quite loses its smack of violence, whereas law promises the extinction of violence. As Cicero put it famously in his speech for Publius Sestius: we want to extinguish violence (*vis*), therefore the law (*jus*) must prevail.

This view has always had to contend with hard-nosed detractors who would mercilessly seek to undermine the dichotomy. Is not law always a thinly veiled instrument of the powerful to keep everyone else in check? Is law, in other words, not simply violence by another name? If we keep the conceptual distinction between law and politics, are we not the naïve victims of mere propaganda—is not law simply epiphenomenal smoke and mirrors, reducible entirely to the hard facts of power politics and violence? Starting with the Greek sophists, these sceptical views have always been with us, finding their most influential expression, perhaps, in St Augustine's sceptical view of states as robber bands in disguise.

The opposing view, always at least as normative as descriptive in its aim, has insisted that the law at least sometimes, under the right circumstances, could indeed aspire to a more autonomous status than the 'realist' Sophists or Augustinians deemed possible. When we attend more closely to this opposing view we realize that it is rarely expressed in terms of a simple dichotomy between politics and law but willing to ascribe an independent causal power to law, a normative pull, even granting that empirically and historically speaking, the law and politics always coexist on a continuum. Where Augustine, on some readings, saw states as robber bands bereft of any juridical underpinning, Cicero in his *On Duties* was willing to see robber bands as at least potential jural communities exhibiting certain juridical traits *in nuce*, observing that 'there are even laws among bandits which they obey and respect'.

One way to figure out which view of the relationship between law and politics is correct is to look to history and try to find out whether or not there has ever existed law, however mixed up with politics, in an even mildly autonomous sense. Such an empirical investigation might show that law could, however mixed up with politics, at least under certain circumstances develop independent normative energy and shape politics. Alternatively, the investigation might reveal that as a matter of contingent historical fact, politics has always ended up forcing its shape onto the law in a kind of causal one-way street.

What better historical context to test these various views than the last few hundred years, which have ostensibly exhibited a 'juridification' of international politics, and what better domain to test these views than what has been called since 1780 'international law'? If there is a domain within which politics can safely be assumed to play a powerful, even overpowering, role to the detriment of law, the realm of modern international relations between sovereign empires and states is surely it. Conversely, if there is as little as a trace of the autonomous normative pull of the law even in this realm, there is at least the possibility that under certain circumstances bandits, too, can be made to sense the tug of norms.

This is where the present volume comes in. It gives us a variegated range of amazingly detailed case studies which together provide a dense array of empirical evidence for the relationship between international law and international politics. These studies are not intended to be representative, for this volume is, as its editors Marcus Payk and Kim Christian Priemel write, not intended to provide 'a synthesis but a template'. But the case studies are ideally suited to bring historical light to the contested relationship between law and politics in that they look to the 'transmission belts' of legal order, to the unsung practitioners of international politics, the in-house government lawyers, diplomats, and legal advisors who applied legal concepts and legal argument on the ground. This is where the causal impact of either law or politics or both must be felt, as this is precisely the level at which a key part of the effect of legal concepts is experienced and where law shapes politics, if it ever does, and vice versa.

As the editors explain, for this kind of investigation individual agency is key. And indeed, the contributions to this volume are united by a keen interest in the 'foot soldiers' of international politics and their actions. This emphasis on individual actors comes at a cost; doctrine, legal substance as well as cultural, political, or economic structures receive far less weight, but, as the readers will see, the editors' resolute decision to focus on case studies of the practice of international law and politics pays off very handsomely. Not only does their approach fill the scholarly gap between histories of legal doctrine, on the one hand, and political practice and international politics, on the other, but it also gives us a far more differentiated view of the respective claims of international-relations 'realists' and international-law 'idealists'. The volume gives us, that is, the empirical means by which we can at least begin to assess the merits of claims on behalf of the efficacy of law in history.

Marcus Payk, in his contribution, points out that there is a 'general tendency to underestimate formalities and technicalities in international politics'. As it turns out, it is these formalities and technicalities, that is to say the professional influence of in-house lawyers of foreign ministries, no less than political bargaining, that still need exploring. Occasionally, as in Payk's contribution, this will lead to the impression that these legal formalities and technicalities carried within them the seeds of an almost Fullerian normativity of law, which could sometimes assume an autonomous weight, seeking to import even into the most political of decisions, such as those pertaining to the Treaty of Versailles, the shape of legal reasoning. Payk concludes by pointing out how 'blurred the boundary between law and politics really was', yet insists on the importance of the *pretence* that this 'boundary actually existed and mattered'. After reading Payk's sensitive description of the influence of the drafting committee at the Paris Peace Conference, one is inclined to think that the drafters of the treaty at times constrained the political agenda and thus, with pretence acquiring momentum, managed to go beyond mere pretence.

This volume shows that it is in the transformation of politics into technical legal language, legal argument, and treaty provisions where the 'secret life of international law' (Daniel Bethlehem) takes place. It is in this transformation, consequently, where normativity can be found in action and where the dark matter of international legal history from the late eighteenth century onwards must reside. Depending on one's baseline, then, the case studies assembled here by Marcus Payk and Kim Christian Priemel provide reasons for pessimism or for hope, for Augustine or for Cicero. The volume is replete with examples of how, through the increasing importance of legal arguments and legal language, normative expectations—the dark matter—that were originally created for contingent and even cynical reasons started to develop a life of their own, capable at times of outrunning political reality and developing a normative gravitational effect that can then become visible in rare glimpses and historical investigations such as those assembled in this volume.

Benjamin Straumann
New York City
3 November 2020

Contents

Contributors

Benjamin Coates is Associate Professor of History at Wake Forest University, North Carolina, United States

Andrew Cobbing is Associate Professor of History at the University of Nottingham, UK

Julia Eichenberg is Freigeist-Fellow and Lecturer in Modern European History at Humboldt University, Berlin, Germany

Gabriela A. Frei is Lecturer in Contemporary History and International Relations at Bundeswehr University, Munich, Germany

Michael Jonas is Lecturer in Modern History at Helmut Schmidt University, Hamburg, Germany, and Adjunct Professor at the University of Helsinki, Finland

Fabian Klose is Professor of International History and Historical Peace and Conflict Research at the University of Cologne, Germany

Marcus M. Payk is Professor of Modern History at Helmut Schmidt University, Hamburg, Germany

Kim Christian Priemel is Professor of Contemporary European History at the University of Oslo, Norway

Morten Rasmussen is Associate Professor of European History at the University of Copenhagen, Denmark

Katharina Rietzler is Lecturer in American History at the University of Sussex, UK

Abbreviations

AHR	American Historical Review
AJIL	American Journal of International Law
BFSP	British and Foreign State Papers
BPP	British Parliament Papers
BWCE	British War Crimes Executive
BYIL	British Yearbook of International Law
CEH	Contemporary European History
CEPAG	Commission des Etudes pour les Problèmes d'Après-Guerre
CFLN	French Committee of National Liberation
CISC	Confédération internationale des syndicats chrétiens
EC	European Community
ECJ	European Court of Justice
ECOSOC	United Nations Economic and Social Council
ECSC	European Coal and Steel Community
ECtHR	European Court of Human Rights
EDC	European Defence Community
EEC	European Economic Community
EJIL	European Journal of International Law
EPC	European Political Community
f.	folder
FO	Foreign Office
fol.	folio
FRUS	Papers Relating to the Foreign Relations of the United States
GPO	Government Printing Office
HA	High Authority
HMG	His Majesty's Government
ICJ	International Court of Justice
IDI	Institut de Droit International
ILA	International Law Association
ILO	International Labour Organization
IMT	International Military Tribunal
IPC	International Prize Court
JCLIL	Journal of Comparative Legislation and International Law
JHIL	Journal of the History of International Law
LG	London Gazette
LJIL	Leiden Journal of International Law
MP	Member of Parliament
MPEPIL	Max Planck Encyclopedia of Public International Law
MRP	Le Mouvement Républicain Populaire

NCO	Nederlandsche Commissie inzake Oorlogsmisdrijven
NGO	non-governmental organization
NJIL	Nordic Journal of International Law
NMT	Nuernberg Military Tribunals
NWCC	Netherlands War Crimes Commission
NY&B	New York and Bermudez Company
OSS	Office of Strategic Services
PCA	Permanent Court of Arbitration
PCAJ	Permanent Court of Arbitral Justice
PCIJ	Permanent Court of International Justice
PDP	Parti Démocrate Populaire
R2P	Responsibility to Protect
TVA	Tennessee Valley Authority
UD	Utrikesdepartementet
UK	United Kingdom
UN	United Nations
UNESCO	United Nations Educational, Scientific and Cultural Organization
UNWCC	United Nations War Crimes Commission

Archives

AD	Archives Diplomatiques, La Courneuve (France)
AGI	Archivo General de Indias, Sevilla (Spain)
AHC	Archives du Centre historique de Sciences Po, Paris (France)
AHN	Archivo Histórico Nacional, Madrid (Spain)
ALMU	Archives of Ludwigs-Maximilians-University, Munich (Germany)
ALSEC	Archive of the Legal Service of the European Commission, Brussels (Belgium)
AN	Archives Nationales, Paris (France)
ASFAE	Archives du Service public fédéral Affaires étrangères, Brussels (Belgium)
BAC	Brussels Archives Commission, Brussels (Belgium)
BAK	Bundesarchiv, Koblenz (Germany)
CAC	Churchill Archives Centre, Cambridge (UK)
CLL	Cornell Law Library, Ithaca, NY (US)
CLS	Columbia Law School, Arthur Diamond Law Library, New York, NY (US)
CU-RMBL	Columbia University, Rare Book & Manuscript Library, New York, NY (US)
FDRL	Franklin Delano Roosevelt Presidential Library, Hyde Park, NY (US)
FJM	Fondation Jean Monnet pour l'Europe, Lausanne (Switzerland)
GUL-SCRC	Georgetown University Library, Special Collections Research Center, Washington, DC (US)
HAEC, BAC	Historical Archives of the European Commission, Brussels Archives Commission, Brussels (Belgium)
HAEU	Historical Archives of the European Union, Florence (Italy)
HIA	Hoover Institution Archive, Stanford, CA (US)
HLL	Harvard Law Library, Cambridge, MA (US)
HSTL	Harry S. Truman Presidential Library, Independence, MO (US)
IALS	Institute of Advanced Legal Studies Archives, London (UK)
JFKL	John F. Kennedy Presidential Library, Boston, MA (US)
KB	Kungliga Biblioteket, Stockholm (Sweden)
LSF	Library of the Society of Friends, London (UK)
LoC	Library of Congress, Washington, DC (US)
NAI	National Archives of India, New Delhi (India)
NARA	National Archives and Records Administration, College Park, MD (US)
NADH	Nationaal Archief, Den Haag (Netherlands)
NLW	National Library of Wales, Aberystwyth (UK)
PAAA	Politisches Archiv des Auswärtigen Amtes, Berlin (Germany)
PA-UK	Parliamentary Archives, London (UK)
SCSC	Smith College Special Collections, Northampton, MA (US)
TNA	The National Archives, Kew (UK)

UAA	University at Albany, M. E. Grenander Departments of Special Collections and Archives, Albany, NY (US)
UM-BHL	University of Michigan, Bentley Historical Library, Ann Arbor, MI (US)
USHMM	United States Holocaust Memorial Museum, Washington, DC (US)
UW-AHC	University of Wyoming, American Heritage Center, Laramie, WY (US)
YULMA	Yale University Library, Manuscripts and Archives, New Haven, CT (US)

1

Introduction

Thinking Law, Talking Law, Doing Law: How Lawyers Craft(ed) the International Order

Marcus M. Payk and Kim Christian Priemel

Between 1950 and 1971 the International Court of Justice (ICJ) passed a string of five advisory opinions and decisions on the territorial status on what was then South West Africa. These belong to the better-known cases brought before the World Court, precisely because of their serial character, as underscored by the odd semantics employed in one jurist's appraisal of them as being 'the single most important moments during the [ICJ's] entire history'.[1] Dealing with an apparently technical question after the South African government had refused to transfer the former mandate into a United Nations Trust Territory, a first decision in 1962 asserted the Court's authority. That gave hope to those in favour of independence, only to see the narrowest possible decision effectively vindicate Pretoria's claim to control over the former German colony in 1966, allowing the extension of its apartheid policy. Yet five years later—by then Namibia had gained independence—the Court sharply reversed course and branded the continued South African presence unlawful, requiring all other countries to withdraw support for what now constituted an illegal occupation.[2]

The South West Africa saga is notorious for its turns (even though the issues in 1966 and 1971 were, strictly speaking, not identical) and for illustrating opposed doctrinal and methodological schools in international law: on the one side the voices of judicial self-restraint, justified by formalist, originalist, or textualist philosophies, on the other more activist judges who were willing to develop the law beyond the confines of travaux préparatoires, wording, and precedent.[3] Their

[1] Ingo Venzke, 'The International Court of Justice during the Battle for International Law (1955–1975)', in Jochen von Bernstorff and Philipp Dann (eds), *The Battle for International Law. South-North Perspectives on the Decolonization Era* (New York, NY: Oxford University Press, 2019), 235–56, at 236.

[2] For an overview of the dispute's stages and contemporary debate as well as legal documents see John Dugard (ed.), *The South West Africa / Namibia Dispute. Documents and Scholarly Writings on the Controversy between South Africa and the United Nations* (Berkeley: University of California Press, 1973). For the background cf. Susan Pedersen, *The Guardians. The League of Nations and the Crisis of Empire* (Oxford: Oxford University Press, 2015), 215–21, 348f., and Ryan M. Irwin, 'Apartheid on Trial: South West Africa and the International Court of Justice, 1960–66', *International History Review* 32 (2010), 619–42.

[3] For example, Lyndel V. Prott, *Der internationale Richter im Spannungsfeld der Rechtskulturen. Eine rechtssoziologische Studie über die Elemente des Selbstverständnisses des Internationalen Gerichtshofs*

Marcus M. Payk and Kim Christian Priemel, *Introduction* In: *Crafting the International Order*. Edited by: Marcus M. Payk and Kim Christian Priemel, Oxford University Press (2021). © The Several Contributors.
DOI: 10.1093/oso/9780198863830.003.0001

respective standard-bearers were Justice Sir Gerald Fitzmaurice from the United Kingdom and his Polish colleague Justice Manfred Lachs, and the story of how they arrived at their different conclusions might well be told differently from the standard narrative of doctrinal and stylistic antagonism if looked at through the lens of their backgrounds: one a prime specimen of the British elite, hailing from a profoundly imperial tradition, the other a diplomat for Communist Poland highly aware of the twin evils of occupation and racism. Such a perspective—further enforced by the fact that the two had sparred before[4]—raises doubts as to the perception of the ICJ, partly self-engineered, as an institution marked by a 'decidedly legalistic ethos'[5] and the all-too-tidy distinction between law, politics, and ethics.

Fitzmaurice's curriculum vitae does not only read like the model career of a British top civil servant, it includes several of the most prestigious jobs in the world of international law. Born in 1901, he was educated at Malvern and read law in Cambridge, became a barrister-at-law at Gray's Inn at the age of twenty-four, and joined the Diplomatic Service four years later. Following a stint at the Ministry of Economic Warfare he returned to the Foreign Office at the end of the war, serving as legal advisor for the next fifteen years and taking silk in 1957. The diplomat-cum-lawyer would be a member of the British delegation at the inauguration of the United Nations (UN) as well as at the peace conferences determining the Axis powers' fate in 1946 and 1951. Fitzmaurice contributed to the drafting of the ICJ statute, was a key player in negotiating the 1958 Geneva Convention on the High Seas, and followed twice in Hersch Lauterpacht's footsteps: first as a member of the International Law Commission from 1955 to 1960, then as a judge at the ICJ until 1973.[6] He would finish his career on yet another bench, this time that

(Berlin: Duncker & Humblot, 1975), 64–6, 74f., 111, 201. The cases appear throughout the jubilee publication by Vaughan Lowe and Malgosia Fitzmaurice (eds), *Fifty Years of the International Court of Justice. Essays in Honour of Sir Robert Jennings* (Cambridge: Cambridge University Press, 1996).

[4] In 1948, Lachs and Fitzmaurice found themselves on opposite sides over the wording of the UN Genocide Convention. While the Polish lawyer argued in favour of a broad rendering which would comprehend 'cultural genocide' and be enforced by an international court, his opposite number on His Majesty's team supported a definition limited to 'physical genocide', relegating other aspects to the sphere of judicially non-enforceable human rights. Fitzmaurice was also at pains to refute Soviet suggestions that British reservations reflected colonial interests; United Nations Radio Interview, Statement by Mr Manfred Lachs (Poland) 8 October 1948, in https://legal.un.org/avl/ha/cppcg/audio_6.html (accessed 18 August 2020); Third Session of the General Assembly, 179th Plenary Meeting, 9 December 1948: Continuation of the discussion on the Draft Convention on Genocide, https://legal.un.org/avl/ha/cppcg/audio_10.html (accessed 18 August 2020).

[5] Ingo Venzke, *How Interpretation Makes International Law. On Semantic Change and Normative Twists* (Oxford: Oxford University Press, 2012), 25. Cf. Venzke, 'Battle' (n 1) 255f.

[6] For a biographical sketch see J. G. Merrills, *Judge Sir Gerald Fitzmaurice and the Discipline of International Law. Opinions on the International Court of Justice, 1961–1973* (The Hague: Kluwer, 1998), 1–101. Cf. Lewis Johnman, 'Playing the Role of a Cassandra: Sir Gerald Fitzmaurice, Senior Legal Advisor to the Foreign Office', *Contemporary British History* 13 (1999), 46–63, and Anthony Carty and Richard Smith (eds), *Sir Gerald Fitzmaurice and the World Crisis: A Legal Adviser at the Foreign Office 1932–1945* (The Hague: Kluwer, 2000).

of the European Court of Human Rights (ECtHR) although, by his own estimate, Strasbourg was not a perfect fit for him and vice versa.[7]

Lachs' biography was no less spectacular. Born in Habsburgian Poland in 1914, Lachs initially embarked on an academic career. His legal studies would take him to Cracow, Nancy, and London, and he had already earned two doctorates when the war stranded him in the United Kingdom where he concluded his education and joined the Polish government-in-exile, one of many cabinets which had sought refuge in the British capital. Lachs, too, would be present at the 1946 Peace Conference at Paris, and he also contributed to the war crimes investigations for the International Military Tribunal at Nuremberg.[8] The young lawyer was appointed to the Polish delegation at the United Nations in 1945, and a few years later—following Fitzmaurice's departure—he would join the prestigious ILC. Here, Lachs was instrumental in the preparatory work for the Vienna Convention on the Law of Treaties, the most fundamental legal document governing international relations.[9] Lachs's work on the law of outer space made him a latter-day Grotius (or would have, had space exploration taken off as rapidly as maritime travel and trade had done four centuries earlier).[10] His crowning achievement was the election to the ICJ whose bench he joined in 1967. He would remain there until 1993 (including a tenure as president from 1973 to 1976), making him one of the longest-serving judges at The Hague ever.[11]

Fitzmaurice and Lachs are as prominent as international lawyers come, and their respective Wikipedia pages attest to the degree of fame they enjoy in afterlife. Yet they are hardly household names these days, and neither has become a seminal, even revered figure in the history of international law as, for instance, Lauterpacht.[12] While their juridical colleagues honour the legacy of the two men as superb craftsmen and authoritative voices, other disciplines do not favour them

[7] See Ed Bates, *The Evolution of the European Convention on Human Rights: From Its Inception to the Creation of a Permanent Court of Human Rights* (Oxford: Oxford University Press, 2010), 364f., and Malgosia Fitzmaurice, 'The Tale of Two Judges: Sir Hersch Lauterpacht and Sir Gerald Fitzmaurice. Human Rights and the Interpretation of Treaties', *Revue Hellénique de Droit International* 61 (2008), 125–70.

[8] Adam Łopatka, 'Foreword', and Lord Elwyn Jones, 'Manfred Lachs', both in Jerzy Makarczyk (ed.), *Essays in International Law in Honour of Manfred Lachs / Études de droit international en l'honneur de Manfred Lachs* (The Hague: Kluwer, 1984), 9–14 and 107–8. On Lachs cf. the chapter by Julia Eichenberg in this volume.

[9] See in Eirik Bjorge, 'The Vienna Rules, Evolutionary Interpretation, and the Intentions of the Parties', in Andrea Bianchi, Daniel Peat, and Matthew Windsor (eds), *Interpretation in International Law* (Oxford: Oxford University Press, 2015), 189–204.

[10] Francis Lyall, 'Manfred Lachs', in Stephan Hobe (ed.), *Pioneers of Space Law: A Publication of the International Institute of Space Law* (Leiden: Nijhoff, 2013), 192–210.

[11] See the biographical information in Edward McWhinney, *Judge Manfred Lachs and Judicial Law-Making. Opinions on the International Court of Justice, 1867–1993* (The Hague: Nijhoff, 1995), 1–84.

[12] The spectrum is wide and includes the chapter in Martti Koskenniemi's enormously influential *The Gentle Civilizer of Nations: The Rise and Fall of International Law 1870–1960* (Cambridge: Cambridge University Press, 2002), 353–412, as well as the bestselling narrative by Philippe Sands, *East West Street: On the Origins of Genocide and Crimes against Humanity* (London: Weidenfeld & Nicolson, 2016).

with any great attention. Political scientists and sociologists have little use for yesterday's judges, and historians of diplomacy and foreign affairs, if asked about Lachs and Fitzmaurice (and not allowed to Google), will usually shrug: the names simply do not ring a bell. And if these two careers—among the most distinguished the twentieth century had to offer both on and behind the international stage—have been largely ignored by historians, it is not surprising that many other, less famous names have fallen into the cracks of grand legal historical narratives.[13]

The Lawyers of the International

While the pre-eminence of lawyers and jurists in the emergence of modern nations and constitutional governments has been studied extensively,[14] far less attention has been paid to their role in foreign affairs, and even less to their practical influence in crafting the international order. Insofar as research exists on lawyering women and men in international contexts, emphasis has been mostly placed on academic protagonists—affiliates of highly visible organizations such as the Institut de Droit International or lone wolves such as Raphael Lemkin, the lifelong campaigner for the criminalization of genocide—and their theoretical contributions to international law. The occasional narrative prominently featuring an international judge, prosecutor, or attorney only goes to illustrate the rule and confines a host of other lawyers all the more firmly to historical obscurity.[15]

While academic jurists and courtroom judges also appear in great numbers in the pages of the present volume, its aim is to cast the net wider and to capture a good share of the 'roving assortment of legal officials',[16] and indeed of private

[13] The fact that they were intertwined with each other both professionally and privately—distinguished international lawyer Malgosia Fitzmaurice is Lachs' daughter and Fitzmaurice's daughter-in-law—makes the story even more intriguing. Cf. Manfred Lachs, 'In Memoriam: Sir Gerald Fitzmaurice', *Netherlands International Law Review* 30 (1983), III–V.

[14] For an overview see Dieter Gosewinkel, 'The Constitutional State', in Heikki Pihlajamäki, Markus D. Dubber, and Mark Godfrey (eds), *The Oxford Handbook of European Legal History* (Oxford: Oxford University Press, 2018) 945–73.

[15] Other disciplines have devoted attention especially to the personnel of international adjudication although here, too, research is enormously lop-sided with judges being the primary focus of interest: See, e.g., Prott, *Der internationale Richter*; Daniel Terris, Cesare P. R. Romano, and Leigh Stewart, *The International Judge. An Introduction to the Men and Women who Decide the World's Cases* (Oxford: Oxford University Press, 2007); Erik Voeten, 'International Judicial Behavior', in Cesare P. R. Romano, Karen Alter, and Yuval Shany (eds), *The Oxford Handbook on International Adjudication* (Oxford: Oxford University Press, 2014), 550–68; Leigh Swigart and Daniel Terris, 'Who Are the International Judges?', ibid., 619–38. For overviews over defence and prosecution organizations and procedures see Colleen Rohan and Gentian Zyberi (eds), *Defence Practices in International Criminal Justice* (Cambridge: Cambridge University Press, 2017), and Eran Sthoeger and Michael Wood, 'The International Bar', in Romano, et al., *The Oxford Handbook on International Adjudication*, 639–54; Antoine Vauchez, 'Communities of International Litigators', ibid., 655–68; Kate Gibson, 'Defense Counsel in International Criminal Trials', ibid., 691–710; Luc Reydams, Jan Wouters, and Cedric Ryngaert (eds), *International Prosecutors* (Oxford: Oxford University Press, 2012).

[16] Lauren Benton and Lisa Ford, *Rage for Order. The British Empire and the Origins of International Law, 1800–1850* (Cambridge, MA: Harvard University Press, 2016), 1f., 20f.

lawyers too, who have been the practitioners of international politics for the past three centuries. Assuming other roles—those of the politician, the diplomat, the legal advisor, the arbitrator, the military officer, the intelligence agency official, among others—and figuring often as national and imperial rather than outwardly 'international' lawyers, these practitioners have received scant attention from historians of both international law and international relations.[17]

In part, this reflects traditional dichotomies which portray 'law' and 'politics' as alternative, if not outright opposed ways of dealing with the same (international) problems and which express a desire for a distance between the sphere of supposedly pure law and the messy realities of politics. The division line has been plainly demarcated by the very protagonists who set out to institutionalize international law on some of its most famous occasions: at the 1907 Hague Conference, US legal adviser James Brown Scott hailed law as an antidote to the brute force of war, and Robert H. Jackson praised Nuremberg's International Military Tribunal, an offspring of The Hague's, in an oft-quoted formula as 'one of the most significant tributes that Power has ever paid to Reason'. Power, of course, is politics, reason law.[18]

Many academic voices have agreed with the practitioners (and, not untypical for the profession, Scott was indeed both). The eminent scholar of international law, Vaughan Lowe, conceives of law as an instrument and of practising law as a craft, suggesting that 'neither can be pushed far beyond its natural limitations'. In this view, lawyers are mere technicians who 'have no special ability or authority to decide whether any such solutions are or are not acceptable'—that is left to politicians, businessmen, or the military.[19] This view is echoed by political professionals and international relations scholars whose hardboiled pragmatism—often self-styled as 'realism'—insists that international power ratios determine and enforce law.[20] By comparison, legalists' allegedly slavish adherence to codified law and the wishful juristic thinking of the *de lege ferenda* type have been easily relegated to

[17] To illustrate the point, in Andraž Zidar and Jean-Pierre Gauci (eds), *The Role of Legal Advisers in International Law* (Leiden: Brill Nijhoff, 2016), the only legal historian to contribute is Martti Koskenniemi and he features in the collection on account of his earlier career as a lawyer attached to the Finnish delegation at the United Nations Security Coucil: Martti Koskenniemi, 'The Place of Law and the Role of Legal Advisers in Collective Security', ibid., 327–36.

[18] Marcus M. Payk, *Frieden durch Recht? Der Aufstieg des modernen Völkerrechts und der Friedensschluss nach dem Ersten Weltkrieg* (Munich: De Gruyter, 2018), 76; Kim Christian Priemel, *The Betrayal. The Nuremberg Trials and German Divergence* (Oxford: Oxford University Press, 2016), 107.

[19] Vaughan Lowe, *International Law* (Oxford: Oxford University Press, 2007), 33; quotations from Vaughan Lowe, *International Law. A Very Short Introduction* (Oxford: Oxford University Press, 2015), 121, 123.

[20] For a classical statement see Hans Morgenthau, 'Review of "The International Law of the Future" and "An International Bill of the Rights of Man" by H. Lauterpacht', *University of Chicago Law Review* 13 (1946), 400–2. Morgenthau's specific brand of realism, it is important to bear in mind, was not one of cynical power politics; see Michael C. Williams, 'Why Ideas Matter in International Relations: Hans Morgenthau, Classical Realism, and the Moral Construction of Power Politics', *International Organization* 58 (2004), 633–65.

the ivory towers of scholarly debate or the public arenas of street protest and activism whose political demands are largely unrelated to the legal forms they intend to assume.[21]

This volume chooses a different perspective. Starting from the premise that law as a social system does not have any 'natural' limitations but indeed is embedded in society (and vice versa) through a contingent process open to historical analysis, it hopes to overcome the dichotomies which result from contrasting 'law' and 'politics', 'theory' and 'practice', or 'legal technicians' and 'legal entrepreneurs'.[22] Instead it is interested in precisely the interplay between the rules of the craft—here understood as the combination of formal skills and informal routines with proven expertise and tacit knowledge gained from practical experience[23]—on the one hand and the autonomous, yet situational agency of individual actors on the other. Lawyers, in this view, are not the 'neutral translators' which Lowe's analogy of international law with a language implies,[24] but authors, writers, editors, and readers of that vast text that is law. They are also, in more contemporary parlance, the users interpreting, applying, and reconfiguring legal information vis-à-vis the realm of international policy-making.[25]

This book therefore sets out to shed light on how lawyers since the eighteenth century have made sense of and engaged in international politics; how politicians and administrators conceived of and considered their tasks in legal terms; and how the large, amorphous field often described as 'international relations' was filled with life in the distinctly legal vernacular of laws and regulations, contracts and treaties, resolutions and conventions, casework and judgments. If 'international law is not a corpus of doctrines but consists in such diffuse phenomena as non-governmental networks and administrative procedures', as Lauren Benton and Lisa Ford have argued, it is an inseparable component of international politics, foreign

[21] Human rights historiography is a pertinent example, see e.g. Samuel Moyn, *The Last Utopia. Human Rights in History* (Cambridge, MA: Belknap Press, 2010); Jan Eckel, *Die Ambivalenz des Guten. Menschenrechte in der internationalen Politik seit den 1940ern* (Göttingen: Vandenhoeck & Ruprecht, 2014).

[22] Cf. Yves Dezalay and Brian Garth, 'Introduction: Lawyers, Law, and Society', in Yves Dezalay and Brian Garth, *Lawyers and the Rule of Law in an Era of Globalization* (London and New York: Routledge, 2011), 1–16, 3f. The distinction between 'legal' and 'norm' entrepreneurs is somewhat opaque although most studies conceive of the former as activist individuals and of the latter as collectives such as international organizations; cf. Stephen Ratner, *The Thin Justice of International Law. A Moral Reckoning of the Law of Nations* (Oxford: Oxford University Press, 2015), 430f.

[23] We are here following the wide understanding as applied in Richard Sennett, *The Craftsman* (London: Allen Lane, 2008); cf. Brett G. Sharffs, 'Law as Craft', *Vanderbilt Law Review* 54 (2001), 2245–347.

[24] Lowe, *Short Introduction* (n 19) 120; Yves Dezalay and Bryant G. Garth, 'Introduction: Constructing Transnational Justice', in Yves Dezalay and Bryant G. Garth (eds), *Lawyers and the Construction of Transnational Justice* (London: Routledge, 2012), 3–12, at 5f.

[25] Our understanding of 'lawyers' and 'lawyering' is akin to the notion of 'players' and 'playing' suggested by the game analysis framework in Bianchi, Peat, and Windsor, *Interpretation in International Law* (n 9). However, 'craft' and 'work' are not metaphors but analytical categories which stress actual professional formation and practical experience.

affairs, and transnational relations, offering different formats and opening different arenas for political action.[26]

To consider these processes of thinking law, talking law, and doing law, and all that in greatly varying contexts, large aggregates will not do: on a systemic level it is virtually impossible to say how 'law' and 'politics' are conceptualized, what bearing notions of the one have on the other, and how theoretical innovation translates into practical action and vice versa. To understand the fashioning of the international order and the mechanisms of international law, we must instead turn to individual protagonists like Fitzmaurice and Lachs, to their professional, often multiple identities, and their tangible (inter)actions in various constellations of national and imperial, international and supranational politics. Looking at lawyers helps to identify how legal concepts and arguments were used, implemented, transformed, or neglected in nations' foreign affairs as well as in transnational fora. By carefully weighing the significance of agency, individuality, or idiosyncrasy against the formative, structural power of political, economic, military, etc., principles and settings, the case studies of this volume provide new insights into the workings of international law itself.

New Histories of International Law

Taking its cue from early reflections by David Kennedy and the influential writings of Martti Koskenniemi, a 'turn to history' has captured the imagination of the international law profession over the past decades.[27] Long dormant, international legal history has seen a great many jurists look for and into the genealogy of their own discipline.[28] While the traditional historiography of legal concepts and doctrines, schools, and scholars continues to attract interest, this rediscovered attention to the field's past is often part and parcel of a methodological soul-searching; turning to history and looking back helps to question the conceptual foundations and apodictic certainties of international law, upending much of its high-minded self-assurance.[29] Among other things, it is now widely accepted how much

[26] Benton and Ford, *Rage for Order* (n 16) 190.

[27] Koskenniemi, *Gentle Civilizer* (n 12); David Kennedy, 'The Move to Institutions', *Cardozo Law Review* 8 (1987), 841–988; David Kennedy, 'International Law and the Nineteenth Century: History of an Illusion', *NJIL* 65 (1996), 385–420. On the debate see the contributions to Matthew Craven, Malgosia Fitzmaurice, and Maria Vogiatzi (eds), *Time, History and International Law* (Leiden: Nijhoff, 2007).

[28] Annalisa Ciampi (ed.), *History and International Law: An Intertwined Relationship* (Northampton: Edward Elgar, 2019); Stephen C. Neff, *Justice among Nations: A History of International Law* (Cambridge, MA: Harvard University Press 2014); Harald Kleinschmidt, *Geschichte des Völkerrechts im Krieg und Frieden* (Darmstadt: WBG, 2013); Bardo Fassbender and Anne Peters (eds), *The Oxford Handbook of the History of International Law* (Oxford: Oxford University Press, 2012); Luigi Nuzzo and Miloš Vec (eds), *Constructing International Law: The Birth of a Discipline* (Frankfurt: Klostermann, 2012); Craven et al., *Time, History and International Law* (n 27).

[29] Matilda Arvidsson and Miriam Bak McKenna, 'The Turn to History in International Law and the Sources Doctrine: Critical Approaches and Methodological Imaginaries', *LJIL* 33 (2020), 37–56; Jean

international law was, and still is, a project based on Western conceptions and categorizations of the world, inseparably connected with the history of European imperialism and of empire.[30]

The implications of this historical insight run deep within the legal profession. They range from stressing the contributions and agency of 'semi-peripheral lawyers'[31] to asking if 'international law is really international'.[32] Yet, historians looking at these same subjects tend to have a different perspective. Determined to no longer leave the history of international law to lawyers and jurists alone, historical scholars of different stripes have begun to supplement the legal profession's auto-historiography. A surge in historical books and articles in the last decade has devoted particular attention to how politics and law were related in the international arena.[33] Many of these writings—if at all interested in legal details—are

d'Aspremont, 'Critical Histories of International Law and the Repression of Disciplinary Imagination', *London Review of International Law* 7 (2019), 89–115; Matthew Craven, 'Theorizing the Turn to History in International Law', in Anne Orford and Florian Hoffmann (eds), *The Oxford Handbook of the Theory of International Law* (Oxford: Oxford University Press, 2016), 21–37; Thomas Skouteris, 'Engaging History in International Law', in José María Beneyto and David Kennedy (eds), *New Approaches to International Law. The European and the American Experiences* (The Hague: Asser, 2013), 99–122; George Radrigo Bandeira Galindo, 'Martti Koskenniemi and the Historiographical Turn in International Law', *EJIL* 16 (2005), 539–59.

[30] Inge van Hulle and Randall Lesaffer, *International Law in the Long Nineteenth Century (1776–1914), From the Public Law of Europe to Global International Law?* (Leiden: Brill, 2019); Jennifer Pitts, *Boundaries of the International: Law and Empire* (Cambridge, MA: Harvard University Press, 2018); Martti Koskenniemi, Walter Rech, and Manuel Jiménez Fonseca (eds), *International Law and Empire: Historical Explorations* (New York, NY: Oxford University Press, 2017); Umut Özsu, *Formalizing Displacement: International Law and Population Transfers* (Oxford: Oxford University Press, 2015); Teemu Ruskola, *Legal Orientalism: China, the United States, and Modern Law* (Cambridge, MA: Harvard University Press, 2013); Nathaniel Berman, *Passion and Ambivalence: Colonialism, Nationalism, and International Law* (Leiden: Nijhoff, 2012); Antony Anghie, *Imperialism, Sovereignty and the Making of International Law* (Cambridge: Cambridge University Press, 2005).

[31] Arnulf Becker Lorca, *Mestizo International Law: A Global Intellectual History 1842–1933* (Cambridge: Cambridge University Press, 2015).

[32] Anthea Roberts, *Is International Law International?* (New York, NY: Oxford University Press, 2017).

[33] Gabriela A. Frei, *Great Britain, International Law, and the Evolution of Maritime Strategic Thought, 1856–1914* (Oxford: Oxford University Press, 2020); Guillaume Mouralis, *Le moment Nuremberg. Le procès international, les lawyers et la question raciale* (Paris: Presses de Sciences Po, 2019); Maartje Abbenhuis, *The Hague Conferences and International Politics, 1898–1915* (London: Bloomsbury Academic, 2019); Fabian Klose, *'In the Cause of Humanity'. Eine Geschichte der humanitären Intervention im langen 19. Jahrhundert* (Göttingen: Vandenhoeck & Ruprecht, 2019); Kerstin von Lingen, *'Crimes against Humanity'. Eine Ideengeschichte der Zivilisierung von Kriegsgewalt 1864–1945* (Paderborn: Schöningh, 2018); Will Smiley, *From Slaves to Prisoners of War: The Ottoman Empire, Russia, and International Law* (Oxford: Oxford University Press, 2018); Juan Pablo Scarfi, *The Hidden History of International Law in the Americas: Empire and Legal Networks* (New York, NY: Oxford University Press, 2017); Benjamin A. Coates, *Legalist Empire: International Law and American Foreign Relations in the Early Twentieth Century* (New York, NY: Oxford University Press, 2016); Susan Pedersen, *The Guardians: The League of Nations and the Crisis of Empire* (New York, NY: Oxford University Press, 2015); Isabel V. Hull, *A Scrap of Paper: Breaking and Making International Law During the Great War* (Ithaca, NY: Cornell University Press, 2014); Aimee Genell, *Empire by Law: Ottoman Sovereignty and the British Occupation of Egypt, 1882–1923* (PhD diss., Columbia University, 2013); Davide Rodogno, *Against Massacre: Humanitarian Interventions in the Ottoman Empire, 1815–1914. The Emergence of a European Concept and International Practice* (Princeton, NJ: Princeton University

less concerned with the doctrinal nitty-gritty and more with what is conveniently called 'the context', meaning, loosely speaking, the assumption that law as social action is determined by its setting and situation at least as much as by its inner logic.

Such imaginative discretion has tended to alarm jurists, including erstwhile proponents of contextualist legal history such as Koskenniemi.[34] Some defend the presentism of their discipline against what they perceive to be the primacy of context resulting from historiographical methods; others bemoan historians' 'painstaking attention to historical details and data' irrelevant to present day concerns, or even see a 'turf war' between lawyers and historians.[35] Considering the different perspectives, the martial vocabulary exaggerates the situation. Neither history nor international law is the prerogative of a single profession, and choosing the most reasonable methodology often depends on whether one is more interested in the historical development of international law itself—the doctrinal lineages within a self-referential 'belief system'[36]—or in the influence it exerted at certain points in time and at places far away from any legal treatise.[37] Finally, methodological and theoretical lines of difference between most academic disciplines have become blurred in recent decades, in the realm of international legal history probably more so than elsewhere.

Stressing the consensual side rather than the differences, there is now agreement that the history of international law encompasses more than compiling treaties and conventions and that it is essential to reconsider its principal actors along with those on the margins, all the more now that the predominance of the (nation) state appears to be severely shaken. New perspectives on who actually 'does' international law, and what constitutes its distinct 'practices' are debated across the field, and both categories have been expanded substantially in the process. They now include jurisprudence in its different forms as well as a variety of

Press, 2012); Francine Hirsch, 'The Soviets at Nuremberg: International Law, Propaganda, and the Making of the Postwar Order', *AHR* 113 (2008), 701–730.

[34] For an excellent overview of the debate, as well as an able repudiation of some of the more eccentric reproaches notably against Cambridge-School inspired intellectual historians of international law, see Andrew Fitzmaurice, 'Context in the History of International Law', *JHIL* 20 (2018), 5–30.

[35] For the different positions see Anne Orford, 'International Law and the Limits of History', in W. G. Werner, Marieke de Hoon, and Alexis Galán (eds), *The Law of International Lawyers. Reading Martti Koskenniemi* (Cambridge: Cambridge University Press, 2017), 297–320; Valentina Vadi, 'International Law and Its Histories: Methodological Risks and Opportunities', *Harvard International Law Journal* 58 (2017), 311–52, quotation at 321.

[36] Jean d'Aspremont, *International Law as a Belief System* (Cambridge: Cambridge University Press, 2017).

[37] Mary L. Dudziak, 'Legal History as Foreign Relations History', in Frank Costigliola and Michael J. Hogan (eds), *Explaining the History of American Foreign Relations* (New York, NY: Cambridge University Press, 2016), 135–50; Frederik Dhondt, 'Looking Beyond the Tip of the Iceberg: Diplomatic Praxis and Legal Culture in the History of Public International Law', *Rechtskultur. Zeitschrift für Europäische Rechtsgeschichte* 2 (2013), 31–42; Gerry J. Simpson, 'International Law in Diplomatic History', in James Crawford and Martti Koskenniemi (eds), *The Cambridge Companion to International Law* (Cambridge: Cambridge University Press, 2012), 25–46.

'jurispractices'—uncodified, even unspoken ways of acting legally—and, logically, cover actors beyond the inner circle of trained lawyers.[38] This breaks with more traditional historiographies that hardly knew any other 'practices' of international law than those of states or, with hazy distinctions between the two, of governments.[39] Likewise, many—though by no means all—international jurists' reluctance to broaden legal personality under international law and include corporations of various kinds along with individuals, is rapidly going out of fashion.[40]

This chimes in with a new appreciation of the influential, yet often invisible, backstage role of individuals, groups, and organizations in creating and contesting the international order which, in recent decades, has manifested itself in a growing number of biographical works.[41] For one, there is strong interest among the legal discipline to look at its forebears as a way to 'inspire and teach' and to show 'the resilience of international lawyers in the face of adversity, how they became masters of their own destiny, and their contributions to the making of the field'.[42] Scholars who see international law as an impartial corrective to power politics would probably agree and share this optimism about principled lawyers as champions of international peace and justice.[43] Others, though, might hit a more sombre note,

[38] Katherine Hermes, '"Justice Will Be Done Us". Algonquian Demands for Reciprocity in the Courts of European Settlers', in Christopher L. Tomlins and Bruce H. Mann (eds), *Many Legalities of Early America* (Chapel Hill, NC: University of North Carolina Press, 2001), 123–49, at 127, fn. 9. Cf. Lauren Benton and Richard J. Ross, 'Empires and Legal Pluralism: Jurisdiction, Sovereignty, and Political Imagination in the Early Modern World', in Lauren Benton and Richard J. Ross (eds), *Legal Pluralism and Empires, 1500–1850* (New York, NY: New York University Press, 2013), 1–17, at 7, and Randall Lesaffer, 'International Law and Its History. The Story of an Unrequited Love', in Craven, et al., *Time, History and International Law* (n 27) 27–43, at 33–7.

[39] Anthony Carty, 'Doctrine versus State Practice', in Bardo Fassbender and Anne Peters (eds), *The Oxford Handbook of the History of International Law* (Oxford: Oxford University Press, 2012), 972–96.

[40] Natasha Wheatley, 'New Subjects in International Law and Order', in Glenda Sluga and Patricia Clavin (eds), *Internationalisms. A Twentieth-Century History* (Cambridge: Cambridge University Press, 2017), 265–86; Martine Julia van Ittersum, *Profit and Principle: Hugo Grotius, Natural Rights Theories and the Rise of Dutch Power in the East Indies, 1595–1615* (Leiden: Brill, 2006); Kim Christian Priemel, 'Corporate Liabilities: A Genealogy of Business Accountability under International Criminal Law', in Eric Brousseau, Jean-Michel Glachant, and Jérôme Sgard (eds), *The Oxford Handbook of Institutions of International Economic Governance and Market Regulation* (Oxford: Oxford University Press, 2019), doi:10.1093/oxfordhb/9780190900571.013.26.

[41] Among others, Arthur Eyffinger, *T.M.C. Asser (1838–1913), 'In Quest of Liberty, Justice, and Peace'*, 2 vols (Leiden: Brill, 2019); Christopher R. Rossi, *Whiggish International Law: Elihu Root, the Monroe Doctrine, and International Law in the Americas* (Leiden: Brill, 2019); Vincent Genin, *Le Laboratoire belge du droit international. Une communauté épistémique et internationale de juristes (1869–1914)* (Brüssel: Académie royale de Belgique, 2018); Felix Lange, *Praxisorientierung und Geme inschaftskonzeption: Hermann Mosler als Wegbereiter der westdeutschen Völkerrechtswissenschaft nach 1945* (Berlin: Springer, 2017); Antoine Prost and Jay Winter, *René Cassin et les droits de l'homme: Le projet d'une génération* (Paris: Fayard, 2011); Jochen von Bernstorff, *The Public International Law Theory of Hans Kelsen: Believing in Universal Law* (Cambridge: Cambridge University Press, 2010); Frank Degenhardt, *Zwischen Machtstaat und Völkerbund: Erich Kaufmann (1880–1972)* (Baden-Baden: Nomos, 2008); Claudia Denfeld, *Hans Wehberg: Die Organisation der Staatengemeinschaft* (Baden-Baden: Nomos, 2008).

[42] Vadi, 'International Law and Its Histories' (n 35) 344.

[43] Oona Hathaway and Scott J. Shapiro, *The Internationalists: How a Radical Plan to Outlaw War Remade the World* (New York, NY: Simon & Schuster, 2017); Jean-Michel Guieu, 'Les juristes internationalistes français, l'Europe et la paix à la Belle Époque', *Relations internationales* 149 (2012),

focusing on how lawyers navigated a racialized and discriminatory international system, or critically examining the claims of universalism no longer self-evident to a discipline once so proud of its allegedly universal values.[44]

The present volume pushes the interest in the practitioners of international law further along these lines. Picking up where most accounts leave off, it puts the entanglement of individuals in international law and foreign affairs centre stage. There are many blank spots left when it comes to the roles of international lawyers, especially with an eye to their participation in diplomatic affairs and their influence as advisors to governments since the eighteenth century. The common-sense assumption that lawyers are somehow important for 'carrying on the everyday functions of government in a law-oriented way'[45] is often picked up, yet seldom scrutinized. Autobiographical and biographical accounts, scattered as they are, tend to be overly confident, arguing that legal professional standards play a crucial role in state compliance with international law.[46] There is little relevant literature to add depth to this widespread notion. Collective biographies and prosopographic studies that outline the lives and career trajectories of various groups of (international) lawyers mostly offer little in terms of analysis.[47] Only a few historical

27–41; Daniel Marc Segesser, *Recht statt Rache oder Rache durch Recht? Die Ahndung von Kriegsverbrechen in der internationalen wissenschaftlichen Debatte 1872–1945* (Paderborn: Schöningh, 2010).

[44] Roberts, *Is International Law International?* (n 32) 51f. Umut Özsu, 'Organizing Internationally: Georges Abi-Saab, the Congo Crisis, and the Decolonization of the United Nations', *EJIL* 31 (2020), 601–19; Meredith Terretta and Benjamin N. Lawrance, '"Sons of the Soil": Cause Lawyers, the Togo-Cameroun Mandates, and the Origins of Decolonization', *AHR* 124 (2019), 1709–14; Sara Dezalay, 'Lawyers' Empire in the (African) Colonial Margins', *International Journal of the Legal Profession* (2016), 1–8; David Kennedy, *A World of Struggle: How Power, Law, and Expertise Shape Global Political Economy* (Princeton, NJ: Princeton University Press, 2016).

[45] Malcolm N. Shaw, *International Law*, 6th edn (Cambridge: Cambridge University Press, 2008), 7.

[46] Michael P. Scharf and Colin McLaughlin, 'Foreign Legal Advisors Roundtable', *Proceedings of the American Society of International Law* 99 (2005), 161–9; Wilhelm Grewe, 'The Role of International Law in Diplomatic Practice', *JHIL* 1 (1999), 22–37; Robbie Sabel, 'The Role of the Legal Advisor in Diplomacy', *Diplomacy & Statecraft* 8 (1997), 1–9; Harold Honju Koh, 'Transnational Legal Process', *Nebraska Law Review* 75 (1996), 181–207; Antonio Cassese, 'The Role of the Legal Advisor in Ensuring that Foreign Policy Conforms to International Legal Standards', *Michigan Journal of International Law* 14 (1992), 139–217; Ronald St. John MacDonald, 'The Role of the Legal Adviser of Ministries of Foreign Affairs', *Recueil des Cours/Académie de Droit International de La Haye* 149 (1977), 377–482; Richard Bilder, 'The Office of the Legal Adviser: The State Department Lawyer and Foreign Affairs', *AJIL* 56 (1962), 633–84; Lester H. Woolsey, 'The Legal Adviser of the Department of State', *AJIL* 26 (1932), 124–6.

[47] For example, James Benjamin Loeffler and Moria Paz (eds), *The Law of Strangers. Jewish Lawyers and International Law in the Twentieth Century* (New York, NY: Cambridge University Press, 2019); Leonie Breunung and Manfred Walther (eds), *Die Emigration deutschsprachiger Rechtswissenschaftler ab 1933. Ein bio-bibliographisches Handbuch* (Berlin: De Gruyter, 2012); Roger K. Newman (ed.), *The Yale Biographical Dictionary of American Law* (New Haven, CT: Yale University Press, 2009); Patrick Arabeyre (ed.), *Dictionnaire historique des juristes français (XIIe–XXe siècle)* (Paris: PUF, 2008); Liora Israël, *Robes noires, années sombre. Avocats et magistrats en résistance pendant la Seconde Guerre mondiale* (Paris: Fayard, 2005); Jack Beatson and Reinhard Zimmermann (eds), *Jurists Uprooted: German-Speaking Émigré Lawyers in Twentieth-Century Britain* (Oxford: Oxford University Press, 2004); Peter Macalister-Smith, 'Bio-Bibliographical Key to the Membership of the Institut de Droit International, 1873–2001', *JHIL* 5 (2003), 77–159; Michael Stolleis (ed.), *Juristen: Ein biographisches Lexikon von der Antike bis zum 20. Jahrhundert* (Munich: Beck, 2001).

studies stand out that explicitly deal with legal advisors in the field of foreign policy, and practically none that investigate the legions of officials who, though not serving in specifically juristic functions, drew on their legal education in fulfilling their daily duties; or, for that matter, those whose 'jurispractices' did not rely on formal training, yet were legally meaningful in their effects.[48] There is much we do not know: about the significance of different traditions of legal and indeed of other forms of professional training; about networks and patronage systems; and about the ever-shifting boundaries both between public and private and between the international in international law and its complements and competitors, the national and the imperial, the supranational and the transnational. With systematic research into these questions only just beginning in legal studies, the sociology of law, in legal anthropology, and in international relations studies,[49] the cases presented in this volume are a first foray from a genuinely historical perspective.

Conceptualizing Practitioners and Practices

To widen the scope of international legal history, the individual chapters of this volume explore how the interaction of individual agency and structures shaped the history of international law; they offer new insights into the role and influence of international lawyers in foreign affairs; and they provide a perspective on the conditions and consequences of the international order as a historical artefact, inevitably contingent upon and confined to specific parameters of time and space. In doing so, and in order to open new directions for and within the larger field, this volume is based on conceptual premises on three distinct levels:

First, our research on lawyers' involvement in and significance to international relations over the past 250 years opens new perspectives on how modern international law was applied. Transcending well-established approaches by legal

[48] Aimee Genell, 'The Well-Defended Domains: Eurocentric International Law and the Making of the Ottoman Office of Legal Counsel', *Journal of the Ottoman and Turkish Studies Association* 3 (2016), 255–75; Ingolf Vislie, *Jens Evensen. Havet, oljen og retten* (Stamsund: Orkana, 2017); Gerhard Stuby, *Vom 'Kronjuristen' zum 'Kronzeugen': Friedrich Wilhelm Gaus. Ein Leben im Auswärtigen Amt der Wilhelmstraße* (Hamburg: VSA, 2008).

[49] Matthew Windsor, 'Consigliere or Conscience? The Role of the Government Legal Adviser', in Jean d'Aspremont, Tarcisio Gazzini, André Nollkaemper, et al. (eds), *International Law as a Profession* (Cambridge: Cambridge University Press, 2017), 355–88; Friedrich Kratochwil, 'Practising Law: Spoudaios, Professional, Expert or "Macher"? Reflections on the Changing Nature of an Occupation', in Werner, et al., *Law of International Lawyers* (n 35) 225–64; Andraž Zidar, 'Interpretation and the International Legal Profession: Between Duty and Aspiration', in Bianchi, et al., *Interpretation in International Law* (n 9) 133–46; Yves Dezalay and Brian Garth, *Dealing in Virtue. International Commercial Arbitration and the Construction of a Transnational Legal Order* (Chicago, IL: University of Chicago Press, 1996); Guillaume Sacriste and Antoine Vauchez, 'The Force of International Law: Lawyers' Diplomacy on the International Scene in the 1920s', *Law & Social Inquiry* 32 (2007), 83–107; Ronald Niezen and Maria Sapignoli (eds), *Palaces of Hope. The Anthropology of Global Organizations* (Cambridge: Cambridge University Press, 2017); James A.R. Nafziger and Thomas B. Stoel (eds), *Comparative Law and Anthropology* (Cheltenham: Edwin Elgar, 2017).

historians and historians of ideas, the individual chapters focus on jurists' practical contributions in different politically contentious but also largely uncharted fields amenable to reform, development, or exploitation. Secular trends of the nineteenth century such as institutionalization, professionalization, and specialization created new spaces for lawyers in international politics but also brought new constraints and expectations. Several chapters highlight how international lawyers were incorporated into the mechanics of foreign ministries and diplomatic services—as in-house advisors as well as external authorities—yet forego convenient narratives of 'juridification' in which politics is simply seen as bending to the force of law. In fact, the relationship between diplomats and lawyers, or sometimes between politically minded lawyers and academic jurists, was often as uneasy as it was unclear, not least due to individual career patterns, elite networks, and the policies of status and prestige. The interplay of these factors created tensions but also opened up new possibilities to formulate and enforce national interests in various international arenas and in the in-between spaces. There remains much research to be done on when, why, and in which contexts legal scholars were called upon, and by whom; how they operated in such assignments and when their expertise was eventually put to use; and which effects, if any, these practical experiences had on academic juristic work.

Second, the contributions to the volume re-evaluate the multifaceted field of international politics by looking at its normative underbelly. While scholars of international history have convincingly shown that nation states' foreign policies since the 1800s have been increasingly formulated in, but also confined by, juridical ideas and institutions whose number, scope, and complexity have been growing to the present day, there exists very little, if any, consensus on whether or not such legal feats actually have had any significant consequences. To what extent decision-makers care for the law is largely unclear. Mirroring individual observers' expectations, the often blatant gaps between the rhetoric of 'ought' and the realities of 'is' are bemoaned, criticized, or ridiculed. In other words, the fact that rules are ignored is said to invalidate them.[50]

The present volume eschews such idealized and at times simplistic correlations of norms and behaviour, and instead enquires into the normative assumptions, legalist premises, and vested interests which inform—or cloak—political decisions in the first place. Rather than finding that national self-interest and universal goals were opposed, this book shows why, and to what effect, legal concepts and legal agents were drawn upon at all. The recourse to juristic expertise and language, several chapters demonstrate, was an irresistible and politically powerful tool. Whether as a strategy to safeguard acceptance in the global arena, to promote national interests, or to exert pressure on friends and foes, being versed in

[50] System theorists beg to differ: 'The mere fact that the law is broken does not mean that it is not the law'; Niklas Luhmann, *Das Recht der Gesellschaft* (Frankfurt: Suhrkamp, 1993), 86 [our translation].

international legalese and commanding a reserve of loyal international lawyers (of cosmopolitan posture, preferably) proved a boon to national governments when engaging in international relations from the eighteenth century onward. It is indicative that multinational enterprises would follow in the nation states' footsteps, literally paying for the legitimacy of international law and the prestige of its practitioners—including international judges such as Mohammed Bedjaoui (ICJ) and Gunner Lagergren (ECtHR)—and increasingly judicializing international commercial arbitration.[51] That this trend often helped foster normative expectations beyond any immediate political control is both an obvious as well as a surprisingly often ignored effect, meriting closer inspection.

Third, and on a more methodological note, the present volume directs attention to practices of international law that go beyond the mere formulation and execution of foreign policy objectives; in fact, 'state practice' in jurisprudence and the 'practice' of actors in historiography point to very different perspectives. Highlighting individual agency rather than focusing on abstract agents such as 'states' or 'governments', all contributions share an interest in the very tangible actions of international politics' foot soldiers. The negotiations leading to an international treaty—with their intellectual, technical, and tactical requirements—are no less important for crafting the international order than interpreting its legal substance. The attention to detail and to agency is not only an antidote to the overwhelming power of structures, whether political, economic, military, or cultural, it also releases individuals from ready-made categorizations as a mere representative of some larger aggregate like nations, institutions, or schools of thought.

To appreciate the agency of the international lawyers, it is essential to keep two trivial facts in mind: first, all lawyers are legally trained and therefore share a communicative code, a common lexicon, and a common syntax.[52] Second, usages differ profoundly, reflecting different semantics, rationales, rationalizations, and contexts. A jurist in an academic study does law differently both from a lawyer at the negotiating table and a government official tucked away in some remote wing of a ministry building. In court, judges and advocates general, attorneys, prosecution, and defence counsel assume different roles and pursue varying, often conflicting agendas. This volume offers some preliminary insights into how these practitioners administered the varieties and vagaries of international law in the ever-changing contexts of international relations, suggesting building blocks for a more comprehensive classification rather than presenting a decisive conclusion or ultimate definition. Importantly, the very notion of 'practitioner' is understood to be a question rather than an answer, and throughout the volume contributions take

[51] See Dezalay and Garth, *Dealing in Virtue* (n 49) 21–9, 55f. Cf. Karen J. Alter, *The New Terrain of International Law. Courts, Politics, Rights* (Princeton, NJ: Princeton University Press, 2014), 170f.

[52] If 'interpreters [of international law] cannot escape its grammar' (Bjorge, 'Vienna Rules' (n 9) 203) their interpretations can and do evolve these rules.

heed of those protagonists who neither were professional lawyers nor would have claimed to be, yet 'did law' none the less.

Crafting the International Order: Case Studies

Following a broadly chronological order and covering a time span from the late eighteenth century to the 1960s, the contributions to this volume focus on individual case studies which have been designed to cover various fields of international law and examples of lawyers in foreign affairs. These run the gamut from arbitration boards in slave trade cases to the intricacies of international treaty-making and from the agonal procedures of judicial trials to the ideas behind constitutionalizing the European Community. The fact that this volume foregrounds case studies from the global north, including Japan, is not intended to continue ingrained international hierarchies by disregarding voices and perspectives from the global south. Instead it enquires into how such hierarchies were established and reproduced within and by actors from the global north as well as adopted and adapted by protagonists elsewhere. In other words, rather than driving home once more the point that the world of international politics and law resonates with the legacies of European rule and Eurocentric epistemologies, the present volume is more interested in tracing the contingencies of these developments and their institutional, cultural, and practical residue.

Chapter 2 exemplifies one such case of adoption and adaption. Andrew Cobbing analyses how Japanese scholars and politicians—rather than lawyers in the strict sense—were confronted with Western understandings of international law and, in the process, began to form a legal profession to match that of their new competitors and partners. After centuries in the Sinosphere, with China as a role model for Japan's foreign affairs and own imperial ambitions, the arrival of Western powers on the shores of East Asia marked a seismic shift. Replacing the Tokugawa regime's politics of isolation which lasted from the seventeenth to the mid-nineteenth century, the Meiji era's growing international engagement after 1868 made it inevitable that legal ideas and terms, which more often than not had no equivalent in Japanese thinking, would be assimilated. Cobbing demonstrates how the first generation of Japanese international lawyers were shaped by this experience, operating both as legal advisers to the state and advocates for their homeland's place in the Eurocentric global order. Ironically, Japanese international lawyers would learn to put the legal foundations of that order to use not only to pursue equality among sovereign nations but to reinforce inequality in East Asia.

In Chapter 3, Fabian Klose sketches how international lawyers were moulded out of a variety of materials. Klose unearths the little-known role of 'Mixed Commissions for the Abolition of the Slave Trade' in the efforts to end the transatlantic slave trade. Beginning in 1817, Great Britain, Portugal, Spain, and the

Netherlands created several such commissions which were authorized to adjudicate on captured slave ships. This first system of international jurisdiction was supposed to operate on a uniform set of practices, functions, and procedures throughout the Atlantic, with courts located in port cities from Cape Town and Rio de Janeiro to New York. The chance of convicting a slave ship, however, largely depended on the local practice of the respective court and thus varied from place to place. To explain this divergence, Klose explores how the members of the Mixed Commissions, whose backgrounds varied greatly, fused international cooperation with national interests. While some commissary judges, mostly appointed by the British, pursued a hard line against slave traders and energetically pursued the abolitionist course of the London government, other members of the commissions took a moderate stance. Notably Spanish, Portuguese, and Brazilian judges often acted as defence counsel or even lobbyists for their slave-trading countrymen. Different self-perceptions and professional engagements accounted for different outcomes of the commissions' work, despite the fact that they adhered to the same letter of the law.

That the British Empire was a key player when it came to creating, interpreting, and instrumentalizing international law in the course of the nineteenth century is also the point of departure of Gabriela Frei's Chapter 4 on the practices of Britain's neutrality policy in the decades before the First World War. But rather than focusing on the imperial dimensions of London's international law politics, this chapter reveals their internal repercussions. After the passing of the Foreign Enlistment Act of 1870, which regulated the involvement and participation of British subjects in foreign wars, the government apparatus' need for structures to supervise and enforce these rules became obvious. In consequence, not only did the traditional means of obtaining legal advice via the Law Offices of the Crown become more formalized, but also the Foreign Office began building up its own expertise in international law matters. Administrative reforms in the course of the 1870s, while failing to establish a full-grown legal department, created the free-floating position of an in-house legal adviser who soon played a constant and important role in daily legal matters. Yet, as Frei shows, the Law Officers were able to preserve their prerogative in all final decision-making processes in Britain's neutrality policy, shaping a consistent state practice that would become crucial for the fierce debates on neutrality in the First World War.

The manifold ways legal expertise was interwoven with imperial politics and policies was not limited to Asia or Africa. As Chapter 5 by Benjamin Coates demonstrates, attempts to establish and maintain US hegemony in Latin America in the early twentieth century were based heavily on international law. Recent research has focused on understanding how Latin American jurists mobilized legal arguments as defensive weapons against US intervention. Yet policy-makers in Washington, DC, were overwhelmingly lawyers themselves, using the concept of the rule of law as a means of asserting and extending US power. As Coates shows, lawyer policy-makers and legal advisers in the US State Department, among them John Bassett Moore, Elihu Root, or James Brown Scott, promoted international law in academic and professional settings at the same time that they were serving in the US government and working as lobbyists for US-based corporations. It was this triple identity that shaped their perception of the conflicts at hand and the solutions they proposed.

National interests and international ambitions were and are never mutually exclusive, of course, but dialectically entwined. One of the arenas where both expectations were pursued, were the Hague Peace Conferences of 1899 and 1907 which Michael Jonas looks into in Chapter 6. Tracing the footsteps of Hjalmar Hammarskjöld, fin-de-siècle Sweden's foremost international legal scholar and practitioner, this chapter adds to the recent surge of interest in the Hague Conferences, yet redirects our attention to mostly forgotten players at the negotiations, often representing smaller nations such as Sweden. Jonas brings to light Hammarskjöld's argument in favour of a codification of small states' rights in the context of the discussions on neutrality, which eventually led to the adoption of two conventions which are fundamental to this day. More generally, the example of Hammarskjöld as well as other Scandinavian law-makers and politicians at The Hague helps to explain how the representatives of small states were able to use legal arguments to great effect in the international arena precisely because legal reasoning could no longer be simply discounted.

Speaking the language of law and knowing its grammar was the key to navigating the ever more complex seas of international politics successfully. Few cases illustrate this point as poignantly as the Treaty of Versailles, arguably one of the most famous peace documents in world history. Yet the complex circumstances of its crafting process are barely known, as Marcus Payk demonstrates in Chapter 7. He directs the spotlight at the drafting committee and gives names and faces to its members, the principal legal advisors of the Allied powers who bore the main responsibility for the actual wording of the treaty. This allegedly 'technical' committee, Payk argues, is crucial to understanding how shaky political compromises could be transformed into legally binding rules and treaty provisions. By taking a look behind the scenes of the peace conference and placing the legal advisors at the centre of peace-making, the chapter explores how blurred the boundary between politics and law is and, at the same time, how important it is to pretend that this boundary actually exists and matters, in 1919 and beyond.

That lawyers often need to operate in uncertain situations is also the topic of Chapter 8 by Julia Eichenberg which takes us to the legal anomaly of exiled governments in London during the Second World War. When government émigrés from Belgium, Czechoslovakia, France, Greece, Luxembourg, Norway, Poland, and Yugoslavia gathered in London, they organized governments-in-exile and strove for their recognition under international law. Legal experts and jurists were indispensable to make this claim, as Eichenberg highlights, and to do so they pursued not only official channels and informal diplomatic avenues but also used academic meetings, discussions, and publications. As at The Hague, scholarly expertise proved a diplomatic resource. The governments-in-exile were officially recognized as legitimate representation of their respective nation within the borders of Great Britain, they managed to establish state-like apparatuses, and they continued to act as political entities. Ousted from the European continent, émigré lawyers, jurists, and legal advisors thus became an influential force in defining and preserving statehood, even devoid of political or military power.

More than a few of the lawyers from the London scene would go on to play a significant role in shaping post-war politics in their respective countries as well as internationally, including through spells at the ICJ and other international courts. Among the first avenues for such endeavours were the policies of retribution directed against Axis criminals, often by employing judicial means. This large programme, but mostly the International Military Tribunal at Nuremberg (and, to a lesser extent, that at Tokyo), has often been praised as a milestone in the evolution of international criminal law, said to be advancing on a 'road' from Nuremberg to The Hague (i.e. the International Criminal Court). On the other hand, critics have chastised what they perceive as double standards and a corruption of the rule of law. But whatever the individual take, both support and rejection have inevitably been phrased in the language of law, as Kim Christian Priemel outlines in Chapter 9. His contribution portrays the so-called Nuremberg lawyers as a variegated lot of theorists and practitioners with a wide spectrum of experiences, motivations, and ambitions, serving different principals and objectives (often at the same time) and fulfilling discrete judicial functions in the process. Identifying which hat which lawyer wore, and at what stage of the trials, Priemel argues, accounts for the enormous differences in what they did at Nuremberg and how they would look back at its legacy.

A closer look at the impact of professional networks of international lawyers is provided by Katharina Rietzler's Chapter 10. Focusing on the International Law Association's (ILA) involvement in brokering the 1960 Indus Waters Treaty between India and Pakistan, this chapter highlights the critical decade of the 1950s, when international lawyers in the West and in the global south sought to formulate universal legal rules amidst the complexities of decolonization, the state-building of post-colonial nations, the proliferation of technological utopias, and the global Cold War. Rietzler pays special attention to the interactions of four jurists from the ILA Rivers Committee: S. M. Sikri, a future Chief Justice of India; Manzur Qadir, Senior Advocate and future Foreign Minister of Pakistan; and two Western advisers to the governments of India and Pakistan respectively, the German scholar Friedrich Berber and the US government official John Laylin. Their contributions and positions in the ILA debates help to understand the way in which post-colonial nations like India and Pakistan used both domestic and imported legal expertise to define sovereignty autonomously and, by extension, to destabilize the consensus within the international legal community on the extent to which international law could be regarded as settled in a post-colonial world.

Returning to Europe in the final chapter, Morten Rasmussen explores the impact of lawyers and legally minded politicians for the transition from international law to European law in the 1950s and 1960s. With European integration and cooperation firmly grounded in international treaties between sovereign nations, Rasmussen argues, it is remarkable that an understanding of the primacy of European law for all member states was already firmly established by the mid-1960s. To explain this 'constitutional breakthrough', the chapter traces the influence of five seminal protagonists: Walter Hallstein, Petrus Serrarens, Michel Gaudet, Robert Lecourt, and Alberto Trabucchi. While these men from four European countries shared an idealist idea of European integration and even federalism, their professional roads and approaches to integration law differed greatly. Yet they all consciously applied law and legal arguments as tools and techniques to ensure closer cooperation and to enforce the integration process. The political battle over the institutional nature of the European community, Rasmussen reminds us, was fought in the domain of law.

The chapters assembled in this volume do not lay any claim to comprehensiveness. Indeed, the very fact that they cover more than three centuries and large parts of the globe make the gaps all the more evident. The dominant focus on European and North Atlantic protagonists rather than those from other regions and hemispheres has already been commented on, and there are equally large lacunae when it comes to other perspectives. The traditionally uneven sexual balance among international lawyers as well as the gendered character of international legal practice, and the question as to what extent past patterns continue to determine today's practices, is an obvious omission.[53] So too is the near absence of international private law and its practitioners, which reflects conceptual limitations of the present volume with its focus on the—somewhat literally understood—international rather than the transnational, but also the fact that the non-public spheres of commercial law are not easily covered by research in public archives.[54] The list of gaps—the role of lawyers in international organizations and transnationally active non-governmental organizations (NGOs) comes to mind[55]—could easily go on. Yet this volume is not a synthesis but a template or, rather, a selection of templates

[53] Cf. Isabelle Delpla, 'Les femmes et le droit (pénal) international', *Clio* 39 (2014), 183–204, and Hilary Charlesworth, 'The Hidden Gender of International Law', *Temple International & Comparative Law Journal* 16 (2002), 93–102.

[54] But see the excellent study on commercial arbitrators by Dezalay and Garth, *Dealing in Virtue* (n 49).

[55] Dzovinar Kévonian, 'Les juristes et l'Organisation internationale du travail, 1919–1939. Processus de légitimation et institutionalisation des relations internationales', *JHIL* 12 (2010), 227–66. For an analogue look at economists and economic thinking in an NGO see Heike Wieters, *The NGO CARE and Food Aid from America 1945–80: 'Showered with Kindness'?* (Manchester: Manchester University Press, 2017).

of how historians can portray the craftsmen and the idiosyncrasies of their assignments without depoliticizing their metier or trivializing their labours.[56] If readers of this collection are willing to engage with it as a guide, pointing out a variety of directions to pursue, it will have served its purpose.

The chapters assembled in the present volume result from a long, continuous debate at several meetings of the international and interdisciplinary research network *Juristen in der internationalen Politik. Praxis und Praktiker des Völkerrechts im 19. und 20. Jahrhundert*, generously funded by the Deutsche Forschungsgemeinschaft. We would like to thank all participants, including those not represented in this volume, for their comments and insights, and we hope that these spirited and collegial discussions are reflected in the following pages.

We would also like to thank those who helped this book on its long way to publication. At Oxford University Press, Merel Alstein, Jack McNichol, and Cathryn Steele were an unfailingly supportive team, wondrously patient, and a pleasure to work with. Two reviewers generously recommended the proposed volume for publication while helpfully pointing us to gaps we could fill while there was still time. Catherine Marshall's precise editing was crucial in polishing the chapters and making them publishable. Mohith Singh's competent management and Janet Walker's copy-editing skills finally helped us over the finish line. The end product, we hope, attests to the efforts of all who have contributed to make it more than the sum of its parts.

56 For a recent critique of such depoliticizing tendencies in analysing international law see Ian Hurd, *How to Do Things with International Law* (Princeton, NJ: Princeton University Press, 2017).

2

Shaping a New Profession

Japanese Encounters with International Law, *c.* 1600–1900

Andrew Cobbing

Japan's reception of Western international law developed across several decades of revolutionary social and political change in the late nineteenth century. These sweeping reforms following the Meiji Restoration in 1868 involved a profound transition from the relatively insular pattern of foreign relations under the Tokugawa regime (1603–1868) to Japan's closer engagement with international society during the Meiji era (1868–1912). Traditionally, the regional model for structuring interstate relations in East Asia had been the Sinocentric order based on the cultural supremacy of China. While still drawing on this framework, Tokugawa shogun rulers had since modified the system to assemble their own Japan-centred world. Under the Tokugawa 'Great Peace' of the early modern period, the emerging law of nations that exercised minds in the turbulent politics of far-off Europe was out of sight, and beneath notice, in Japan.

This insular world view was rocked to its foundations by the increasingly frequent European and US incursions in the nineteenth century. Commercial treaties were imposed under duress in 1858, dismantling the Tokugawa state's edifice of self-imposed isolation and establishing treaty ports that marked the 'opening' of Japan. Suddenly forced to operate within the parameters of an alien world order, scholar-officials scrambled to familiarize themselves with the unknown West. This chapter traces the challenges they faced in assimilating terms that often had no cultural equivalent in their own society. To understand how the Japanese understood the world at this juncture first requires a brief review of the long-standing impact of continental ideas, introduced through the ebb and flow of relations with China over the previous millennium (600–1600). One belief still prevalent under Tokugawa rule, for example, was the assumption that the more remote a society was from the civilizing influence of Chinese culture, the more barbarian its people were. In this design, Europe was beyond the pale.[1]

[1] On the concept of civilization, the idea of China, 'central efflorescence', 'order of manifest civility', and perceived category of barbarian, see David C. Kang, *East Asia Before the West: Five Centuries of Trade and Tribute* (New York, NY: Columbia University Press, 2010), 29–30, 33–5.

Andrew Cobbing, *Shaping a New Profession* In: *Crafting the International Order.* Edited by: Marcus M. Payk and Kim Christian Priemel, Oxford University Press (2021). © The Several Contributors.
DOI: 10.1093/oso/9780198863830.003.0002

Japan and the West were thus still worlds apart when the treaty ports opened in 1859. While the European diplomat deplored the 'barbarous' customs of this non-Christian society, the Japanese were appalled by the intrusion of this unlettered foreign 'barbarian' whose arrival defiled the sacred soil of their imperial land. Furthermore, the concept of a legal profession had yet to be really introduced in Japan, let alone the architecture of international law. This chapter traces how the Japanese encountered and grappled with translating the new language of Europe's law of nations. It then explores how it was rapidly deployed by the new Meiji state, on the one hand to undermine the Sinocentric regional order and project Japan's status in East Asia, on the other to campaign for full recognition in the eyes of the Western treaty powers. In a formative process that produced Japan's first international lawyers, a new generation of specialists appeared with the training essential to operate both as legal advisers to the state and advocates for their homeland's place in the emerging global order.

Such was the tenacity of the Tokugawa regime that there was practically no knowledge of Western international law until it was finally imposed by treaty in the mid-nineteenth century. This was surprisingly late, given the intensity of Japan's first encounters with Europe several hundred years earlier. They may have lived on the other side of the globe, but during the so-called Christian Century (1543–1639), all the signs had been that the Japanese, like others, were already becoming entangled in European politics. First of all, Portuguese and Spanish merchants and missionaries had spread their influence in these islands; Dutch and English servants of the newly formed East India Companies then set up factories as footholds for trade.[2]

Iemitsu himself, the third shogun of the new Tokugawa dynasty founded in 1603, was not averse to playing on the religious loyalties then dividing Europe in the Thirty Years War. During the Shimabara Rebellion in 1637–1638, he ordered the Dutch to assist the siege on Hara Castle, where over 20,000 Japanese peasants, many of them inspired by Iberian padres, held out before the uprising was suppressed.[3] In 1639 the Portuguese were then expelled, concluding the flurry of seclusion edicts that Iemitsu had issued in recent years. All Europeans were henceforth excluded from Japan bar a handful of Dutch East India Company servants incarcerated on the man-made island of Dejima in Nagasaki Bay. In previous decades, trade with the Portuguese had been so sought after that in 1571 the local warlord had let the coastal village there become a Jesuit colony. Now these Dutch merchants were allowed to stay in Nagasaki, but only by permission of the shogun. Although a highly controlled trade endured, Japan eschewed all diplomatic relations with

[2] See C. R. Boxer, *The Christian Century in Japan, 1549–1650* (Berkeley, CA: University of California Press, 1951). Grant K. Goodman, *Japan and the Dutch, 1600–1853* (Richmond: Curzon, 2000).

[3] Adam Clulow, *The Company and the Shogun: The Dutch Encounter with Tokugawa Japan* (New York, NY: Columbia University Press, 2014), 121–2.

European states, and by extension all contact with their theories of international law, for the next 200 years.[4]

In the Tokugawa dynasty's world view, outside interference was unwelcome. Even as wars raged in Europe and colonial expansion transformed the Americas, Africa, and parts of Asia, these islands enjoyed centuries of peace and political stability. Europe also played little part in the way the Japanese defined foreign relations or conceptualized their place in the world. For more than a thousand years, they had been incorporated into the cultural orbit of Chinese civilization, the Sinosphere.[5] Their writing script employed Chinese characters imported from the continent, while Buddhism and Confucianism, the belief systems that helped early rulers of the Yamato state impose their authority across the Japanese archipelago, were introduced from China in the sixth and seventh centuries.[6]

Due to this influx of foreign cultural influence, Japan had long since been drawn into the Chinese political universe. During the Sui (581–618) and Tang (618–907) dynasties in particular, tributary relations were established, enabling diplomatic exchange in the form of sporadic missions. Japanese rulers submitted to the Emperor of China as the 'son of heaven' and peerless ruler on earth; in return they received the reflected kudos and glory they needed to secure their political legitimacy at home. Under these arrangements for investiture, often called the tribute system, Japan was situated among a cluster of neighbouring satellite states in East Asia—usually viewed as 'barbarian' by the Chinese—whose monarchs drew their authority from official recognition by the celestial ruler of the Middle Kingdom.[7]

There were times when diplomatic relations lapsed or were even severed. In the late ninth century, for instance, political instability abroad prompted the Heian court in Japan to abandon sending further missions to Tang China. In the sixteenth century, the Ming authorities were so exasperated by Japanese pirates (*wakō*) raiding the coast that they finally refused further trade. There were also overtures to restore these ties, some more successful than others. Notoriously in 1401, the shogun Ashikaga Yoshimitsu earned himself the censure of future patriots by consenting to the subordinate title of 'king of Japan' in order to secure trade relations with China. In the thirteenth century, by contrast, Kublai Khan's failure to gain the Kamakura shogunate's consent to this status had led to war, albeit with two unsuccessful Mongol invasions of Japan in 1274 and 1281.[8]

In the early seventeenth century as well, the first Tokugawa shoguns saw good reason for repairing the relations with China so catastrophically damaged during

[4] On the founding of Nagasaki see Reinier H. Hesselink, *The Dream of Christian Nagasaki: World Trade and the Clash of Cultures, 1540–1640* (Jefferson, NC: MacFarland & Co., 2016), 55.

[5] Joshua Fogel, *Articulating the Sinosphere: Sino-Japanese Relations in Space and Time* (Cambridge, MA: Harvard University Press, 2009), 7–18.

[6] H. Paul Varley, *Japanese Culture*, 4th edn (Honolulu, HI: University of Hawai'i Press, 2000), 19–21.

[7] Ronald P. Toby, *State and Diplomacy in Early Modern Japan: Asia in the Development of the Tokugawa Bakufu* (Stanford, CA: Stanford University Press, 1984), 170–1.

[8] Varley, *Japanese Culture* (n 6) 105–7, 113–14.

the recent Imjin War with Toyotomi Hideyoshi's invasions of Korea in 1592 and 1597. While such external recognition might help shore up their initially fragile political authority, however, their enthusiasm was tempered by the Ming rulers' insistence on reducing them to the same status they had conferred on Yoshimitsu. Just as they shied away from state-level ties with Europe, Tokugawa rulers eschewed diplomatic relations with China, even though both Dutch ships and junks (*tōsen*) continued to put into port at Nagasaki, now the sole designated enclave for foreign trade.[9] No longer active participants in the orbit of the tribute system focused on China, instead they assembled a conceptually similar order of their own, a system of foreign relations described by Ronald Toby as a 'Japan-centred world'.[10]

Tokugawa Japan's Own International Order

There always remained a certain awareness that civilization had once emanated from China, but in the Tokugawa narrative Japan had outgrown this heritage. With the continent now consumed by conflict as Manchu invaders from the north threatened and destroyed the Ming dynasty, the new regime in Japan set about imposing order after a century of endemic conflict among rival warlords. This host of local magnates, the *daimyō*, were forced to pledge loyalty to the shogun, ushering in the Tokugawa 'Great Peace'. Ironically, the neo-Confucian philosophy these shogun rulers used to control society and justify their political legitimacy was itself only recently imported from China.[11] Nevertheless, Japanese scholars devised some creative arguments to naturalize these foreign ideas and explain how China's ancient 'Way of the Sages' found its purest expression in the harmonious society of contemporary Japan.[12] The known universe had also contracted to some extent, since Iemitsu's decrees included the draconian measure of prohibiting all overseas travel. Inheriting the mantle from China, the notional hub of civilization in the Tokugawa world view was now situated in the shogun's new capital at Edo (modern-day Tokyo).

Just as in China's tribute system, Japan would be orbited by satellite states, perceived to varying extents as barbarians. This parallel could be seen as only natural in the case of the Ryukyu Islands. Although conquered by the Satsuma domain in 1609, the king of Ryukyu was kept in situ as the nominal ruler of a puppet state, partly to preserve the kingdom's tributary relations with China, which provided

[9] On the Tokugawa regime's policy of self-imposed seclusion, see Tashiro Kazui and Susan Downing Videen, 'Foreign Relations during the Edo Period: Sakoku Reexamined', *Journal of Japanese Studies* 8/2 (1982), 283–306. Ronald P. Toby, 'Reopening the Question of Sakoku: Diplomacy in the Legitimation of the Tokugawa Bakufu', *Journal of Japanese Studies* 3/2 (1977), 323–63.

[10] Toby, *State and Diplomacy* (n 7) xix, 88–9, 173, 228.

[11] Luke S. Roberts, *Performing the Great Peace: Political Space and Open Secrets in Tokugawa Japan* (Honolulu, HI: University of Hawai'i Press, 2012), 3; Varley, *Japanese Culture* (n 6) 171–3.

[12] Conrad Totman, *Early Modern Japan* (Berkeley, CA: University of California Press, 1993), 172–6.

a useful alternative gateway for overseas trade. Moreover, the crown prince of Ryukyu led a grand retinue on a courtesy visit to Edo each time a new shogun was sworn into office or a new king was invested in Naha. These embassies made the journey twenty-one times in all, presenting the inhabitants of Edo with a powerful reminder of the shogun's prestige abroad. Similarly, exotic processions of envoys from Korea marched through the streets of Edo on twelve occasions under Tokugawa rule. In 1609 diplomatic relations were restored with the kingdom of Korea, on essentially equal terms, but such visits reinforced the impression that all roads led to Edo.[13]

To complete this effect, Tokugawa rulers studiously avoided sending their own envoys abroad for as long as they could, until reluctantly prompted by their treaties with the Western powers in 1858. Meanwhile, a smaller retinue led by the *opperhoofd* (head) of the Dutch trading post at Dejima, was also escorted to Edo each year where they paid homage to the shogun, just as *daimyō* processions were required to make regular journeys there under the alternate attendance system enforced in Tokugawa Japan.[14] The cumulative effect of these embassies served to 'create the illusion of an East Asian world order that was Japanese in design and Japanese in focus'.[15]

With their outlandish dress and ignorance of Chinese letters, the Dutch were naturally considered the most barbarian visitors of them all. In this respect, they were simply following in the footsteps of the Portuguese and Spanish, the 'southern barbarians' (*nanbanjin*) of previous centuries. Reading Dutch texts was thus described as 'barbarian studies' (*bangaku*), confined at first to a handful of interpreters in Nagasaki. In generations to come, the Dutch would also be joined in this pantheon of outsiders beyond the pale of civilization by 'red barbarians' (*akaezo*), the Russian traders and migrants who began appearing in the Kuril Islands and sporadically off the coast of Ezo—now Hokkaido in northern Japan—in the last decades of the eighteenth century.[16]

In this Japan-centred world order, there was no incentive to engage with Europe's law of nations. Moreover, the scholar-officials who later chanced upon, studied, translated, and introduced this body of thought had no real legal training themselves. A Japanese bar for professional lawyers with recognized qualifications would not appear until the last decade of the nineteenth century. In early modern Japan there was also a cultural aversion to litigation, as the neo-Confucian pursuit of harmony in Tokugawa society discouraged people from seeking recourse to a

[13] Toby, *State and Diplomacy* (n 9) 36–7, 48–9.

[14] Goodman, *The Dutch in Japan* (n 2) 26–31; Constantine N. Vaporis, *Tour of Duty. Samurai, Military Service in Edo and the Culture of Early Modern Japan* (Honolulu, HI: University of Hawai'i Press, 2008), 2–3.

[15] Toby, *State and Diplomacy* (n 9) 234.

[16] Donald Keene, *The Japanese Discovery of Europe: Honda Toshiaki and Other Discoverers, 1720–1798* (London: Routledge, 1952), 14, 47.

court. Nor could they call upon a lawyer when they did, as the concept of a litigant's right to representation was not imported until the 1880s. There was just some recognition that a guarantor, perhaps a respected figure within the litigant's community, might accompany them to court. Litigants (*kujinin*) who travelled to court in Edo, for example, might thus be escorted by their innkeeper, who in the process took on the role of a *kujishi*, perhaps the closest precursor of a modern lawyer to be found in early modern Japan. Throughout the hearing this *kujishi* advised his clients, prepared the necessary documents, detained them in his establishment, and guided them to and from the *shirase* court. He was tolerated rather than welcomed by the presiding magistrates, however, and widely suspected of dragging cases out simply to increase the fees he charged his guests. Writing in 1956, Richard Rabinowitz explained, '[i]t is no accident that the lawyer in contemporary Japan takes as his model the European or American practitioner rather than the indigenous *kujishi*'.[17]

The *shirase* courts themselves were situated within the authorities' general administrative buildings. Often in a courtyard open to the sky, they took their name from a layer of white gravel, symbolizing purity, spread across the floor. Magistrates called *bugyō* presided on a raised platform, where instruments of torture might be kept in view, not so much for use but to remind litigants of the gravity of the occasion. They were not professional jurists, however, as these judicial duties formed only part of their roles as senior government officials, combined with those of police chief, tax collector, and mayor. The *yoriki* officials who acted as their assistants might have a deeper understanding of the legal process, as these appointments often ran in the family among higher-ranking retainers. All these officials came from the ruling samurai class that comprised 6–7 per cent of the total population (including women and children of samurai status).[18] They weighed the merits of each case collectively, and reached their judgment in accordance with the moral guidance of neo-Confucian philosophy, which formed the bedrock of samurai education in early modern Japan. When passing sentences, they could also draw on the *kōjiikata osadamegaki*, a law code compiled in the mid-eighteenth century by order of the eighth shogun, Tokugawa Yoshimune, which covered procedure and precedents with specified punishments in relation to the severity of the crime. This was for officials' eyes only, however, so Tokugawa justice was hardly transparent, but it did allow a more humane approach, limiting the use of torture during interrogation, and curbing the practice of extending punishment to the guilty party's relatives.[19]

[17] Richard W. Rabinowitz 'The Historical Development of the Japanese Bar', *Harvard Law Review* 70 (1956), 64.

[18] Eiko Ikegami, *The Taming of the Samurai, Honorific Individualism and the Making of Modern Japan* (Cambridge, MA: Harvard University Press, 1995), 162.

[19] Marius B. Jansen, *The Making of Modern Japan* (Cambridge, MA: Harvard University Press, 2000), 238.

While these courts operated in lands directly controlled by the Tokugawa shogunate, the administrative practices in early modern Japan were fragmented and decentralized, with cases in large parts of the empire left to the jurisdiction of other authorities. Beyond the Tokugawa heartland and a few major cities under direct rule from Edo, over 260 *daimyō* lords still held their own semi-autonomous domains, not unlike the principalities of the Holy Roman Empire. In each domain comparable judicial arrangements were in place, with magistrates appointed from the local *daimyō*'s own ranks of samurai retainers. Moreover, powerful domains such as Satsuma would subsequently play a key role in the overthrow of the Tokugawa regime and creation of the Meiji state. In the late nineteenth century, therefore, it was often samurai from these regions who went on to fill senior posts in the new government ministries like foreign affairs and justice that engaged most closely with questions of international law.[20]

Despite their proud heritage as descendants of illustrious warriors, the samurai had little outlet for their training in martial arts during the Tokugawa 'Great Peace', which spared Japan from war for over 200 years. It was rather their education in neo-Confucian lore from their years spent at the domain's school that prepared them for the bureaucratic duties of government posts. For those in coastal domains, however, this hardly prepared them for a new threat that appeared in the last decades of the eighteenth century as unfamiliar European sails were sighted on the horizon. Initially, this consisted of Russian incursions to the north, and then, during the Napoleonic Wars, forays by the British, among others, from the south. Over following decades, the explosive growth of the opium trade brought more ships into the China Seas, and by the mid-nineteenth century the North Pacific Ocean had become a magnet for British and US whalers, who viewed the coasts of Japan as an inhospitable 'double-bolted land'.[21]

By this stage, an academic curiosity in European ideas was taking hold within Japan, but it was medicine rather than international law that first piqued the interest of scholars. Studying European books had already been rehabilitated by Tokugawa Yoshimune in the 1720s, as long as they contained nothing on Christianity. The pursuit of 'barbarian studies' (*bangaku*) was now reconfigured as 'Dutch Studies' (*rangaku*), a niche field often dominated by doctors, and would later develop into 'Western Studies' (*yōgaku*), as the increased contact with foreign ships demanded some acquaintance with European languages other than Dutch. Technical fields besides medicine also gained currency, notably navigation, geography, and the science of casting cannon.[22]

[20] The first four Meiji diplomats sent to represent Japan at the Court of St James in London, for example, were all from Satsuma. Andrew Cobbing, 'Opening Legations: Japan's First Resident Minister and the Diplomatic Corps in Europe', *Diplomacy & Statecraft* 28 (2017), 195–214, at 202.

[21] Herman Melville, *Moby-Dick or The Whale* (New York, NY: Harper & Brothers, 1851), 122.

[22] Keene, *The Japanese Discovery of Europe* (n 16) 32.

It was this select group of *rangaku* scholars who, through their exposure to Dutch texts, first showed some awareness of Europe's law of nations. When a British whaling ship ran aground off the coast not far from Edo in 1824, Takahashi Kageyasu, the most brilliant *rangaku* scholar of the day, was charged with investigating and producing a response to the growing threat posed by foreign vessels.[23] Takahashi drew on European protocol to draft the notorious 1825 Expulsion Edict, ordering officers manning coastal defences to shoot on sight, expressed in terms such as 'shell and repel' or 'don't blink twice', whenever a foreign sail was seen approaching the shore. As Takahashi explained,

> According to the laws of European nations, cannons are mounted along the coast, and when ships of a nation with whom trade relations are maintained enter the harbour, signals are exchanged by flag. When ships from a nation with whom diplomatic relations are not maintained try to enter, blank rounds are fired from the nearest cannon on shore. It is customary for those ships to leave the harbour after thus being informed that entry is not permitted.[24]

Takahashi was thus aware of, and willing to incorporate, such elements from the Law of the Sea as he had gleaned directly from Dutch East India Company officials in Nagasaki, or possibly from Dutch texts. It was the Dutch, after all, who had promoted the practical and now widely used cannon shot rule defining a state's territorial seas as the coastal waters within range of cannon on the shore.[25] It was also conventional to fire a blank warning shot across the bow of any unidentified vessel as a prompt to confirm identity by raising the ship's colours, at the same time threatening the use of force in the event of belligerence or non-compliance. Takahashi's mistake was to assume that all foreign ships would be as pliant as the Dutch had been to date. In reality, states with powerful navies like Britain and the United States were unlikely to accept such hostile terms imposed by Edo and, as time would prove, would seek to impose unequal terms of their own.[26]

To maintain the cohesion of Japan's Middle Kingdom, for instance, in the decades prior to the 1825 Expulsion Edict any foreign ships making overtures for trade had been routinely redirected to Nagasaki, as far as possible from the shogun's seat of power at Edo. It fell to the governor of Nagasaki, the Tokugawa regime's closest equivalent of a foreign minister, to humour such visitors before turning them away. In 1805, for example, Nikolai Rezanov was kept waiting and his request for trade

[23] Takahashi Kageyasu (1785–1829): from Edo, followed in his father's footsteps in joining the shogunate's astronomy department. Also involved in surveying and cartography, was placed in charge of translating barbarian books from 1811.

[24] Translation by Bob Tadashi Wakabayashi, *Anti-Foreignism and Western Learning in Early Modern Japan: The New Theses of 1825* (Cambridge, MA: Harvard University Press, 1986), 103.

[25] 'At present the whole space of the sea within cannon-shot of the coast is considered as making a part of the territory.' Emer de Vattel, *The Law of Nations* (London: Robinson, 1797), 129.

[26] Wakabayashi, *Anti-Foreignism and Western Learning* (n 24) 105–6.

with Russia finally refused only after months of correspondence between Nagasaki and Edo. Similarly, any foreign sailors cast ashore when their ships ran aground on Japan's coasts were sent to Nagasaki and interred there while arrangements were made for their rescue. Japanese castaways were likewise treated with suspicion if they somehow made it back to their homeland, having transgressed Iemitsu's now 'ancestral law' prohibiting travel abroad.[27] When attempting to return nine such castaways in 1837, the USS *Morrison* was thus driven away forcibly from the shore of Uraga Bay (close to Edo), in compliance with Takahashi's 'don't blink twice' policy. Even the more knowledgeable critics of this hostile approach, such as Takano Chōei and Watanabe Kazan, voiced their concern more out of a practical fear of reprisals from powerful foreign states than any real appetite for overhauling Japan's existing world order.[28]

Shortly afterwards, China's defeat in the First Opium War (1839–1842) heralded a seismic shift in the power dynamics of East Asia. While keenly aware, however, even then the Tokugawa authorities were not moved to alter Japan's foreign relations and simply modified their 'shell and repel' policy in 1842. This pragmatic decision drew praise from King Willem II of Holland when the Dutch made their first diplomatic overture by sending the warship *Palembang* to deliver a letter to the shogun, sovereign to sovereign, in 1844. Written in flattering terms, Willem did not really allude to international law but did warn that 'a nation preferring to remain in isolation at this time of increasing relationships could not avoid hostility with many others'.[29] This Dutch initiative was rejected, however, and in 1846 as well, Commodore James Biddle was met with the standard instruction to take his petition to faraway Nagasaki when he reached Uraga Bay with two US Navy ships in the hope of negotiating a treaty like the ones recently signed with China.

Captain James Glynn experienced more success in 1849 when he managed to rescue fifteen US sailors who had been imprisoned in Nagasaki after being shipwrecked off the northern island of Ezo the previous year. He relied on Dutch help to negotiate their release, but in forcing his way into Nagasaki Bay despite attempts to block his ship's path, Glynn demonstrated a level of resolve not seen since 1808

[27] On the treatment of Japanese castaways see Andrew Cobbing, *The Japanese Discovery of Victorian Britain. Early Travel Encounters in the Far West* (Folkestone: Japan Library, 1998), 4–5.

[28] Takano Chōei (1804–1850): from the Sendai domain, followed in his father's footsteps studying Dutch-style medicine, later in Nagasaki, then opening his own academy of Dutch Studies in Edo. Watanabe Kazan (1793–1841): from a prominent family in the small domain of Tabara, studied Confucian thought and Dutch Studies and became a noted artist, rising to rank of *karō* (senior advisor) in Tabara. Both Takano and Watanabe were imprisoned in 1839 for criticizing the government's response to the USS *Morrison*. Watanabe was placed under house arrest but committed suicide in 1841 to prevent reputational damage extending to Tabara. Takano escaped and became a fugitive for six years but died under torture on his recapture in 1850. Donald Keene, *Frog in the Well: Portraits of Japan by Watanabe Kazan (1793–1841)* (New York, NY: Columbia University Press, 2006), 153–7.

[29] United States, *Treaties and Other International Acts of the United States of America: Documents, 1852–4* (Washington, DC: GPO, 1931), 531. Robert Hellyer, *Defining Engagement: Japan and Global Contexts, 1640–1868* (Cambridge, MA: Harvard University Press, 2009), 145–7.

when the HMS *Phaeton* had entered this harbour.[30] The harsh conditions these sailors suffered during their internment, moreover, made headlines on their return to the United States, framing the agenda of the Perry mission that followed. The message from US President James Buchanan that Commodore Matthew Perry delivered to the Japanese in 1853 again made no direct reference to international law, but in his own address he demanded that US castaways 'shall be treated with humanity', pointing out that, among all Christian peoples, 'it is considered a sacred duty to receive with kindness, and to succour, and protect all, of whatever nation, who may be cast upon their shores'.[31]

The Treaty of Amity and Commerce signed with Perry in 1854, albeit under duress, was Japan's first ever treaty with a foreign power, and as such eroded the conceptual framework of the Japan-centred world. Despite Perry's reputation for 'opening' Japan, however, this agreement did not yet really provide for trade, being more a 'tentative pact' than a revolution in Tokugawa diplomacy.[32] Nevertheless, it was couched in the rhetoric of the law of nations and Western diplomatic protocol that, over the following decades, would transform Japan's foreign relations. It included, for example, a most favoured nation clause, securing for the United States any further privileges subsequently granted to other states.[33] Article XI also allowed a US consul 'to reside in S[h]imoda', heralding the arrival of the resident diplomat, a hitherto unknown concept, in the shape of Townsend Harris in 1856.[34]

To the consternation of Japanese translators, moreover, these first treaties were peppered with a whole new vocabulary of specialist terms with no existing counterpart or even concept in Japanese. Western diplomatic agents were just called *kanri* or *riin* in these texts, simply meaning an official, and it was not until 1867 that a Japanese term for consul was devised.[35] Fathoming the exact meaning of such loaded terms, and deploying new combinations of Chinese characters to convey their effect would be, over the following decades, the most daunting challenge facing Japanese linguists' efforts to understand international law.

It was also such semantic minutiae that preoccupied Tokugawa officials during their negotiations with Harris and European diplomats ahead of signing the commercial treaties in 1858 with America, then Britain, Russia, the Netherlands, and France, paving the way for the opening of treaty ports the following year. What they

[30] See Noell Wilson, 'Tokugawa Defense Redux: Organizational Failure in the "Phaeton" Incident of 1808', *Journal of Japanese Studies* 36/1 (2010), 1–32.

[31] Commodore M. C. Perry to His Imperial Majesty the Emperor of Japan, 7 July 1853. W. G. Beasley, *Select Documents in Japanese Foreign Policy* (Oxford: Oxford University Press, 1955), 101.

[32] Michael Auslin, *Negotiating with Imperialism: The Unequal Treaties and the Culture of Japanese Diplomacy* (Cambridge, MA: Harvard University Press, 2004), 17.

[33] Convention between the United States of America and Japan, signed at Kanagawa, 31 March 1854. Beasley, *Select Documents*, 121.

[34] Technically Jan Hendrik Donker Curtius was the first resident diplomat in Japan. Already in situ as the *opperhoofd* of the Dutch trading post at Dejima, Curtius was appointed 'Dutch Commissioner in Japan' in 1855 to negotiate a treaty, but this was only after the treaty with Perry had been signed.

[35] Auslin, *Negotiating with Imperialism* (n 32) 25.

did not yet realize, and so did not concern them, was just how these treaties were framed in terms that incorporated Japan not so much into the family of nations but in a subordinate rank of semi-civilized, barbarous, usually non-Christian empires, ineligible for the full sovereign rights of an independent state.[36] Since this notional hierarchy was largely a product of the recent positive turn in international law, they also had no way of knowing the relative inequality such terms imposed. Only in subsequent decades, when Japanese scholars acquired the necessary European language skills to absorb such details of international law, would their invidious implications be revealed.[37]

Key terms that would later be decried as 'unfair' during the Meiji period were thus waved through by Tokugawa negotiators in the 1850s. Extraterritoriality, for example, was not considered out of the ordinary in East Asia. Comparable arrangements had existed for centuries in the region, often in tightly controlled trading enclaves for foreign merchants located at a suitable distance from the capital, such as Canton (China), Busan (Korea), and Nagasaki (Japan). Even before Harris requested such a clause, moreover, Tokugawa officials had started codifying extraterritorial arrangements for inclusion in their new treaties with Western powers, hence his pleasant surprise when they so readily agreed.[38] Similarly, the most favoured nation clause had already become a feature of foreign relations in the region since Britain signed the Treaty of the Bogue with China in 1843. Like the Chinese, the Japanese viewed this rather in terms of their own traditional customs as a convenient mechanism for 'using barbarians to control barbarians'.[39] The low tariffs imposed by the treaties, meanwhile, simply reflected the free trade values prevalent in the mid-nineteenth century, particularly among the British merchant community then dominant in the treaty ports. It was only in subsequent decades when higher rates set in as protectionism was reinforced in the United States, and then Europe, that Meiji Japan's inability to adjust these fixed tariffs became a burning issue.

The overriding concern for Tokugawa negotiators in 1858 was rather the indignity of signing treaties with foreign barbarians at all. They also kept one eye fixed on the political impact at home, given that even the remit of the shogun—his full title meant barbarian-quelling generalissimo (*seii tai-shōgun*)—was to keep such intruders at bay. They nevertheless saw the treaties as a price reluctantly worth paying for the sake of preserving Japan's territorial sovereignty. It also spared their land, as Katō Yuzō emphasizes, from the more onerous treaties of defeat that were recently imposed on China.[40] Even after the treaty ports opened, therefore, there

[36] Jennifer Pitts, *Boundaries of the International. Law and Empire* (Cambridge, MA: Harvard University Press, 2018), 30–38.

[37] Auslin, *Negotiating with Imperialism* (n 32) 139.

[38] Ibid., 26–7.

[39] Ibid., 20.

[40] Katō Yūzō, *Kurofune zengo no sekai*, 2nd edn (Tokyo: Chikuma Gakugei Bunko, 1994), 167.

were many who still clung on to the belief that their Japan-centred world had not yet been fatally compromised. This was borne out by much of the political rhetoric at the time, most notably the imperial edict ordering the shogun to expel the foreign 'barbarian' in 1863. The edifice did not crumble, moreover, until 1865 when, under pressure from foreign warships in Hyōgo Bay, the court in Kyoto was coerced into ratifying the treaties. On their first meeting with the foreign representatives following the Meiji Restoration in 1868, officials of the new imperial regime also promised to honour the existing treaties, irrevocably locking Japan into the Western international order. Now even acknowledged by the court, no longer could citizens and subjects of the treaty powers be just dismissed as foreign barbarians.

The Reception of International Law in Meiji Japan

The challenge facing the men who had just seized power was to explain how an essentially European concept of international relations could possibly determine Japan's place in the world. Some attempts had already been made to naturalize these alien ideas, using familiar expressions like the Way of Heaven (*tiendao*) from the neo-Confucian concept of universal order.[41] Under the tutelage of Harris and other foreign representatives, Tokugawa officials had also acquired some practical knowledge of diplomatic protocol and the law of nations. The new Meiji leaders drew on such templates, and the 'public law of the universe' (*udai no kōhō*) was soon invoked in an imperial proclamation early in 1868, ordering subjects to exercise restraint towards foreigners in Japan.[42] The same phrase reappeared on several occasions as the fledgling regime took responsibility for attacks on foreigners caught in the crossfire of the Boshin civil war, which stamped out Tokugawa resistance by June 1869.[43] Even the Charter Oath, the mission statement imposed on *daimyō* lords across Japan in April 1868, included an article endorsing 'the path of justice on Heaven and Earth' (*tenchi no kōdō*). Sometimes interpreted as alluding to international law, the phrase was so nebulous that it might also appeal to adherents of Japan's nativist Shinto religion.[44] Nevertheless, the author of this article, Kido Takayoshi, is known to have already familiarized himself with Uryū Mitora's translation of Henry Wheaton's *Elements of International Law*.[45]

[41] Ōhira Zengo, 'Japan's Reception of the Law of Nations', *The Annals of the Hitotsubashi Academy* 4 (1953), 55–66, at 57 and 64.

[42] Ibid., 65.

[43] Yasuoka Akio, 'Bankoku kōhō to meiji gaikō', *Seiji keizai shigaku* 200 (1983), 188–90.

[44] Sumiyoshi Yoshihito, 'Meiji shoki ni okeru kokusaihō no dōnyū', *Kokusaihō gaikō zasshi* 71 (1973), 33–58, at 39.

[45] Kido Takayoshi (1833–1877): senior retainer of Chōshū domain, played key role in sealing the Satsuma-Chōshū alliance that led to overthrow of the Tokugawa regime. A prominent early Meiji statesman, influential in the abolition of the domains in 1871, but health failed and died in his forties. Uryū Mitora (1842–1913): from Fukui domain, studied English under Guido Verbeck in Nagasaki

Translating such key works played an important role in Japan's reception of international law, but absorbing these culturally unfamiliar ideas was a slow, painstaking process. At first the only materials available were imported Chinese translations of Western texts. Fragments of Vattel's *Law of Nations* (1777), for example, featured in Wei Yuan's *Haiguo tzuhi* (*Illustrated Treatise on the Maritime Kingdoms*), a gazetteer read widely in Japan in the 1850s.[46] The first full text to appear was Wheaton's *Elements of International Law* (1836) in Chinese translation, a work completed by US missionary William A. P. Martin in Beijing in 1864.[47] Reprinted in Edo the following year by the Institute for Investigating Barbarian Books (*Bansho shirabesho*), Uryū's Japanese translation was available by 1868.[48] Several decades later, Soejima Taneomi, a former foreign minister, would tell a Chinese exile in Japan how much he and other Meiji diplomats owed to Wheaton in Chinese translation.[49]

From the mid-1860s onwards, a surge in Japanese translations fostered a growing awareness of international law. These were often produced by language experts who had recently been to Europe themselves. As such, they were a by-product of the rapid growth in Japanese overseas travel in the years following the opening of the treaty ports, as both Tokugawa officials and retainers of individual domains ventured abroad to study or tour foreign lands on diplomatic missions.[50] The notes that Nishi Amane wrote up from lectures delivered by Professor Simon Vissering at the University of Leiden, for example, were published in 1868 as *Bankoku kōhō* (*Public Law of All Nations*).[51] Similarly, Fukuchi Gen'ichirō, an interpreter on two Tokugawa overseas missions, returned with Hudson's English edition of Charles de Martens' *Guide Diplomatique*, which he then translated and published in 1869.[52]

A steady stream of publications was soon familiarizing the Meiji intelligentsia with key works in the field. Mitsukuri Rinshō, head of the Translation Bureau, for

before becoming English teacher at shogunate's English college in Edo. Later served Meiji government in several ministries; Yasuoka, 'Bankoku kōhō to meiji gaikō' (n 43) 66.

[46] These were translated under the auspices of Commissioner Lin Zexu shortly before the First Opium War. Shin Kawashima, 'China' in Bardo Fassbender and Anne Peters (eds), *The Oxford Handbook of the History of International Law* (Oxford: Oxford University Press, 2012), 451–74, at 458.

[47] Martin undertook this translation after witnessing British violations of international law in 1858. Ibid., 460.

[48] Auslin, *Negotiating with Imperialism* (n 32) 138–9.

[49] Soejima Taneomi (1828–1905): from Hizen (Saga) domain which, together with Tosa, joined Satsuma and Chōshū to complete the alliance of south-western domains that defeated Tokugawa forces in 1868–1869 and founded the Meiji state. A noted scholar of Chinese classics. Yasuoka, 'Bankoku kōhō to meiji gaikō' (n 43) 196–7.

[50] Cobbing, *The Japanese Discovery of Victorian Britain* (n 27) 28–37.

[51] Nishi Amane (1829–1897): from the small domain of Tsuwano, son of the *daimyō* lord's physician. Trained in Chinese and Dutch Studies at domain school, then served at shogunate's new Bansho shirabesho in Edo before studying in Holland. Later a prominent figure in *bunmei kaika* (civilization and enlightenment) movement.

[52] Fukuchi Gen'ichirō (1841–1906): born in Tokugawa-controlled Nagasaki, son of a doctor and neo-Confucian scholar, trained in Chinese and Dutch Studies, then English before serving as an interpreter on Bakufu and then Meiji overseas missions. Later a prominent journalist in Meiji Japan.

example, produced Japanese versions of T. Woolsey's *Introduction to the Study of International Law* (1860) in 1873; and by order of the government, J. Kent's *Commentaries on International Law* (1873) in 1876.[53] In the process, he is credited with coining the Japanese term for 'international law' (*kokusaihō*) still in use today.[54] In 1877 alone, there were translations of A. W. Heffter, *Das europäische Völkerrecht der Gegenwart auf den bisherigen Grundlagen* (1866) and H. Halleck, *Elements of International Law* (1877). A Chinese translation of J. K. Bluntschli, *Das moderne Völkerrecht als Rechtsbuch* (1868), then appeared in 1879, and was published with Japanese annotations in 1881.[55] In the headlong rush for Western inspiration during the 1870s, intellectuals who played prominent roles in the 'civilization and enlightenment' (*bunmei kaika*) movement would also invoke the law of nations (*bankoku kōhō*) and authorities like Kent and Bluntschli in respectful, almost reverential, tones.[56]

For the Meiji government, the adoption of international law meant acknowledging the overhaul of the Japan-centred world order. At the same time, it presented a political opportunity to distance the new regime from the Tokugawa policy of seclusion that had previously earned Japan near-pariah status as Western powers clamoured for trade. For all the xenophobic undercurrents still prevalent among some supporters of the imperial restoration in 1868, therefore, the public invocation of international law helped project the political legitimacy of the fledgling Meiji state at a time when its hold on power was still tenuous. Just as the Yamato state had once bathed in the reflected glory of Chinese culture, international recognition could have its uses.

The opportunity was not lost on Meiji officials, moreover, of deploying this alien code of international law to gain some leverage over Japan's neighbours in East Asia. If a key motive of the Tokugawa seclusion policy had been to insulate Japan from its traditionally subordinate status to China, international law provided a powerful tool for undermining the entire world order of the Sinosphere. Even now, the kingdoms of Korea and Ryukyu were both still tributary states of China, and the original Middle Kingdom continued to resist adhering to Western diplomatic protocol, despite the 'unequal' treaties of defeat imposed after two Opium wars. The case of Ryukyu in particular was incompatible with Western norms as, despite

[53] Mitsukuri Rinshō (1846–1897): born in Edo, grew up in noted family of government-employed scholars, training in Dutch Studies before joining Bansho shirabesho. Accompanied Tokugawa mission to 1867 Paris Exposition, then served in Meiji government's Translation Bureau, working with Gustave Boissonarde on drafting Japan's new commercial and civil law codes. Yasuoka, 'Bankoku kōhō to meiji gaikō' (n 43) 191.

[54] Sumiyoshi, 'Meiji shoki ni okeru kokusaihō no dōnyū' (n 44) 43.

[55] Kinji Akashi, 'Japan—Europe' in Fassbender and Peters (eds), *The Oxford Handbook of the History of International Law* (n 46) 724–43, at 732; Sumiyoshi, 'Meiji shoki ni okeru kokusaihō no dōnyū' (n 44) 43, 51–5.

[56] For examples of Meiji intellectuals referencing the law of nations and international lawyers see William R. Braisted (transl.), *Meiroku Zasshi: Journal of the Japanese Enlightenment* (Cambridge, MA: Harvard University Press, 1976).

remaining under *de facto* Japanese rule for centuries, this island kingdom had retained its official status as a tributary state. The Meiji regime actively used precepts of international law to loosen China's grip, including a short military campaign to Formosa (Taiwan) in 1874, and managed to incorporate Ryukyu (now Okinawa) within the Japanese state by 1879. Similarly, by stipulating the equal status of Japan and Korea in negotiating the Treaty of Gangwha in 1876, the Meiji regime eroded China's traditional suzerain authority over the peninsula.

Japan also signed its first ever treaty with China in 1871, but although this was agreed on equal terms, Qing officials continued to show Meiji diplomats the cultural superiority and condescending attitude befitting envoys from a tributary state. If anything, the treaty relations now imposed by the Western powers had reinforced China's determination to cling on to the protocol of the Sinocentric tribute system. In 1873, Foreign Minister Soejima Taneomi at last managed to break through this impasse by calling on his knowledge of both international law and Confucian literature to secure a diplomatic victory for Japan. On his visit to China as ambassador extraordinary and minister plenipotentiary, he became the first foreign representative from a non-tributary state in eighty years to receive an imperial audience. Symbolically, he wore Western dress with a sword at his side for the occasion, and bowed only three times, rather than the traditional kowtow accorded to the Son of Heaven.[57]

For the Meiji government, however, international law was a double-edged sword; more effective in asserting Japan's equality with China than gaining recognition from the Western powers. Rather than conferring on Japan entry to the family of nations, there was now an emerging awareness of just how asymmetric, or non-reciprocal, some terms of the treaties were. The entire treaty port regime, for example, was predicated on the assumption of only Western merchants trading in designated ports in East Asia, such as Yokohama in Japan, and Tokugawa negotiators themselves had not explored the possibility of Japanese trade overseas. This anomaly was only exposed in 1866 when, under pressure from the foreign representatives, the Tokugawa regime repealed its long-standing ban on overseas travel. Although Western merchants held privileges in Japan like the right to consular jurisdiction, these were denied to Japanese travellers in the West.[58]

From the outset, the Meiji regime had signalled its desire for treaty revision, at the very least to change the signatory to the emperor, but it was only now with their growing awareness of international law that Japanese officials perceived in these treaties violations of their sovereign rights. Particularly conspicuous was the continued presence of foreign troops, for in the volatile political climate in the early years of the treaty ports, French and British garrisons had been established

[57] Wayne McWilliams, 'East Meets East: The Soejima Mission to China, 1873', *Monumenta Nipponica* 30 (1975), 237–75, at 269.

[58] Cobbing, 'Opening Legations' (n 20) 199–200.

in Yokohama, in 1863 and 1864 respectively, to protect the international community there. Michael Auslin traces 'the intellectual beginning of [treaty] revision' to a letter in March 1869 from Iwakura Tomomi to Sanjō Sanetomi, two court nobles at the heart of the Meiji government.[59] 'We must guard our country's independence', Iwakura wrote, 'it is the greatest insult to our empire that foreign troops have landed on our territory and Western residents breaking our laws are punished by their own countries' officials.'[60]

For all their enthusiasm for international law in imperial edicts, or in relations with neighbouring states, therefore, Meiji officials showed more circumspection about this new legal language in their relations with the West. In the same letter Iwakura described international law as 'merely a cover for the use of imperialist force'.[61] He had clearly been comparing notes with Kido Takayoshi, then a Meiji councillor of state who, after a long meeting with British Minister Sir Harry Parkes three months earlier, confided to his diary,

> One cannot depend on international law without having a well-prepared military force. Many countries use the cloak of international law to seek their own interest in dealing with weaker nations. This is why I call international law a mere tool for depriving a weak nation of its rights.[62]

Kido was thus already articulating an outlook that would gain traction in the twentieth century in the context of postcolonial discourse. Focusing on the experience of colonized peoples, for example, Antony Anghie has described international law as a tool 'devised specifically to ensure their disempowerment and disenfranchisement'.[63]

Iwakura seemed in more positive mood in 1871 when, on his appointment as ambassador extraordinary charged with leading a grand embassy to America and Europe he declared, 'we must rely on international law if we wish to revise the treaties'.[64] He was disappointed, therefore, by the outcome of a series of interviews with Foreign Secretary Lord Granville in November 1872, when he was told that

[59] Iwakura Tomomi (1825–1883): lower-ranking but influential court noble, exiled after helping forge controversial alliance between imperial court and shogunate, returned to join forces with Satsuma and play leading role in Meiji Restoration. Served as equivalent of vice-president in new Meiji government, famously led Iwakura Embassy around America and Europe in early 1870s. Sanjō Sanetomi (1837–1891): higher-ranking court noble, also exiled after supporting Chōshū domain's efforts to secure imperial directive to 'expel the barbarian' (*jōi*). Like Iwakura, returned to take up leading position in Meiji government, serving as president until the 1880s. Auslin, *Negotiating with Imperialism* (n 32) 157.

[60] Iwakura Tomomi, *Iwakura kō jikki* vol. 1 (Tokyo: Iwakura kō kyūseki hozonkai, 1927), 699.

[61] Ibid.

[62] Sidney Devere Brown and Akiko Hirota (transl.), *The Diary of Kido Takayoshi*, vol. 1, 1868–1871 (Tokyo: University of Tokyo Press, 1985), 168.

[63] Antony Anghie, *Imperialism, Sovereignty and the Making of International Law* (Cambridge: Cambridge University Press, 2004), 31.

[64] Yasuoka, 'Bankoku Kōhō to Meiji Gaikō' (n 43), 195.

extraterritoriality would remain in Japan for the foreseeable future. As Granville explained, 'the policy of the British Government was to yield [to] the local authorities jurisdiction over British subjects in precise proportion to their advancement in enlightenment and civilization'.[65]

Gerrit Gong has used an English School approach to show how a perceived standard of civilization was imaginatively constructed and consciously employed in the nineteenth century to keep eastern, non-Christian states, in a subordinate status within the international community, even after entering into treaty relations with the Western powers.[66] While such treaties theoretically welcomed them into the family of nations, this did not confer full recognition as civilized states. Thirty years later, it was this commonly accepted mentality of exclusion from a notional inner circle that prompted Alexander von Siebold, a former adviser to the Meiji government, to choose the title *Japan's Accession to the Comity of Nations* for his short account of Japan's achievement in ending the treaty port regime by 1899. Noting that the Ottoman Empire's symbolic entry to the Concert of Europe with the 1856 Treaty of Paris 'carried with it only a theoretical value', Siebold stressed the importance of Japan's success by claiming, '[i]n the field of public law this is quite a new departure; but more than this it marks a new epoch in the relations of West to East'.[67]

As Douglas Howland points out, however, to all intents and purposes, Japan had always been a sovereign state under the natural law of nations and so the standard of civilization was 'merely a point of political rhetoric'.[68] Martti Koskenniemi has also demonstrated that the concept of a measurable standard of civilization only ever amounted to 'conjectural policy'.[69] Even so, Western diplomats and international lawyers clung to this tenuous theory. The mercantile community in Japan's foreign settlements, who stood to lose most from the removal of treaty privileges, also saw the preservation of consular jurisdiction in particular as almost an article of faith.

Japan's claim to be a full-fledged member of international society, meanwhile, was reinforced by the Meiji state's policy of sending resident ministers abroad to establish legations in the capitals of Europe and America. This was an ambitious project because, like other non-European states, Japan had no cultural tradition of maintaining permanent missions abroad. In the former Japan-centred world,

[65] 'Memorandum of an Interview between Earl Granville and Iwakura', 27 November 1872, The National Archives, Kew (TNA), FO 881/2138.

[66] Gerrit W. Gong, *The Standard of Civilization and International Society* (Oxford: Clarendon Press, 1984).

[67] Alexander von Siebold, *Japan's Accession to the Comity of Nation* (London: Paul, Trench, Trubner & Co., 1901), 1–3.

[68] Douglas Howland, *International Law and Japanese Sovereignty: The Emerging Global Order in the 19th Century* (New York, NY: Palgrave Macmillan, 2016), 4.

[69] Martti Koskenniemi, *The Gentle Civilizer of Nations: The Rise and Fall of International Law, 1871–1960* (Cambridge: Cambridge University Press), 134–5.

foreign envoys had always made the journey to the shogun's seat of government at Edo, but Tokugawa officials stayed at home. And while the new treaties provided for the reciprocal exchange of resident diplomats, this was viewed as window dressing in 1858. Western consuls soon arrived in the treaty ports to provide support for foreign merchants, but there were no plans yet for Japanese resident diplomats abroad. This dynamic soon changed, however, with the rapid rise in the number of Japanese students living overseas from the mid-1860s onwards.

In an age of unfavourable exchange rates, it represented a huge commitment for the new Meiji state to set up permanent missions abroad. Nevertheless, the first Japanese legations were opened in Paris and Washington, DC in 1871, London in 1872, Vienna and Berlin in 1873, followed by St Petersburg and Rome in 1875. By the end of the decade Japan also had legations in the Benelux countries and Iberian Peninsula.[70] This development was welcomed universally as a sign that Japan was now subscribing to Western modes of diplomacy. Yet the project was not just a costly expression of compliance with European customs but calculated also to serve Japan's political ends. As the treaty port press soon noticed, the appointment of Japanese resident ministers had the effect of containing the influence of their counterparts in Tokyo. In 1876, for example, an article in the *Japan Gazette*, an English newspaper in Yokohama, pointed out how their presence served to diminish the standing of the foreign representatives:

> The fact of there being *Japanese* Ministers Plenipotentiary, who are recognized as on an equality with those of other nations, the Government, and it may be added, the more educated people generally, have come to consider ministers much as other men, and not as formerly in the light of ministering or destructive angels sustained by heaven-like power.[71]

Meiji diplomats, therefore, were not simply acting as 'passive adopters', because their studied use of Western forms also subverted some of the prevailing norms in international society.[72] In effect, they challenged the overarching narrative of Western expansion in East Asia over previous decades as the mere presence of permanent Japanese officials in Europe augured a more reciprocal footing for diplomatic relations in future. Moreover, they paved the way for others, as the only other eastern diplomats already in situ when they arrived were there on behalf of the Ottoman Empire (since the 1830s) and Persia (since the 1850s), both states with a far longer history of relations with Europe. The Japanese example was soon followed by other eastern states that had recently signed treaties but were yet to embrace Western customs of diplomatic exchange. For China, in particular,

[70] Cobbing, 'Opening Legations' (n 20) 197–8.
[71] 'Treaty Revision', *The Japan Gazette*, 18 February 1876.
[72] Howland, *International Law and Japanese Sovereignty* (n 47) 5.

consigning a Manchu official to the indignity of a post so far removed from the Middle Kingdom was a reluctant admission of the irrevocable changes now forced upon the traditional world order in East Asia. The first Chinese legation opened in London in 1877, while the first minister from Siam was in residence by 1881, embedding a trend that, over time, would reshape the profile of the diplomatic corps in Europe.

These new legations also served as a platform for participating in the non-government organizations that were then transforming global communications. Japan joined the Universal Postal Union in 1877 and the International Telegraph Union in 1879.[73] By the end of the 1870s, the last remaining British and French post offices had closed down in treaty ports like Yokohama, and the postal service was controlled entirely by the Meiji state. In 1874 Ueno Kagenori, the newly appointed minister to Britain, also became the first Japanese member of the Association for the Reform and Codification of the Law of Nations, subsequently renamed the International Law Association (ILA).[74] By contrast, it would be several decades before the other international law society formed in 1873, the Institut de Droit International (IDI), also admitted Japanese members.

Demonstrating Meiji Japan's Credentials as a Civilized State

With treaty revision now the top foreign policy objective for the Meiji government, both the ILA and IDI provided a forum for exploring, as Iwakura had hoped, the possibility of a legal solution. In practice, however, they often found their path blocked by what they saw as European international lawyers' insistence on setting an impossibly high bar for the abolition of consular jurisdiction in Japan. In Europe, moreover, the dominant narrative for legal reform in 'semi-civilized states' was now the system of mixed courts that had just been implemented in Egypt in 1875, and at this stage was often viewed as 'a success'.[75] This compromise solution had taken years of negotiations to prepare, and was seen as a practical option in those states, like Japan, where the judicial system was not yet developed enough to warrant the removal of consular courts. On meeting Iwakura in 1872, for example, Lord Granville had also 'referred to the case of Egypt where the extra-territorial jurisdiction had formerly prevailed, but where the experiment was being tried of allowing Egyptian tribunals to administer the law in civil cases'.[76] As a result,

[73] Ibid., 80–5.

[74] Ueno Kagenori (1845–1888): from Satsuma domain, studied Dutch and then English in Nagasaki before joining new government as a Meiji diplomat, serving as envoy to Hawai'i, deputy minister, and minister to Britain. On the ILA cf. Katharina Rietzler's chapter in this volume.

[75] Jasper Y. Brinton, *The Mixed Courts of Egypt* (New Haven, CT: Yale University Press, 1968), 27. For example, Lord Granville commented, '[t]he establishment of Mixed Courts has worked well in Egypt'. Granville to Plunkett, 11 January 1884, TNA, PRO 30/29/313.

[76] Granville went on, 'if this experiment succeeded, it would be tried in criminal cases also, and there was no reason why a similar course should not be taken with Japan'. Memorandum of an Interview

Fukuchi Gen'ichirō was sent to investigate the mixed courts in Turkey and Egypt the following year, and several Japanese reports on mixed courts followed. In the event, however, such a scheme was never taken up, partly because of reservations expressed over key differences between Egypt and Japan.[77] Mixed courts did feature in Inoue Kaoru's strategy in the 1880s when, as foreign minister, he hosted two Tokyo conferences on treaty revision, but the project was then abandoned due to public unrest over the prospect of foreign judges in Japanese courts.[78]

Meiji diplomats like Ueno Kagenori were initially encouraged when the IDI set up a commission in 1874 to conduct a survey on whether 'Eastern nations' could be admitted to 'the general community of international law'. The outcome in 1878 was dispiriting, however, as Sir Travers Twiss simply reported to the fourth conference in Paris that they shared a common 'awareness of obligations' with Europeans, and the question was then shelved in favour of focusing on the regulation of consular tribunals.[79] In the same year, a discussion on extraterritoriality in East Asia was held at the ILA conference in Frankfurt, but this also concluded that foreign jurisdiction should remain in place for the foreseeable future. Present at this meeting were Guo Songtao and Ueno, the Chinese and Japanese ministers to Britain; so dissatisfied was Ueno with this resolution that he pursued the issue, 'pressing for an opinion from the jurists of the west as to the touching point between the system of civilization and that of Orientalism'.[80]

By the end of the 1870s, therefore, a decade of presenting grievances with the treaties had sown a sense of distrust in Japan, not so much with international law itself but its perceived manipulation by the Western powers. This disappointment was compounded by the failure of the Yoshida–Evarts Treaty in 1878, an agreement with the United States that promised lower tariff rates, only to be vetoed by the British as it required the endorsement of all the treaty powers.[81] In the same year, the official chronicle of the Iwakura Embassy's travels to the West was published in Japan, including an account of the advice the Japanese ambassadors had received

between Earl Granville and Iwakura, Chief Japanese Ambassador, at the Foreign Office, 27 November 1872, TNA, PRO 881/2138.

[77] In 1873, for example, the ministry of Justice concluded that Japan already enjoyed more rights than Egypt. Naganuma Hideaki, 'Naigai shosō kara mita nihon no saibanken mondai', *Rekishi hyōron* 604 (August 2000), 37.

[78] Inoue Kaoru (1836–1915): from Chōshū domain, one of the 'Chōshū Five' who escaped to England in 1863 and studied at University College London. Later became a prominent Meiji oligarch in the new regime, serving as finance minister and, during 1880s, foreign minister.

[79] Jennifer Pitts, 'Boundaries of Victorian International Law', in Duncan Bell (ed.), *Victorian Visions of Global Order: Empire and International Relations in Nineteenth-Century Political Thought* (Cambridge: Cambridge University Press, 2007), 68–88, at 75. On Twiss cf. the chapter by Gabriela Frei in this volume.

[80] 'Extra-territoriality', *Japan Weekly Mail*, 13 October 1878.

[81] Yoshida Kiyonari (1845–1891): from Satsuma domain, one of nineteen retainers covertly sent to England in 1865, most studying at University College London. Later a Meiji diplomat, served as Minister to United States.

from Bismarck during a dinner party in Berlin five years earlier. As the view of a seasoned European statesman, it offered a perspective that was often referenced in Japan during the last decades of the nineteenth century. Recalling his childhood when Prussia was a weaker and poorer state, Bismarck had told Iwakura that

> From the very beginning, the so-called international law, which was supposed to protect the rights of all nations, afforded us no security at all. In cases involving a dispute, a great power would invoke international law and stand its ground if it stood to benefit, but if it stood to lose it would simply change tack and use military force, so that it never limited itself to defence alone.[82]

There was now also increasing criticism from the Meiji intelligentsia. In 1878, for example, Fukuzawa Yukichi declared that 'treaties of peace and amity or the law of nations are all very fine words, but these are just formalities, and the reality of international relations is no more than the contest for power and pursuit of profit'. Echoing Bismarck, he stressed, 'a hundred volumes of the law of nations do not compare with a few pieces of cannon'.[83] By 1881, Fukuzawa had refined his critique, possibly in response to the ongoing debate over extraterritoriality and Japan's aspirations for treaty revision. 'The word "nation" in the law of nations,' he decried, 'does not refer to all the nations of the world but applies only to Christian states'.[84]

The tortuous negotiations with the treaty powers over the following decade would only entrench such views among Japanese patriots. The year before the breakthrough finally came in the shape of the 1894 Anglo-Japanese Treaty, the influential journalist Kuga Katsunan even declared, 'international law is actually [just] the family code of Europe and not the public law of the world. To receive the benefits of this code there is no option but to transform the entire nation into a European state.'[85] Kuga had been particularly critical of Inoue Kaoru's attempts to win over foreign diplomats during a 'reign of Euromania' at the Rokumeikan, a two-storey guesthouse designed by British architect Josiah Conder, which had opened in Tokyo in 1883. Even members of the government and their wives had been reduced to acting like a 'dancing cabinet', as Western fashion was enforced at

[82] Kume Kunitake (ed.), *The Iwakura Embassy, A True Account of the Ambassador Extraordinary & Plenipotentiary's Journey of Observation Through the United States of America and Europe*, vol. 3: *Continental Europe* 1 (Tokyo: The Japan Documents, 2002), 323–4.

[83] Fukuzawa Yukichi (1835–1901), from Nakatsu domain, studied Dutch and then English before serving as interpreter on several Tokugawa overseas missions. Later founded Keio University, became leading figure in *bunmei kaika* (civilization and enlightenment) movement, and face still adorns the 10,000-yen banknote. Yasuoka, 'Bankoku kōhō to meiji gaikō' (n 43) 196.

[84] Ibid.

[85] Kuga Katsunan (1857–1907): born in Hirosaki domain, son of the *daimyō* lord's physician, went to school in early Meiji period, then served in several government posts before becoming a journalist and founding *Nippon*, a newspaper critical of westernization and outspoken in defence of Japanese tradition.

the banquets and masquerades held there.[86] Kuga also added an interesting comparison with the arbitrary laws once used under Tokugawa rule in Japan. 'Their invariable use of consular jurisdiction against us is much like the privilege that samurai once had to cut down [insolent] commoners.' Expressing a view then gaining currency in Japan he concluded, 'I wish international law was based on natural justice, so the family code of Europe could become the public law of the world'.[87]

The first generation of Japanese international lawyers was thus trained in a climate where Meiji statesmen sought foreign recognition and intellectuals questioned the integrity of the treaty powers. A programme of legal institutionalization, meanwhile, was launched in the early 1870s to pursue the dream of treaty revision, framing the agenda from the start. The aim was to articulate and translate a raft of new civil, criminal, and commercial codes so as to satisfy the treaty powers that Japan had become sufficiently civilized to dispense with consular courts in the treaty ports. European experts were employed to steer this process, French jurist Gustave Boissonarde arriving in 1872 to set about compiling the first draft of a new civil code. Similarly, German legal scholar Hermann Roesler turned his mind to the commercial code in the early 1880s. Boissonarde also taught at the ministry of Justice's own law school, while the Imperial University in Tokyo was soon staffed by Japanese lecturers who had studied law in Europe, usually in England, France, or Germany.

Legislation also lent new credibility to the legal profession; an amendment to the Criminal Code in 1880 recognized a defendant's right to representation in court, while each district court was now required to have a formal bar association, and the 'Lawyer's Law' of 1893 then set standard rules for examinations and qualifications.[88] In the words of Alexander von Siebold, '[n]ot only … did Japan have to create a bench but also a bar as a consequence of its adoption of European forms of procedure'. It was a herculean task to train such a body of judges and advocates given that there had been no clear separation of administration and justice under the previous Tokugawa regime. Nevertheless, by the end of the nineteenth century, there was already a supreme court, 7 superior district courts, 49 district courts, and 98 county courts, besides 1,201 other tribunals.[89]

Arnulf Becker Lorca calls Meiji Japan the 'paradigmatic example' of elites being trained at home and abroad to become experts in the Western canon of law.[90] These Japanese scholars were certainly among the 'semi-peripheral lawyers' he describes

[86] Junesay Idditie, *The Life of Marquis Okuma Shigenobu* (Tokyo: Hokuseido Press, 1956), 247–8; Ian Buruma, *Inventing Japan* (New York, NY: Modern Library, 2002), 57.

[87] Yasuoka, 'Bankoku kōhō to meiji gaikō' (n 43) 196.

[88] David Hood, 'Exclusivity and the Japanese Bar: Ethics or Self-Interest?' *Washington International Law Journal* 6 (1997), 199–218, at 201–2.

[89] Siebold, Japan's *Accession to the Comity of Nations*, 68–9.

[90] Arnulf Becker Lorca, *Mestizo International Law: A Global Intellectual History 1842–1933* (Cambridge: Cambridge University Press, 2014), 21.

as emerging at a distance from the metropole. To some extent, however, their heritage differed from other cases, as the legacy of the Japan-centred world still lingered in Meiji society. A Confucian worldview remained a familiar outlook in Japan, notwithstanding recent efforts to impose the new Western-style order. Within living memory, moreover, many Japanese intellectuals had viewed Europeans as barbarian intruders, exploiting the technological power that had come their way in the course of their rapacious expansion across the globe to threaten Japan. Sporadic backlashes against Western influence would thus become a recurrent feature in Meiji Japan, often in response to perceived slights by the Western powers and would feature again in the twentieth century en route to the Pacific War.

Japan's international lawyers still acknowledged their debt to Europe, but there was now less cultural deference than guarded respect. Becker Lorca outlines how this first generation responded to the puzzle presented by Japan's struggle for full recognition by either internalizing or challenging the standard of civilization.[91] In this sense they reflected the shifts in opinion among the Meiji intelligentsia, whose articles on current affairs including treaty revision were widely read. Kaneko Kentarō, for example, a prominent diplomat and jurist who received a law degree from Harvard, produced a compelling case for Japan in the 1893 volume of the *Revue de droit international et de législation comparée*.[92] First he enumerated the various legal reforms implemented by the Meiji government to date, an achievement he described as 'a legislative monument that has called the attention of the scientific community'.[93] In Kaneko's narrative, however, a long history of legal development in the past, including the compilation of codes in the seventh century had already prepared Japan for the challenge of modernization and assimilating Western law in the Meiji period. If Japan could absorb Confucian philosophy in the formative decades of Yamato rule, the reception of Western international law was not beyond the Meiji state. In a similar vein, in 1901 Takahashi Sakuye asserted that while modern legal standards had recently been introduced from Europe, 'in general it may be said that if the graft was from Europe, the stock was an ancient one, deeply rooted in Japan from the earliest times'.[94]

By contrast, in 1897 Senga Tsurutarō questioned the prevailing adherence to the idea of a standard of civilization altogether. In his view, the very concept was 'unscientific and deceitful', given that a term like 'civilization' was intrinsically cultural

[91] Ibid., 69, 73.

[92] Kaneko Kentarō (1853–1942): from Fukuoka domain, attended the domain school before travelling with Iwakura Embassy to America, where he was left behind to enrol at Harvard, graduating in law in 1878. Later taught at Tokyo Imperial University, also Minister of Justice, and then special envoy to America liaising with Theodore Roosevelt during Russo-Japanese War.

[93] Becker Lorca, *Mestizo International Law* (n 90) 68.

[94] Takahashi Sakuye (1867–1920): born in Takatō domain on eve of Meiji Restoration, went to Tokyo Imperial University Preparatory School and then university, graduating in law in 1894. Served as legal advisor to Meiji government during Sino-Japanese and Russo-Japanese Wars, and became professor of international law at Tokyo Imperial University. Ibid., 69.

by nature, and so clearly lay beyond the competence of jurisprudence.[95] 'Which science has defined this expression?' he asked, 'None!' Instead he drew on ethnographic terms to explain how this was a culturally specific outlook, and so could vary depending on the worldview (*Weltanschauung*) of any particular writer. As he put it, 'each religious denomination or philosophical school cherishes a peculiar conception of civilization'. Highlighting what he saw as the parochial outlook of his colleagues in the West, he declared, '[w]hen European international law scholars speak about "civilization" or "civilized states", they do so likewise from the subjective standpoint of their own *Weltanschauung*'.[96]

Over time, European training, publication of articles, and contact with renowned lawyers in the West also allowed Japanese scholars to gain a measure of international recognition. In an early case, Baba Tatsui spent some months enrolled at Middle Temple and would go on to a political career in Japan's then growing movement for freedom and popular rights.[97] While still in London in 1876, he wrote a scathing article on *The Treaty Between Japan and England* (1876), one of the first works in English to highlight Japanese perspectives on the injustice of consular jurisdiction. Similarly, while a student at Middle Temple in 1878, Hozumi Nobushige gave an impassioned address at the ILA conference in Frankfurt on the great strides taken in Japan to modernize since the Meiji Restoration.[98] At this time French law was still a prevalent model in Japan, under the influence of Boissonarde, but in 1885 Hozumi was among the founders of the English Law School (Igirisu Hōgakkō) in Tokyo, a forerunner of Chuo University.

Hozumi was also the first Japanese jurist to speak at an ILA conference, but others followed, and they generally found a sympathetic audience there. By contrast, the subject of Japan's claims for membership of civilized states for years received a cooler reception by the IDI. Paolo Paternostro, another legal advisor to the Meiji government, produced a detailed report at the 1891 IDI conference, where he explained why mixed courts would be inappropriate for Japan, and reiterated the country's now long-standing case against consular jurisdiction. Paternostro even went so far as to moot the possibility of Japan unilaterally abrogating from the treaties altogether, a threat that drew a reproach from Travers Twiss. Not until 1893

[95] Senga Tsurutarō (1857–1929): born in Okayama domain, attended the domain school, and then studied at Keio University. Later stayed in Germany for fifteen years, studying at Berlin University and graduating in law in 1897. Then taught Roman law at Kyoto Imperial University, receiving his doctorate in law in 1901.

[96] Becker Lorca, *Mestizo International Law* (n 90) 73.

[97] Baba Tatsui (1855–1888): from Tosa domain, learnt English under Guido Verbeck in Nagasaki before being sent to England in 1870, where he studied law at Middle Temple. Later became a prominent activist for liberal rights and critic of Meiji government.

[98] Hozumi Nobushige (1855–1926): born in Uwajima domain to a family of senior retainers, went on to study at Kaiseigakkō school of Western Studies (a forerunner of Tokyo University). Enrolled at Middle Temple in 1876, graduating in 1879, then stayed in Germany. Later taught at Tokyo Imperial University and received doctorate in law in 1888. Howland, *International Law and Japanese Sovereignty* (n 47) 41.

was a Japanese member first admitted to the IDI, when it was finally 'recognized that Japan had produced meritorious scholars of international law'.[99]

Other examples of international recognition soon followed as Japanese scholars began producing substantial original works in Western languages. Takahashi Sakuye was sent to Europe in 1897 and produced a work in English, *Cases on International Law*, which was published by Cambridge University Press two years later. The introduction, moreover, was contributed by John Westlake, who had now modified his earlier outlook on the perceived bar required by the standard of civilization, commenting that 'Japan presents a rare and interesting example of the passage of a state from the oriental to the European class'. Similarly, T. E. Holland excluded Japan from the family of civilized nations in all the editions of his international law treatise until 1900, after he met Takahashi.[100]

For the most part, early Japanese international lawyers were preoccupied with the task of proving Japan's compliance with the general principles of law and adherence to universal treaties. Takahashi, for example, tried to project Japan's status overseas by reminding international lawyers of the law-abiding spirit recently shown by the Imperial forces during the Sino-Japanese War (1894–1895). Significantly, Takahashi distinguished Japan's approach from what he called Chinese 'barbarian' behaviour.[101] By demeaning China and creating distance between two states hitherto seen by many international lawyers as essentially indistinguishable, he was hoping that the achievements of the Meiji government could be viewed in isolation.

A key element in this project was the theme of torture, which in European minds had long been associated with all non-Christian states. The entire rationale for constructing and retaining a system of consular jurisdiction, in fact, was based on the premise that foreigners in Japan were in danger of being subjected to inhumane conditions in the event of being arrested and detained by local police. On its creation, therefore, Japan's new Ministry of Justice soon banned torture in an effort to dissociate itself from the often draconian, routinely opaque system of criminal justice previously in effect under the Tokugawa regime. Torture also featured prominently in the narrative Japanese international lawyers then presented to demonstrate the progress made by the Meiji state.

Something of a propaganda war followed during the Satsuma Rebellion in 1877, the final samurai revolt against the sweeping early Meiji reforms, and to this day the last civil war on Japanese soil. Some Western journalists in the treaty port press latched on to any rumour of torture resurfacing during the fighting, as if to reinforce the argument that a non-Christian society like Japan was incapable of dispensing with this inhumane practice. The Meiji government, meanwhile, sought to draw

[99] Ibid., 28.
[100] Becker Lorca, *Mestizo International Law* (n 90) 135.
[101] Ibid., 71.

attention to the launch of its own humanitarian organization, the Philanthropic Society (*Hakuaisha*). After the Meiji government signed the Geneva Convention in 1886 this was renamed the Japanese Red Cross Society (*Nippon Sekijūjisha*) the following year. By the start of the Russo-Japanese War it was the largest Red Cross organization in the world and received plaudits from Western journalists for its role in the benevolent treatment of Russian prisoners.

Japanese international lawyers experienced mixed results in the early years of the twentieth century, the last decade of the Meiji period. Little resistance was experienced in asserting the privileges of a great power, since this followed the now ingrained hierarchy in this age of empire. An unequal treaty was imposed on China after the Sino-Japanese War, and Korea became a Japanese protectorate after the Russo-Japanese war in 1905. In the same year, however, the Permanent Court of Arbitration rejected the Meiji government's right to tax properties held in Japan by foreigners under perpetual leases dating back to the old treaties. A further blow would follow at the Paris Peace Conference with the failure of Japan's racial equality clause in 1919. Japanese international lawyers thus experienced more success in terms of reinforcing inequality in East Asia than their own pursuit of equality in the international order. In some respects, it seemed that Japan's vaunted new status as a supposed member of civilized states was still not enough to confer parity among the powers.[102]

Conclusion

Japan's reception of international law coincided with the formative years at the end of Tokugawa rule and the onset of the Meiji state. Until treaty relations were imposed in the 1850s, and even during the civil unrest in the decade that followed, there was still a desire to retain the Japan-centred world of the previous two centuries. The new Western-style international order was viewed as a threat not only to stability but Japanese cultural identity as well, creating a strain of scepticism that would resurface at times in the Meiji period and beyond. Whenever there was public outrage over an injustice handed down by a consular court in Japan, the entire superstructure of international law as conceived by European states was subject to criticism in the Meiji press.

Japan's first generation of international lawyers was thus raised and trained in a volatile intellectual climate. As government officials soon recognized, only familiarity with this new language could enable Japan to build a judicial system that could ever meet the treaty powers' vague criteria of a standard of civilization. Equipping scholars to raise awareness of Meiji Japan's grievances was also the only

[102] Ibid., 168–9.

way to confront Western international lawyers with the injustices of the treaty port regime. Some headway was made in the early decades of Meiji rule, but it was in the 1890s, when Britain and the other treaty powers were finally persuaded to relinquish their treaty privileges, that Japan's own international lawyers first gained some recognition overseas.

Their perspectives on international law were tempered not just by a still prevalent Confucian outlook in Meiji society but the memory of a Japan-centred world that had maintained social stability until the Western intrusion in the nineteenth century. A mood of distrust also developed as the government encountered obstacles in its pursuit of an elusive standard of civilization in the quest for treaty revision. Nevertheless, the treaties at least gave Japan's international lawyers a platform to develop their arguments on the progress achieved by the Meiji state. These scholars were also now in a position to challenge the status quo from an innovative standpoint of strategic compliance, by articulating their case in the language of Western-style international law. Results may not have been immediate, but this approach did begin to undermine some of the long-standing assumptions that, even at the end of the Meiji period, still prevented Japan from receiving full recognition by the international community.

The outcome was, by the onset of the twentieth century, a small but vocal group of Japanese international lawyers sufficiently conversant with the language and terms of their field to engage directly with colleagues in the West. Those who taught in Japan's new faculties of law, moreover, were now passing on the lessons from their own training in Europe to a new generation including growing numbers of overseas students, notably from China. Despite their own specialist background, however, they always remained aware that their field was, in effect, a system of ideas grafted from a distant social universe. They knew that international law had been consciously imported with the intention of enabling Meiji Japan to contend with the challenges posed by a rapidly shrinking international environment as modern transport and communications brought far-flung communities closer together than ever before. Sensitive to, and often sceptical of, the premise that international law was inherently universal in application, they found themselves strategically placed to promote Japan's role in shaping the emerging global order.

3

Legal Practitioners

Nineteenth-Century International Jurisdiction and the Ambiguous Role of the Members of the Mixed Commissions

Fabian Klose[*]

In December 1856, Edmund Gabriel, the British Commissioner at the Mixed Commission in Loanda, emphasized the singularity and uniqueness of the court system of which he was an acting member. Gabriel explicitly stressed the international character of the tribunals in his correspondence with the Portuguese Governor General of the colony of Angola regarding the much debated procedure of appointing a new Portuguese commissioner and secretary of the aforementioned mixed commission:

> The Mixed Commissions established under the Treaty between Great Britain and Portugal of the 3rd July, 1842, are, I venture to submit, international Courts, created for a definitive and special purpose, and existing solely in consequence of precise Treaty stipulations; as such, they cannot, in my opinion, be constituted or governed by the laws of either country. The only law which can serve to regulate the organization and proceedings of those Courts is the Treaty referred to.[1]

This early system of international jurisdiction, to which Gabriel referred, emerged in the wake of the efforts to fight the transatlantic slave trade during the course of the nineteenth century. Beginning with the first treaties of 1817/18, Great Britain, Portugal, Spain, and the Netherlands founded the Mixed Commissions for the Abolition of the Slave Trade, which was joined by additional nations at a later

[*] This chapter is based on the research for my book *In the Cause of Humanity. Eine Geschichte der humanitären Intervention im langen 19. Jahrhundert* (Göttingen: Vandenhoeck & Ruprecht, 2019). This chapter profited from the suggestions of many, for which I am grateful. I specifically want to thank Jakob Vogel, Paul-André Rosental, and the participants of the Seminar 'Histoire de l'Europe' at the Centre d'Histoire at Sciences Po Paris.

[1] Letter by Edmund Gabriel to Governor-General of the Province of Angola, 4 December 1856, in Foreign Office (ed.), *Correspondence with the British Commissioners at Sierra Leone, Havana, The Cape of Good Hope, and Loanda; and Reports from British Naval Officers, Relating to the Slave Trade, From April 1, 1857, to March 31, 1858* (London: Harrison and Sons, 1858), 58. The mentioned Treaty of 3 July 1842 between the United Kingdom and Portugal replaced earlier treaties that approved measures for the abolition of the slave trade, but largely followed the stipulations of the earlier Treaty of 1817.

Fabian Klose, *Legal Practitioners* In: *Crafting the International Order.* Edited by: Marcus M. Payk and Kim Christian Priemel, Oxford University Press (2021). © The Several Contributors. DOI: 10.1093/oso/9780198863830.003.0003

date. From 1839 to 1841, for example, newly independent states in South America such as Chile, the Argentine Confederation, Uruguay, Bolivia, and Ecuador also joined the system of the mixed commissions. Due to high maintenance costs, however, this took place only nominally as they did not send their own representatives to the existing tribunals or establish tribunals on their territory.[2] Finally, after a long period of intense diplomatic resistance, even the United States under the Lincoln administration at the time of the American Civil War announced its participation in the system and created the last mixed commission in New York City in 1862.[3]

The creation of the mixed commissions as stipulated in the treaties was to guarantee the conviction of captured slave ships. In a similar way to the regulation of military executive measures, the treaty partners also established a practice of standardization for all of the mixed commissions established throughout the entire Atlantic region which stipulated a uniform set of practices, functions, and procedures. These courts were located in port cities throughout the entire Atlantic area, namely in Freetown, Loanda, Cape Town, Boa Vista in Cape Verde, Rio de Janeiro, Paramaribo in Surinam, Spanish Town in Jamaica, Havana, and New York. They were in place for over fifty years, specifically from 1819 to 1871, and liberated over 80,000 Africans from various captured slave ships.[4]

The history and significance of the mixed commissions regarding international law and international relations has been neglected by academic scholars for many years.[5] It has long been assumed by legal historians that the creation of the Permanent Court of Arbitration in 1899 and the Permanent Court of International Justice in 1921 in The Hague marked the beginning of international jurisdiction.[6]

[2] Letter from Aberdeen 'Commission of Appointment under the Treaty with the Oriental Republic of the Uruguay', 2 August 1842, in Foreign Office (ed.), *British and Foreign State Papers* (hereafter BFSP) 32 (London 1857), 149–50; Letter from Aberdeen 'Commission of Appointment under Treaty with Chile', 13 October 1843, in ibid., 147–8; Letter from Aberdeen 'Commission of Appointment under Treaty with Bolivia', 13. October 1843, in ibid., 135–6; Letter from Mandeville to Aberdeen, 26 November 1842, in ibid., 310–11; Letter from Mandeville to Aberdeen, 18 July 1843, in ibid., 311–12; See also: Leslie Bethell, 'The Mixed Commissions for the Suppression of the Slave Trade in the Nineteenth Century', *The Journal of African History* 7 (1966), 83–8; Dennis A. Lypka, 'The Slave Trade Department of the British Foreign Office and the Suppression of the Transatlantic Slave Trade 1819–1854' (unpublished MA thesis, Calgary: University of Calgary, 1977), 147–8.

[3] Jean Allain, 'The Nineteenth Century Law of the Sea and the British Abolition of the Slave Trade', *BYIL* 78 (2007), 368–76; Eugene Kontorovich, 'The Constitutionality of International Courts: The Forgotten Precedent of Slave Trade Tribunals', *University of Pennsylvania Law Review* 158 (2009), 95–9.

[4] Despite these measures, one must note here that the number of slaves forcibly deported to the Americas in the course of the nineteenth century still remained high, at over 3 million people. See David Eltis and David Richardson, *Atlas of the Transatlantic Slave Trade* (New Haven, CT: Yale University Press, 2010), 274; Seymour Drescher, *Abolition. A History of Slavery and Antislavery* (Cambridge: Cambridge University Press, 2009), 245.

[5] An exception is the article: Bethell, 'Mixed Commissions' (n 2) 79–93.

[6] See for instance: Eric A. Posner and John C. Yoo, 'Judicial Independence in International Tribunals', *California Law Review* 93 (2005), 8–10; Timothy L. H. McCormack, 'From Sun Tzu to the Sixth Committee: The Evolution of an International Criminal Law Regime', in Timothy L. H. McCormack and Gerry J. Simpson (eds), *The Law of War Crimes. National and International Approaches* (The Hague: Kluwer Law International, 1997), 43–58.

It is only recent studies, mainly undertaken by legal scholars, which now investigate the role of these slave-trade tribunals as forerunners of a multi-national legal system, as the dawn of international courts, and as forgotten precedents regarding the constitutionality of international courts, especially in the context of US history.[7] Some legal scholars, such as Jenny Martinez, even go so far as to argue that international human rights law derives its origins from the fight against the slave trade and these related 'Courts of Mixed Commission for the Abolition of the Slave Trade'.[8] For Martinez, the mixed commissions were the 'first international human rights courts' and a significant forerunner of international criminal justice of the twentieth and twenty-first centuries.[9]

However, this rather idealistic picture which draws a direct line from the mixed commissions of the nineteenth century to international human rights law of the twentieth century invites a counter-argument: the mixed courts were the judicial part of the enforcement machinery not in regard to human rights, but in regard to maritime prize law and the internationally agreed humanitarian norm of abolition. Furthermore, the mixed commissions were far from being an institution in which all members closely cooperated to fight for a common cause such as universal rights and for the prosecution of human rights violations. On the contrary, the mixed commissions were a fiercely contested place, where each participating country sought to defend and enforce its own national interests in regard to one of the most controversial diplomatic issues of this time, the abolition of the slave trade.

In the following, I will focus closely on the members of the mixed commissions and the ambiguous role they often fulfilled. Officially, each member served in the system of the mixed commissions as a jurist and diplomatic representative of his

[7] For these legal studies see: J. P. van Niekerk, 'British, Portuguese, and American Judges in Adderley Street: the International Legal Background to and Some Judicial Aspects of the Cape Town Mixed Commissions for the Suppression of the Transatlantic Slave Trade in the Nineteenth Century (Part 1)', *The Comparative and International Law Journal of Southern Africa* 37, 1 (2004), 1–39; J. P. van Niekerk, 'British, Portuguese, and American Judges in Adderley Street: the International Legal Background to and Some Judicial Aspects of the Cape Town Mixed Commissions for the Suppression of the Transatlantic Slave Trade in the Nineteenth Century (Part 2)', *The Comparative and International Law Journal of Southern Africa* 37, 2 (2004), 196–225; Mark Lewis, *The Birth of the New Justice. The Internationalization of Crime and Punishment, 1919–1950* (Oxford: Oxford University Press, 2014), 14–15; Kontorovich, 'Constitutionality of International Courts' (n 3) 39–115; Seymour Drescher and Paul Finkelman, 'Slavery', in Bardo Fassbender and Anne Peters (eds), *The Oxford Handbook of the History of International Law* (Oxford: Oxford University Press, 2012), 904; Cornelisen G. Roelofsen, 'International Arbitration and Courts', in ibid., 162–3.

[8] Jenny S. Martinez, 'Antislavery Courts and the Dawn of International Human Rights Law', *The Yale Law Journal* 117, 4 (2008), 550–641; Jenny S. Martinez, *The Slave Trade and the Origins of International Human Rights Law* (Oxford: Oxford University Press, 2012).

[9] 'Though all but forgotten today, these slave trade courts were the first international human rights courts' in Martinez, *Slave Trade* (n 8) 6 and especially chapter 8 'A Bridge to the Future. Links to Contemporary International Human Rights Law', in ibid., 148–57. Farida Shaikh also speaks in the context of the Mixed Commissions of 'one of the earliest attempts to enforce international human rights law'. See Farida Shaikh, 'Judicial Diplomacy. British Officials and the Mixed Commission Courts', in Keith Hamilton and Patrick Salmon (eds), *Slavery, Diplomacy and Empire. Britain and the Suppression of the Slave Trade, 1807–1975* (Brighton: Sussex Academic Press, 2009), 42.

country according to the stipulations of the signed international treaties. These individuals were mainly recruited from the diplomatic circles of each state. As former civil servants, diplomats, and colonial officials they were hardly in possession of a specific legal education, which makes it difficult to designate them as professional jurists in a classical sense. Thus, far from being well-trained jurists or even legal scholars of the theory of international law, the members of the mixed commissions can be best described as legal practitioners, who as diplomatic as well as judicial agents had to implement the stipulations of international treaties on the abolition of the slave trade.[10]

However, apart from this official function as legal practitioners, the members of the mixed commissions also fulfilled another important role: they were lobbyists for the national interest of their respective country in regard to the slave trade, competing with lobbyists from other nations. While British representatives in these international tribunals were clearly dedicated to the new abolitionist agenda of the United Kingdom and acted accordingly, members from slave-trading nations such as Portugal, Spain, and Brazil sought to defend the interests of the slave traders and the slave owners. In this respect, the members of the mixed commissions simultaneously occupied different roles and functions, which makes it difficult to clearly define their role as research reveals a rather multifaceted picture. Thus, the purpose of this chapter is to focus on the somewhat ambiguous character of the mixed commissions and its members. In a first step, it analyses how the system of the mixed commissions emerged and functioned in the Atlantic world of the nineteenth century. It then moves on to concentrate on the ambiguous role of the commission members as jurists, diplomats, and lobbyists in order to present the first system of international courts as a fiercely contested body of early international cooperation.

The British Intervention against the Slave Trade and the Idea of International Enforcement

The passage of the Abolition Act by the British Parliament on 25 March 1807 transformed the once leading slave-trading nation into the exact opposite, the nation leading the fight to end the transatlantic slave trade. According to the Act of the British Parliament for the Abolition of Slave Trade,[11] every British citizen was

[10] Farida Shaikh uses the term 'judicial diplomacy' in the context of the system and function of the mixed commissions. For this see: Shaikh, 'Judicial Diplomacy' (n 9) 42–64.

[11] Act of the British Parliament for the Abolition of the Slave Trade, 25 March 1807, *BFSP* 5, 559–68; Stephen Farrell, 'Contrary to the Principle of Justice, Humanity and Sound Policy: The Slave Trade, Parliamentary Politics and the Abolition Act, 1807', in Stephen Farrell, Melanie Unwin, and James Walvin (eds), *The British Slave Trade: Abolition, Parliament and People* (Edinburgh: Edinburgh University Press, 2007), 141–71. There has been an intensive research debate with various explanations concerning the background of British abolition. For an overview see, for example, Thomas Bender (ed.), *The Antislavery Debate: Capitalism and Abolitionism as a Problem in Historical Interpretation* (Berkeley, CA: University of California Press, 1992).

forbidden to engage, directly or indirectly, in any aspect of the slave trade on the threat of a heavy fine of 100 pounds[12] per slave. The particular importance of this decision lay, above all, in the fact that the struggle against the transatlantic slave trade had now become an official matter of state. Before this, the abolitionists had conducted the struggle only at the level of civil society by petitioning parliament and mobilizing public opinion. With this Act, the government in London had committed itself to take action using state means to target human trafficking. Accordingly, the Abolition Act stipulated measures for British authorities on the seizure and sequestration of slave ships as described in the following:

> And be it further enacted, that all Ships and Vessels, Slaves or Natives of Africa, carried, conveyed, or dealt with as Slaves, and all other goods and effects that shall or may become forfeited for any offence committed against this Act, shall and may be seized by any Officer of His Majesty's Customs or Excise, or by the Commanders or Officers of any of His Majesty's Ships or Vessels of War.[13]

Thus, the Abolition Act served as the legal foundation for the military deployment of the Royal Navy off the coast of West Africa to enforce the ban on the transatlantic slave trade. For this reason, the British Admiralty sent two warships to African waters in 1808, the year immediately following the passage of the Act. This step was at first no more than a symbolic act, but it marked the start of the first and longest humanitarian intervention in history. In 1811, the number of ships was increased to that of a small fleet, and Great Britain continued to demonstrate its permanent military presence along the infamous Slave Coast of West Africa until the middle of the 1860s. At the highpoint of its engagement in the 1840s, the British fleet consisted of more than thirty ships.[14] Abolition thereby became a fundamental foreign policy paradigm of the United Kingdom in the course of the nineteenth century.

From the beginning, this maritime intervention raised a key problem, namely the question of mandate which was insufficiently addressed at the time: was it legitimate for the Royal Navy to capture slave ships of other nations, to confiscate them, and turn them over for court trial? Such questions touched upon sensitive rights of national sovereignty and fundamental issues of emerging international law. For the duration of the Napoleonic Wars, the British government justified its unilateral operations against foreign slave ships by referring to the right to search as set down in maritime law in times of war. Accordingly, officers of the Royal Navy handed over

[12] In 1787, a British pound had the purchasing power of about USD 140 today.

[13] Act of the British Parliament, *BFSP* 5, 567.

[14] On the deployment of the Royal Navy against the slave trade, see Christopher Lloyd, *The Navy and the Slave Trade: The Suppression of the African Slave Trade in the Nineteenth Century* (London: Longmans, Green, 1949); William E. F. Ward, *The Royal Navy and the Slavers: The Suppression of the Atlantic Slave Trade* (London: Allen and Unwin, 1969); Siân Rees, *Sweet Water and Bitter: The Ships that Stopped the Slave Trade* (London: Chatto & Windus, 2009).

captured slave ships for trial to the British prize court in Freetown, Sierra Leone, which had been established there for precisely this purpose.[15]

However, with the peace agreement of 1814, this situation altered fundamentally, leaving Britain with the need for a new internationally agreed legal basis for the right to capture, search, and convict slave ships sailing under a foreign flag in times of peace.[16] In the wake of the first international condemnation of the slave trade, the 'Declaration des 8 Cours, relative à l'Abolition Universelle de la Traite des Nègres', agreed by the European great powers in February 1815 at the Congress of Vienna, the British government initiated diplomatic negotiations to install an international machinery of enforcement.[17] The proposed model set out the crucial idea of combining military and legal enforcement measures.[18] The first treaties in what would become a comprehensive international network[19] between the United Kingdom and various countries were the legally binding agreements in 1817 with Portugal and with Spain, followed by an agreement in 1818 with the Netherlands.[20]

[15] See especially, Tara Helfman, 'The Court of Vice-Admiralty at Sierra Leone and the Abolition of the West African Slave Trade', *Yale Law Journal* 115 (2006), 1122–56. For the later established Vice-Admiralty Court on St Helena see: J. P. van Niekerk, 'The Role of the Vice-Admiralty Court at St Helena in the Abolition of the Transatlantic Slave Trade: A Preliminary Investigation, Part 1', *Fundamina: A Journal of Legal History* 15, 1 (2009), 69–111; and J. P. van Niekerk, 'The Role of the Vice-Admiralty Court at St Helena in the Abolition of the Transatlantic Slave Trade: A Preliminary Investigation, Part 2', *Fundamina: A Journal of Legal History* 15, 2 (2009), 1–56.

[16] On this, from a contemporary point of view see Henry Wheaton, *A Digest of the Law of Maritime Captures and Prizes* (New York, NY: R. M'Dermut & D.D. Arden, 1815), 227–30. Additionally see Allain, 'Nineteenth Century Law of the Sea' (n 3) 348–54; Maeve Ryan, 'The Price of Legitimacy in Humanitarian Intervention: Britain, the Right of Search, and the Abolition of the West African Slave Trade, 1807–1867', in B. Simms and D. J. B. Trim (eds), *Humanitarian Intervention: A History* (Cambridge: Cambridge University Press, 2011), 234–5; Lauren Benton, 'Abolition and Imperial Law 1790–1820', *Journal of Imperial and Commonwealth History* 39 (2011), 361–4.

[17] Declaration des 8 Cours, relative à l' Abolition Universelle de la Traite des Negres, 8 February 1815, *BFSP* 3, 971–2.

[18] Fabian Klose, 'Humanitäre Intervention und internationale Gerichtsbarkeit—Verflechtung militärischer und juristischer Implementierungsmaßnahmen zu Beginn des 19. Jahrhunderts', *Militärgeschichtliche Zeitschrift* 72, 1 (2013), 1–21.

[19] For this international treaty regime against the slave trade, see Ethan A. Nadelmann, 'Global Prohibition Regime: The Evolution of Norms in International Society', *International Organization* 44 (1990), 491–8; Edward Keene, 'A Case Study of the Construction of International Hierarchy: British Treaty-Making Against the Slave-Trade in the Early Nineteenth Century', *International Organization* 61 (2007), 311–39; Matthew Mason, 'Keeping Up Appearances. The International Politics of Slave Trade Abolition in the Nineteenth-Century Atlantic World', *The William and Mary Quarterly* 66, 1 (2009), 809–32; Robin Law, 'Abolition and Imperialism. International Law and the British Suppression of the Atlantic Slave Trade', in Derek R. Peterson (ed.), *Abolitionism and Imperialism in Britain, Africa, and the Atlantic* (Athens, OH: Ohio University Press, 2010), 150–174. For an overview of all treaties concerning the slave trade in the period between 1776 and 1863, see 'Slave Trade Suppression Tables; or A Chronologically arranged Statement of the Measures taken by different Nations for the Abolition of the Slave Trade', in Her Majesty's Stationery Office (ed.), *Slave Trade Instructions, being Instructions for the Guidance of the Commanders of Her Majesty's Ships of War employed in The Suppression of the Slave Trade* (London: HMSO, 1865), 131–42.

[20] Additional Convention for the Purpose of Preventing Their Subjects from Engaging in Any Illicit Traffic in Slaves, between Great Britain and Portugal, 28 July 1817, The National Archives, Kew (TNA), FO 84/2; Tratado Para la Abolicion del Trafico de Negros, between Spain and Great Britain, 23 September 1817, Archivo General de Indias, Sevilla (AGI), ULTRAMAR, Legajo 32, N. 20; Treaty for Preventing Their Subjects from Engaging in Any Illicit Traffic in Slaves, between Great Britain and the Netherlands, 4 May 1818, *BFSP* 5, 125–35.

Referring explicitly to the term 'in the cause of humanity', each of the respective treaty parties agreed to grant the other a mutual 'right to visit' their merchant ships in international waters during peacetime. In other words, these treaties provided the navies of the respective countries with the right in specified zones to stop ships suspected of slave trade, search them, and—if slaves were found on board—to confiscate them.

Only warships with the required special authority, documented in the languages of both parties to the treaty, were allowed to engage in such activity under strict adherence to the common instructions.[21] These detailed instructions were integral parts of the treaties and created an obligatory manual of operations for the British, Portuguese, Spanish, and Dutch navies.[22] In this way, a remarkable standardization in the use of military executive force by the navies of four different countries was created, with the clear aim to avoid diplomatic complications from the outset and to conduct international abolitionist cooperation as smoothly as possible. This intention was expressed particularly clearly in the following article from the agreement: 'Whenever a ship of war shall meet a merchant vessel liable to be searched, it shall be done in the most mild manner, and with every attention which is due between allied and friendly nations; and in no case shall the search be made by an officer holding a rank inferior to that of lieutenant in the navy.'[23] The inspection of foreign ships was designated as the responsibility of higher-ranking officers because only this circle of individuals was trusted to have sufficient diplomatic tact to conduct such a politically delicate task. Since all three treaties also contained a mutual liability to redress any treaty infringements, officers were compelled to follow a correspondingly exact perpetuation of evidence. This meant that they were required to write an affidavit on every case in which a ship was captured and to include the circumstances of the seizure, the exact nautical position in which the confiscated ship was found, and the flag under which it was sailing at the time.[24] The purpose of this was to prevent any cover-up of the nationality and the travel route of the alleged slave traders. Overall, the Royal Navy clearly shouldered the heaviest burden of these naval operations; in other words, Great Britain was the organizer and leader of the maritime measures. From the British outpost in Freetown, Sierra Leone, English captains launched their hunt for slave ships for over fifty years, driven by the prospect of financial gain through the prize money awarded for captured ships. In addition to this, the Abolition Act stipulated the payment of bounties for every slave they freed: forty pounds for a man, thirty pounds for a woman, and ten pounds for a child.

[21] Instructions Intended for the British and Portuguese Ships of War Employed to Prevent the Illicit Traffic in Slaves, TNA, FO 84/2; Instructions for the British and Spanish Ships of War Employed to Prevent the Illicit Traffic in Slaves, ibid.

[22] Ibid.

[23] Article 7 and Article 5, respectively, of the 'Instructions' as cited in the previous footnote.

[24] Form of Declaration of the State of the Vessel at the Time of Capture, TNA, FO 313/1.

However, at this point it must be noted that the capture of a slave ship did not automatically mean the liberation of the people found penned in below deck. The naval forces only had the military executive authority to inspect and, if necessary, to confiscate a suspected ship and escort it to the nearest port. In port, the future fate of the confiscated slave ship and its 'human freight' was dependent on the verdict handed down by the Mixed Commissions for the Abolition of the Slave Trade.

The Mixed Commissions for the Abolition of the Slave Trade as International Jurisdiction

The agreements of 1817/18 between Great Britain, Portugal, Spain, and the Netherlands also included a decisive judicial component, namely the creation of the 'Mixed Commissions for the Abolition of the Slave Trade'[25] as stipulated in each treaty:

> In order to bring to adjudication, with the least delay and inconvenience, the vessels which may be detained for having been engaged in an illicit traffick of Slaves, there shall be established, within the space of a year at furthest from the exchange of the ratifications of the present convention, two mixed commissions, formed of an equal number of individuals of the two nations, named for this purpose by their respective sovereigns.[26]

Located in port cities such as Freetown, Luanda, Cape Town, Boa Vista in Cape Verde, Rio de Janeiro, Paramaribo in Surinam, Spanish Town in Jamaica, Nassau, Havana, and New York, the purpose of these international commissions was to guarantee the adjudication of cases of captured slave ships.[27] Hereby these international tribunals replaced the British prize court in Freetown, Sierra Leone, which had been established during the Napoleonic wars to convict captured foreign slave ships according to maritime law in times of war.[28] Under the leadership of the United Kingdom an international enforcement machinery was thus developed, based on the idea that an internationally stipulated humanitarian norm was to be implemented by combined military and judicial means. Over the course of several decades of diplomatic negotiations, Great Britain successfully managed to establish a comprehensive international treaty network to enforce international abolition.

[25] Other terms used were 'Mixed Courts of Justice' and 'Courts of Mixed Commission'.

[26] Article 8 of the Additional Convention, 28 July 1817, TNA, FO 84/2; Article 12 of the Additional Convention, 23 September 1817, ibid.

[27] Bethell, 'Mixed Commissions' (n 2) 79–93; Shaikh, 'Judicial Diplomacy' (n 9) 42–64.

[28] See especially, Helfman, 'Court of Vice-Admiralty' (n 15) 1122–56.

Similar to the regulation of military executive measures, the treaty partners also established a practice of standardization for all of the mixed commissions established throughout the entire Atlantic area. The treaty countries were equally represented on each commission by a commissary judge and a commissioner of arbitration, whereas the state on whose territory the mixed commission was seated appointed a judicial secretary.[29] The court costs, which amounted to several thousand pounds annually, were divided equally among the treaty parties.[30] In the British case, the mixed commissions were under the administrative responsibility of the Foreign Office. The personnel of the tribunals was mainly recruited from the diplomatic circles of each country. As former diplomats, colonial administrators, and civil servants, they possessed hardly any specialized judicial training, which made their degree of professionalization rather low.[31] It is difficult to label them as professional jurists in a classical sense or even as legal scholars advancing the theory of international law. Instead, they are best described as legal practitioners who, as diplomatic as well as judicial agents, were obliged to implement the stipulations of international treaties on the abolition of the slave trade.[32]

The payment varied according to the location of the mixed commission. For instance, a British commissary judge in Freetown earned 3,000 pounds per year, while the salary of a commissioner of arbitration was 2,000 pounds and for a judicial secretary it was 1,000 pounds.[33] In order to avoid bribery, the common regulations for the mixed commissions strictly prohibited each member from receiving any further emolument from other parties.[34] Despite the generous salary—even compared to modern standards—the appointment of members was often a rather difficult task, especially in West Africa which, due to its harsh climate and tropical diseases, was regarded by contemporaries as the 'white man's grave'. In the case of death or absence of a member of the mixed commission, high-ranking officials such as the governor and the consul of the relevant country were designated to take over the position ad interim, so that the operability of each commission was guaranteed at all times. In this respect, the contracting parties further agreed to fill any vacancy as soon as possible.[35]

The standardized regulations clearly defined a common procedure in each case which had to be observed as closely as possible. Immediately after the arrival in the harbour, the responsible prize officer had to provide an affidavit including all necessary information regarding the circumstance of the capture, the ship, its crew,

[29] Article 2, Regulations for the Mixed Commissions, TNA, FO 84/2.
[30] Shaikh, 'Judicial Diplomacy' (n 9) 42–64.
[31] Lypka, *Slave Trade Department* (n 2) 120–1 and 126–7.
[32] Shaikh, 'Judicial Diplomacy' (n 9) 42–64.
[33] Slave Trade Restriction Commission, TNA, FO 96/34.
[34] Article 11, Regulations for the Mixed Commissions, TNA, FO 84/2.
[35] Article 14, Regulations for the Mixed Commissions, TNA, FO 84/2.

and its cargo, with a detailed list about the slaves found on board.[36] Furthermore, he had to hand over all means of evidence such as the logbook and the ship's papers. In addition, the judicial secretary of each mixed commission surveyed the crew according to a special interrogatory to gain further evidence, in particular on the nationality, the owner, the travelling route, and the cargo of the captured vessel.[37] Subsequently, both judges received all documents for their final assessment with a deadline of twenty days in which to complete the procedure. According to the common regulations, the official form of process was as follows:

> The Commissary Judges of the two nations shall, in the first place, proceed to the examination of the papers of the vessel, and to receive the depositions on oath of the Captain and of two or three, at least, of the principal individuals on board of the detained vessel, as well as the declaration on oath of the captor, should it appear necessary, in order to be able to judge and to pronounce if the said vessel has been justly detained or not, according to the stipulations of the Additional Convention of this date, and in order that, according to this judgement, it may be condemned or liberated.[38]

Following the review of the evidence, both judges were to hand down a unanimous decision. Should they be unable to agree, then one of the two commissioners of arbitration was chosen by lot to cast the third and tie-breaking vote, thus deciding the final verdict.[39]

Thus, two different scenarios could result. In the case of acquittal, the ship, its crew, and its cargo were to be released immediately, whereby the court was also to rule on the amount of reparations to be paid to the defendant for the resulting damages and losses—included the death of slaves—during the internment period.[40] In the case of conviction, however, the ship and all of its material freight were confiscated and sold at public auction. Sometimes the British Admiralty even bought these vessels and integrated them into its own naval squadron, thus transforming former slave ships such as the Brazilian brig *Henriquetta* into a successful slave hunter under its new name *HMS Black Joke*.[41] The proceeds from this were equally divided between the two treaty partners and were often used to finance the mixed

[36] Article 3, Regulations for the Mixed Commissions, ibid.; Form of Proceedings, and Steps to Be Taken On Arrival in Port, *BFSP* 8, 30; Mode of Process, or Form of Procedure for the Mixed Court at Surinam, in *BFSP* 10, 473–5.

[37] Interrogatories for the Use of the British Commissioners, to Be Administered to the Witnesses Belonging to the Vessel Taken, 1819, TNA, FO 313/1.

[38] Article 3, Regulations for the Mixed Commissions', TNA, FO 84/2.

[39] Ibid.

[40] Article 6, Regulations for the Mixed Commissions, ibid.; Article 8, Regulations for the Mixed Commissions, ibid.

[41] Lloyd, *The Navy and the Slave Trade* (n 14) 71–3.

commissions.[42] If slaves were on board the ship, these were only taken from board following the conviction and released to freedom in each area with a 'Certificate of Emancipation'. Each contracting party explicitly bound itself to guarantee the freedom of the liberated slaves.[43] However, it is important to note that the mixed commissions had no jurisdiction at all over the crew, captain, and owner of a convicted vessel, who could only be handed over to their respective national authorities for trial. The commissions thus functioned as a proto-system of international jurisdiction, in which judges of different nationalities made rulings together concerning the detained ships and the slaves on board.

Still, successfully implementing this legal theory into practice, that is, convicting a slave ship, was dependent on the respective court and varied from place to place. Whereas only 1.8 per cent of the cases brought before the court in Freetown ended in acquittal, the rate in Havana was 10 per cent and in Rio de Janeiro even an astonishing 32 per cent.[44] The reason for this was that the mixed commissions were not only a body of early international cooperation but also a fiercely contested place. Each member sought to defend and enforce the specific national interest of their country in relation to the controversial issue of the transatlantic slave trade.

The Ambiguous Role of the Commission Members

Officially, each member served in the system of the mixed commissions as a legal agent of his country according to the stipulations of the signed international treaties. British judges were bound by judicial principles to uphold impartiality, and 'to combine a fair conscientious zeal for the prevention of the illegal traffick in slaves, with the maintenance of the strictest justice towards the parties concerned, and with the promotion of a spirit of conciliation and harmony between His Majesty's Subjects and those of the Kings of Spain and Portugal'.[45] However, in practice, the British judges usually pursued a hard line against the slave traders and often turned their official role as impartial judge into that of prosecutor.[46] In this way, they zealously carried through the abolition course laid out by their government on the judicial level and acted as vanguard of London's abolitionist policy.

[42] See, for example, the proceeds in regard to the convicted Brazilian slave-ship Calliope, 31 December 1839, TNA, FO 84/273.

[43] Article 7, Regulations for the Mixed Commissions, TNA, FO 84/2.

[44] Shaikh, 'Judicial Diplomacy' (n 9) 51.

[45] Letter from Commissary Judge Thomas Gregory to Viscount Castlereagh, Sierra Leone, 21 June 1819, *BFSP* 8, 53. See also: Letter from Viscount Castlereagh to Commissary Judge Thomas Gregory, 19 February 1819, TNA, FO 315/1.

[46] Luis Martínez-Fernandéz, 'The Havana Anglo-Spanish Mixed Commission for the Suppression of the Slave Trade and Cuba's Emancipados', *Slavery and Abolition* 16, 2 (August 1995), 207; Bethell, *Mixed Commissions* (n 2) 85–6, Shaikh, 'Judicial Diplomacy' (n 9) 51; van Niekerk, 'British, Portuguese, and American Judges' (Part 2) (n 7) 200–1.

In addition to their official function, the British members of the commission also undertook an additional task, which closely resembled the actions of abolitionist activists and was clearly dedicated to the abolitionist agenda of the United Kingdom. In innumerable reports, they supplied the Foreign Office with valuable information from their locations across the entire Atlantic region. In doing so, they not only fulfilled their obligation to report on the various specific activities and the financial matters concerning the mixed commissions, but compiled useful information of all kinds with reference to the slave trade. From their port of station, they put together lists of slave ships in which the name, departure and arrival dates, point of destination, and crew size, as well as the number of the transported and deceased slaves were documented in minute detail.[47] Moreover, in their accounts, they listed the slave traders by name, reported on the size and weaponry of their ships, described their tactics, and pinpointed their outposts along the African coast.[48]

The British commissioners assumed the role of monitoring the extent to which other parties adhered to the treaty in so far as they persistently revealed the collaboration between slave traders and local authorities. For example, the representative of the Mixed Commission in Sierra Leone reported in March 1822 on the common practice of Spanish colonial authorities to extend—meaning to forge—time and again the royal licences for legal slave trade that had been permitted by the treaty agreements, but with time limitations.[49] Based on this information, the Foreign Office turned directly to the Spanish government and demanded unambiguously that such practices by its subjects be stopped immediately and the stipulations of the 1817 treaty upheld. Thanks to the news supplied by its commissioners, the government in London had access to a tightly woven network of information that made possible its detailed knowledge on the transatlantic slave trade and the corresponding coordination of military and diplomatic measures.[50] Thus, the British

[47] On this point, see, for example, List of Slave Ships and Slaves Arrived at Rio de Janeiro During the Months of January, February and March 1823, TNA, FO 84/23; Result of Voyages of 32 Vessels Which Sailed from the Port of Havannah for the Coast of Africa During the Year 1825, *BFSP* 15, 229.

[48] On this point, see for example: Charles MacCarthy, Memorandum of the Present Actual State of the Slave Trade on the Coast of Africa, Sierra Leone, 14 January 1822, *BFSP* 9, 164–6; Report of the British Commissioners in Sierra Leone to Foreign Secretary Canning, 15 Mai 1824, *BFSP* 12, 56–71; Report of the British Commissioners in Sierra Leone to Foreign Secretary Canning, 10 April 1825, *BFSP* 13, 30–40; Report by John Tasker Williams, Commissary Judge in Sierra Leone, to Foreign Secretary Canning, 30 March 1826, *BFSP* 14, 21; Lypka, *Slave Trade Department* (n 2) 136.

[49] Letter from the Marquess of Londonderry to Lionel Hervey, 10 March 1822, *BFSP* 9, 61. On the forgery of licences by Portuguese authorities, see for example: Report of the British Commissioners in Sierra Leone to Viscount Palmerston, 2 January 1836, *BFSP* 24, 10; Report of the British Commissioners in Sierra Leone to Viscount Palmerston, 5 January 1837, *BFSP* 25, 17–18.

[50] A very good example for the brisk flow of information is a letter from Viscount Palmerston to the British commissioners, in which he adds the most recent reports on the slave trade from the various locations. On this see Letter from Viscount Palmerston to the British Commissioners, 11 August 1841, *British Parliament Papers* (*BPP*) 21 Class A, 217.

commissioners played an important part in influencing London's international anti-slave trade policy and helped shape abolitionist strategy in a significant way.[51]

In return, the Spanish, Portuguese, and later Brazilian members of the commission also performed a dual function, albeit of a thoroughly different kind. They took a very moderate stance toward the slave traders during the trials and tended to adopt the role of the defence lawyer. Often their main concern was to protect the economic interests of their fellow compatriots against any British intervention considered too detrimental for trade, including the trafficking of humans. In part, they even maintained close contact to known slave traders, whose property was a matter over which they actually were supposed to rule in court.[52]

There were even some extreme cases in which the appointed judges themselves actually belonged to the lobby of the slave traders and supported these interests accordingly. People like José Maria Herrera y Herrera and José Buenaventura Esteva not only held the office of the Spanish judge in the Mixed Commission in Cuba in the 1840s and 1850s, but were simultaneously among the largest slave owners on the island.[53] In his dual role as judge and slaveholder, Bueanventura Esteva also recruited manpower for his own plantations from the ranks of the slaves liberated by the commission. Because of these activities, the British foreign minister, Lord Palmerston, instructed the Foreign Office in August 1846, to inquire critically 'whether the Marques de las Delicias [Buenaventure Esteva], being so great a slave-holder, is well fitted to be a member of the Mixed Commission'.[54] In Palmerston's view, the Madrid government should instead have given the office to a person who had the least possible connections to the criminal practices that the judges were to sentence.[55]

Furthermore, as the British commission reports documented, the local Spanish, Portuguese, and Brazilian authorities and Commission members often lacked any measure of political will to enforce the international ban on the slave trade.[56] As a rule, public opinion in these countries perceived abolitionism as an instrument of power politics used by Great Britain to intervene in the domestic affairs of sovereign states. The first British Commissar Judge in Cuba, Henry Kilbee, reflects upon the attitude of the Cuban public in January 1825 by noting '[i]t is universally believed that the Abolition was a measure which Great Britain, under the cloud

[51] Lypka, *Slave Trade Department* (n 2) 125–6.

[52] David Turnbull, *Travels in the West: Cuba with Notices of Puerto Rico and the Slave Trade* (London 1840), 77–8.

[53] Luis Martínez-Fernández, *Fighting Slavery in the Caribbean. The Life and Times of a British Family in Nineteenth Century Havana* (Armonk: Sharpe 1998), 47.

[54] Letter from Viscount Palmerston to H. L. Bulwer, 14 August 1846, *BFSP* 35, 402.

[55] Letter from Viscount Palmerston to H. L. Bulwer, 10 December 1846, in ibid., 408.

[56] On this, see for example: Report of the British Commissioners in Sierra Leone to Foreign Secretary Canning, 15 May 1824, *BFSP* 12, 58; Report of the British Commissioners in Sierra Leone to Viscount Palmerston', 14 December 1833, *BPP* 14 Class A, 10–11; Report of the British Commissioners in Sierra Leone to Viscount Palmerston, 5 January 1837, *BFSP* 25, 16; David R. Murray, *Odious Commerce. Britain, Spain and the Abolition of the Cuban Slave Trade* (Cambridge: Cambridge University Press, 1980), 76–7.

of philanthropy, but really influenced by jealously of the prosperity of this Island, forced upon Spain'.[57] In his estimation, the slave trade was not understood by the Spanish to be criminal activity; on the contrary, it was seen as an instrument to advance the economic interests of the island with which one could also thwart British politics, which were perceived as self-seeking. Kilbee's conclusion was, plain and simple, that Spain had officially agreed to the abolition of the slave trade but took no practical steps to enforce the ban.[58]

In their letter to the Foreign Office from January 1827, Kilbee and his colleague W. L. Macleay repeat these accusations. The slave trade in Cuba was being continued undeterred and in full public view, despite the ban.[59] Slave ships left Havana headed for Africa and returned to port without generating any measure of attention and reaction by the island authorities, who only became active when the British commissioner requested an inspection from the Spanish Capitan General. The standard procedure of the official investigation would be formally to clear the ship in question of all suspicion, and the case would then be closed. In the view of Kilbee and Macleay, the collaboration went so far that slaves could be unloaded in the public port of Havana and herded through the city in the middle of the day without it being possible to produce a single witness to corroborate this in court. Therefore, both commissioners claimed that 'we are justified by past experience in believing, that the legal authorities will exert all their ingenuity to evade the fulfillment of whatever orders may be received from Spain, the object of which is the suppression of the Slave-trade'.[60] This inactivity of the Spanish authorities was reflected in the large number of Africans slaves—namely 43,000—smuggled illegally into Cuba just in the years between 1822 and 1829, despite the international ban.[61]

Another weakness of the commissions lay also in the lack of jurisdiction they held over the perpetrators. The crews of the seized ships continued to fall under the jurisdiction of the national courts of their respective countries of origin, where a lack of legislative prerequisites and often political will meant that they went unpunished and were therefore free to resume their participation in the slave trade. The mixed commissions only had the right to detain the crews and to turn them over to their home countries.[62] The jurisdiction of the commissions was restricted to the ship and its cargo. Except for the material loss suffered, the deterrent effect remained correspondingly small. This becomes particularly clear in an excerpt

[57] Letter from Kilbee to Foreign Secretary Canning, 1 January 1825, *BPP* 10 Class A, 143.

[58] Ibid.

[59] Report of the British Commissions in Havana to Foreign Secretary Canning, 1 January 1827, TNA, FO 313/10. See also the Report of the British Commissioners in Havana to Foreign Secretary Viscount Dudley, 1 January 1828, in ibid.

[60] Report of the British Commissioners in Havana to Foreign Secretary Canning, 1 January 1827, TNA, FO 313/10.

[61] Murray, *Odious Commerce* (n 56) 80.

[62] This point, in particular, is a strong argument against the thesis of Jenny Martinez, that the mixed commissions were forerunners of international criminal justice of the twentieth and twenty-first centuries. On this see especially Martinez, *Slave Trade* (n 9) 148–57.

from the British Commission's report from 15 May 1824, in which the case is described of Mr Brandão, the leading Portuguese slave trader of the region around the Cape Verde islands. After his ship, the Conde de Villa Flor, was captured by the Royal Navy in February 1822, then confiscated and subsequently legally convicted, the Portuguese slave trader blatantly announced 'that it was his intention to have retired from the [slave] trade, but that he is determined now, out of a spirit of defiance, to pursue the Slave Trade with all the means in his power'.[63] Despite Brandão's public challenge, the Mixed Commission in Freetown could not take any steps against him and could only hope for a conviction and imprisonment by the Portuguese authorities. However, such hopes proved to be no more than wishful thinking. A commission report in the following year confirmed that the Portuguese slave trader had resumed his business with new ships and greater determination and thereby even enhanced his position as the leading trader in the Cape Verde islands.[64] Even though the British commissioners time and again reminded the foreign authorities of their national legal commitments, the domestic prosecution of convicted slave traders by these countries was not pursued, as demonstrated in this significant case.

The effectiveness of the mixed commissions was therefore highly dependent on the support of the local authorities and each of the respective members of the commission, which is also illustrated by the statistics for each location. The special tribunal in Sierra Leone played a clearly dominant role in enforcing the treaty measures, handling 528 cases in the years between 1819 and 1845. In the same period, its counterparts in Havana and Rio de Janeiro handed down only fifty and forty-four decisions respectively, while the British-Dutch commission in Surinam heard only a single case.[65] One reason for these differences was certainly related to the fact that the main operations area of the Royal Navy targeting slave ships lay in West African waters and that the captured ships fell into the jurisdiction of the tribunal in Freetown, Sierra Leone. Another reason lay in the vehemence with which British authorities attempted to follow the treaty stipulations to the letter and to use the mixed commissions as a legal weapon in the struggle against the slave trade.

However, even when the court decided in favour of the slaves, their freedom was not always guaranteed and again was dependent on the location. In Sierra Leone, the 'certificate of emancipation' did indeed mean the reinstatement of their freedom and their registration as new subjects of the British crown.[66] An agency,

[63] Report of the British Commissioners in Sierra Leone to Foreign Secretary Canning, 15 May 1824, *BFSP* 12, 57.

[64] Report of the British Commissioners in Sierra Leone to Foreign Secretary Canning, 10 April 1825, *BFSP* 13, 31.

[65] Bethell, *Mixed Commissions* (n 2) 84.

[66] Bethell, *Mixed Commissions* (n 2) 89; Shaikh, 'Judicial Diplomacy' (n 9) 48; Hugh Thomas, *The Slave Trade: The History of the Atlantic Slave Trade 1440–1870* (London: Phoenix, 2006), 688. Numerous examples of detailed registration lists of the slaves liberated by the Mixed Commission in Freetown are found under TNA, FO 315/31.

the Liberated African Department, was established specifically to deal with liberated slaves.[67] It first supplied the liberated people with much needed clothing, food, shelter, and, when necessary, medical care. Then the authorities offered the new arrivals building material and seeds in order to settle them in the vicinity of Freetown.[68] As a result, entire new villages sprang up, populated by liberated Africans from various ethnicities who contributed to the colonization of the region through their farming. As free labourers, several were also employed in public projects in the city or found work such as court messengers[69] for the mixed commissions. Many were recruited to military service in the Royal African Corps in the British West Indies.[70] Although there were also cases in Sierra Leone in which former slaves were again abducted and illegally sold into slavery, the liberation through the courts in Freetown usually meant that a person had escaped the fate of slavery.[71]

Fate was not as kind to liberated slaves in Rio de Janeiro and Havana. Once they were officially liberated, these so-called emancipados[72] were subsequently compelled to undergo many years of forced labour under the pretence of an 'apprenticeship'.[73] The Spanish and Brazilian colonial authorities thus rented out the new labourers initially for seven years to the highest bidder, whereby the prices in Cuba, according to British Consul David Turnbull, varied 'from three to six ounces of gold for women, and from six to ten ounces for men'.[74] Politically influential persons were often given preference during the process of distribution. Ironically, among these were prominent members of the mixed commissions. For instance, the above-mentioned Spanish Judges Herrera y Herrera and Buenaventura Esteva received 35 and 400 'emancipados' respectively for forced labour on their estates, the very same slaves they had liberated before through their ruling at the Mixed Commission in Havana.[75]

[67] Originally, the name was the Captured Negro Department, but it was changed in August 1822 to Liberated African Department for political reasons.

[68] On this, see Richard Meyer-Heiselberg, *Notes from Liberated African Department* (Uppsala: Scandinavian Institute of African Studies, 1967); Christopher Fyfe, *A History of Sierra Leone* (London: Oxford University Press, 1962), 138–9; Christopher Fyfe, *A Short History of Sierra Leone* (London: Longman, 1979), 39–44 and 48–55.

[69] Letter by the British Commissioners in Sierra Leone to Viscount Palmerston, 20 September 1841, in *BPP* 21 Class A, 31.

[70] Ibid., 219, 224–5, 230; Fyfe, *History of Sierra Leone* (n 68) 118–19 and 178.

[71] On these abduction cases, see Meyer-Heiselberg (n 68) *Notes*, XI; Fyfe, *History of Sierra Leone* (n 68) 183–4.

[72] In Brazil the name for the 'emancipados' was 'africanos livres'.

[73] Robert Conrad, 'Neither Slave nor Free: The Emancipados of Brazil, 1818–1868', *The Hispanic American Historical Review* 53, 1 (1973), 51–2.

[74] Turnbull, *Travels in the West* (n 52) 162.

[75] Luis Martínez-Fernández, 'The Havana Anglo-Spanish Mixed Commission for the Suppression of the Slave Trade and Cuba's Emancipados', *Slavery and Abolition* 16, 2 (1995), 210–11; Letter by Viscount Palmerston to Bulwer, 3 August 1846, Archivo Histórico Nacional, Madrid (AHN), Estado, Esclavitud, Legajo 8040.

This practice meant enormous profits for the colonial authorities and these involved commission members. Furthermore, they found a way to multiply this profit at the end of such an 'apprenticeship' by arbitrarily extending service by another seven years and again profitably renting out the surviving 'liberated' slaves.[76] In particularly dreadful cases, the abuse was taken a step further. In Cuba and Brazil, 'emancipados' would be declared dead, then given new identities and forged papers and condemned to a life of outright slavery.[77]

The decision of the mixed commissions in Rio de Janeiro and in Havana in favour of the slaves did not mean their liberation; it meant instead euphemistically veiled and state-organized slave labour. The 'emancipados' found themselves in a type of limbo in which they were not free but also did not belong to the slave population and therefore could not expect any support from other slaves.[78] According to the British Consul, David Turnbull, their situation was even worse than that of the common slaves, 'because the term of their apprenticeship is for seven years only, and because the parties to whom they are bound have therefore no interest in their existence after the period for which their services have been purchased'.[79] Consequently, the 'parties to whom they were bound' exploited the labour of the 'emancipados' with no regard for the consequences to their health; in many cases, the 'emancipados' were simply worked to death.[80] Despite repeated diplomatic interventions and strong protest by the United Kingdom against this practice, the situation for the 'emancipados' only changed in Cuba in the 1850s and in Brazil in the 1860s.[81]

Conclusion

In the wake of the efforts to fight the transatlantic slave trade in the course of the nineteenth century, the first system of international jurisdiction emerged. The 'Mixed Commissions for the Abolition of the Slave Trade' were, as British

[76] Turnbull, *Travels in the West* (n 52) 161–2; William Dougal Christie, *Notes on Brazilian Questions* (London: Macmillan, 1865), 47–9; Conrad, 'Neither Slave nor Free' (n 73) 61; Franklin W. Knight, *Slave Society in Cuba During the Nineteenth Century* (Madison, WI: University of Wisconsin Press, 1970), 103.

[77] Martínez-Fernández, 'Mixed Commission' (n 75) 213; Conrad, 'Neither Slave nor Free' (n 73) 59, 60–1; Letter from Crawford to Lord Clarendon, 3 January 1855, *BPP* 41 Class B, 563; Letter from Crawford to Lord Clarendon, 1 June 1855, AHN, Estado, Esclavitud, Legajo 8048; Letter from Stephen to Backhouse, 19 January 1839, *BPP* 17 Class A, 24; Letter from Strangways to Stephen, 4 February 1839, in ibid., 125.

[78] Ibid., 214.

[79] Turnbull, *Travels in the West* (n 52) 75.

[80] Ibid., 76; Conrad, 'Neither Slave nor Free' (n 73) 62.

[81] See Christie, *Notes on Brazilian Question* (n 76) 1–50; Martínez-Fernández, 'Mixed Commission' (n 75) 217–20; Conrad, 'Neither Slave nor Free' (n 73) 67–9; Leslie Bethell, *The Abolition of the Brazilian Slave Trade. Britain, Brazil and the Slave Trade Question 1807–1869* (Cambridge: Cambridge University Press, 1970), 383.

Commissioner Edmund Gabriel described in his correspondence of December 1856, international courts, which were not governed by any national law but by the stipulations of international treaties.[82] Their purpose was to guarantee the conviction of captured slave ships by a uniform set of practices, functions, and procedures for all of the mixed commissions established throughout the entire Atlantic area. During their existence from 1819 to 1871, 11 countries participated and co-operated in this first standardized system of international jurisdiction, which dealt with far more than 600 cases and thereby freed about 80,000 slaves from various captured ships.

However, the mixed commissions were far from being a body of frictionless international cooperation. They cannot even be described as the 'first international human rights courts' and therefore cannot be seen as significant forerunners to systems of international criminal justice of the twentieth and twenty-first centuries.[83] In fact, the opposite is true: the slave-trade tribunals were a fiercely contested place where each member state sought to defend and enforce its own national interests concerning the abolition of the slave trade, competing with the national interests of other parties. The ambiguous roles and functions of its members illustrates this rather multifaceted picture. Officially, the commission members served at the tribunals as practitioners, who as diplomatic as well as judicial agents had to implement the stipulations of international treaties regarding the abolition of the slave trade. Beside this official function, they simultaneously performed competing roles as activists and lobbyists for the national interest of their respective country. Britain's representatives were strongly committed to the abolitionist agenda and acted accordingly. By contrast, commissioners of slave-trading nations such as Portugal, Spain, and Brazil actively defended the interest of the slave traders and the slave owners. In extreme cases they themselves belonged to this interest group and even benefited from selling and receiving 'emancipados' for forced labour on their estates, whom they had previously liberated through their ruling. Thus, the effectiveness of the mixed commissions was highly dependent on the support and commitment of the respective members from different countries. In this respect, the slave-trade tribunals as an early form of international cooperation highlights a major problem international organizations are still facing today: international bodies are only as strong and effective as the political will and capacity of the participating member states to implement a commonly agreed cause.

[82] Letter by Edmund Gabriel to Governor-General of the Province of Angola, 4 December 1856, in Foreign Office (ed.), *Correspondence with the British Commissioners at Sierra Leone, Havana, The Cape of Good Hope, and Loanda; and Reports from British Naval Officers, Relating to the Slave Trade, From April 1, 1857, to March 31, 1858* (London 1858), 58.

[83] Martinez, *Slave Trade* (n 9) 6 and 148–57; Shaikh, 'Judicial Diplomacy' (n 9) 42.

4

Legal Advice, the Foreign Office, and Britain's Neutrality Policy, 1870–1914

Gabriela A. Frei

In the nineteenth century, neutrality became a significant issue in international politics. As the dominant sea power at the time, Britain shaped the international understanding of neutrality at sea. While recent literature has highlighted the importance of neutrality as a concept in the long nineteenth century,[1] this chapter focuses mainly on the practice of the law of neutrality. It examines in particular the role of legal advisers who shaped Britain's neutrality policy from 1870 to 1914, a crucial period in which Britain applied a strict policy of neutrality in most conflicts.[2] Britain's neutrality policy provides thus a good example of how legal advice worked within the British government.

The Making of Britain's Neutrality Policy

Britain's neutrality policy was formulated in the aftermath of the American Civil War, in which the Unionists accused Britain of 'unneutral' behaviour for engaging in contraband trade and selling blockade runners, such as the CSS *Alabama*, to the Confederates. The Alabama Claims Arbitration condemned Britain's 'unneutral' behaviour. In 1871, the Treaty of Washington defined under Article 6 the 'Three Rules' of neutrality. The 'Three Rules' consisted of first, to 'prevent the fitting out, arming or equipping' of vessels for belligerents. Second, neutrals had to ensure that belligerents did not use their waters and ports for naval operations, and third, to prevent its citizens from engaging in 'unneutral' behaviour.[3] Britain also actively

[1] Maartje M. Abbenhuis, *An Age of Neutrals. Great Power Politics, 1815–1914* (Cambridge: Cambridge University Press, 2014); Maartje M. Abbenhuis, 'A Most Useful Tool for Diplomacy and Statecraft: Neutrality and Europe in the "Long" Nineteenth Century, 1815–1914', *The International History Review* 35 (2013), 1–22.

[2] The Boer War of 1899 to 1902 was an exception.

[3] Annexed to Article 6 of Treaty of Washington (Confidential), 8 May 1871, The National Archives, Kew (TNA), FO 881/7040. See also: Tom Bingham, 'The Alabama Claims Arbitration', *The International and Comparative Law Quarterly* 54 (2005), 1–25; Stephen C. Neff, *Justice in Blue and Gray. A Legal History of the Civil War* (Cambridge, MA: Harvard University Press, 2010); Stephen C. Neff, *The Rights and Duties of Neutrals. A General History* (Manchester: Manchester University Press, 2000), 105–8.

Gabriela A. Frei, *Legal Advice, the Foreign Office, and Britain's Neutrality Policy, 1870–1914* In: *Crafting the International Order.* Edited by: Marcus M. Payk and Kim Christian Priemel, Oxford University Press (2021). © The Several Contributors.
DOI: 10.1093/oso/9780198863830.003.0004

changed its neutrality policy by reforming domestic legislation, in particular, the Foreign Enlistment Act. On the outbreak of the Franco-Prussian War one year earlier, the British government adopted a revised Foreign Enlistment Act, which outlined Britain's neutrality policy. Enacted on the 9 August 1870, this Act made it a punishable offence for a British subject to enlist in foreign services, or to engage in 'illegal shipbuilding' activities, including equipping, arming, or fitting out of vessels.[4] The revised domestic legislation marked a shift in British politics towards neutrality and, together with the 'Three Rules' formulated under Article 6 of the Treaty of Washington, provided the legal basis for Britain's neutrality policy until the outbreak of the First World War.[5]

The Foreign Office was responsible for the implementation and enforcement of Britain's neutrality policy. Yet, as the Foreign Office had no designated legal department before 1914, it relied on various sources for legal advice.[6] These structures raise a number of questions: who provided legal advice from within and outside the Foreign Office? How influential were these legal advisers? Did they actively shape decision-making processes or were they just bystanders in policy-making? By investigating Britain's state practice in the application of the Foreign Enlistment Act, this chapter will shed light on these questions. It will also reveal the inner-workings of legal advice within the context of Britain's neutrality policy in a crucial period before the outbreak of the First World War. The chapter will focus on three significant historical events—the Franco-Prussian War of 1870–1871, the Sino-French War of 1884–1885, and the Russo-Japanese War of 1904–1905—in order to reveal Britain's state practice and show how Britain shaped the understanding of neutrality at sea. The chapter will also deal with the administrative reforms which took place to reorganize legal advice within the British government in this period.

[4] Foreign Enlistment Act, 1870 (33 and 34 Vict., cap. 90), in http://www.legislation.gov.uk/ukpga/1870/90/pdfs/ukpga_18700090_en.pdf (accessed 18 August 2020).

[5] For a detailed analysis of Britain's neutrality policy, see: Nir Arielli, Gabriela A. Frei, and Inge Van Hulle, 'The Foreign Enlistment Act, International Law, and British Politics, 1819–2014', *The International History Review* 38, 4 (2016), 636–56; Gabriela A. Frei, *Britain, International Law, and the Evolution of Maritime Strategic Thought, 1856–1914* (Oxford: Oxford University Press, 2020).

[6] For an overview of legal advice for the British government, see: Brian Simpson, 'The Rule of Law in International Affairs', *Proceedings of the British Academy* 125 (2004), 221–7; Kate Jones, 'Marking Foreign Policy by Justice: The Legal Advisers to the Foreign Office, 1876–1953', in Robert McCorquodale and Jean-Pierre Gauci (eds), *British Influences on International Law, 1915–2015* (Leiden: Brill Nijhoff, 2016), 28–55; Clive Parry, 'United Kingdom. Background Paper', in Herbert Christian Laing Merillat (ed.), *Legal Advisers and Foreign Affairs* (Dobbs Ferry, NY: Oceana Publications, 1964), 101–52; Clive Parry, 'Foreign Policy and International Law', in Francis H. Hinsley (ed.), *British Foreign Policy under Sir Edward Grey* (Cambridge: Cambridge University Press, 1977), 89–110; Ray Jones, *The Nineteenth-Century Foreign Office. An Administrative History* (London: Weidenfeld and Nicolson, 1971).

The Franco-Prussian War and the Organization of Legal Advice

Shortly after the outbreak of the Franco-Prussian War in August 1870, the British government publicly announced its revised Foreign Enlistment Act.[7] The Queen's Proclamation warned British citizens against engaging in 'unneutral services'. However, the war between France and Prussia offered many opportunities for British citizens to engage in contraband trade, in particular the arms trade and the re-coaling of warships from both belligerent parties.[8] The Prussians as well as the French frequently accused the British government of breaching neutrality. Britain's revised domestic legislation offered the Foreign Office a legal tool to enforce neutrality within its jurisdiction and over its citizens. In a public announcement directed at the Lord Commissioners, as well as at belligerents, the Foreign Office outlined restrictions, including the stipulation that warships would only be allowed to take on coal in British ports once every three months—a practice which the British government had adopted in the American Civil War.[9] More generally, Article 11 of the Foreign Enlistment Act prohibited coaling because it was regarded as part of the 'fitting out' of warships. Since neither belligerent party possessed enough steam coal for their warships, coaling became a lucrative business for British citizens and several cases of illegal coaling were brought to the attention of the Foreign Office during the war.

In the Foreign Office, the Librarian and Keeper of the Archives, Edward Hertslet, prepared documentation pertaining to the proclamation of neutrality and related questions.[10] Hertslet joined the Foreign Office in 1857, stepping into the footsteps of his father, Lewis Hertslet who had worked for the Foreign Office for fifty-six years. Together the Hertslets shaped the institutional memory of the Foreign Office for almost a century.[11] A principal task of the librarian was to collect treaties, prepare documents for publication, and organize the Foreign Office archive.[12] The

[7] 'A Proclamation of Neutrality by the Queen Victoria', *The London Gazette*, No. 23642, 9 August 1870, 3743–5.

[8] Michael Howard, *The Franco-Prussian War. The German Invasion of France, 1870–1871* (London: Routledge, 1961; reprint: London, 2000).

[9] 'Copy of a Letter from Earl Granville (Foreign Office) to the Lords Commissioners of the Admiralty and other Government Departments', *The London Gazette*, No. 23635, 19 July 1870, 3432–3.

[10] Memorandum by E. Hertslet as to the Time when British Proclamations of Neutrality were Issued in Cases of Wars between Foreign States (Confidential), 16 July 1870, TNA, FO 881/3362.

[11] Despite the anecdotal character of the book, Hertslet's memoirs contain valuable information as to the inner-workings of the Foreign Office, see: Edward Hertslet, *Recollections of the Old Foreign Office* (London: John Murray, 1901). See also: Shirley Hall, *Sir Edmund Hertslet and his Work as Librarian and Keeper of the Papers of the Foreign Office from 1857–1896* (unpublished Masters Thesis, University of London, 1958).

[12] Duties imposed on Librarian's Department of Foreign Office, and Salaries by Edward Hertslet, 19 March 1871, TNA, FO 881/1869; Librarian's Department by Edward Hertslet, 9 March 1872, TNA, FO 881/2459; Clive Parry and Gerald Fitzmaurice (eds), *A British Digest of International Law Compiled Principally from the Archives of the Foreign Office. Part VII: Organs of States* (London: Stevens & Sons, 1965), 170–5.

Hertslets regularly published collections of treaties and state papers, making these available to the public.[13]

As the Foreign Office had no legal adviser at the time, it regularly consulted the Law Officers of the Crown for legal advice on the matter of coaling of warships. The Law Officers consisted of the Attorney General, Robert Porrett Collier; the Solicitor General, John Duke Coleridge; and the Queen's Advocate, Travers Twiss. If the British government required legal advice, it would hand papers to Twiss as Queen's Advocate first, before the other two advisers received the material for consideration.[14] The Attorney General and the Solicitor General were both Members of Parliament (MPs), appointed to these positions by the Prime Minister, William E. Gladstone. While they were the chief legal advisers of the British government, they were not always members of the Cabinet. Their primary task was to advise the British government and the different government offices on all legal matters, both non-contentious and contentious. The two Law Officers were barristers who were based in the Inns of Court and who worked primarily on private cases, and they only advised the British government on a case-by-case basis, upon request.[15]

The Queen's Advocate as the third Law Officer of the Crown served at Her Majesty's pleasure. Unlike the other two Law Officers, the Queen's Advocate was not a barrister but a member of the Doctors' Commons, a distinction in degree rather than in competency. He specialized in civil and cannon law, which included international law.[16] Travers Twiss was to be the last Queen's Advocate, and one of the most prolific international lawyers of his time. He was Professor of International Law at King's College, London when he was appointed Queen's Advocate in 1867. Due to a scandal, Twiss resigned in 1872. He remained, however, active, and served at one point as legal counsel to King Léopold of Belgium.[17] Following Twiss' resignation, the position of the Queen's Advocate was no longer filled, and subsequently, the Law Officers of the Crown consisted of only the Attorney General and the Solicitor General.[18]

[13] For instance: Edward Hertslet, *Treaties and Tariffs regulating the Trade between Great Britain and Foreign Nations: And Extracts of Treaties between Foreign Powers, Containing Most-Favoured-Nation Clauses Applicable to Great Britain, 6 vols.* (London: Butterworth's, 1875–1879); Hall, *Hertslet* (n 11) 38–45.

[14] Brunson MacChesney, 'The *Alabama* and the Queen's Advocate—A Mystery of History', *Northwestern University Law Review* 62, 4 (1967/68), 572–3.

[15] John Ll. J. Edwards, *The Law Officers of the Crown. A Study of the Offices of Attorney-General and Solicitor-General of England, with an Account of the Office of the Director of Public Prosecutions of England* (London: Sweet & Maxwell, 1964); Parry and Fitzmaurice (n 12) *British Digest, Part VII*, 246–8.

[16] Parry and Fitzmaurice (n 12) *British Digest, Part VII*, 243–6.

[17] Andrew Fitzmaurice, *Sovereignty, Property and Empire, 1500–2000* (Cambridge: Cambridge University Press, 2014), 276–84; Monica Garcia-Salmones, *The Project of Positivism in International Law* (Oxford: Oxford University Press, 2014), 20–6; Martti Koskenniemi, *The Gentle Civilizer of Nations. The Rise and Fall of International Law 1870–1960* (Cambridge: Cambridge University Press, 2001), 108, 22, 32–3; Casper Sylvest, '"Our Passion for Legality": International Law and Imperialism in Late Nineteenth-Century Britain', *Review of International Studies* 34, 3 (2008), 408–15.

[18] Edwards, *Law Officers of the Crown* (n 15) 133–8.

When the Law Officers dealt with the coaling of warships during the Franco-Prussian War, they advised the Foreign Office to adopt the practice that

> if colliers are chartered for the purpose of attending the French fleet and supplying them with coal to enable them to pursue their hostile operations, such colliers become 'store-ships' employed in their service, and (if this fact be established) that they should be detained under the provisions of the Foreign Enlistment Act.[19]

A few months later, the Admiralty enquired about the circumstances under which the supply of coal to a belligerent from government stores was legal. In this case, Twiss as Queen's Advocate alone replied that 'if a belligerent steam-vessel should come into a neutral port in distress of fuel, it may fairly be regarded as an obligation of neutral hospitality to allow a reasonable supply of coals to be furnished to her'.[20] Yet, coal should only be provided from government stores if no commercial coal was available.

Despite warnings from the British government and clarifications from the Law Officers, British citizens were actively engaged in contraband trade.[21] When the Prussian Ambassador to Britain, Count Bernstorff, protested against British colliers sailing from Newcastle for neutral Denmark to coal French warships in international waters, the Foreign Office asked the Law Officers for legal advice. After studying the briefs and documents sent to them, the three lawyers advised the Foreign Office to 'remind' Bernstorff that 'Her Majesty's Government are but pursuing the same course which they took during the American war, and the continental wars of 1859 [Italian War] and 1866 [Austro-Prussian War]' which included a friendly warning to its citizens of not engaging in contraband trade or they 'risk ... hostile capture'.[22] Only a few days later, the Law Officers had to look into the matter again as Bernstorff insisted that the British government should take precautionary measures with regard to coaling and suggested it levy a 'bond for double the value of the cargo', which should only be returned after proof had been received that the cargo actually reached the indicated neutral port. Such a request was unacceptable for the British government, and the Law Officers advised that such a request 'would entail an interference with trade such as no neutral country can be called upon to undertake'.[23]

The example of coaling during the Franco-Prussian War shows the growing importance of legal advice for use in diplomatic argument as a means to underscore

[19] The Law Officers of the Crown (R. P. Collier, J. D. Coleridge, and T. Twiss) to Earl Granville, 25 July 1870 (No. 1), TNA, FO 881/8508.

[20] The Queen's Advocate (T. Twiss) to Earl Granville, 19 November 1870 (No. 152), TNA, FO 834/9.

[21] Howard (n 8) *Franco-Prussian War.*

[22] Law Officers of the Crown (R. P. Collier, J. D. Coleridge, and T. Twiss) to Earl Granville, 25 July 1870 (No. 199), TNA, FO 934/9.

[23] Law Officers of the Crown (R. P. Collier, J. D. Coleridge, and T. Twiss) to Earl Granville, 10 August 1870 (No. 200), TNA, FO 934/9.

Britain's new policy of neutrality. Importantly, the Law Officers' references to past conflicts highlighted Britain's consistency in state practice. Moreover, the Law Officers were not only the principal legal advisers to the Foreign Office but also gave advice to other government departments, such as the Admiralty. Typically, the Foreign Office would write to the Law Officers with a specific legal question and provide them with the necessary documents and papers. In the case of Bernstorff's protest, the Law Officers studied Bernstorff's letter and, within a day or two, replied with a comprehensive legal opinion as to the argument which the Foreign Office should pursue, referring to state practice.

Since the Law Officers had no government office, they worked from their offices in the Inns of Court using a courier service to exchange briefs and opinions. At times, this was a cumbersome business as the Foreign Office did not always provide full documentation, and consequently, they had to request additional material to form an opinion.[24] The Law Officers' opinions were always constructed in the same way. First, they repeated the context in which a question was posed, followed by their opinion, referring to British state practice, to general principles of international law, or to specific treaties. Their legal advice was at all times confidential which ensured the independent nature of their advice.[25] In cases where a question exceeded the Law Officers' competency, they referred it to the Cabinet for a political decision.[26]

Administrative Reforms and the Creation of the Office of Legal Adviser

With the discontinuation of the position of the Queen's Advocate after Twiss' resignation, the role and position of the Law Officers came under review from the Treasury. In December 1871, the Treasury had already suggested that the Law Officers should be remunerated based on an annual salary for non-contentious business and retain fees payment only for contentious business.[27] The Law Officers Fees Act, which parliament adopted on 10 August 1872 introduced this new scheme.[28] In the same year, the Treasury also decided, in lieu of a Queen's Advocate,

[24] Hertslet, *Foreign Office* (n 11). See also: Patrick Polden, 'The Legal Professions', in William Cornish, J. Stuart Anderson, Ray Cocks et al. (eds), *The Oxford History of the Laws of England: Volume XI: 1820–1914 English Legal System* (Oxford: Oxford University Press, 2010), 1071.

[25] See clarification of the Speaker: Speaker on Law Officers' Opinion, Hansard, 5th series, Vol. 24, HC Deb. 25 April 1911, c. 1602–1603.

[26] References to the Law Officers, and Printing of their Reports, 20 March 1880, TNA, FO 881/4104.

[27] Treasury Minute, 14 December 1871, in Legal Business Committee. Return to an Order of the Honourable The House of Commons, dated 10 May 1877; Copy of the First, Second, and Third Reports made by a Departmental Committee Appointed in 1875, to Inquire into the System upon which the Legal Business of the Government is Conducted, with Minutes of Evidence and Appendices, House of Commons Papers, 199, XXXVII. 1 [Legal Business Committee, 1877], 52.

[28] Law Officers (England) Fees, 35&36 Vict., 10 August 1872.

to appoint James Parker Deane as legal adviser for all legal matters connected with the Foreign Office, and to work alongside the Law Officers to 'fill in some measure the position of the late Queen's Advocate'.[29] Deane, who was also Attorney General of the Admiralty at the time, was familiar with the business of the Law Officers, and was therefore well-suited to the position.[30]

In 1875, the Treasury attempted to limit still further the expense of legal advice to the British government and appointed a committee headed by Sir George Jessel, Master of the Rolls. The Jessel Committee's main task was to review the role of legal advisers within the government administration, and to determine whether or not it was necessary to create new appointments for legal advisers in government offices. The Treasury clearly positioned itself at the outset of the review, stating it was against the creation of new positions, and suggesting that the Treasury Solicitor should take over the work and, if necessary, 'employ' experts to deal with specific legal questions.[31]

The Treasury committee requested information from all government offices regarding their fees and a description of their legal business. During the hearing, the Attorney General, Richard Baggallay, voiced his discontent with the current system, arguing that a lot of legal business was treated as non-contentious whereas much of it was contentious and for which a different remuneration should apply. Second, Baggallay thought that the fees applicable in contentious cases were far below 'the usual professional scale'. Third, he added that the Law Officers' workload had increased heavily because the Treasury had withdrawn funds to pay for an assistant or junior counsel to relieve the Law Officers from some of their duties.[32] Baggallay also complained that since the discontinuation of the Queen's Advocate, the Foreign Office and Colonial Office had been sending all their legal business to the Law Officers. He further criticized the government's 'zeal for economy' in terms of reducing expenditure for departmental solicitors or counsels, which meant that offices could no longer prepare a case thoroughly and gather enough evidence to support a case, with the consequence that he, as Attorney General, had to make further enquiries.[33] Following his statement, Baggallay urged the committee to consider the appointment of a law clerk for support. He also remarked that he was decidedly against giving up private practice as this would mean 'his prospects of successfully following his profession on his retirement from office [as Law Officer] would be materially diminished'.[34]

[29] Treasury Minute, 14 March 1875, in Legal Business Committee, 1877 (n 27) 50–1, at 50.

[30] Parry and Fitzmaurice, *British Digest, Part VII* (n 12) 253; Beth F. Wood, 'Sir James Parker Deane', in *Oxford Dictionary of National Biography* (Oxford: Oxford University Press, 2004).

[31] Treasury Minute, 14 March 1875, in Legal Business Committee, 1877 (n 27) 50–1, at 51.

[32] Richard Baggallay (Attorney General) to Treasury, 26 May 1875, in Legal Business Committee, 1877 (n 27) 54–7, at 56.

[33] Examination of Sir Richard Baggallay (Attorney General), 3 May 1875, in Legal Business Committee, 1877 (n 27) 10–22, at 15–16, 21–2.

[34] Memorandum by the Attorney General (Richard Baggallay) as to the Suggested Modes of Remunerating the Law Officers, 31 May 1875, in Legal Business Committee, 1877 (n 27) 48–9, at 49.

The role of James Parker Deane as replacement for the abolished position of the Queen's Advocate raised quite a few questions during the committee work. Deane complained about his workload, which had considerably exceeded his expectations of what the position would entail. Rather than just dealing with cases brought forward by the Foreign Office, Deane also had to deal with cases from the Colonial Office and the Board of Trade, which were, in his opinion, not part of his job. He suggested the restitution of the position of a Queen's Advocate with an adequate salary.[35]

The evidence gathered during the Jessel committee's work showed diverging opinions between the Treasury, the Attorney General, and Deane, yet the Treasury ignored the suggestions of the latter. Instead, the committee put forward a number of changes to the ways in which legal advice for the British government should be organized in the future. For instance, they suggested the abolition of the departmental legal advisers in the War Office, replacing them with the Treasury Solicitor, and in the Admiralty with the permanent secretary of the Admiralty. The committee also argued that much more work should be concentrated within the Treasury. The only exception to this was the Foreign Office, for which the committee proposed the creation of a legal assistant under-secretary to ease the workload of the Law Officers and Deane.[36]

As a result of the committee's work, the Foreign Office appointed Sir Julian Pauncefote as first legal assistant under-secretary on 14 July 1876. As a barrister and former Attorney General of Hong Kong, and experienced in international law, Pauncefote's tasks were as broad as the distribution of business documented in the Foreign Office list. He was assigned to several departments, providing legal advice on matters of the slave trade, international cases, and treaties, as well as general correspondence within and outside the government.[37] He was responsible for the Foreign Office's legal business, which included the compilation of cases for consideration by the Law Officers and Deane. Beyond that, Pauncefote had broad responsibilities in political matters, and was also an effective reformer of the Foreign Office. In 1882, Pauncefote rose to the position of permanent under-secretary, a post he held until 1889. As permanent under-secretary, Pauncefote advanced internal reforms, and yet the Treasury was reluctant in appointing a new legal adviser

[35] Examination of Sir James Parker Deane, 3 June 1875, in Legal Business Committee, 1877 (n 27) 33–7.

[36] Third Report, 3 December 1875, in Legal Business Committee, 1877 (n 27) 62–70. See also: Edwards, *Law Officers of the Crown* (n 27) 82–9.

[37] Edward Hertslet, *The Foreign Office List, Forming a Complete British and Consular Handbook with Maps, Shewing where Her Majesty's Ambassadors, Ministers, Consuls, and Others are Resident Abroad: Together with a List of Foreign Diplomatic and Consular Representatives Resident within The Queen's Dominions, January 1877* (London: Harrison, 1877). See also: Jones, 'Foreign Policy by Justice' (n 6) 29–32.

as Pauncefote's successor. Instead, he had to continue dealing with legal business in addition to his new duties.[38]

The Foreign Office reforms were necessary as part of a growing demand to increase government efficiency. At the same time, legal advice became indispensable for the smooth running of the Foreign Office's daily business. Pauncefote was an excellent barrister and his promotion was the result of his political ambitions, yet neither his promotion nor the government efficiency drive would improve the situation in the Foreign Office, which was still overwhelmed by legal matters.

The Sino-French War and Legal Advice under Pressure

Britain's neutrality policy in the 1880s, which was applied to the Sino-French War of 1884–1885, illustrates well how legal advice operated after the administrative reforms. The far distant theatre of war made it difficult for the Foreign Office to gain a complete picture of the events unfolding there. Britain's neutrality policy focused on the British Crown colony, Hong Kong, which was a significant financial and trading centre in the region. Due to the geographical location of Hong Kong with its direct connection to the Chinese hinterland, it was attractive for contraband trade. When war broke out in September 1884, neither France nor China formally declared war. In the absence of a formal declaration of war, the British government were hesitant to issue a proclamation of neutrality and so could not readily enforce the Foreign Enlistment Act.[39] There was no international obligation to declare war but there was a certain expectation, particularly from the side of neutrals to do so. With the growing importance of neutrality in international politics, the issue of declarations of war became more frequent.[40] The Law Officers at the time, Henry James and Farrer Herschell, together with James Parker Deane agreed that a 'state of war' existed between France and China and suggested that the British government enforce 'strict neutrality'. However, the British government was hesitant in following their legal advice, not least because the French government denied that a general state of war existed, insisting that the conflict was of 'limited character'. Despite reassurances from the French government, the Law Officers and Deane advised that instructions be sent to Hong Kong and other colonies affected by the

[38] Keith Neilson and Thomas G. Otte, *The Permanent Under-Secretary for Foreign Affairs, 1854–1946* (New York, NY: Routledge, 2009), 62–77.

[39] Law Officers of the Crown (H. James, F. Herschell) and Dr Deane to Earl Granville, 2 September 1884 (No. 29), TNA, FO 834/14.

[40] Memorandum by E. Hertslet as to the Time When British Proclamations of Neutrality Were Issued in Cases of Wars between Foreign States (Confidential), 16 July 1870, TNA, FO 881/3362. See also: John Frederick Maurice, *Hostilities without Declaration of War. An Historical Abstract of the Cases in which Hostilities Have Occurred between Civilized Powers Prior to Declaration or Warning. From 1700 to 1870* (London: Her Majesty's Stationary Office, 1883); William E. Hall, *A Treatise on International Law*, 5th edn, J. B. Atlay (ed.) (Oxford: The Clarendon Press, 1904), 377–95, 574–5.

conflict to obey strict neutrality.[41] The British government remained reluctant to proclaim neutrality, a stance which the Law Officers and Deane described as 'perplexing', and urged the British government to apply 'strict neutrality'.[42]

When the conflict continued, the British government considered the enforcement of the Foreign Enlistment Act and on 11 December 1884, Pauncefote prepared a case for the Law Officers and Deane to examine. It took the Law Officers more than ten days to come to a legal opinion. When they finally replied, they suggested amending the Foreign Enlistment Act under the consideration of the lack of a declaration of neutrality.[43]

While the Law Officers and Deane were chiefly involved in the decision-making processes of how the British government could apply its neutrality policy, the Foreign Office was responsible for coordinating the implementation of the policy together with the Colonial Office. The latter had the role of communicating this policy to the Governors of the 'Eastern Colonies', which included Hong Kong, the Straits Settlements, and Ceylon. Lord Derby, the Colonial Secretary at the time, wanted to send a telegram at once to the Governors in the colonies to inform them about the British governments' decision. However, the Foreign Secretary, Lord Granville, insisted that the instructions first be sent to the Foreign Office.[44] Obeying the orders of the Foreign Office, Sir Edward Wingfield, the legal assistant under-secretary of the Colonial Office sent Pauncefote the draft telegram.[45] Derby decided to send a telegram with instructions to the Governor of Hong Kong on 21 January 1885 as he thought it was a matter of urgency. This was before Granville had formally approved the instructions.[46]

While the Foreign Office pondered the right course and moment of publication, rumours spread quickly throughout the British colonies as to Britain's intention on implementing the Foreign Enlistment Act, leading the French Consul in Singapore to ask whether the British could delay the publication for twenty-five days while French warships passed through Singapore. Neither Derby nor Granville saw a reason for the British government to comply with such a request. However, pressure grew in Singapore to publish the instructions when the Governor of the Straits

41 Law Officers of the Crown (H. James, F. Herschell) and Dr Deane to Earl Granville, 5 September 1884 (No. 30), TNA, FO 834/14; Law Officers of the Crown (H. James, F. Herschell) and Dr Deane to Earl Granville, 27 September 1884 (No. 31), TNA, FO 834/14.

42 Law Officers of the Crown (H. James, F. Herschell) and Dr Deane to Earl Granville, 25 October 1884 (No. 32), TNA, FO 834/14.

43 Law Officers of the Crown (H. James, F. Herschell) and Dr Deane to Earl Granville, 22 December 1884 (No. 36), TNA, FO 834/14.

44 John Bramston (CO) to Sir Julian Pauncefote (FO), 12 January 1885 (No. 7), TNA, FO 881/5163; Mr P. Currie (FO) to Sir Robert Herbert (CO), 15 January 1885 (No. 9), TNA, FO 881/5163.

45 Sir Edward Wingfield (CO) to Sir Julian Pauncefote (FO), 20 January 1885 (No. 13), TNA, FO 881/5163.

46 Sir Edward Wingfield (CO) to Sir Julian Pauncefote (FO), 23 January 1885 (No. 14), TNA, FO 881/5163. Sir Julian Pauncefote (FO) to Sir Edward Wingfield (CO), 23 January 1885 (No. 16), TNA, FO 881/5163; Sir Julian Pauncefote (FO) to the Law Officers of the Crown and Dr Deane, 23 January 1885 (No. 18), TNA, FO 881/5163.

Settlements reported to the Colonial Office that French warships had approached the port of Singapore for coaling and repairs.[47]

The Colonial Office told the Governors not to publish the instructions until the Law Officers had approved the final wording, but it was too late. The Governor of Hong Kong had already published the instructions on 23 January because French warships were expected to enter Hong Kong Harbour.[48] As soon as the instructions were published, the French government protested against them because of an earlier understanding with the British that it would not exercise belligerent rights against British ships during the conflict and in return, the British would allow French warships into ports for repair and coaling.[49] The British government argued that it had acted 'upon the authority of our legal advisers, in order to protect ourselves not only from Parliamentary attacks, but from very serious pecuniary claims'. The Foreign Office tried to smooth diplomatic tensions, indicating that the British government would be willing to alter the Foreign Enlistment Act, allowing French warships into ports for repairs and coaling under the provision that they were not 'used in a hostile operation'.[50] It could also be argued that the British government used the legal advisers' opinion to gain time to find an adequate course in dealing with the issue.

The Law Officers' opinion reached the Foreign Office only after the instructions had already been sent to and published in the colonies. The Law Officers and Deane were not entirely satisfied with the phrasing and suggested changes to the instructions, which were sent to the colonies at once.[51] At that point, the French government had already responded and announced the exercise of belligerent rights, which meant the search and capture of British neutral ships as well as the blockade of ports and coastlines. The French government was particularly alarmed about the arms trade to China via Hong Kong, and argued that the exercise of belligerent rights was a measure to stop contraband trade.[52] The Law Officers and Deane acknowledged France's belligerent rights, and advised the British government against a relaxation of the Foreign Enlistment Act, arguing that this could

[47] Sir Robert Herbert (CO) to Sir Julian Pauncefote (FO), 24 January 1885 (No. 19), TNA, FO 881/5163; Sir Julian Pauncefote (FO) to Sir Robert Herbert (CO), 24 January 1885 (No. 21), TNA, FO 881/5163.

[48] Sir Robert Herbert (CO) to Sir Julian Pauncefote (FO), 26 January 1885 (No. 23), TNA, FO 881/5163.

[49] Sir Julian Pauncefote (FO) to the Law Officers of the Crown and Dr Deane, 27 January 1885 (No. 25), TNA, FO 881/5163.

[50] Earl Granville to Viscount Lyons (British Ambassador to France), 28 January 1885 (No. 26), TNA, FO 881/5163.

[51] Law Officers of the Crown (H. James, F. Herschell) and Dr Deane to Earl Granville, 28 January 1885 (No. 28), TNA, FO 881/5163; Sir Julian Pauncefote (FO) to Sir Robert Herbert (CO), 29 January 1885 (No. 30), TNA, FO 881/5163.

[52] William Henry Waddington (French Ambassador to Britain) to Earl Granville, 29 January 1885 (No. 29), TNA, FO 881/5163; Earl Granville to William Henry Waddington (French Ambassador to Britain), 31 January 1885 (No. 31), TNA, FO 881/5163.

more generally damage Britain's neutrality policy.[53] Accordingly, Pauncefote informed the Colonial Office, the Admiralty, and other government offices about the French government's decision on exercising belligerent rights, which ended the turbulent process of the implementation of the Foreign Enlistment Act.[54]

The example of the implementation of Britain's neutrality policy during the Sino-French War shows how central the Law Officers and Deane were in the decision-making processes. Their legal opinion provided the basis for the principal decisions which shaped the course of the British government's policy. Pauncefote was a crucial figure in the Foreign Office as he was not only in close contact with the Foreign Secretary, Granville, but also with colleagues from the Colonial Office. Pauncefote mainly dealt with barristers in the Colonial Office, who had prepared, for instance, the telegram instructions which were sent to the Governors in the colonies. In fact, the position of legal advisor to assistant under-secretary was already established in the Colonial Office in 1870 and, despite resistance from the Treasury, the Colonial Office managed to appoint three assistant under-secretaries, two of whom should be qualified barristers. This arrangement secured the Colonial Office's legal expertise in dealing with the complex legal arrangements in the colonies.[55] At the time, Wingfield and Bramston were the two assistant under-secretaries dealing with the legal business of the Colonial Office.[56] Sir Robert Herbert, the permanent under-secretary of state for the Colonies, was another barrister and a good friend of John Bramston. Bramston and Pauncefote were both former attorneys-general of Hong Kong, and thus, familiar with the situation in the Crown colony.

The correspondence between the Colonial Office and the Foreign Office during the Sino-French War suggests that the Foreign Office was officially in charge but when an urgent situation arose, the Colonial Office or local governors in the colonies acted without the approval of the Foreign Office. The Colonial Office retained a certain degree of independence, and particular notice should be given its legal advisers, who prepared the drafts and questions for the Law Officers and Deane. Their pre-emptive decision to send instructions to the colonial governors also occurred because it took the Law Officers and Deane five days to formulate a legal opinion. Time was an important factor in the decision-making process, and while telegraphic communications allowed the colonial governors and the

[53] Law Officers of the Crown (H. James, F. Herschell) and Dr Deane to Earl Granville, 28 January 1885 (No. 32), TNA, FO 881/5163.

[54] Sir Julian Pauncefote (FO) to Sir Robert Herbert (CO), 2 February 1885 (No. 35), TNA, FO 881/5163; Sir Julian Pauncefote (FO) to Admiralty, 2 February 1885 (No. 36), TNA, FO 881/5163.

[55] R. B. Pugh, 'The Colonial Office, 1801–1925', in E. A. Benians, James Butler, and C. E. Carrington (eds), *The Cambridge History of the British Empire. Vol. III: The Empire-Commonwealth 1870–1919* (Cambridge: Cambridge University Press, 1959), 711–68, at 740–1, 744–5. See also John M. Carland, *The Colonial Office and Nigeria, 1898–1914* (London: Macmillan, 1985), 1–47.

[56] Edward Fairfield, *The Colonial Office List for 1881: Comprising Historical and Statistical Information Respecting the Colonial Dependencies of Great Britain, and an Account of the Services of the Officers in the Colonial Service. A Transcript of the Colonial Regulation, and Other Information. With Maps.* (London: Harrison, 1881), 12, 15.

commanding officers to communicate quickly with London and receive timely instructions, legal advice was not effectively organized within the British government.[57] One reason for this delay was certainly that the documents first had to be sent to the Law Officers at the Inns of Court, who then needed time to read through the large amount of correspondence to understand the context in which a question had been asked. In a time when methods of communication were changing rapidly, legal practitioners were also obliged to adapt to a much faster-paced world, in which news of conflicts spread much more quickly.

During the Sino-French War, the Foreign Office frequently requested legal advice on Britain's neutrality policy and, in particular, with regard to the infringement of the Foreign Enlistment Act.[58] When the conflict ended in late April 1885, the Foreign Office wanted to lift the Act and allow coaling of warships in British ports again. The Law Officers and Deane were hesitant about this suggestion but eventually approved it.[59] The French government, however, protested, arguing that it had not stopped exercising belligerent rights. The Foreign Office requested further advice from the Law Officers and Deane.[60] They suggested a strong formulation as in their opinion '*de facto* state of war now no longer exists' and, thus, 'Her Majesty's Government cannot, therefore, assent to the contention that the French Government are entitled to exercise belligerent rights against neutral vessels unless hostilities should be renewed'. The two Foreign Office clerks, J. H. G. Bergne and Philipp Currie, were surprised at the strong wording, and thought that 'a reply of a more temporizing nature … would be more politic' and thought it advisable to consult the Lord Chancellor in the matter.[61]

The office of the Lord Chancellor performed important duties for all branches of the government, particularly in overseeing the independence of the different government branches. As a senior Cabinet member, the Lord Chancellor was usually only involved in legal business in cases of disagreement within the government offices or in principal political decisions that demanded the advice of a higher ranking member of the government.[62] Lord Selborne, who was Lord Chancellor

[57] Daniel R. Headrick, *The Invisible Weapon: Telecommunications and International Politics, 1851–1945* (New York, NY: Oxford University Press); Robert Kubicek, 'British Expansion, Empire, and Technological Change', in Andrew Porter (ed.), *The Oxford History of the British Empire*, Vol. 3: *The Nineteenth Century* (Oxford: Oxford University Press, 1999), 247–69.

[58] Frei, *Britain, International Law, and the Evolution of Maritime Strategic Thought* (n 5) 46, 51, 66.

[59] F. Herschell (Attorney General) to Mr Currie (FO), 6 May 1885 (No. 352), TNA, FO 881/5163; Minute by Mr Bergne, 6 May 1885 (Inclosure of No. 352), TNA, FO 881/5163; Earl Granville to M. Waddington, 8 May 1885 (No. 356), TNA, FO 881/5163; Mr Currie (FO) to Mr Godley (CO), 8 May 1885 (No. 354), TNA, FO 881/5163.

[60] M. Waddington to Earl Granvillle, 15 May 1885 (No. 363), TNA, FO 881/5163; Mr P. Currie to the Law Officers of the Crown (H. James, F. Herschell) and Dr Deane, 18 May 1885 (No. 365), TNA, FO 881/5163.

[61] The Law Officers of the Crown (H. James, F. Herschell) and Dr Deane to Earl Granville, 22 May 1885 (No. 95), TNA, FO 834/15.

[62] Quintin Hogg, Lord Hailsham of St. Marylebone, *The Office of Law Officer of the Crown, and the Office of Lord Chancellor* (London: Child&Co., 1978); Parry and Fitzmaurice, *British Digest, Part VII* (n 12) 248–51.

at the time of the Sino-French War, did not share the Law Officers' opinion, and thought that the Foreign Enlistment Act had been lifted too early before all hostilities had terminated, and thought it best to reinforce the Act.[63] The Law Officers and Deane, however, insisted on their legal opinion, arguing that the 'peculiar' circumstances of the Sino-French War, in which 'the declaration of war was not accidentally but designedly withheld', led to their decision.[64] The following day, on 9 June 1885, France and China signed a peace treaty at Tientsin, and hence, the decision of the Lord Chancellor was not implemented. This example not only illustrates how Britain applied its neutrality policy through the Foreign Enlistment Act but also shows the connected legal challenges. Selbourne's intervention certainly demonstrated the limitation of the Law Officers' opinion, but also showed that the Foreign Office could involve the Lord Chancellor in difficult and politically sensitive matters.

The Russo-Japanese War and the Emancipation of Legal Advice in the Foreign Office

In 1890, a Royal Commission inquired into the inner-workings of the Foreign Office and examined whether any changes were necessary in terms of efficiency. W. E. Davidson, a former private secretary to the Lord Chancellor, and assistant to Pauncefote from 1886 after Deane's retirement, and later a legal adviser to the Foreign Office, was also invited to give evidence.[65] Describing his work in 1890, Davidson stated that 'the great majority of the legal questions at the Foreign Office are settled without any reference to the Law Officers.... I should say at least four-fifths, and probably many more, of the cases I advise on do not go to the Law Officers at all.' Davidson explained that he would refer a case to the Law Officers if he thought it necessary. Yet, Davidson pointed out that he needed the consent of the Foreign Secretary to seek the advice of the Law Officers. This was because he was only a legal counsel rather than a legal assistant under-secretary, which meant that he had no executive powers to do so.[66] In fact, Davidson, who was a barrister, was the only lawyer in the Foreign Office after Pauncefote's departure in 1889.[67] In

[63] Memorandum by the Lord Chancellor (Lord Selborne), 1 June 1885 (No. 99), TNA, FO 834/15.

[64] Law Officers of the Crown (H. James, F. Herschell) and Dr Deane to Earl Granville, 8 June 1885 (No. 101), TNA, FO 834/15.

[65] Jones, 'Foreign Policy by Justice' (n 6) 32–4.

[66] Evidence of W. E. Davidson, 14 February 1890, in Fourth Report of the Royal Commission Appointed to Inquire into the Civil Establishments of the Different Offices of State at Home and Abroad, Command Papers (1890), C. 6172 C. 6172-I, 109–11.

[67] Neilson and Otte, *Permanent Under-Secretary* (n 38) 69. See also: John Tilley and Stephen Gaselee, *The Foreign Office* (London: G. P. Putnam's Sons Ltd., 1933), 115–120. Tilley/Gaselee's judgement of Davidson is not very flattering as they argue that Davidson confined himself of only giving legal advice.

the end, the Royal Commission decided that no changes were necessary with regard to the organization of legal advice in the Foreign Office.

The role of the Law Officers was also scrutinised by the Treasury in the early 1890s. The workload was huge as the example of the Sino-French War has illustrated. During this period, the Law Officers would receive several cases a day from the Foreign Office for consideration. The extensive correspondence demanded close reading and the Law Officers' replies were not always provided in time, which delayed decisions or caused decisions to be made without a legal opinion. In 1892, the Treasury suggested limiting the private practice of the Law Officers. A year later it then called for a fundamental change to the system of legal advice by demanding the creation of an office at the Royal Courts of Justice and the appointment of two permanent clerks. This was to 'ensure a complete record' of the Law Officers' opinion, and 'establish as far as possible uniformity of practice in the manner in which papers are submitted to and dealt with by them'.[68] To this end, the Treasury suggested increasing the Law Officers' salaries in order to compensate for the loss of income from private practice.[69] An overview of the British government's expenses for the services of the Law Officers between 1880 and 1895 shows that the fees for contentious business varied greatly from year to year, which meant it was difficult for the Treasury to predict exact figures for the expenses of the Law Officers.[70] It was only in 1902 that it was deemed necessary to appoint a legal assistant under-secretary. This was the barrister Sir Cecil Hurst. He had previously worked for the Attorney General, Sir Robert Finlay, and it was here that Hurst first became interested in international law. The strengthening of the number of legal advisers in the Foreign Office can be seen as an acknowledgement of the increasing importance of legal matters in international politics.[71]

The reforms of the 1890s also shifted the dynamics between the Foreign Office and the Law Officers, as the example of the Russo-Japanese War of 1904–1905 illustrates. Britain again proclaimed neutrality in this war and enforced the Foreign Enlistment Act of 1870 on 11 February 1904 as a domestic measure.[72] When the Russian fleet sailed from the Baltic through the Channel, the Mediterranean, and the Suez Canal to reach the theatre of war in the Pacific, the fleet required regular re-coaling, which provided a lucrative business for British and foreign colliers. The

[68] Treasury Minute, 5 December 1892, in Law Officers of the Crown (Remuneration and Staff), House of Commons Papers 62 (1893–94), L. 465; Treasury Minute, 12 January 1893, in Law Officers of the Crown (Remuneration and Staff), House of Commons Papers 62 (1893–94), L. 465.

[69] Treasury Minute, 29 June 1894, in Law Officers of the Crown (Remuneration), House of Commons Papers 191 (1894), Ll. 201.

[70] Return of the Sums Paid in Salaries and Fees to the Law Officers of the Crown in England, Ireland, and Scottland since 1880, 21 August 1895, in Law Officers of the Crown (Salaries), House of Commons Papers 429 (1895), LXI. 215.

[71] Eric Beckett, 'Sir Cecil Hurst's Service to International Law', *BYIL* 26 (1949), 1–5. On Hurst also see Marcus Payk's chapter in this volume.

[72] 'A Proclamation of Neutrality by the King Edward', *The London Gazette*, No. 27644, 11 February 1904, 931–4.

Foreign Secretary, Lord Lansdowne, had already sent a telegram on 10 February 1904 to Sir Charles Eliot, Commissioner of East Africa, and others, stating that no coal should be provided to belligerent warships in Zanzibar waters, which were close to the Suez Canal.[73] Eliot responded to the instructions, reporting that 'Indians were buying up coal', and asking whether private firms were also affected by the provisions of the Foreign Enlistment Act.[74] Willoughby Maycock, a senior clerk, who had worked in the Treaty Department of the Foreign Office since 1896, thought that the answer was clear as the Foreign Enlistment Act was 'applicable to all persons', and this also applied to a British Protectorate such as Zanzibar.[75] Davidson concurred with Maycock's views. To clarify the situation in Zanzibar, Maycock suggested that the Sultan of Zanzibar issue a proclamation of neutrality to ensure British neutrality. Davidson, on the other hand, disagreed with Maycock on this point and ordered the compilation of a case for the Law Officers to consider as he thought that only the British government could issue a proclamation of neutrality.[76] Maycock also asked whether the British custom that belligerent ships were only allowed to coal in British neutral ports once every three months also applied in this context. While Davidson thought that it indeed did, he was sceptical about 'whether these neutrality rules can be enforced in the case of recalcitrant private British subjects, who insist on breaking them'. Augustus Henry Oakes, who had been Hertslet's successor as Librarian and Keeper of the Archives of the Foreign Office since 1896, provided useful information regarding precedents but Davidson was convinced that the British government did not have sufficient control over all citizens of Zanzibar.[77]

Due to the legal complexity, Davidson asked Hurst for a second legal opinion. Hurst agreed with Davidson's suggested course and immediately drew up a bill to extend the Foreign Enlistment Act to Protectorates. Since there was not enough time to get a bill through Parliament, Hurst suggested implementing the bill as a 'local enactment' of which he also drew up a draft.[78] Only after the Foreign Office had weighed up all options, did Davidson contact the Solicitor General, Edward Carson on 15 February 1904, suggesting a meeting with the Attorney General, the Colonial Office and himself to discuss the options available.[79] For the Law Officers,

[73] The Marquess of Lansdowne to Sir Charles Eliot (Telegraphic), 10 February 1904 (No. 15), TNA, FO 834/21.

[74] Sir Charles Eliot to the Marquess of Lansdowne (Telegraphic), 10 February 1904 (No. 15), TNA, FO 823/21.

[75] Minute of W. Maycock, 11 February 1904 (No. 15), TNA, FO 834/21.

[76] Minute of W. Maycock, 12 February 1904 (No. 15), TNA, FO 834/21; Minute of W. E. Davidson, 11 February 1904 (No. 15), TNA, FO 834/21; Minute of W. E. Davidson, 12 February 1904 (No. 15), TNA, FO 834/21.

[77] Three Months' Rule as to Coaling, and its Application to British Protectorates by W. E. Davidson, 12 February 1904 (No. 15), TNA, FO 834/21; Breach of Neutrality Rules by Private Individuals by W. E. Davidson, 12 February 1904 (No. 15), TNA, FO 834/21.

[78] Minute by C. J. B. Hurst, 14 February 1904 (No. 15), TNA, FO 834/21.

[79] W. E. Davidson (FO) to E. Carson (Solicitor General), 15 February 1904 (No. 15), TNA, FO 834/21.

Finlay and Carson, the case was clear and in their brief legal opinion provided on 25 February 1904, they stated that the Foreign Enlistment Act was sufficient and no colonial legislation was required.[80]

The above case illustrates the prominent role of the legal adviser Davidson, and to a lesser extent that of Hurst in discussing legal matters within the newly created structures of the Foreign Office. Davidson and Hurst were primarily concerned with the implementation and execution of Britain's neutrality policy. More generally, the correspondence of the Foreign Office during the Russo-Japanese War showed that there was much more debate amongst Foreign Office officials than had previously been the case, while the Law Officers were consulted less frequently.[81] This suggests that the Foreign Office had strengthened the position of the in-house legal advisers, which was paramount for it to gain independence from the Law Officers,[82] yet the legal advice of the Law Officers was still indispensable for approving the course of action, which the Foreign Office legal advisers suggested.

The Second Hague Peace Conference and the Codification of the Law of Neutrality

After the Russo-Japanese War, the Foreign Office faced further reforms which aimed to increase its efficiency.[83] However, the influence of the Foreign Office within the British government diminished prior to 1914. This became apparent when, shortly after the Russo-Japanese War, an inter-departmental committee was formed to prepare the Second Hague Peace Conference, where the question of neutrality was raised. The chair of the committee was Sir John Lawson Walton, who had been the Attorney General since 1905.[84] Although Hurst, Davidson, and others from the Foreign Office were present, two non-lawyers, Charles L. Ottley as Director of Naval Intelligence and George S. Clarke as Secretary to the Committee of Imperial Defence, determined Britain's legal position regarding the laws of war. To a large extent, the examination focused on Britain's capacity as a belligerent sea power rather than on its previous experience as a neutral sea power. Yet as Britain had shaped the international understanding of neutrality at sea in the decades after 1856, the committee suggested obtaining 'international sanction' for its state

[80] Memorandum by the Law Officers (R. B. Finlay, E. Carson), 25 February 1904 (No. 15), TNA, FO 834/21.

[81] For instance, see discussion of Maycock, Hurst, and Campbell about dynamite as contraband, in Sir E. Satow to the Marquess of Lansdowne (Telegraphic), 9 September 1904 (No. 724), TNA, FO 881/8433.

[82] Tilley and Gaselee, *Foreign Office* (n 67) 266–7; Parry, 'Foreign Policy' (n 6) 98–9.

[83] Tilley and Gaselee, *Foreign Office* (n 67) 159–71. See also: Thomas G. Otte, 'Old Diplomacy: Reflections on the Foreign Office before 1914', *Contemporary British History* 18, 3 (2004), 37–9; Parry, 'Foreign Policy' (n 6) 99–100; Zara S. Steiner, *The Foreign Office and Foreign Policy, 1898–1914* (Cambridge: Cambridge University Press, 1969), 79–81.

[84] Parry, 'Foreign Policy' (n 6) 89–110.

practice at the Hague Peace Conference.[85] For Clarke, Britain's goal had to be that 'our interests as neutrals require uniformity of procedure on the part of neutrals generally'.[86] Hence, the committee suggested the international adoption of the 'Three Rules' of the Treaty of Washington and a slightly revised Foreign Enlistment Act. The Russo-Japanese War had shown that British shipbuilders were disadvantaged due to the strict provisions of the Foreign Enlistment Act, which in Article 8 forbade the 'building', 'equipping', or 'dispatching' of ships for employment in naval operations. Because of this, Ottley suggested loosening the provisions of Article 8 so that British shipbuilders were no longer disadvantaged, while, at the same time, provide there would still remain a basis for an international agreement. In the scenario that no agreement could be reached with other states, the British government should no longer feel bound to implement the Foreign Enlistment Act, unless the other states 'act reciprocally'.[87]

The committee report showed that new actors shaped Britain's neutrality, in particular the Committee of Imperial Defence and the Admiralty. Both had a strong interest in assessing British neutrality policy from the point of view of a belligerent power, and thus pushed to relax the provisions of the Foreign Enlistment Act, which was too stringent in their opinion. The Foreign Office, which had significantly shaped Britain's neutrality policy in previous decades, stood on the sidelines. This highlights that the Foreign Office and its legal advisers were primarily responsible for the implementation and enforcement of Britain's neutrality policy, rather than deciding the course of the British government.

Nevertheless, the composition of the British delegation at the Second Hague Peace Conference showed the growing importance of legal advice in diplomacy. The Foreign Office sent its senior members, Sir Edward Fry, a former judge of the Court of Appeal, and Sir Ernest Satow, a senior diplomat with expertise in the Far East. Hurst and Eyre Crowe, another senior clerk at the Foreign Office who worked for the Western Department, were sent as technical advisers.[88] While Fry and Satow had not been involved in the preparations of the Second Hague Peace Conference, Hurst and Crowe had been an integral part of that process, which not

[85] John W. Coogan, *The End of Neutrality. The United States, Britain, and Maritime Rights, 1899–1915* (Ithaca, NY: Cornell University Press, 1981), 90–103; Frei, *Britain, International Law and the Evolution of Maritime Strategic Thought* (n 5); Nicholas A. Lambert, *Planning Armageddon. British Economic Warfare and the First World War* (Cambridge, MA: Harvard University Press, 2012), 85–103, Jan M. Lemnitzer, *Power, Law and the End of Privateering* (Houndmills: Palgrave, 2014).

[86] Report of the Inter-Departmental Committee Appointed to Consider the Subjects which may Arise for Discussion at the Second Peace Conference (Confidential), 21 March 1907, TNA, FO 881/9041X, 23.

[87] Memorandum by Captain Charles Ottley on the Question of Contraband of War in its Relation to Ships sold by a Neutral to a Belligerent (Appendix 11), n.d., in Report of the Inter-Departmental Committee appointed to consider the Subjects which may arise for Discussion at the Second Peace Conference (Confidential), 21 March 1907, TNA, FO 881/9041X, 80–3.

[88] For a detailed analysis of the role of Crowe, see: Zara S. Steiner, 'Grey, Hardinge and the Foreign Office, 1906–1910', *The Historical Journal* 10, 4 (1967), 432–6.

only guaranteed continuity but also showed the significance of expert knowledge. This development marked a new departure in diplomacy.[89]

At the Hague Peace Conference, Satow was part of the commission which drafted Convention XIII concerning the Rights and Duties of Neutral Powers in Naval War. While most provisions reflected British state practice, some articles were controversial and Britain made reservations at the conference to some provisions.[90] When the Inter-Departmental Committee assessed Convention XIII in the aftermath of the Hague Peace Conference, it suggested its adoption despite the compromises, arguing that it would help consolidate the understanding of neutrality at sea more generally. The new agreement endorsed a concept of neutrality which was significantly less strict and enabled the British government to loosen the Foreign Enlistment Act, reflecting Britain's current national interests.[91] While various government officers were involved in the decision-making process, the Foreign Office was responsible for the amendment of the Foreign Enlistment Act. The changes particularly concerned Article 8 of the Foreign Enlistment Act, and the Law Officers accepted them.[92]

After 1906, the British government increasingly evaluated Britain's neutrality policy from a strategic and economic point of view, bringing in new actors, mostly non-lawyers, to define Britain's legal position towards the laws of war, balancing Britain's interest as a belligerent with that of a neutral power in a potential future war.[93] When the First World War broke out in August 1914 and the British government decided to enter it, Britain's neutrality policy came to an end, and the Foreign Office and its legal advisers had to adapt to new legal challenges arising from that conflict.[94]

[89] Maartje Abbenhuis, Christopher Barber, and Annalise Higgins (eds), *War, Peace and International Order? The Legacies of the Hague Peace Conferences of 1898 and 1907* (London: Routledge, 2017); Stanislas Jeannesson, Fabrice Jesné, and Éric Schnakenbourg (eds), *Experts et expertises en diplomatie. La mobilisation des compétences dans les relations internationales du congrès de Westphalie à la naissance de l'ONU* (Rennes: PUR, 2018).

[90] 'Convention (XIII) concerning the Rights and Duties of Neutral Powers in Naval War. The Hague, 18 October 1907', in Dietrich Schindler and Jiří Toman (eds), *The Laws of Armed Conflicts. A Collection of Conventions, Resolutions and other Documents* (Dordrecht: Martinus Nijhoff, 2004), 1407–16; Frei, *Britain, International Law and the Evolution of Maritime Strategic Thought* (n 5) 131–3, 137–8.

[91] Final Report by the Inter-Departmental Committee on the Second Peace Conference, 28 May 1908, TNA, FO 881/9325X.

[92] F. A. Campbell (FO) to the Law Officers of the Crown (W. S. Robson, S. T. Evans), 16 January 1909 (No. 4), TNA, FO 881/9638.

[93] Frei, *Britain, International Law and the Evolution of Maritime Strategic Thought* (n 5) 114, 119–25.

[94] Isabel V. Hull, *A Scrap of Paper. Breaking and Making International Law during the Great War* (Ithaca, NY: Cornell University Press, 2014); Jones, 'Foreign Policy by Justice' (n 6) 34–8.

Conclusion

In summary, the period prior to the First World War was one of great changes for the British government, not only politically but also with regard to the workings of its administration. The various administrative reforms of the second half of the nineteenth century aimed to increase efficiency within the government offices by creating structures to deal with ever more complex and demanding tasks of a modern interconnected world.[95] The reforms also acknowledged the importance of legal advice for the British government, which tied the chief legal advisers, the Law Officers, more strongly to the government administration. The reforms also created the position of an in-house legal adviser to the Foreign Office to build up legal expertise there. The reforms, however, failed to create a more integrated and permanent legal department within the Foreign Office, which meant that the Foreign Office still relied on legal advice from the Law Officers, particularly on questions of legal principle.

The reforms reflected the demand of the British government for professional legal advice on how to deal with questions concerning international politics. More generally, the professionalization of international law in the mid-nineteenth century was closely intertwined with the growing importance of legal advice in diplomacy.[96] The example of Britain's neutrality policy shows that legal advice to the British government was given and received through a complex government structure, which had to adapt to deal with the growing tasks of the government.

The Foreign Office was principally responsible for the implementation of Britain's neutrality policy, and the Foreign Enlistment Act of 1870 gave the Foreign Office a legal instrument to enforce it. The Foreign Office was thus a powerful actor when it came to implementing and enforcing Britain's neutrality policy. The in-house legal advisers played a constant and important role in dealing with daily legal matters in the Foreign Office. They not only gathered essential legal information, but also analysed it and provided a possible course for the Foreign Secretary to pursue. Yet, the Law Officers decisively shaped the decision-making processes in Britain's neutrality policy. They displayed a flexible and practical approach to the application and enforcement of the articles under the Foreign Enlistment Act. In this way, they built a consistent state practice, which significantly contributed to Britain's successful neutrality policy prior to the First World War. Consequently, the Law Officers can rightly be called the chief architects of Britain's neutrality policy.

95 Otte, 'Old Diplomacy' (n 83) 37–9.

96 Jean d'Aspremont, 'Professionalisation of International Law', in Jean d'Aspremont, Tarcisio Gazzini, André Nollkaemper et al. (eds), *International Law as a Profession* (Cambridge: Cambridge University Press, 2017), 19–37; Stephen C. Neff, *Justice Among Nations: A History of International Law* (Cambridge, MA: Harvard University Press, 2014).

5

The First R2P

US Legal Advisers and the Right to Protect Citizens in the Early Twentieth-Century Americas

Benjamin A. Coates

Around the middle of 1912, US solicitor J. Reuben Clark, Jr set to work on an unwanted task: a legal brief justifying potential US intervention in Mexico. Amidst revolutionary violence, US citizens clamoured for protection and restitution for lost property.[1] President William Howard Taft had mostly stiff-armed pleas for intervention, but with his prospects for re-election in doubt, he began to explore a military response. Taft's secretary of state, Philander C. Knox, tasked Clark with justifying such a policy.[2]

Clark accepted the assignment even though he opposed the intervention. Unlike many other international lawyers whose family backgrounds and elite educations primed their interest in global affairs, Clark was born to a humble Mormon family in the Utah territory and did not step foot in a classroom until the age of ten.[3] Clark had come east in 1903, at the age of thirty-two, to attend Columbia Law School. Although he had intended to focus on mining law, his studies with two leading international lawyers, John Bassett Moore and James Brown Scott, changed his mind. In 1906 Scott took a position in the State Department and hired the newly graduated Clark as his assistant.[4] By 1910 Clark had been promoted to solicitor, the department's top legal officer.

The early twentieth-century State Department was increasingly dependent on legal advice to navigate the diplomatic consequences of globalization. When US investors and entrepreneurs clashed with foreign governments, they turned to Washington for assistance. Thus, pecuniary claims generated by the accelerating transnational flows of money, goods, and capital occupied most of the time of Clark

[1] John Mason Hart, *Empire and Revolution: The Americans in Mexico since the Civil War* (Berkeley, CA: University of California Press, 2002), 271–92.

[2] Frank W. Fox, *J. Reuben Clark: The Public Years* (Provo, UT: Brigham Young University Press, 1980), 195–6.

[3] David H. Yarn, Jr, 'Biographical Sketch of J. Reuben Clark, Jr', *Brigham Young University Studies* 13, 3 (1973), 235.

[4] Fox, *Clark* (n 2) 40–1.

Benjamin A. Coates, *The First R2P* In: *Crafting the International Order*. Edited by: Marcus M. Payk and Kim Christian Priemel, Oxford University Press (2021). © The Several Contributors. DOI: 10.1093/oso/9780198863830.003.0005

and his more than a dozen clerks and assistants. As Frederick Dunn, a former legal adviser himself, noted in 1932: while

> [w]ars and alliances and balances of power have the appeal of grandeur ... the average foreign office official or diplomatist discovers ... [that the] subject-matter of his daily note-writing and his conferences is apt to be concerned primarily with the safeguarding of the interests of his fellow-citizens in their activities that extend beyond the borders of their own country.[5]

Above all, the legal department weighed the public implications of private activities.

Clark believed strongly that governments must protect foreigners and pay their debts.[6] He also deplored the violence against US citizens in Mexico. But Clark expected that a US invasion would make things much worse by inviting retaliation: the thousands of his countrymen in northern Mexico (including many Mormons) would be at the mercy of 'roving bands of insurrectionists ... and an equal number of bands of highway robbers ... all willing and eager to loot, to rape, and to murder'.[7] In later years Clark would expand his critique of war beyond pragmatic rationales. He criticized the 1846 Mexican-American War as a case of US aggression and deemed the 1898 Spanish-American War an unfortunate accident.[8] During the interwar period he promoted the peaceful settlement of international disputes and condemned war as a sin.[9] But as a lawyer, Clark believed he had a duty to his client, so in August 1912 he delivered a memorandum running to seventy-eight printed pages explaining that both international law and the Constitution justified what his client proposed to do: intervene in the affairs of another sovereign state.[10]

At the heart of Clark's argument lay a crucial assertion. Sending troops into Mexico to protect US citizens would not be intervention, he claimed, but merely 'interposition'. Interventions, Clark explained, were political: actions designed to influence or change governments. International lawyers disagreed on their legality.

[5] Frederick S. Dunn, *The Protection of Nationals: a Study in the Application of International Law* (Baltimore, MD: The Johns Hopkins Press, 1932), 12–13.

[6] Gene A. Sessions, *Prophesying Upon the Bones: J. Reuben Clark and the Foreign Debt Crisis, 1933–39* (Urbana, IL: University of Illinois Press, 1992). Sessions focuses on Clark's leadership of the Foreign Bondholders Protective Council in the 1930s.

[7] Quoted in Fox, *Clark* (n 2) 187–8.

[8] Martin B. Hickman and Ray C. Hillam, 'J. Reuben Clark, Jr.: Political Isolationism Revisited', *Brigham Young University Studies* 13, 3 (1973), 438; James B. Allen, 'J. Reuben Clark, Jr., on American Sovereignty and International Organization', *Brigham Young University Studies* 13, 3 (1973), 355.

[9] Allen, 'J. Reuben Clark, Jr., on American Sovereignty and International Organization' (n 6) 347–72; Edwin Brown Firmage and Christopher L. Blakesley, 'J. Reuben Clark, Jr., Law and International Order', *Brigham Young University Studies*13, 3 (1973), 273–346. In 1934 Clark became a member of the First Presidency of the Mormon Church. Yarn, 'Biographical Sketch' (n 3) 241.

[10] J. Reuben Clark, Jr, *Right to Protect Citizens in Foreign Countries by Landing Forces* (Washington, DC: GPO, 1934 (1912)).

But to intervene 'merely to protect citizens where the local government is either unable or unwilling to give such protection' was not really to intervene at all. In fact, it was not only a 'right' but perhaps even a 'duty' under international law.[11]

In reality, sending troops across the border nearly always had political implications, a fact of which Clark must have been aware. In 1910, for instance, US marines landed in Nicaragua ostensibly to protect US citizens. But since those citizens were supporting a rebellion, the intervention bolstered opposition forces and led to the ouster of the Nicaraguan government. Not long after, US marines began an occupation of the country that lasted roughly two decades.[12] 'Interposition' or not, Clark's legal justifications underwrote the kind of informal imperialism about which Latin Americans so often complained.

Controversies over law and intervention still linger today. Since the late 1990s, some scholars, activists, and policy-makers have embraced a 'Responsibility to Protect' (R2P). They contend that willing states, representing the international community, ought to be able to bypass state sovereignty in order to intervene to prevent genocide, ethnic cleansing, and mass killing. At the United Nations World Assembly in 2005, world leaders unanimously embraced the broad outlines of R2P.[13] In 2011, many supporters of military intervention in Libya cited the principle in support.[14] R2P justifies intervention on neutral and universal grounds: the use of force to benefit humanity. Critics charge that political calculations still drive the choice to intervene and contend that R2P simply reinforces the unequal distribution of global power.[15] When J. Reuben Clark invoked the 'right to protect' in 1912, he had US citizens rather than foreign civilians in mind. But in using the language of international law he nevertheless defended intervention as promoting a universal rule of law. Still, just as with modern debates, the first 'R2P' also generated political controversies.

This chapter explores the work of men like Clark to illuminate the role of US legal advisers in managing US interventions in the early twentieth-century Caribbean and Central America. It finds that international legal argumentation served to enable intervention. Lawyer policy-makers hoped that asserting the supremacy of

[11] Clark, *Right to Protect Citizens* (n 8) 3, 24–5.

[12] Lars Schoultz, *Beneath the United States: A History of U.S. Policy Toward Latin America* (Cambridge, MA: Harvard University Press, 1998), 213–19; Michel Gobat, *Confronting the American Dream: Nicaragua Under U.S. Imperial Rule* (Durham, NC: Duke University Press, 2005). Clark referenced the Nicaraguan intervention in his memorandum. See Clark, *Right to Protect Citizens* (n 8) 75–7.

[13] Gareth Evans, *The Responsibility to Protect: Ending Mass Atrocity Crimes Once and for All* (Washington, DC: Brookings, 2008); Ramesh Thakur, *The United Nations, Peace and Security: From Collective Security to the Responsibility to Protect*, 2nd edn (New York, NY: Cambridge, 2017).

[14] Aidan Hehir, *The Responsibility to Protect: Rhetoric, Reality and the Future of Humanitarian Intervention* (London: Palgrave Macmillan, 2012), 12–17. Some members of the Barack Obama administration cited the failure to protect Rwandan citizens in 1994 while calling for intervention in Libya. Michael Crowley, 'Susan Rice, Samantha Power, Rwanda and Libya', *Time*, 24 March 2011, http://swampland.time.com/2011/03/24/susan-rice-samantha-power-rwanda-and-libya/ (accessed 18 August 2020).

[15] Rajan Menon, *The Conceit of Humanitarian Intervention* (New York, NY: Oxford, 2016).

international judgment over national sovereignty could make coercive diplomacy and the use of force compatible with the rule of law. Yet in practice, I suggest, they found that enduring political controversies over sovereignty and capitalism made legal argumentation insufficient without deft diplomacy. In part because international law proved too amenable to intervention, it could not secure an ordered world for capital expansion on its own.

Clark may have found justifying an invasion of Mexico distasteful, but he did not find it difficult. Supporting legal arguments were plentiful. Clark cited a number of (mostly European) legal treatises, written by authors including Bluntschli, Bonfils, Hall, Lawrence, Oppenheim, Phillimore, Pradier-Fodéré, and Westlake, who all agreed that protecting one's own nationals by force was justified even as they differed on the legality of 'intervention' in general. The problem was thus one of definition: which practices constituted 'intervention' rather than some other category of state action? The 'perplexities, difficulties, and disagreements' over intervention, wrote Clark, were 'at least in part [due] to the failure of most writers to appreciate or make the distinction made by Mr. [John Bassett] Moore in his *Digest* between political intervention and non-political intervention'.[16] Embracing the categorization of Moore (his former law professor), Clark suggested that 'non-political' intervention had wide legal support.

Clark also found justification in precedent. He appended to his memorandum a list of US interventions, documenting forty-eight separate instances between 1811 and 1911 when US troops landed in foreign countries to protect US citizens or secure compensation for wrongs committed against them. This long record, in Clark's eyes, made the United States a leader in the field of what Clark defined as 'interposition'. The nation lacked an extensive empire of its own, he claimed, and had mostly refrained from participating in great power politics. Yet 'no nation, it would seem, has with more frequency than has this Government used its military forces for the purpose of occupying temporarily parts of foreign countries in order to secure adequate safety and protection for its citizens and their property'.[17]

There still remained a potential constitutional problem. Could the president dispatch US troops without congressional assent? Here Clark turned to his other Columbia mentor, James Brown Scott. True, the US Constitution gave Congress—and only Congress—the right to declare war, Clark admitted, but it also gave the president the power to enforce the law. And, as Scott had 'elaborately argued' in a series of articles, 'international law is law and is a part of the law of the land'.[18] Scott had written those articles in order to promote support for international law as a means for establishing world peace.[19] Now, however, Clark was mobilizing

[16] Clark, *Right to Protect Citizens* (n 8) 24.
[17] Clark, *Right to Protect Citizens* (n 8) 33.
[18] Clark, *Right to Protect Citizens* (n 8) 33, 44.
[19] Benjamin A. Coates, *Legalist Empire: International Law and American Foreign Relations in the Early Twentieth Century* (New York, NY: Oxford University Press, 2016), chapter 3.

international law to justify unilateral intervention: if international law permitted the use of force on behalf of citizens abroad, then in authorizing such force the president was merely fulfilling his duties to execute the law.

Thus, international law as interpreted by the United States (and most European countries) made it easy to justify intervention to protect citizens abroad. Yet the domestic and international politics of intervention were anything but simple. Intervention rarely escaped domestic criticism, especially when its beneficiaries appeared to be politically connected corporations. Political opponents attacked Taft's policy of 'dollar diplomacy' as the corruption of diplomacy by private interests.[20] Hoping to avoid controversy, in 1912 Taft opted not to invade Mexico. Clark's memorandum, however, was immediately published, and would be cited in interventionist writings for decades.[21]

By citing both Moore and Scott, Clark's memorandum invoked not only his legal mentors but arguably the two most important figures in the early twentieth-century US international law profession. Moore and Scott approached international law from different perspectives, but both touted its contributions to world peace.[22] Citing the influence of law and lawyers—in particular the fact that every secretary of state in the early twentieth century was a lawyer—scholars have identified this period as a 'legalist era' in US foreign relations.[23] However, as I have argued elsewhere, a legalist foreign policy was not necessarily a peaceful one. International lawyers played important roles in administering and justifying the expansion of US power in the early twentieth century.[24]

Since that time many scholars have addressed questions of claims, diplomatic protection, and intervention. Much of this scholarship concerns legal doctrine, and it tends not to explore how this doctrine functioned in the hands of legal advisers themselves.[25] Historical writing has also focused on how legal writers at the

[20] Emily S. Rosenberg, *Financial Missionaries to the World: The Politics and Culture of Dollar Diplomacy, 1900–1930* (Durham, NC: Duke University Press, 2003), 67–9.

[21] See, for example, Evelyn Speyer Colbert, *Retaliation in International Law* (New York, NY: King's Crown Press, 1948), 72; William Warner Bishop, *International Law: Cases and Methods* (Boston: Little, Brown, 1962), 746. In 1928 the *New York Times* reported that Clark's volume 'stands in the Department of State as the classic authority on the subject'. 'New Under-Secretary has had Active Career', *New York Times*, 28 October 1928, sec. 10, 13.

[22] Richard Megargee, 'The Diplomacy of John Bassett Moore: Realism in American Foreign Policy' (PhD diss., Northwestern University, 1963); John Hepp, 'James Brown Scott and the Rise of Public International Law', *Journal of the Gilded Age and Progressive Era* 7, 2 (April 2008), 151–79; Ralph Dingman Nurnberger, 'James Brown Scott: Peace Through Justice' (PhD diss., Georgetown University, 1975); Paolo Amorosa, *Rewriting the History of the Law of Nations: How James Brown Scott Made Francisco de Vitoria the Founder of International Law* (Oxford: Oxford University Press, 2019).

[23] Jonathan Zasloff, 'Law and the Shaping of American Foreign Policy: From the Gilded Age to the New Era', *New York University Law Review* 78 (April 2003), 240–373; Francis Anthony Boyle, *Foundations of World Order: The Legalist Approach to International Relations, 1898–1922* (Durham, NC: Duke University Press, 1999).

[24] Coates, *Legalist Empire* (n 14).

[25] Some examples include Milton Offutt, *The Protection of Citizens Abroad by the Armed Forces of the United States* (Baltimore, MD: Johns Hopkins University Press, 1928); Edwin Borchard, 'Protection of Foreign Investments', *Law and Contemporary Problems*, 11, 4 (1946), 835–47; J. Gillis Wetter,

time mobilized legal and diplomatic arguments to promote or parry intervention.[26] Most of the literature sees intervention, claims, and protection as an international phenomenon—a matter of discussion between and among states.[27] This chapter begins by examining international struggles over the law of intervention in the early twentieth century, and emphasizes how the debate in practice—if not in principle—came to revolve around problems of definition and classification.[28] US legal scholars and policy-makers were willing to rule some interventions out of bounds but nearly always defended the legitimacy of diplomatic and even military intervention in cases of fraud, denial of justice, or anarchy. The task for those seeking intervention—US overseas citizens as well as corporations and their representatives—then became convincing the government that their claims fit into these categories.

The second half of this chapter focuses on the role of legal advisers in the US government's response to these claims. Dealing with claims actually relied on two separate techniques: legal staff had to both *evaluate* claims by nationals and then *pursue* them against other nations. State Department reformers hoped that an expanded cadre of qualified legal professionals could vet claims and avoid politically risky intervention on behalf of undeserving claimants. But because of the nature of international legal discourse—especially its cultural and ideological components—finding legal justifications for intervention proved too easy. Rather than serving as a restrictive hurdle between claimants and the coercive machinery of the state, legal advisers became enablers. Thus, while disputes over international claims took place in the language of law, their resolution depended on politics.

Debating Intervention

Clark had little difficulty finding precedents in international law to support intervention. European states long had claimed the right to intervene on behalf of their nationals. As the influential writer Emerich de Vattel put it in his 1758 *Le Droit des Gens*, 'whoever ill-treats a citizen indirectly injures the State, which must protect

'Diplomatic Assistance to Private Investment: A Study of the Theory and Practice of the United States during the Twentieth Century', *University of Chicago Law Review*, 29 (1962), 275–326; Philip C. Jessup, *A Modern Law of Nations: An Introduction* (New York, NY: The MacMillan Company, 1948), chapter 5.

[26] Martti Koskenniemi, *The Gentle Civilizer of Nations: The Rise and Fall of International Law 1870–1960* (Cambridge: Cambridge University Press, 2002); Antony Anghie, *Imperialism, Sovereignty and the Making of International Law* (Cambridge: Cambridge University Press, 2004).

[27] Lauren Benton and Lisa Ford offer an exception, showing how protection functioned within the British Empire. Lauren Benton and Lisa Ford, *Rage for Order: The British Empire and the Origins of International Law, 1800–1850* (Cambridge, MA: Harvard University Press, 2016), 88–91.

[28] This argument echoes claims made by Kathryn Greenman about the law of state responsibility for rebels. Kathryn Greenman, 'Aliens in Latin America: Intervention, Arbitration and State Responsibility for Rebels', *Leiden Journal of International Law* 31 (2018), 617–39.

the citizen'.[29] The nineteenth-century invention of rapid communication technologies and the gunboat made intervention more common. In 1850, in the so-called Don Pacifico Affair, the British navy blockaded the port of Athens to compel payment for injuries suffered to a British citizen. Foreign secretary Lord Palmerston defended intervention as necessary to protect citizens in areas without proper judicial systems. Nonetheless many contemporaries condemned Palmerston's actions as an attempt to spread British power.[30]

In addition to the use of diplomatic intercession and the threat of force, European empires also relied on 'unequal treaties' to protect their nationals. These had their origins in the decisions of Ottoman rulers to grant European merchants and travellers some immunity from local laws. By the nineteenth century, European powers had bent these compacts to their advantage.[31] In the Ottoman Empire and in East Asia, European travellers who committed crimes would be tried through 'consular jurisdiction' or 'extraterritoriality'—that is, by representatives of their own countries. Thus, they were immune from local authorities. These treaties became contentious symbols of imperialism by the late nineteenth century.[32]

In Asia and the Pacific, the United States eagerly embraced the use of consular jurisdiction and military intervention. In the 1844 Treaty of Wanghia, China extended to US citizens the same rights as it had grudgingly granted British subjects after the Opium Wars.[33] The United States also compelled Japan and Korea to sign similar agreements.[34] Throughout the Pacific, US whalemen, merchants, and missionaries looked to the US navy and US diplomats to protect them from what they viewed as unjust treatment by locals.[35] Protection could range from delicate diplomatic intercession to the razing of entire villages suspected of harbouring bandits.[36]

When not justifying these kinds of intervention and unequal treaties through the language of state interest, lawyers and statesmen in Europe and the United

[29] Emerich de Vattel, *Le Droit des Gens, ou Principes de le Loi Naturelle, appliqués à la Conduite et aux Affaires des Nations et de Souverains*, transl. Charles Fenwick (Washington, DC: Carnegie Institution, 1916), 136.

[30] Benton and Ford, *Rage for Order* (n 22) 113–16; Greenman, 'Aliens in Latin America' (n 23) 620–1; Dolphus Whitten, Jr, 'The Don Pacifico Affair', *The Historian* 48, 2 (1986), 255–67.

[31] On the changing meanings of the so-called Capitulations, see Jennifer Pitts, *Boundaries of the International: Law and Empire* (Cambridge, MA: Harvard University Press, 2018), 30–8.

[32] Shogo Suzuki, *Civilization and Empire: China and Japan's Encounter with European International Society* (New York, NY: Routledge, 2009). Pär Cassel emphasizes the multilateral elements of extraterritoriality and the ways in which especially Chinese rulers before the late nineteenth century integrated consular jurisdiction into a broader system of legal pluralism. Pär Kristoffer Cassel, *Grounds of Judgment: Extraterritoriality and Imperial Power in Nineteenth-Century China and Japan* (New York, NY: Oxford University Press, 2012).

[33] Teemu Ruskola, 'Canton is Not Boston: The Invention of American Imperial Sovereignty', *American Quarterly* 57, 3 (2005), 859–84.

[34] Cassel, *Grounds of Judgment* (n 27) 90; Gordon H. Chang, 'Whose "Barbarism"? Whose "Treachery"? Race and Civilization in the Unknown United States–Korea War of 1871', *Journal of American History* 89, 4 (2003), 1331–65.

[35] Nancy Shoemaker, 'The Extraterritorial United States to 1860', *Diplomatic History* 42, 1 (2018), 36–54.

[36] For a brief account of armed interventions, see Clark, *Right to Protect Citizens* (n 8) 51–76.

States turned to what became known as the 'Standard of Civilization'.[37] Borrowing from contemporary social scientific tracts like Henry Morgan's 1877 *Ancient Society*, lawyers argued that human societies could be ranked hierarchically on a scale from 'savage' to 'civilized' (with 'barbarous' sometimes used to describe a middle position).[38] A nation's treatment in international society then depended on whether or not it met the standards of civilization. As the Scottish lawyer James Lorimer argued, 'civilized' states were full members of the society of nations, entitled to equal international rights. 'Barbarous' states, which included Persia and Turkey, could assert internal sovereignty but must grant extraterritorial jurisdiction to foreigners. And 'savage' peoples had few rights at all.[39]

The precise characteristics that made one 'civilized' were never fully defined nor static. Attaining a certain level of socio-political organization and maintaining the 'rule of law' seemed to matter, but so did blunter racial (white) and cultural ('Western') characteristics. Throughout most of the nineteenth century, religion factored heavily: the map of 'Christian' states tended to overlap the map of 'Civilized' humanity quite neatly.[40] Descended from Catholic Spain and Portugal, Latin American states were considered civilized.[41]

In practice, however, Latin America's international citizenship was distinctly second-class. Britain pressed its claims by blockading Nicaraguan ports in 1842 and 1844, and El Salvador in 1851; in 1838–1839 France bombarded a fortress in Veracruz when Mexico denied the pecuniary demands of a French pastry chef.[42] The legality of these actions depended on essentially Vattelian arguments: states had the right to use force if necessary to defend citizens and their property abroad.

Beginning in the late nineteenth century, Latin American elites challenged these rationales.[43] In a two-volume 1868 treatise, *Derecho Internacional: Teórico y Práctico*

[37] Gerrit W. Gong, *The Standard of 'Civilization' in International Society* (Oxford: Clarendon Press, 1984); Brett Bowden, *The Empire of Civilization: The Evolution of an Imperial Idea* (Chicago, IL: University of Chicago Press, 2009); Georg Schwarzenberger, 'The Standard of Civilisation in International Law', *Current Legal Problems* 8, 1 (1955), 212–35.

[38] Bowden, *Empire of Civilization* (n 32) 33.

[39] James Lorimer, *The Institutes of the Law of Nations: A Treatise of the Jural Relations of Separate Political Communities*, vol. 1 (Edinburgh: William Blackwood and Sons, 1883), 101–2.

[40] On the importance of Christianity to developing European ideas of civilization and international law, see Alexander Orakhelashvili, 'The Idea of European International Law', *EJIL* 17, 2 (2006), 315–47. Racial classifications mattered too: Abyssinia's Christianity did not necessarily afford it international equality.

[41] Carlos Calvo pointed out in 1883 that European treatises ranked Latin America 'among civilized nations'. Quoted in Christina Duffy Burnett [Ponsa], 'Contingent Constitutions: Empire and Law in the Americas' (PhD diss., Princeton University, 2010), 299–300.

[42] Christopher Ernest Barber, 'Gunboat Diplomacy', in Gordon Martel (ed.), *The Encyclopedia of Diplomacy* (Chichester: Wiley, 2018), online at https://onlinelibrary.wiley.com/doi/10.1002/9781118885154.dipl0114 (accessed 18 August 2020).

[43] Latin American states had a long engagement with international law. For instance, a recent study finds that Latin American states were signatories to 40 per cent of all arbitral agreements between 1794 and 1914. Steven M. Harris, 'Between Law and Diplomacy: International Dispute Resolution in the Long Nineteenth Century' (PhD diss., University of California, Davis, 2015), 17. On Latin America and international law, see Greg Grandin, 'The Liberal Traditions in the Americas: Rights, Sovereignty, and the Origins of Liberal Multilateralism', *AHR* 117 (2012), 68–91; Max Paul Friedman and Tom

de Europa y América, Argentine historian, diplomat, and publicist Cárlos Calvo criticized European states—namely the United Kingdom, France, and Spain—for their interventions in Latin America. These states had meddled in Argentina's affairs in the 1830s and 1840s, Calvo complained, and in the early 1860s France had gone so far as to topple the government of Mexico and install an Austrian prince as Emperor Maximilian I. Calvo contended that not only were European monetary claims generally exaggerated, if not wholly invented, but that the very notion that a state could use force against another for the purpose of gaining compensation for its own citizens was wrong. For Calvo, international law began with the basic belief that states were independent and juridically equal.[44] To grant foreigners the right to appeal to their home governments would be to grant 'un privilegio injustificable a favor de los extranjeros y contrario a los naturales'.[45] The application of the principle of diplomatic protection had been 'notoriamente injusta'.[46] Europeans did not sanction such a practice amongst themselves, he noted. Their claim that they could do so in Latin America suggested that they had not yet fully come to grips with the region's independence from colonial rule.[47]

Calvo's ideas found many champions among Latin American diplomats and publicists. Latin American delegates to the first Pan-American Conference in 1889–1890 complained that '[t]he foreigner should not appear like a spoiled child, always encircled by the arms of the Government of his nationality to prevent him from stumbling and injuring himself'.[48] Argentine foreign minister Luis M. Drago gained international attention when he proposed in late December 1902 what came to be known as the Drago Doctrine: the contention that states must not use force to collect debts owed to their citizens.

The Drago Doctrine responded to a European intervention against Venezuela in 1902. After Venezuelan President Cipriano Castro refused to address their citizens' claims of mistreatment, Britain, Germany, and Italy blockaded and bombarded the country. Noting that the Europeans had justified their intervention partly on the grounds that Venezuela had refused to deliver payments owed to bondholders,

Long, 'Soft Balancing in the Americas: Latin American Opposition to U.S. Intervention, 1898–1936', *International Security* 40, 1 (2015), 120–56; Juan Pablo Scarfi, *The Hidden History of International Law in the Americas: Empire and Legal Networks* (Oxford: Oxford University Press, 2017); Arnulf Becker Lorca, *Mestizo International Law: A Global Intellectual History, 1842–1933* (Cambridge: Cambridge University Press, 2014).

[44] Cárlos Calvo, *Derecho Internacional: Teórico Y Práctico de Europa Y América*, vol. 1 (Paris: D'Amyot, 1868),134.

[45] Calvo, *Derecho Internacional* (n 44) 358.

[46] Calvo, *Derecho Internacional* (n 44) 393.

[47] Calvo, *Derecho Internacional* (n 44) 392–5.

[48] International American Conference, *Reports of committees and discussions thereon. Rev. under the direction of the Executive Committee by order of the conference, adopted March 7, 1890* (Washington, DC: GPO, 1890), vol. 2, 936.

Drago argued that 'public debt can not occasion armed intervention'.[49] Lenders already priced risk—hence their ability to demand high interest rates—and defaults already drew punishment from bond markets, Drago noted. Military intervention was therefore unnecessary. It was also wrong. Issuing bonds was a sovereign act. Although a state could not escape its *liability* to pay, foreign states could not *compel* it to pay at any particular time. To do so not only violated the principle of sovereign equality but also led ineluctably to territorial occupation: a new colonization of the poor by the rich.[50]

Some Latin Americans opposed Drago's proposal, fearing that it would depress investment in their capital-hungry countries.[51] Many others rallied to his banner. Calvo himself—now seventy-nine years old—translated Drago's message into French and pressed European legal scholars to endorse Drago's claims.[52] At the 1906 Pan-American Conference in Rio de Janeiro, Brazil, Latin American delegates pushed to enshrine the Drago Doctrine as a hemispheric principle.[53]

US Americans had a mixed reaction to Drago. Although many US newspapers praised Drago's initial proposal in 1902 and US secretary of state John Hay endorsed peaceful settlement of international disputes, Hay was unwilling to commit to non-intervention generally.[54] In 1904, president Theodore Roosevelt's 'Corollary' to the Monroe Doctrine promised that the United States would intervene in cases of 'chronic wrongdoing' in the hemisphere. Implicitly, Roosevelt suggested that the United States might use force to collect European debts in the Caribbean.[55]

But by 1906, US policy seemed to be shifting. Elihu Root, who replaced Hay as secretary of state, pursued a more conciliatory policy toward Latin America. He travelled to Rio in 1906 for the Pan-American Conference, and proclaimed '[w]e wish for no victories but those of peace; for no territory except our own; for no sovereignty except sovereignty over ourselves'. Equal sovereignty of all states offered the 'chief guaranty of the weak against the oppression of the strong'.[56] Root's official instructions to US delegates agreed with Drago that the collection of international debts by force was 'injurious in its general effect upon the relations of nations' and

[49] Luis M. Drago to Martin García Mérou, 29 December 1902, *Papers Relating to the Foreign Relations of the United States 1903* (Washington, DC: GPO, 1904), 4.

[50] Ibid.

[51] Albert de Lapradelle and Ellery C. Stowell, 'Latin America at the Hague Conference.' *Yale Law Journal* 17 (1907–1908), 274–5.

[52] Becker Lorca, *Mestizo International Law* (n 38) 153; Friedman and Long, 'Soft Balancing in the Americas' (n 38) 141

[53] Scarfi, *Hidden History* (n 38) 73.

[54] Hay to García Mérou, 17 February 1903 and Ames to Hay, 5 May 1903, in *FRUS 1903* (n 49), 5–6.

[55] Theodore Roosevelt, 'Message of the President to the Senate and the House of Representatives', 6 December, 1904, in *Papers Relating to the Foreign Relations of the United States, 1904* (Washington, DC: GPO, 1905), esp. xli.

[56] 'Speech of Elihu Root, Secretary of State of the United States of America, Honorary President of the Conference', given at an extraordinary session of the 3rd Conference of American republics held in Rio de Janeiro, 31 July 1906, in *Speeches Incident to the Visit of Secretary Root to South America, 4 July to 30 September 1906* (Washington, DC: GPO: 1906), 12.

'offered frequent temptation to bullying and oppression and to unnecessary and unjustifiable warfare'.[57] However since most American nations were debtors, Root argued, European creditor states would be likely to dismiss any convention passed solely by them. The Latin Americans agreed to table the issue and raise it instead at the upcoming Second Hague Peace Conference of 1907.[58]

Drago travelled to The Hague as a delegate for Argentina and proposed that the conference adopt a convention banning the use of force to collect debts. Sovereign acts like the issuance of government bonds could not be made the subject of international coercion. Even compulsory arbitration of such debts should be out of the question.[59] The US delegation disagreed.[60] Delegate Horace Porter instead submitted a resolution that the conference eventually adopted instead. The so-called Porter Convention prohibited the 'recourse to armed force for the recovery of contract debts'.[61] However, if a debtor nation refused to submit to arbitration or comply with the decision of an arbitral tribunal, military coercion would then be permitted. This was, in the words of one scholar, a loophole 'through which a fleet of warships could sail'.[62] Indeed, in 1912 when the New Orleans businessman Sam 'the Banana Man' Zemurray inquired at the State Department about attaining security for a loan to the Honduran government, J. Reuben Clark assured him that the 'Hague Convention' continued to grant a good 'right to use force'. Zemurray 'seemed very pleased upon learning of this Hague Convention, and seemed to think that it afforded a satisfactory guaranty'.[63]

Scholars have interpreted the debate over the Drago doctrine in different ways. Some paint Drago's actions as largely successful. Even the watered-down Porter Resolution, argues Martha Finnemore, led to the end of the use of force to collect debts.[64] Other scholars are less sanguine.[65] Gerry Simpson even contends that

[57] Quoted in Amos S. Hershey, 'The Calvo and Drago Doctrines', *AJIL* 1 (1907), 26–45, at 40.

[58] 'Resolution: Public Debts', in James Brown Scott (ed.), *The International Conferences of American States, 1889–1928* (New York, NY: Oxford University Press, 1931), 135–6.

[59] Lapradelle and Stowell, 'Latin America' (n 46) 273.

[60] Elihu Root, *Instructions to the American Delegates to the Hague Conference* (Washington, DC: GPO, 1907).

[61] James Brown Scott (ed.), *The Hague Conventions and Declarations of 1899 and 1907* (New York: Oxford University Press, 1918), 89; Edwin M. Borchard, 'International Contractual Claims and Their Settlement', *Judicial Settlement of International Disputes* 13 (August 1913), 51–2.

[62] Donald R. Shea, *The Calvo Clause: A Problem of International Law and Diplomacy* (Minneapolis, MN: University of Minnesota Press, 1955), 15.

[63] Memorandum of Mr Pierrepont of the Division of Latin-American Affairs of the Department of State concerning an interview with the Agent of Honduras, 11 June 1912, *Papers Relating to the Foreign Relations of the United States with the Annual Message of the President Transmitted to Congress 3 December 1912* (Washington, DC: GPO, 1912), 616–17. On Zemurray, see Lester D. Langley and Thomas Schoonover, *The Banana Men: American Mercenaries & Entrepreneurs in Central America, 1880–1930* (Lexington, KY: University Press of Kentucky, 1995).

[64] Martha Finnemore, *The Purpose of Intervention: Changing Beliefs About the Use of Force* (Ithaca, NY: Cornell University Press, 2003), chapter 2.

[65] Becker Lorca, *Mestizo International Law* (n 38) 157; Carsten-Andreas Schulz, 'Accidental Activists: Latin American Status-Seeking at The Hague', *International Studies Quarterly* 61 (2017), 612–22.

debates at The Hague led lawyers themselves to question the value of sovereign equality.[66] In any case, the debate over the Drago Doctrine is often framed as one of imperialism versus resistance or intervention versus sovereignty.

However, focusing too much on the Drago Doctrine distorts the nature of the practical debate over intervention. US Americans largely agreed with the ban on forceful debt collection.[67] As early as 1886, a US secretary of state declared that 'a contractual claim is held as a rule not to be the subject of diplomatic treatment'.[68] At a dinner with Drago in Buenos Aires in 1906, Root himself declared that the United States had 'never deemed it suitable' to collect 'ordinary contract debts' by force.[69] By 1907 there was broad consensus among US policy-makers and legal elites that intervention to collect debts merely based on an inability to pay was wrong. Yet intervention might be appropriate in cases of fraud, 'arbitrary' treatment, or the denial of justice, morally opprobrious acts that violated individual rights. Action in these cases simply represented an act of national self-defence, since an injury to a citizen constituted an injury to the state. The important debate then turned not on whether certain categories of claims (government loans) provided grounds for intervention but on how to categorize any particular claim.[70]

A 1910 meeting of the American Society for International Law highlights how US international lawyers opposed intervention for simple economic purposes while leaving the door open to intervene in order to protect US citizens. Elihu Root delivered an address on 'The Basis of Protection to Citizens Residing Abroad'. He complained that the landing of forces to protect Americans abroad

> leads to many abuses, especially in the conduct of those nationals who, feeling that they are backed up by a navy, act as if they were superior to the laws of the country in which they are residing and permit their sense of immunity to betray them into arrogant and offensive disrespect.

Yet Root also condemned the mistreatment of foreigners by unjust court systems that failed to meet international standards. In such cases, he declared, 'there is a failure on the part of the government to perform its international duty, and a right on the part of the government whose citizen has failed to secure justice to demand

66 Gerry Simpson, *Great Powers and Outlaw States: Unequal Sovereigns in the International Legal Order* (Cambridge: Cambridge University Press, 2004), 135.

67 So too did Great Britain. See Kate Miles, The Origins of International Investment Law: Empire, Environment and the Safeguarding of Capital (New York, NY: Cambridge University Press, 2013), 53.

68 Francis Wharton, *A Digest of the International Law of the United States*, 3 vols (Washington, DC: GPO, 1888), vol. 2, 660.

69 *Speeches Incident to the Visit of Secretary Root* (n 51) 157–8.

70 Drago admitted that debt was not the only issue at stake in the 1902 Venezuelan blockade. He noted in his original communiqué of December 1902 that the European powers intervened in part because of 'the damages suffered by subjects of the claimant nations during the revolutions and wars'. However, he proceeded to ignore this for the remainder of his message. Drago to García Mérou (n 49).

reparation'.[71] Other speakers offered broadly similar conclusions. Edwin Borchard, for instance, said that only when 'Latin-American states raise the standard of their judicial organization so that the courts will perform their international duty as measured by the standard of international law' would intervention cease.[72]

In the discussion that followed, philanthropist and peace advocate Theodore Marburg argued that the United States should never use force to collect debts. Advanced nations no longer had debtor's prisons, and neither should the international order, he contended. But C. L. Bouvé objected. Ought the United States simply to leave its citizens abroad unprotected? Marburg hastened to say that he referred merely to the non-payment of debts, not other forms of mistreatment. But what if a US citizen had a contract that was 'arbitrarily' cancelled? In that case Bouvé contended that he should be entitled to damages. A Mr Larrinaga from Puerto Rico disputed the charge of 'arbitrary' takings. He claimed that foreigners happily made a 'very good business out of some deal which they knew was illegal' and only when 'the business failed to be so good' did they 'cling to the protection of their country'. Bouvé retorted that '[t]he State Department will not entertain such cases', as did R. Floyd Clarke, who added that such a case 'would never lead to diplomatic intervention, or open rupture'.[73] In fact as we will see US intervention in practice did embrace such murky cases.

US international lawyers thus agreed that sovereignty did not present an impermeable barrier to intervention. Under the right circumstances—a failure of protection, 'arbitrary' treatment of businessmen or investors, a 'denial of justice'—intervention became a right and a duty. These criteria were uncertain.[74] How to determine where a state crossed the line between mere inability to pay and an arbitrary rejection of a contract? When a US corporation lost a trial in a Latin American court, was this evidence of 'denial of justice,' or simply proof that the company lacked a good case?

Critics of intervention often contended that powerful governments answered these questions through extralegal means, ignoring the substance of the law to maximize their material interests.[75] A government would claim 'denial of justice', then, when in its interests to do so. Yet this 'imperialistic hypothesis' lets international law off the hook too easily.[76] While top policy-makers had to decide how

[71] Elihu Root, 'The Basis of Protection to Citizens Residing Abroad', *American Society of International Law Proceedings* (1910), 16–27, at 20 and 25.

[72] Edwin Borchard, 'The Question of the Limitation of Protection by Contract between the Citizen and a Foreign Government or by Municipal Legislation', *American Society of International Law Proceedings* (1910) 46–62, at 62.

[73] *American Society of International Law Proceedings* (1910) 187–92.

[74] As Kathryn Greenman shows, on the issue of state responsibility for the actions of rebels, Latin American and US lawyers essentially agreed in principle that government negligence might justify intervention. However, their disagreements on what constituted negligence in practice were so great that in essence the two sides embraced incompatible views on state responsibility and sovereign immunity. Greenman, 'Aliens in Latin America' (n 23) 639.

[75] Dunn, *Protection of Nationals* (n 5) 24–6.

[76] Dunn, *Protection of Nationals* (n 5) 25.

to intervene, it was the lawyers who ruled whether or not a dispute justified intervention in the first place. Policy-makers hoped that legal expertise might manage the behaviour of their own citizens abroad while preserving a US hegemonic order in the circum-Caribbean. Yet owing to the nature of international law and the international legal profession, such an attempt proved only partially successful.

Lawyers, Claims, and the Politics of Intervention

At the centre of the attempt to bring legal expertise to bear on the problem of claims stood Elihu Root. The son of a Hamilton College maths professor, he had made his way to New York City in 1864 to attend NYU Law School, and soon became a well-respected and well-remunerated corporate lawyer.[77] In 1899, William McKinley asked him to become secretary of war, famously because, as McKinley's aide put it '[the president] has got to have a lawyer to direct the government of these Spanish islands, and you are the lawyer he wants'.[78] From his position as head of the War Department, Root oversaw the US colonization of the Philippines as well as the military occupation of Cuba. He then returned to his lucrative private law practice in New York where in 1904 he billed his clients USD 100,000 (equivalent to nearly USD 3 million in 2019 prices).[79]

In 1905 Root returned to Washington, somewhat grudgingly, at the request of Theodore Roosevelt to take the position of secretary of state. Roosevelt's foreign policy—especially his 'taking of Panama' and his announcement of a 'Corollary' to the Monroe Doctrine—had provoked opposition. The president sought a new strategy. As a corporate lawyer, Root had made it his mission to find ways to reconcile his clients' interests with the law. As he put it pithily, 'a lawyer's chief business is to keep his clients out of litigation'.[80] He applied this approach to his new client, the US government. 'The main object of diplomacy', he wrote, was 'to keep the country out of trouble.'[81]

The circum-Caribbean region was the area most likely to get the United States into 'trouble' in 1905. The combination of unstable Caribbean and Central American governments with rapacious foreigners led to frequent conflicts and allegations of mistreatment. The threat of European intervention—a repeat of the

[77] The best biography of Root remains Philip C. Jessup, *Elihu Root*, 2 vols (New York, NY: Dodd, Mead & Company, 1938).

[78] Elihu Root, 'The Lawyer of Today, Address before the New York Country Lawyers Association, New York City, 13 March 1915', in Robert Bacon and James Brown Scott (eds), *Addresses on Government and Citizenship* (Cambridge, MA: Harvard University Press, 1916), 503–4.

[79] Jessup, *Root* (n 77), vol. 2, 431. Currency comparisons are based on the consumer price index as calculated by MeasuringWorth at https://www.measuringworth.com/calculators/uscompare/index.php (accessed 28 December 2020).

[80] Jessup, *Root* (n 77), vol. 1, 133.

[81] Richard W. Leopold, *Elihu Root and the Conservative Tradition* (Boston, MA: Little, Brown and Company, 1954), 50.

Venezuelan blockade and bombardment—loomed. The resolution of that conflict raised even greater fears because an arbitral panel of the Permanent Court of Arbitration had ruled that citizens of those nations that had used force against Venezuela deserved to be paid first.[82] This seemed likely to encourage further violence.

Root held US investors and businessmen partially responsible for this state of affairs. He knew that the Roosevelt Corollary had been prompted in part by a concern that European states would intervene in the Dominican Republic on behalf of their nationals who owned government bonds. Dominican debt had been managed by a US corporation (the San Domingo Improvement Company) which had provoked European opposition by mismanaging Dominican resources, driving the country into insolvency and then pocketing the bulk of government reparations.[83]

Root recognized this combination of malfeasance and incompetence as part of a larger pattern. '[O]ne of the most remarkable facts' about foreign claimants, he noted in 1907, 'was the largeness of the claims presented and the smallness of the awards made when passed upon by a judicial tribunal'.[84] Examples abounded: British claims against the United States during the latter's civil war totalled USD 96 million (about USD 1.55 billion in 2019), but an arbitral tribunal awarded less than USD 2 million; French claims of USD 35 million received just USD 625,000. An 1869 US-Mexican mixed commission decided that US claims of USD 470 million were actually worth about USD 4 million, while Mexican claims of USD 86 million were reduced to USD 150,000. And a 1903 mixed commission reduced US claims against Venezuela from VEB 81.4 million to VEB 2.3 million.[85]

The State Department frequently managed crises involving US citizens overseas. Increased foreign investment after the Civil War forced bureaucratic innovations in the department. In 1866 secretary of state William Seward hired an 'Examiner of Claims'; in 1891 this position became 'Solicitor for the Department of State'.[86] Seward's successor, Hamilton Fish, promoted international arbitration as an alternative to armed intervention. In 1868 he appointed Francis Lieber as the first professional international lawyer to umpire an international arbitration. As noted earlier, arbitrations often trimmed the claims of US investors. Yet they remained ad

[82] James Brown Scott (ed.), *The Hague Court Reports* (New York, NY: Oxford University Press for the Carnegie Endowment for International Peace, 1916), 55–61.

[83] Cyrus Veeser, *A World Safe for Capitalism: Dollar Diplomacy and America's Rise to Global Power* (New York, NY: Columbia University Press, 2002).

[84] 'Meeting of the American Commission to the Second Hague Conference, Held on 20 April 1907, in the Diplomatic Room of the Department of State', Box 20, Joseph H. Choate Papers, Library of Congress.

[85] Hershey, 'Calvo and Drago Doctrines' (n 57) 43–4.

[86] Gaillard Hunt, *The Department of State of the United States; Its History and Functions* (New Haven, CT: Yale University Press, 1914), 202.

hoc affairs that sometimes produced fraudulent outcomes.[87] Latin American states often resented paying even reduced amounts.

After 1900, some international lawyers pushed for the codification of international law and the professionalization of international adjudication.[88] In China, as Eileen Scully has noted, when disruptive US 'sojourners' troubled diplomatic relations, Root created a new US Court for China in order to 'save imperialism from itself'.[89] To deal with US investors in the Caribbean, Root aimed to reform the State Department, in part by hiring more lawyers: diplomatic problems became opportunities for legal solutions. Despite previous reforms, by 1900, the department legal staff consisted solely of the solicitor and two clerks. By 1906, two assistant solicitors and four more clerks had joined. Five years later the solicitor's office employed fifteen assistants and clerks, and a separate Office of the Counselor had a staff of three.[90] Department lawyers earned high pay checks: the counsellor received USD 7,500 annually and the solicitor's salary of USD 5,000 equalled that of the first assistant secretary of state.[91] In addition, the department spent USD 49,000 in 1909 alone on outside legal counsel (USD 1.42 million in 2019 values).[92] Legal expertise was expensive, but necessary.

In hiring legal staff, Root looked beyond patronage appointments. James Brown Scott offers a case in point. When the State Department's solicitor retired in 1905, Scott sent Root an unsolicited letter wondering if 'you might care to make a nonpolitical appointment of some one who has specialized in International Law'. Citing his credentials—Harvard class of 1890, a graduate degree from Heidelberg in 1894, faculty appointments at Illinois and Columbia—Scott proposed: 'If so, I would suggest that you give me a passing thought'.[93] Root was, it turned out, just so motivated, and he hired Scott as solicitor in 1906 despite the fact that the law professor lacked the kinds of political connections often necessary to obtain a government sinecure.[94]

Scott would build an international reputation for his work in the peace movement and his leadership of the American Society of International Law and other

[87] Tzvika Alan Nissel, 'A History of State Responsibility: The Struggle for International Standards (1870–1960)' (PhD diss., University of Helsinki, 2016), 44–52, 96, 125.

[88] David S. Patterson, *Toward a Warless World: The Travail of the American Peace Movement, 1887–1914* (Bloomington, IN: Indiana University Press, 1976), chapter 8.

[89] Eileen P. Scully, *Bargaining with the State from Afar: American Citizenship in Treaty Port China, 1844–1942* (New York, NY: Columbia University Press, 2001), 105–7. On the broader context of diplomatic protection in the Pacific, see Shoemaker, 'The Extraterritorial United States to 1860' (n 30).

[90] Sources for these figures are in *Register of the Department of State* (Washington, DC: GPO, 1900, 1906) and Department of State, *Outline of the Organization and Work of the Department of State* (Washington, DC: GPO, 1911).

[91] *Register of the Department of State* (1910); Graham Stuart, *The Department of State: A History of its Organization, Procedure and Personnel* (New York, NY: MacMillan, 1949), 219.

[92] Richard Hume Werking, *The Master Architects: Building the United States Foreign Service, 1890–1913* (Lexington, KY: University of Kentucky Press, 1977), 150.

[93] Nurnberger, *James Brown Scott* (n 17) 130.

[94] See Coates, *Legalist Empire* (n 14) chapter 3.

professional organizations. His edited volumes of the proceedings of the Hague Peace Conferences are still widely cited.[95] But when Scott arrived in Washington, Root explained that his immediate task was to evaluate a series of acrimonious claims against Venezuela—a murky conflict that Roosevelt had 'cheerfully unload[ed]' on his secretary of state.[96] The Venezuelan claims represented only a few of the many claims requiring State Department attention.[97] But a case study of one of the claims against Venezuela is worth pursuing here because it highlights the complexities in using law to resolve claims both domestically and internationally.

The conflict traced to a US corporation—the New York and Bermudez Company (NY&B)—which had obtained a concession to mine asphalt from a large tar lake in Venezuela in 1893.[98] Soon the NY&B became part of the so-called Asphalt Trust which controlled 85–90 per cent of the market for the paving of America's expanding cities.[99] (Unlike today, when asphalt is produced through petrochemical processes, at the turn of the century most asphalt was mined from surface tar deposits like the one in Venezuela.) The Asphalt Trust controlled other sources of supply and thus had an interest in not fully exploiting its Venezuelan concession. Combined with difficulties in production, this meant that by 1900 the company had generated less than USD 30,000 in revenue for the Venezuelan government.[100] Thus Venezuelan president Cipriano Castro had incentives to support rival US entrepreneurs who challenged the validity of the NY&B's titles and attempted to gain access to a supply of asphalt with which to challenge the Trust's monopoly.

Believing that Castro was plotting to revoke their claim to the asphalt, in 1901 the NY&B conspired with Manuel Antonio Matos—said to be Venezuela's richest man, and a rival of Castro—to overthrow Castro's government.[101] The company spent USD 145,000 to purchase a gunboat for Matos's forces and provided ammunition

[95] See, for example, Chiara Giorgetti, *The Rules, Practice, and Jurisprudence of International Courts and Tribunals* (Leiden: Martinus Nijhoff, 2012), 37–8; Mary Ellen O'Connell, *The Power and Purpose of International Law* (New York, NY: Oxford University Press, 2008), 154; or the chapter by Michael Jonas in this volume.

[96] Nurnberger, *James Brown Scott* (n 17) 132; Schoultz, *Beneath the United States* (n 10) 191.

[97] A card index for the solicitor's office, which begins in 1910, identifies the protection of US interests abroad as the largest category of correspondence for the office. See Solicitor Name Card Index, available by requesting 59/250/16/24 'Decimal File 1910–1929 Source Card Index Solicitor', National Archives and Records Administration, College Park (NARA), Box 1346.

[98] *Correspondence relating to Wrongs Done to American Citizens by the Government of Venezuela*, 60th Cong., 1st sess., 1908, S. Doc. 413, 161–3. The account of the NY&B and Venezuela is explored at greater length in Benjamin A. Coates, 'Securing Hegemony through Law: Venezuela, the U.S. Asphalt Trust, and the Uses of International Law, 1904–1909', *Journal of American History* 102, 2 (2015), 380–405.

[99] Nikita Harwich Vallenilla, *Asfalto y Revolución: la New York & Bermudez Company* (Caracas, Venezuela: Monte Avila Editores, 1992), 160; Brian S. McBeth, *Gunboats, Corruption, and Claims: Foreign Intervention in Venezuela, 1899–1908* (Westport, IN: Greenwood Press, 2001), 43–44.

[100] Charles E. Carreras, *United States Economic Penetration of Venezuela and its Effects on Diplomacy, 1895–1906* (New York, NY: Garland Publishing, 1987), 39.

[101] William Maurice Sullivan, 'The Rise of Despotism in Venezuela: Cipriano Castro, 1899–1908' (PhD diss., University of New Mexico, 1974), 248–9; McBeth, *Gunboats, Corruption, and Claims* (n 99) 62–4.

and other supplies.[102] The Matos rebellion lasted for two years, leading to perhaps 15,000 Venezuelan deaths, but Castro ultimately triumphed.[103] Upon being informed of the NY&B's complicity in the rebellion by disgruntled former NY&B official Ambrose Carner, in 1904 Castro's Attorney General filed suit against the NY&B for violating the terms of its original concession. Another suit, based on the company's support for revolutionary forces, followed soon after.[104] At the same time, Venezuelan forces seized the NY&B's asphalt deposits, and Castro appointed Carner to act as receiver for the sequestered property. Following a preconceived plan, Carner then began to sell asphalt to the Trust's rivals in the United States.[105]

The NY&B immediately appealed to Washington, seeking military and diplomatic backing. The company counted several powerful Republicans among its board of directors but knew that political connections would not suffice on their own. As their lawyer explained: 'Secretary [of State John Hay] in my judgment certainly would not make peremptory demand without legal opinion from Department's Solicitor advising such action, nor probably without also obtaining approval of President'.[106] Thus the company hired John Bassett Moore to lobby on its behalf in Washington. In addition to his reputation as a legal expert (Moore, recall, had taught J. Reuben Clark at Columbia), he was well connected, having served as assistant secretary of state in 1898–1899 and as an informal legal adviser since then. Moore had a particularly close relationship with the man initially charged with evaluating the company's claim, solicitor Walter Penfield.[107]

Solicitor Penfield at first advised against intervention on behalf of the company. Venezuela's case against the NY&B was still proceeding in local courts, and thus a US display of force would violate procedural norms. As Penfield noted, 'we deal with semi-barbarous states in that manner, on the theory that they are outside the pale of international law'. But 'European and American states' required that justice run its course before the government could consider intervening.[108]

John Bassett Moore therefore needed to demonstrate that the NY&B had not simply experienced an adverse legal judgment but had been the victim of a 'denial of justice'. This concept was difficult to disentangle from broader civilizational

[102] Avery Andrews to John Bassett Moore, 2 January 1906, Columbia University, Rare Book & Manuscript Library, New York (CU-RMBL), John Bassett Moore Papers, Box 13; Thurber, *Asphalt Trust*, 21–31.

[103] Judith Ewell, *Venezuela and the United States: From Monroe's Hemisphere to Petroleum's Empire* (Athens, GA: University of Georgia Press, 1996), 101. In fact it was this conflict that produced many of the damage claims that Britain, Germany, and Italy cited when blockading Venezuela in 1902.

[104] Nicolás Bello to Cipriano Castro, 19 March 1901, *Boletín del Archivo Histórico de Miraflores (Caracas)*, 19 (nos 98–100, 1977), 93; Vallenilla, *Asfalto y revolución* (n 94) 323–37; Andrews to Moore, 27 July 1906, CU-RMBL, box 13, Moore Papers; *Correspondence relating to Wrongs Done to American Citizens* (n 93) 133–6, 217.

[105] Andrews to Moore, 3 January 1905, CU-RMBL, Moore Papers, box 62.

[106] Moore to Andrews, 22 August 1904, CU-RMBL, Moore Papers, box 63.

[107] See, for example,, Penfield to Moore, 6 December 1904, ibid.

[108] Walter Penfield, 'Memorandum', August 1904, ibid.

discourses. In a series of briefs submitted to the State Department, Moore simultaneously drew on European legal expertise while implicitly challenging Venezuela's membership in the society of civilized nations. Moore cited publicists like Cressy and Hall to demonstrate that international law permitted states to intervene to protect the property of their citizens when local legal systems could not be trusted. Intervention constituted 'the true rule ... which is observed by civilized governments on this subject', Moore concluded.[109]

Perhaps more importantly, Moore also painted Venezuela as uncivilized by impugning the nature of its justice system. He criticized the 'arbitrary and irregular character of the recent "judicial" proceedings' against his client and was 'delighted' when Venezuela arrested two NY&B agents under questionable circumstances.[110] Here was more proof, he argued, of Castro's despotic tendencies. The seizure of the company's property before final judgment, 'without emergency, without any allegation of urgency, and upon a stale default', was, Moore argued, 'nothing less than monstrous'. While never explicitly saying that Venezuela was uncivilized, Moore's use of terms like 'monstrous' appealed to racial prejudices against Latin Americans widely shared by US policy-makers.[111] By embedding his legal arguments in broader cultural assumptions, Moore implied that any Venezuelan judgment against his client was *ipso facto* devoid of justice.

Moore's arguments convinced Penfield that the NY&B's claim had merit. And though secretary of state John Hay considered the company 'shady', he nevertheless forwarded the matter to the US Attorney General, whose February 1905 report called Venezuela's suit against the NY&B 'not a bona fide judicial proceeding but ... part of a scheme of spoliation'.[112] The State Department then sent an ultimatum to Venezuela, promising to 'take such measures as it may deem necessary in order to obtain complete reparation'.[113] The British minister in Caracas reported to London that 'the question of American intervention in this country will, I am convinced, eventually become an accomplished fact'.[114]

Indeed, President Roosevelt considered dispatching the marines. Although sceptical of business monopolies at home, the president liked Castro even less, but he recognized the political danger of military intervention. The Asphalt Trust was not a sympathetic litigant. 'Even the Big Stick would not look pretty all dripping

[109] Moore to Secretary of State, 23 January 1904, CU-RMBL, Moore Papers, box 62.

[110] Moore to Andrews, 1 September 1904, CU-RMBL, Moore Papers, box 63; Moore to Lindsay, 25 November 1904, ibid.

[111] James William Park, *Latin American Underdevelopment: A History of Perspectives in the United States, 1870–1965* (Baton Rouge, LA: Louisiana State University Press, 1995); Fredrick B. Pike, *The United States and Latin America: Myths and Stereotypes of Civilization and Nature* (Austin, TX: University of Texas Press, 1992).

[112] John Hay, Diary Entry, 30 December 1904, Reel 1, John Hay Papers, Library of Congress; Moore to Lindsay, 24 February 1905, CU-RMBL, Moore Papers, Box 62.

[113] Hay to Bowen, 10 March 1905, CU-RMBL, Moore Papers, Box 63.

[114] McBeth, *Gunboats, Corruption, and Claims* (n 99) 123.

with asphalt', quipped one newspaper editorial.[115] The case became a headache for the Roosevelt administration, a headache that only worsened when Herbert Bowen, the US minister to Caracas, accused assistant secretary of state Francis Loomis of taking a bribe from the NY&B.[116] To 'secure an unbiased and dispassionate view' of the situation, Roosevelt sent Judge William Calhoun to Caracas in August 1905. Calhoun described the judgment against the NY&B as 'a travesty, a farce ... not justified by any principle of law, by any rule of practice known to the courts of any civilized country, or by any principle of common sense or common justice'. Yet his report also cast doubt on some of the company's contentions, and asserted that the NY&B's claim could not 'properly be disposed of by a simple demand'.[117]

Root inherited this situation when he took office and, based on Calhoun's findings, declined to back intervention. Yet he did not reject the company's claim entirely. The new secretary concluded that the Venezuelan courts had proceeded 'in an exceedingly harsh manner', one 'hardly consistent with that sense of justice which should control nations in their treatment' of foreigners.[118] As we have seen, Root aimed to bring stability to the hemisphere (thereby minimizing challenges to US dominance) in part through Pan-American initiatives. Legalist policies formed an important part of this outreach. In addition to convincing European states to include Latin American nations at the 1907 Hague peace conference, Root pushed for expanded arbitration and the creation of an international court. He also promoted the creation of a Central American Court of Justice in 1907. Along with his leadership of the American Society of International Law, this formed part of a broader strategy to substitute adjudication for force and thereby preserve a stable global environment for capital accumulation.[119]

Yet in Root's legalist vision, international law did not necessarily prohibit intervention. States had 'duties' as well as 'rights' under international law, Root often said, and must uphold a 'standard of international conduct'.[120] One of these duties consisted in the fair treatment of foreigners and their property. '[T]he United States possesses the inherent right to protect its property and enforce its rights wherever located and wherever imperiled,' he stated in 1906.[121] If the NY&B's claims

[115] *NY Evening Post*, 24 December 1904, cited in Harwich Vallenilla, *Asfalto y Revolución* (n 94) 365.

[116] *In the Matter of the Charges of Mr. Herbert W. Bowen, United States Minister to Venezuela, against Mr. Francis B. Loomis, First Assistant Secretary of State, and the Counter Charges of Mr. Loomis against Mr. Bowen* (Washington, DC: GPO, 1905).

[117] *Correspondence relating to Wrongs Done to American Citizens* (n 93) 154, 530.

[118] Elihu Root to Minister Russell, 10 November 1905, *Papers Relating to the Foreign Relations of the United States 1905* (Washington, DC: GPO, 1906), 1003.

[119] On Root's legalism, see Coates, *Legalist Empire* (n 14) chapter 4.

[120] Elihu Root, 'The Relations between International Tribunals of Arbitration and the Jurisdiction of National Courts', *AJIL* 3 (1909), 529–36, at 35.

[121] Root to the Secretary of War, 21 February 1906, in United States Department of State, *Papers Relating to the Foreign Relations of the United States with the Annual Message of the President Transmitted to Congress December 3, 1906* (Washington, DC: GPO, 1906), vol. 2, 1205.

had merit, then dropping the case risked not only alienating several influential Republicans but also contradicting international law.

Root thus had Scott, his new solicitor, review the case anew. Previous policy was widely regarded as having been driven by 'pressure from private interests of a not unimpeachable character'. A more professional brief might either provide a rationale for dropping the case or else justify its continued pursuit.[122]

Scott produced a lengthy opinion concluding that Venezuela had violated the NY&B's 'property rights' through 'gross misuse of judicial and executive authority'. He added that 'the company's claim is perfect, not only from a legal standpoint, but, more important still, from the standpoint of equity and the broad principles of right and fair play'.[123] Neutral legal expertise, then, had backed the sketchy claims of a revolution-instigating corporation. 'We want you to understand', wrote the company's counsel, John Lindsay in a 1909 note preserved in Scott's personal papers, 'how much we appreciate the splendid work done both in the Department and at Caracas in the assertion and protection of our client's rights in which your share formed so conspicuous a part.'[124]

Root submitted Scott and Calhoun's reports to the Senate.[125] Although the secretary doubted that a congressional report would rally public support for intervention, this strategy had the benefit of tabling the NY&B's insistent demands while still keeping the government officially in support of the company's rights. Even when the Asphalt Trust's US rivals hired lawyers of their own to undermine the NY&B—lawyers led by former secretary of state John W. Foster and his son-in-law, future secretary of state Robert Lansing—Root refused to abandon his support for the company's claim.[126]

All of this legal writing failed to convince Castro to yield, however. The Venezuelan government held fast to the assertion—echoing Calvo—that US citizens had no right to take 'la vía diplomática' and call on the US government for support.[127] The Caracas newspaper *El Constitucional* claimed that the NY&B's actions overrode 'the most elementary principles of international law' and set aside 'sacred canons of universal civilization'.[128] Castro also refused to submit the matter to arbitration, in part because Moore had insisted on the return of the NY&B's property as a precondition.[129]

[122] McBeth, *Gunboats, Corruption, and Claims* (n 99) 143.

[123] *Correspondence relating to Wrongs Done to American Citizens* (n 93) 143, 154.

[124] Lindsay to Scott, 2 March 1909, Georgetown University Library, Special Collections Research Center (GUL-SCRC), James Brown Scott Papers, Box 13.

[125] *Correspondence relating to Wrongs Done to American Citizens* (n 93).

[126] 'Plead for Venezuela; John W. Foster Argues against Government Aiding Claimants', *New York Times*, 16 April 1908.

[127] Ministro de Relaciones Exteriores, *Libro Amarillo de la República Venezuela* (Caracas, Venezuela: Imprenta Nacional, 1905), xxxiv.

[128] 'The New York & Bermudez Company: Its Proceedings and Methods', *El Constitucional*, 4 March 1905, transl. copy in Box 62, Moore Papers.

[129] For a copy of Moore's draft protocol, see Box 63 of Moore Papers.

Ultimately a combination of US pressure and patience secured the return of the NY&B's property. Although Roosevelt proposed seizing a customhouse to 'show those Dagos that they will have to behave decently', Root instead severed diplomatic relations in June 1908.[130] Six months later, while Castro was undergoing surgery in Europe, his army chief Juan Vicente Gómez seized power.[131] Root sped the diplomat William I. Buchanan to Caracas with orders to demand arbitration of outstanding claims in exchange for diplomatic recognition. 'The essential quality of arbitration', Root cabled Buchanan, 'is the substitution of a tribunal, which is international and therefore unprejudiced for a tribunal which is national and therefore partial.'[132] Root's suggestion seemed to imply the possibility of creating a global rule of law above politics. In such a world, outside interference with domestic legal processes would be unproblematic because it would be motivated by neutral principles of justice rather than political self-interest. Property rights were central to this vision of the rule of law; indeed, it had as one of its primary goals the depoliticization of property itself. If foreign claims could be understood in the language of rights rather than contests over resources, then a national 'duty' to protect such rights could be inferred. That this rule of law would tend to benefit international investors went unsaid but was clearly key to Root's endorsement of it in the first place.

Whether Gómez agreed with this vision is unclear, but he certainly understood the language of money and power. Recognition meant access to foreign capital, and settling foreign claims was part of the deal. In an agreement signed on 13 February 1909, the NY&B secured a return of its property and confirmation of its titles (although it agreed to pay a fine).[133] NY&B directors were 'jubilant', they told Root.[134]

The NY&B's regaining of its property would have been more difficult if international law did not provide so many precedents supporting the right of intervention. Moore was able to mobilize these arguments to sway US legal advisors. He more than earned the USD 27,000 that he billed his clients.[135] With legal advisors providing briefs that supported their case, the company could apply pressure to the government to pursue its claims against Venezuela. Yet without Root's diplomatic finesse they might not have triumphed in the end since public opinion frowned on the use of force on behalf of an unpopular trust. As Roosevelt lamented,

[130] Stephen G. Rabe, *The Road to OPEC: United States Relations with Venezuela, 1919–1976* (Austin, TX: University of Texas Press, 1982), 10; Embert J. Hendrickson, 'Root's Watchful Waiting and the Venezuelan Controversy', *The Americas* 23, 2 (1966), 120–1.

[131] McBeth, *Gunboats, Corruption, and Claims* (n 99) 233.

[132] Harold F. Peterson, *Diplomat of the Americas: A Biography of William I. Buchanan* (Albany, NY: State University of New York Press, 1977), 333.

[133] See copy of settlement in Box 14, Moore Papers. Ministro de Relaciones Exteriores, *Libro Amarillo de la República Venezuela* (Caracas, Venezuela: Imprenta Nacional, 1909), v–vii.

[134] Peterson, *Diplomat of the Americas* (n 127) 338.

[135] This figure represents the sum of payments attested to by letters and receipts in Boxes 13, 28, 62, 63, Moore Papers.

> It is literally true that if I started to deal with him [Castro] as he deserves, the enormous majority of my countrymen would be so absolutely amazed and so absolutely out of sympathy with me as if I undertook personally to run down and chastise some small street urchin who yelled some epithet of derision at me while I was driving.[136]

Root's policy of 'watchful waiting', as one historian described it, was therefore vital.[137] It permitted the triumph of the NY&B's claim without the need for violence. Having a supporting legal opinion enabled this outcome, but it was Root's patience that made recovery possible in a political sense.

Root's successors did not share his political acumen. Philander Knox, William Howard Taft's secretary of state, eagerly pressed US claims. His State Department's legal arguments in favour of US claimants were no less polished than those of his predecessors. Yet they had no more success convincing Latin Americans to embrace the US vision of intervention under international law.

Take for example the so-called Alsop claim. The dispute dated back to the 1870s, when a US firm chartered in Chile disputed contracts with Bolivia. After Chile annexed Bolivian territory in the War of the Pacific, the former agreed to accept responsibility for claims against the latter, including that of Alsop. However, Chile refused to arbitrate the claim, arguing that since the firm was legally a Chilean company it remained subject to Chilean laws. In 1909 the United States and Chile had agreed on the outlines of a compromise, but Knox discarded the deal, demanded that Chile submit to arbitration, and threatened to sever relations when Chile refused.[138] Root and the British ambassador convinced the parties to de-escalate their conflict and the case went to arbitration before King George V of England.[139] J. Reuben Clark, serving as assistant solicitor, filed nearly 1,000 pages worth of briefs (plus an even lengthier collection of appendices), and the US claimants were awarded over USD 900,000—at that point the largest personal claim ever granted.[140] The Chileans unhappily paid up.

Though complying with legal process, the Taft–Knox strategy made few friends in Latin America. 'When dealing with weak Latin-American countries, the United States cares as much about international law as about a radish', complained Manuel

[136] Ewell, *Venezuela and the United States* (n 98) 105–6.

[137] Hendrickson, 'Root's Watchful Waiting' (n 130) 115–29.

[138] Henry F. Munro and Ellery C. Stowell, *International Cases: Arbitrations and Incidents Illustrative of International Law as Practised by Independent States* (Boston, MA: Houghton-Mifflin, 1916), 326–34; Frederick B. Pike, *Chile and the United States, 1880–1962* (Notre Dame, IN: University of Notre Dame Press, 1963), 141–2.

[139] It was not uncommon to choose a head of state to serve as umpire for an arbitral tribunal. European monarchs often served in this position, and US presidents occasionally did so in arbitrations between two Latin American countries. For an overview, see Alexander M. Stuyt, *Survey of International Arbitrations*, 3d edn (Hague: Nijhoff, 1939). For a list of arbitrations between 1794 and 1918, see Harris, 'Between Law and Diplomacy' (n 38) 362–87.

[140] Fox, *Clark* (n 2) 75–7.

Foster Recabarren, Chile's agent in the Alsop claims arbitration.[141] Unlike Root, who had carefully wooed Latin American elites, Knox 'did not conceal the fact that he considered them inferior'.[142] Taft and Knox intervened throughout the Caribbean and Central America, earning criticism abroad and at home. President Woodrow Wilson vowed to end 'dollar diplomacy', and in his first foreign policy speech promised to respect 'the consent of the governed'.[143] But while Wilson's Fourteen Points sparked enthusiasm among colonized peoples in Asia, in Latin America he compiled an unprecedented record of military interventions.[144]

Conclusion: Law and Non-intervention

Although US occupying troops remained in some countries until 1934, US interventionism wound down after the First World War.[145] This development had multiple causes, including concerns over the high cost of military occupation, the rise of anti-imperialist movements in the United States and Latin America, disagreements between US businesses over how to respond to Latin American defaults, and the emergence of dictators who cooperated with Washington.[146] International law, however, remained a potential enabler of intervention.

The experiences of J. Reuben Clark once again illuminate the situation. Clark remained a firm believer in international law after the First World War. He advocated for compulsory international arbitration, for the codification of international law, and for enhanced international adjudication.[147] However, he vigorously opposed the League of Nations which, he believed, was far too harsh on Germany.[148] Moreover, Clark argued, the League was 'founded upon the recognition of force as a lawful and valid means of settling international disputes', and it would draw the United States into foreign squabbles. America was and ought to remain a

[141] Pike, *Chile and the United States* (n 133) 142.

[142] Walter V. Scholes and Marie V. Scholes, *The Foreign Policies of the Taft Administration* (Columbia, MO: University of Missouri Press, 1970), 12.

[143] Woodrow Wilson, 'A Statement on Relations with Latin America' (12 March 1913), *Papers of Woodrow Wilson* vol. 27, 172.

[144] Erez Manela, *The Wilsonian Moment: Self-Determination and the International Origins of Anticolonial Nationalism* (New York, NY: Oxford University Press, 2007); Schoultz, *Beneath the United States* (n 10) 220–52.

[145] See generally Schoultz, *Beneath the United States* (n 10) 253–71. The US intervention in Nicaragua against Sandino is an important exception.

[146] Long and Friedman, 'Soft Balancing' (n 38) 148; Noel Maurer, *The Empire Trap: The Rise and Fall of U.S. Intervention to Protect American Property Overseas, 1893–2013* (Princeton, NJ: Princeton University Press, 2013), 188–9.

[147] Firmage and Blakesley, 'J. Reuben Clark, Jr., Law and International Order' (n 7) 275.

[148] 'The Treaty of Versailles' (1921), in J. Reuben Clark, *Selected Papers on International Affairs*, David H. Yarn, Jr (ed.) (Provo, UT: Brigham Young University Press, 1987), 183–91. On the nature of opposition between Wilson and many international lawyers, see Stephen Wertheim, 'The League That Wasn't: American Designs for a Legalist-Sanctionist League of Nations and the Intellectual Origins of International Organization, 1914–1920', *Diplomatic History* 35, 5 (2011), 797–836.

peace-loving nation, he believed, and thus he supported as a substitute the growing 'Outlawry of War' movement which would eventually culminate in the Kellogg–Briand Pact of 1928.[149] Yet Clark's commitment to eliminating aggressive war did not extend to banning 'interposition'. Well into the interwar period, both Clark and the US government remained committed to the claim that international law protected the right to intervene to protect US citizens and property.

This commitment persisted in the face of increasing Latin American opposition. In the 1920s and early 1930s, Mexican diplomats joined Argentine publicists in advocating for the principle of absolute non-intervention.[150] At the 1928 Pan-American Conference in Havana, the Salvadoran delegate Gustavo Guerrero proposed a resolution 'That no state has the right to intervene in the internal affairs of another'. US secretary of state Charles Evans Hughes withheld his endorsement. While stating that '[w]e do not wish to intervene in the affairs of any American Republic', Hughes defended action in the case of threats to US citizens. Drawing on Clark's writings, Hughes explained: 'it is a principle of international law that in such a case a government is fully justified in taking action—I would call it interposition of a temporary character—for the purpose of protecting the lives and property of its nationals… I could say that that is not intervention. One can read in text books that that is not intervention.' Hughes concluded by affirming that '[i]nternational law cannot be changed by the resolutions of this Conference. International law remains'.[151]

That same year Clark wrote a lengthy memorandum on the Monroe Doctrine. Because it repudiated Theodore Roosevelt's claim that the doctrine justified intervention in Latin America, scholars have sometimes portrayed the memorandum as an important predecessor of the Good Neighbor Policy and an endorsement of non-intervention. Yet, citing his 1912 memo on the right to protect citizens, Clark defended US intervention on different grounds: self-defence, including the protection of US citizens and property.[152] The Roosevelt corollary might not be 'justified by the terms of the Monroe Doctrine', Clark explained, but it was a legitimate 'application of the doctrine of self-preservation'.[153]

Matters came to a head in 1933 at the Seventh Pan-American Conference in Montevideo, Uruguay. Secretary of state Cordell Hull named Clark to the US delegation. The conference would again take up the question of non-intervention and

[149] 'Some Elements of an American Foreign Policy' (4 April 1925), in J. Reuben Clark, *Selected Papers on International Affairs*, David H. Yarn, Jr (ed.) (Provo, UT: Brigham Young University Press, 1987), 366.

[150] Friedman and Long, 'Soft Balancing' (n 38) 145–50.

[151] *Report of the Delegates of the United States to the Sixth International Conference of American States, held at Habana, Cuba, January 16 to February 20, 1928* (Washington, DC: GPO, 1928), 13–15.

[152] Department of State, *Memorandum on the Monroe Doctrine*, Prepared by J. Reuben Clark, Jr, 17 December 1928 (Washington, DC, GPO: 1930), ix–xxv, esp. xviii–xix and xx–xxv; Gene A. Sessions, 'The Clark Memorandum Myth', *The Americas* 34, 1 (1977), 40–58.

[153] Department of State, *Memorandum* (n 147) xxiii–xxiv.

Clark was determined to oppose it.[154] Clark did not favour more US interventions in the region necessarily, but he strongly believed both that foreign nations had an obligation to repay US investors and that established international law gave governments the right to support their citizens.[155] To renounce this right would be to invite abuse. As he told his son, '[w]e know we're not going to intervene, and they know we're not going to intervene, and we know they know—but you just can't bind yourself legally'.[156]

However, facing intense pressure from Latin American delegates, Hull decided to endorse an agreement that '[n]o state has the right to intervene in the internal or external affairs of another'. (The conference also endorsed the Calvo Doctrine, resolving that 'foreigners may not claim rights other or more extensive than those of ... nationals'.[157]) With Clark's encouragement, Hull explained that notwithstanding this new agreement, the United States would continue to follow 'the law of nations as generally recognized and accepted'. As Hull explained to Washington, '[t]his statement preserves to any government the right to protect lives and property where government has broken down and anarchy exists'.[158] If new barriers to intervention had emerged, Hull suggested, these did not come from international law.

Geopolitical developments finally led the United States to abandon its insistence on the right of intervention. With fascist threats on the rise, President Franklin D. Roosevelt sought closer ties with Latin America in the hope of protecting the hemisphere from German influence. In 1936, he personally attended the Pan-American Conference in Buenos Aires, during which the United States signed—without reservations—a unanimous resolution prohibiting intervention 'directly or indirectly, and for whatever reason, in the internal or external affairs of the parties'.[159] This did not mean the end of intervention in practice, especially during the Cold War, when the Central Intelligence Agency plotted the overthrow of Guatemalan President Jacobo Árbenz in 1954 and the failed invasion of Cuba in 1961. The political and ideological concerns that motivated these actions could be difficult to separate from the desire to protect US businesses.[160] Nevertheless it is

[154] Long and Friedman, 'Soft Balancing' (n 38) 150–1; Fox, *Clark* (n 2) 592–4.

[155] An excellent example of Clark's combination of insistence on repayment and reticence for intervention is his leadership of the Foreign Bondholders Protective Council in the 1930s. See Sessions, *Prophesying Upon the Bones* (n 6).

[156] Fox, *Clark* (n 2) 591.

[157] Convention on the Rights and Duties of States (1933), Arts 8–9, http://avalon.law.yale.edu/20th_century/intam03.asp (accessed 18 August 2020).

[158] Fox, *Clark* (n 2) 594; Hull to Acting Secretary of State, 18 December 1933, *Papers Relating to the Foreign Relations of the United States 1933* (Washington, DC: GPO, 1950), vol. 4, 193–4.

[159] Friedman and Long, 'Soft Balancing' (n 38) 151.

[160] On the historiographical disagreement over the role of the United Fruit Co. in the Guatemalan operation, see Stephen M. Streeter, 'Interpreting the 1954 U.S. Intervention in Guatemala: Realist, Revisionist, and Postrevisionist Perspectives', *The History Teacher* 34, 1 (2000), 61–74.

significant that these operations took place covertly: the US did not claim the legal right to intervene.[161]

Other forms of intervention nevertheless persisted. In the 1950s and 1960s, the US threatened to cut off economic aid to nations that expropriated US property without paying compensation.[162] By the late 1960s, the creation of the International Centre for the Settlement of International Disputes and the growing popularity of Bilateral Investment Treaties made it possible for corporations to bring suits against other nations directly in international courts, thus reducing the incentive for governments to intervene directly.[163] However, given imbalances in power between global corporations and smaller states, the governance of international investment remains politically controversial.[164] In any event, as the experience of the early twentieth-century Americas reveals, so long as the powerful shape the law, the law will have difficulty in restraining the powerful.

[161] Grandin, 'The Liberal Traditions in the Americas' (n 38) 89.
[162] Maurer, *Empire Trap* (n 141) chapters 8–10.
[163] Kenneth J. Vandevelde, 'A Brief History of International Investment Agreements', *U.C. Davis Journal of International Law & Policy* 12 (2005–2006), 157–94.
[164] For an overview, see Miles, *Origins of International Investment Law* (n 62).

6

Hammarskjöld at The Hague

Sweden and the Peace Conference of 1907

*Michael Jonas**

It is rare that Swedes feature prominently in the arena of global politics, and when they do it is as international negotiators and peace mediators. Dag Hammarskjöld—the UN secretary general widely considered the 'perfect person for this impossible job'[1]—is usually perceived as the archetype of the Swedish internationalist, succeeded by the other celebrated exemplar of this kind, the country's long-term prime minister and political figurehead of internationalism, Olof Palme. The actual archetype, however, seems to have been another Hammarskjöld: Hjalmar, Dag's father and—in his own time—a figure of equal standing, in particular in the troubled arena of European politics. At the beginning of the twentieth century, Hammarskjöld senior was Sweden's foremost international legal scholar and practitioner, his country's chief delegate to the Second Hague Peace Conference in 1907 and prime minister during the First World War. Unlike his son, Hjalmar Hammarskjöld is largely forgotten today, pushed aside by the 'Age of Social Democracy' that shaped Sweden's twentieth century.[2] Hammarskjöld features at best as a footnote, as the last remnant of an outlived, soon obsolete age, if not as 'Hungerskjöld', the pitiless prime minister whose period in government saw one of the greater crises in supply of foodstuffs in modern Swedish history.[3] The central transitional figure between Hjalmar and Dag Hammarskjöld is undoubtedly Dag's older brother Åke (1893–1937), the first Registrar of the Permanent Court

* I would like to acknowledge gratefully the generous support of Kungliga biblioteket (KB), the National Library of Sweden in Stockholm, whose excellent staff has provided me with access to the voluminous private archive of Hjalmar Hammarskjöld and scans of the relevant files.

[1] Paul Kennedy, *The Parliament of Man, The Past, Present, and Future of the United Nations* (New York, NY: Vintage, 2006), 60.

[2] The phrase is inspired by Francis Sejersted's grand apologia of that development: *The Age of Social Democracy. Norway and Sweden in the Twentieth Century* (Princeton, NJ: Princeton University Press, 2011).

[3] With the publication of Mats Svegfors' balanced but brief biography of Hammarskjöld, critics emphasized the 'Hungerskjöld' dimension of the prime minister's tenure. Cf. Mats Svegfors, *Sveriges statsministrar under 100 år*, vol. 3: *Hjalmar Hammarskjöld* (Stockholm: Bonnier, 2010), and the reviews by, among others, Hans Lindblad, 'Radiochefen skönmålar "Hungerskjöld"', *Gefle Dagblad*, 5 October 2010, as well as Olov Abrahamsson, 'Om regeringen "Hungerskjöld"', *Norrländska Socialdemokraten*, 20 August 2011.

Michael Jonas, *Hammarskjöld at The Hague* In: *Crafting the International Order.* Edited by: Marcus M. Payk and Kim Christian Priemel, Oxford University Press (2021). © The Several Contributors.
DOI: 10.1093/oso/9780198863830.003.0006

of International Justice and—just before his untimely death—a judge at the same court. Åke bridges the pre-1914 and the post-1945 careers and dispositions of his father and his younger brother respectively, thereby somewhat mending the inner-familial polarity that seems to separate the legal from the political internationalist, the allegedly heartless political automaton the older Hammarskjöld was often held to be from the lively, engaging, and charismatic son.[4]

In any case, it is not only the figure of Hjalmar Hammarskjöld who seems to have been forgotten today but also the larger international context in which he moved. At their inauguration in 1899 and 1907, the Hague Conferences were celebrated as global events. Within a few years, however, and despite their undoubted role in the evolution of modern international law, their significance was overshadowed by the Versailles peace process, the League of Nations, and the collapse of the international order in the late 1930s. In the post-1945 historiography of the period, 'The Hague' hardly figured.[5] Interest in the Peace Conferences seems only lately to have reawakened, accompanied by a general reinvigoration of the history of international law and politics as research fields.[6] The rekindled interest in the Hague Conferences and the more recent approaches to international history, however, suffer from a certain lack of balance. Most works on the history of international politics of the early twentieth century tend to ignore the small and middle-sized states and their respective contributions to the development of international law or the establishment and running of international institutions.[7] At times, it seems as if the almost pathological emphasis on the great powers in today's scholarship merely perpetuates the self-conceptions of the major players of the nineteenth century, largely at the expense of acknowledging the role of the smaller players

[4] On Åke Hammarskjöld cf. the brief remarks by Astrid Kjeldgaard-Pedersen, 'Nordic Judges of the Permanent Court of International Justice and the International Court of Justice', in Astrid Kjeldgaar-Pedersen (ed.), *A Nordic Approach to International Law?* (Leiden: Brill Nijhoff, 2016), 334–47, at 337–9; see as well the obituary by Max Huber, 'Åke Hammarskjöld in Memoriam', *Nordisk Tidsskrift for International Ret* 8 (1937), 133–7; Ole Spiermann, *International Legal Argument in the Permanent Court of International Justice: The Rise of the International Judiciary* (Cambridge: Cambridge University Press, 2010).

[5] A substantial exception is Jost Dülffer, *Regeln gegen den Krieg? Die Haager Friedenskonferenzen 1899 und 1907 in der internationalen Politik* (Berlin: Ullstein, 1981).

[6] Isabel V. Hull, *A Scrap of Paper: Breaking and Making International Law in the First World War* (Ithaca, NY: Cornell University Press, 2014); Marcus M. Payk, *Frieden durch Recht? Der Aufstieg des modernen Völkerrechts und der Friedensschluss nach dem Ersten Weltkrieg* (Berlin: de Gruyter, 2018), 27–148. In 2007, two special journal issues were devoted to the centenary of the conference, *Die Friedens-Warte: Journal of International Peace and Organization* 82, 4 (2007), 100 Jahre Zweite Haager Friedenskonferenz von 1907, and *Netherlands International Law Review* 54, 2 (2007); Maartje Abbenhuis, Christopher Barber, and Annalise Higgins (eds), *War, Peace and International Order? The Legacies of the Hague Peace Conferences of 1898 and 1907* (London: Routledge, 2017). Abbenhuis has recently provided a new history of the Hague Conferences, entitled *The Hague Conferences and International Politics, 1898–1915* (London: Bloomsbury, 2019).

[7] This applies to Dülffer's comprehensive study (n 5) only partly, as he, at 184–202, probes rather convincingly, if generally, into the positioning of small states at The Hague. The historiographical neglect can, in any case, be seen in the more recent literature on the subject, such as the otherwise excellent works by Mark Mazower's *Governing the World: The History of an Idea* (London: Allen Lane, 2012), and William Mulligan, *The Great War for Peace* (New Haven, CT: Yale University Press, 2014).

in the international system. From the 'big picture'—as well as from the tableau of the Hague Conferences—the small states seem to have disappeared.[8] This also applies to the Scandinavian states, even in Nordic international and legal historiography. This indifference appears even more puzzling as Denmark and Sweden, in particular, but also Norway and Finland (within their imperial entities, the United Kingdoms of Sweden and Norway respectively the Russian Empire), possessed vibrant traditions in the study of international law and sent high profile representatives to The Hague.[9]

This exploratory chapter intends to help redress that balance. It probes into the segment of small-state representatives at The Hague by focusing on the views and activities of one of the more vocal and influential among the delegates, Hjalmar Hammarskjöld (1862–1953). The analysis of Hammarskjöld's role, presence, and activities at The Hague serves thereby as a prism of international legal diplomacy and politics, and the distinct contribution the northern neutrals made. The chapter thereby explores not only Hammarskjöld's conduct and record at The Hague but also the leeway and limits of small-state agency and the position of small states in international politics more generally.[10] Against such a backdrop, the emphasis shifts from the hegemonic powers of the international system to its more peripheral components. By accompanying Hammarskjöld and his delegation through the proceedings of the 1907 Peace Conference, a range of new questions can be asked and suppositions tested about the function of international law for less powerful states, about the self-conception, international legal tradition, and spectrum of expectations of small-state representatives at the Peace Conferences, about their diplomatic and political ways and means to exercise influence and mould the proceedings, and about the effect and persistence of their experiences at The Hague in their future careers and conduct. The Hague arena of 1899 and 1907 was eminently suited to function as a forum for a new type of legal and political internationalism that permitted and encouraged the participation of 'states at the periphery of power', as Madeleine Herren has conceptualized the role of powers such as Belgium

[8] Paraphrasing a research project by Samuël Kruizinga at the University of Amsterdam: 'Getting the Big Picture on Small States: Towards a New Research Agenda for Small State Studies, 1815–present day'.

[9] *Nordic Journal of International Law* 85 (2016), 'Special issue: A Nordic Approach to International Law?', Astrid Kjeldgaard-Pedersen (ed.), 261–413, especially the contributions by Martti Koskenniemi, Astrid Kjeldgaard-Pedersen, and Gregor Noll; for Norway and—by implication—Sweden, the obvious exception is Nils Ivar Agøy, '"It Will Serve to Increase Our Union Difficulties": Norway, Sweden and the Hague Peace Conference of 1899', *Historisk tidsskrift* (Oslo) 79 (2000), 181–208, whose approach is primarily centred on the bilateral domestic-imperial politics of the United Kingdoms' participation at The Hague.

[10] For review of the pertinent literature and an historical approach to 'smallness' in international politics cf. the introduction of my recent book: Michael Jonas, *Scandinavia and the Great Powers in the First World War* (London: Bloomsbury, 2019), 9–16. Cf. as well Samuël Kruizinga's first probing on that issue, largely focused on the Netherlands: 'A Small State? The Size of the Netherlands as a Focal Point in Foreign Policy Debates, 1900–1940', *Diplomacy and Statecraft* 27 (2016), 420–36; R. van Dijk, S. Kruizinga, V. Kuitenbrouwer, et al. (eds), *Shaping the International Relations of the Netherlands, 1815–2000: A Small Country on the Global Scene* (London: Routledge, 2018).

and Switzerland (and the United States) prior to the First World War—states that appear by and large comparable to the position of Sweden at the time.[11] Taking its cues from Martti Koskenniemi's explorations, the present chapter also makes a contribution to a deliberately 'de-centred' comparative analysis of international law in its historical context.[12]

The Making of a Swedish Jurist: Hammarskjöld and the German Influence on Nordic Legal Culture

In order to situate Hammarskjöld's thought and activities in the broader transformation of international politics and law before, during, and after the First World War, a few remarks on his biographical origins as well as his intellectual and political formation are indispensable. Descending from an old southern Swedish aristocratic family of landowners, Hammarskjöld first studied the humanities, then law at Sweden's oldest and most prestigious university in Uppsala. After graduation in 1884, he received a stipend to further his legal studies in Germany. By then, the German university had entirely replaced other orientations within the Swedish academia.[13] For the law faculties in late nineteenth-century Scandinavia and even more so those of Sweden, the academic treatment of law was to no small extent a reception and variant of German legal discourse, especially of the so-called historical and conceptual schools of German jurisprudence.[14] The dynamic between

[11] Madeleine Herren-Oesch, *Hintertüren zur Macht. Internationalismus und modernisierungsorientierte Außenpolitik in Belgien, der Schweiz und den USA* (Munich: Oldenbourg, 2000), 5–6. With regard to Denmark, Karen Gram-Skjoldager has developed this approach further, cf. Karen Gram-Skjoldager, *Fred og Folkeret. Dansk internationalistisk udenrigspolitik 1899–1939* (Copenhagen: Tusculanum, 2012), especially 17–34.

[12] Martti Koskenniemi, 'Diplomats, Professors, and Then Some: Notes for a History of International Law in 20th Century Finland', *NJIL* 85 (2016), 322–33, at 323, speaks of 'comparative international law' in a historical perspective. In a recent collection of essays, Marja Jalava, Stefan Nygård, and Johan Strang have described this approach as 'decentering European intellectual space', cf. especially the introduction by the editors 'At the Periphery of European Intellectual Space', 1–15, and Nygård's and Strang's stimulating contribution 'Facing Asymmetry: Nordic Intellectuals and Center-Periphery Dynamics', in Marja Jalava, Stefan Nygård, and Johan Strang (eds), *Decentering European Intellectual Space* (Leiden: Brill, 2018), 19–42; the latter is based on an earlier article of the same title in *Journal of the History of Ideas* 77 (2016), 75–97.

[13] This is evident by the annual reports of the British minister to Sweden, Cecil Spring Rice, submitted to the Foreign Office (henceforth FO), Spring Rice to Grey, 23 January 1911, The National Archives, Kew (TNA), FO 371/1225: Political: Sweden Files 147–24927: 1911.

[14] Most forcefully argued by Lars Björne, *Den konstruktiva riktningen—Den nordiska rättsvetenskapens historia, vol. III: 1871–1910* (Stockholm: Institutet för rättshistorisk forskning, 2002). On the debate of a distinct Nordic law tradition for the late nineteenth and early twentieth century cf., besides Björne's four-volume Nordic legal history, Jakko Husa, Kimmo Nuotio, and Heikki Pihlajamäki (eds), *Nordic Law—Between Tradition and Dynamism* (Cambridge: Intersentia, 2007); Pia Letto-Vanamo, Ditlev Tamm, and Bent Ole Gram Mortensen (eds), *Nordic Law in European Context* (Cham: Springer, 2019), especially the introduction 'Nordic Legal Mind', 1–19; Pia Letto-Vanamo, 'Nordische Rechtsgeschichte—eine europäische Variante?', *Zeitschrift für Neuere Rechtsgeschichte* 35 (2013), 112–24.

German university culture and its much smaller Swedish pendant mirrors a rather typical centre-periphery relation and this also applied to the field of international law. In his historical genealogy of international law, Koskenniemi has gone as far as to describe it as a 'German discipline'; for legal scholars in fin-de-siècle Scandinavia, it certainly appeared that way—an aspect only too symptomatic for the academic hegemony of the classic German university model in Sweden and the rest of the North.[15] The stipend Hammarskjöld received had been instituted by the Swedish government in order to educate the country's future juridical elite at what was commonly perceived to be the best institutions for the study of law in the world.[16] On that basis, Hammarskjöld spent a term at Freiburg University, before moving on to Strasbourg for half a term. In Freiburg, he seemed to have been greatly influenced by Germany's foremost legal historian, Karl von Amira.[17] In Strasbourg, he studied under Paul Laband, one of the most innovative legal thinkers in the field of constitutional law at the time. It was Laband who suggested to Hammarskjöld that he should systematize his interest in the laws of carriage by writing his dissertation on the subject. Once back at Uppsala, he duly submitted a well-received thesis entitled 'Om fraktaftalet och dess vigtigaste rättsföljder' [On the law of carriage and its most important legal consequences], whose merits brought him the title of docent in 1886 and five years later—aged twenty-eight—a full professorship with an emphasis on private law at Uppsala University.[18] After a decade at the university, as a judge in different courts, and as regional governor, Hammarskjöld moved into politics and government, becoming Minister of Justice (from 1900), then Minister of Education, and chief negotiator in the negotiations on Norway's separation from the union with Sweden (in 1905). In the same year, he entered the Swedish diplomatic service and became minister to Copenhagen. As one of Sweden's high-profile jurists, Hammarskjöld also served—between 1904 and 1906—as a member of the Permanent Court of Arbitration (PCA), an institution set up by the First Hague Peace Conference.[19]

In Hammarskjöld's legal thinking, the experiences of Freiburg and Strasbourg and especially Laband's influence, nurtured and consolidated an approach that prioritized legal positivism over less formal traditions of political philosophy. Furthermore, his specialist background in private law seems to have left a significant imprint upon his perception of international law as the law governing

[15] Martti Koskenniemi, 'Between Coordination and Constitution: International Law as a German Discipline', *Redescriptions: Political Thought, Conceptual History and Feminist Theory* 15 (2011), 45–70.

[16] Jan-Olof Sundell, *Tysk påverkan på svensk civilrättsdoktrin 1870–1914* (Stockholm: Nordiska bokhandeln i distribution, 1987), 198–200; Marius Kohler, *Die Entwicklung des schwedischen Zivilprozessrechts—Eine rezeptionshistorische Strukturanalyse der Grundlagen des modernen schwedischen Zivilverfahrensrechts* (Tübingen: Mohr, 2002), 149–50.

[17] Sundell, *Tysk påverkan* (n 16) 198–9; Kohler, *Entwicklung des schwedischen Zivilprozessrechts* (n 16) 149–50, especially note 718.

[18] Svegfors, *Hammarskjöld* (n 3) 18.

[19] Ibid., 14–27.

relations among equals. In such an understanding, the intricate relationship between law and power appears artificially separated, and international legal interaction appears as the thing any realist would say it can never be: communication among equals.[20] The legal conception Hammarskjöld cultivated would resurface in his activities both in the context of The Hague and—later on—in his allegedly 'legalist' approach to Swedish neutrality during the First World War.[21] In the diplomatic contexts of both The Hague and the First World War, Hammarskjöld could furthermore claim expertise in areas that certainly exceeded the capacities of many contemporary diplomats and even legal scholars. There was, to begin with, hardly anyone to be found in the legal community who was able to combine expertise in international law, politics, and diplomacy with the specifics of cargo and contraband regulations. Considering the centrality of these issues for the deliberation of The Hague and thereafter, Hammarskjöld justifiably emerged as the natural head of Sweden's 1907 delegation.[22]

The Swedish 1907 Delegation: the Swedish-Norwegian Conflict and the International Background of Swedish Foreign Policy

On being appointed in the spring of 1907, Hammarskjöld—by then in his second year as Swedish ambassador to Copenhagen—immediately began to sound out what the conference had in store for him. Stockholm's instructions were clear and in their scope and ambition were comparatively limited. This supposed timidity related to the domestic and geo-political circumstances that shaped the conditions of Swedish foreign policy in the early twentieth century, which is summarized as follows.

There was, first, an aggravating sense of insecurity and fear of the supposed 'Russian menace', shared—with few exceptions—by the country's political,

[20] I would like to acknowledge gratefully that I owe the substance of this thought to Kim Priemel. On the dichotomy cf., among others, Klaus Schlichte, 'Das formierende Säkulum. Macht und Recht in der internationalen Politik des 19. Jahrhunderts', in Ulrich Lappenküper and Reiner Marcowitz (eds), *Macht und Recht: Völkerrecht in den internationalen Beziehungen* (Paderborn: Schöningh, 2010), 161–80; recent tendencies, pointing to law and (political) power as intricately, indeed constitutively linked categories, are aptly discussed by Payk, *Frieden durch Recht?* (n 6) 5–12, the classic reference being Martti Koskenniemi, 'Between Apology and Utopia. The Politics of International Law [1990]', in Martti Koskenniemi, *The Politics of International Law* (Oxford: Oxford University Press, 2011), 35–62.

[21] Esme Howard, *Theatre of Life*, vol. II: 1905–1936 (London: Hodder & Stoughton, 1936), 239. For the evolution of constitutional law in Germany, which Sweden more or less emulated, and especially on Laband cf. Werner Frotscher and Bodo Pieroth, *Verfassungsgeschichte* (Munich: Beck, 1999), 446–7; Kohler, *Entwicklung des schwedischen Zivilprozessrechts* (n 16) 149–50.

[22] Hammarskjöld's appointment seemed to have been communicated to him slightly earlier than the first mention in his correspondence with the ministry. Cf. Foreign Office [signature illegible] to Hammarskjöld, 30 April 1907, KB, Hjalmar Hammarskjölds arkiv: SE S-HS L175: 1: vol. 164–5: Internationella organ för fred och folkrätt: Fredskonferensen 1907.

military, and cultural elites.[23] This Russophobic disposition certainly fed into the reception of Tsar Nicholas II peace initiative to invite governments to an international conference on peace and disarmament. This scepticism was a general phenomenon and applied particularly to the 1899 conference, but also in 1907, when the foundation by the Tsar of a Peace Palace was largely greeted with 'grim irony', as the US president Theodore Roosevelt observed at the time.[24] For contemporaries, it was difficult to square Russia's imperialist policies and expansionism with the concern for peace echoed in the Tsar's manifestos. Against the background of the 1899 conference, all too often the general efforts for peace and international regulation instigated by the Tsar were dismissed as 'advertising work for the Russian government'.[25] Even if scepticism was made somewhat relative by the experiences and results of The Hague in 1899, the international situation had worsened further since then, with the Finnish question and Russian policies in the Baltic generally looming large in the Swedish government's perception of foreign threat.[26] During the First Peace Conference, for instance, the Swedish foreign ministry called off an attempt by the country's first delegate, Carl N. D. Bildt, and a number of other small-state representatives to secure the inviolability of the small states of Western Europe. Three years later, even a well-intentioned initiative by Russia's foremost international legal scholar, Friedrich Martens, and the Russian foreign ministry in 1902 in favour of a permanent neutralization of the Scandinavian countries 'through a joint great power declaration' was met with 'marked distrust'.[27]

Second, the Swedish government's attitude towards the evolution of international law around 1900 remained cautious and thereby markedly contrasts with the country's engagement in international legal discourse in the course of the twentieth century.[28] In a world dominated by great powers, initiatives for a more encompassing and effective character of international law were not easily separated from their origins and naturally infringed upon accustomed policies and practices of self-reliance. With Russia and France as the driving forces behind The Hague process, scepticism and the adoption of a wait-and-see attitude by the Swedish government appears unsurprising. The misgivings of Stockholm's successive conservative-led governments even exceeded those of their Norwegian counterparts. In fact, as early as 1899, the rift between the governments in Kristiania and Stockholm had become obvious, with the Norwegian liberal

[23] Gunnar Åselius, *The 'Russian Menace' to Sweden: The Belief System of a Small Power Security Elite in the Age of Imperialism* (Stockholm: Almqvist&Wiksell, 1994).

[24] Dülffer, *Regeln* (n 5) 280.

[25] Abbenhuis, *Hague Conferences* (n 6) 100, cites the Swedish foreign minister, Ludvig Douglas, in an exchange with the Dutch ambassador to Stockholm.

[26] Åselius, *'Russian Menace'* (n 23) 275–323.

[27] Ibid., 170–1.

[28] Ibid., 168–9, referring to Per Ahlin's PhD: *Folkrätten i svensk säkerhetspolitik*, Stockholm: Juristförlaget, 1993, 45–57, whose emphasis is less historical and largely limited to the postwar period.

government repeatedly arguing for binding arbitration rules and a proper codification of the United Kingdoms' neutrality policy.[29] In principle, both Bildt in 1899 and Hammarskjöld in 1907 could undoubtedly relate to this tradition of international legal thought, thereby carefully dissociating themselves from their governments' more ideological position. The liberal participatory Norwegian course of policy, however, was viewed by Bildt and Hammarskjöld alike as naïve and annoyingly futile.[30]

That assessment and indeed the sentiment that went with it, originated, third, with the changed circumstances in the North. Norway's break-away from the union in 1905 had left Sweden in a rather unstable domestic and regional position, with hardly any capacity for a more ambitious foreign policy or strategic initiatives. Geostrategically, the former hegemon of northern Europe had been reduced to a small state comparable to Denmark and Norway. With the dissolution of the union, even the post-imperial notion of Sweden as a regional power coveted by Stockholm's security-political elites was a thing of the past. As chief Swedish negotiator in the Karlstad negotiations, which eventually settled the conflict, Hammarskjöld had himself been closely involved in averting war between the agitated member states of a collapsing union.[31] The Hague formed one of the first instances since the establishment of the Union in 1814 where Swedish and Norwegian diplomats and negotiators represented completely separate entities. In particular, the Swedish diplomats' view of their Norwegian counterparts remained fundamentally clouded by the experience of 1905, not least Hammarskjöld's own. In an exchange with his predecessor Bildt after the conclusion of the 1907 conference, the latter gleefully recalls the lack of competence among the Norwegian delegation, as reported to him by observers, and contrasts this with Hammarskjöld's own allegedly impeccable performance at The Hague.[32] Hammarskjöld, Bildt

[29] Agøy, 'Norway, Sweden and the Hague Peace Conference' (n 9) 191–8, discusses the twin questions of representation and instruction excellently.

[30] Agøy, 'Norway, Sweden and the Hague Peace Conference' (n 9) 198–202, for the 1899 conference.

[31] On the overall process cf. the source edition by Arne Wåhlstrand, *Karlstadkonferensen 1905. Protokoll och aktstykken* (Stockholm: Almqvist & Wiksell, 1953), including the Norwegian edition by Andreas Urbye, ibid., 87–175; on Hammarskjöld's involvement as Swedish delegate see—besides frequent references in the above-mentioned edition—Hammarskjöld's private papers: KB, Hammarskjölds arkiv: SE S-HS L175:1: vol. 161: Offentliga uppdrag och åtaganden: Unionskommittén (1896–1905), Unionsupplösningen 1905 (1892–1906). The centenary brought about a revival of research on the subject, inter alia Bo Stråth, *Union och demokrati. De Förenaderikena Sverige-Norge 1814–1905* (Nora: Nya Doxa, 2005); Thorbjørn Nilsson and Øystein Sørensen (eds), *1905—unionsupplösningens år. Nya perspektiv på ett svensk-norskt drama* (Stockholm: Carlssons, 2005); on the legal implications see Michael Stolleis, 'The Dissolution of the Union between Norway and Sweden within the Context of International Law—Hundred Years Later', in Ola Mestad and Dag Michalsen (eds), *Rett, nasjon, union. Den svensk-norske unionens rettslige historie 1814–1905* (Oslo: Universitetsforlaget, 2005), 35–48, Kjell Å. Modéer, 'Svenska jurister och unionsupplösningen', in ibid., 197–210, and Cecilie Schjatvet, 'Internasjonal voldgift og unionsoppløsningen—arven til den norske foregangspolitikken', in ibid., 49–78.

[32] Bildt to Hammarskjöld, 2 December 1907, KB, Hammarskjölds arkiv: SE S-HS L175: 1: vol. 164; cf. and Hammarskjöld's reply, Hammarskjöld to Bildt, 15 December 1907 (transcript), SE S-HS L175: 1: vol. 165.

concluded, was to be congratulated on not having any 'Norwegian co-helpers' [*norska medhjälpare*] around this time, as he had found them mostly troublesome in 1899.[33] The ad hominem dimension of Bildt's remark should not obscure the fundamental differences in opinion and conceptual approach that divided—crudely speaking—liberal, internationally engaged Norwegians and largely conservative, wary, and insecure Swedes from one another. Besides the international political arena, both Hammarskjöld and Bildt shared the profound, close to traumatic distrust of Norway's political elites so endemic to Stockholm's political circles, especially on the right of Swedish politics.[34]

The recent loss of tangible resources (and less tangible influence) and a pervasive sense of insecurity following Norwegian independence would interact with an older strand in Swedish foreign policy at the Peace Conference, the country's well-established neutrality policy. Two political camps increasingly fought over the actual course and character of Swedish neutrality. There was the traditionalist-conservative wing of the country's political landscape, represented by the right-wing cabinet led by prime minister Arvid Lindman with Eric Trolle as foreign minister, for whom the question of a sustainable neutrality was intrinsically connected to Sweden's capacity for military self-defence. In opposition to government and the established elites, the international peace movement attempted to seize upon The Hague as the central harbinger of a peaceful global future. In 1907, the mobilization for peace was greater and more vehement than ever before. This also applied to Sweden, where the centrally organized peace associations lobbied the government on the main programmatic issues that would shape the Second Hague Conference.[35] The peace movement's demands were underscored by a significant number of peace marches and gatherings in the weeks and months leading up to the conference, mobilizing around 8,000 people in a total of 34 towns throughout Sweden.[36] The instructions of the Swedish government addressed these multiple policy dimensions and anxieties in a nutshell. As delegate designate,

[33] Bildt to Hammarskjöld, 22 May 1907, KB, Hammarskjölds arkiv: SE S-HS L175: 1: vol. 164.

[34] Cf. Dag Hoelseth, '"En svensk-norsk union av det rätta slaget". Forholdet mellom kongehusene i Norge og Sverige 1905–1929', in Øystein Sørensen and Torbjörn Nilsson (eds), *Norsk-svenske relasjoner i 200 år* (Oslo: Aschehoug, 2005), 41–56; Ruth Hemstad, *Fra Indian Summer til nordisk vinter. Skandinavisk samarbeid, skandinavisme og unionsoppløsningen* (Oslo: Akademisk publisering, 2008); Jonas, *Scandinavia and the Great Powers* (n 10) 35–54.

[35] Edvard Wawrinsky, Emilie Broomé, and Sydney Alrutz (Sveriges fredsföreningars samarbedskommittee) to the Swedish king, 15 April 1907, KB, Hammarskjölds arkiv: SE S-HS L175: 1: vol. 164–165: Internationella organ för fred och folkrätt: Fredskonferensen 1907. For the context see Abbenhuis, *Hague Conferences* (n 6) 155–6, who refers to the resolution of 15,000 Swedish citizens addressed to the conference. On the context cf. the transnational history of the Nordic peace movements by Per Jostein Ringsby, *40 års kamp for fred: tre fredsforeninger i Skandinavia* 1882–1922 (Phil. diss. University of Oslo, 2010).

[36] Ibid., Edvard Wawrinsky, Emilie Broomé, and Sydney Alrutz (Sveriges fredsföreningars samarbedskommittee) to the Swedish king, 12 May 1907, with Sundsvall (800 participants), Göteborg, Helsingborg (each 500), and Malmö (400) among the major demonstrations. The associations claimed to have about 5,000 organized members in ca. 25 local committees.

Hammarskjöld must have been familiar with his instructions as he seems to have co-written them himself.[37] On the sensitive issue of armaments, which eventually did not feature at the Second Hague Conference, Stockholm's ambivalent position mirrored that of the great powers. Whilst Hammarskjöld was instructed to 'stress strongly the Swedish government's and the Swedish people's concordant sympathy with everything that might further the cause of peace', he was also supposed to make sure that Swedish defence capabilities would not be internationally restricted by the conference and its results.[38] Stockholm's line of reasoning accentuated the almost other-worldly character of Sweden's alleged position in the international system. As a neutral small state whose military's only purpose was the defence of the country's independence and territorial integrity, Swedish armaments, no matter whether increasing or decreasing, bore no relation whatsoever to international politics and were therefore irrelevant to the defence policies of other powers and—by implication—to any regime of restriction.[39] The position assumed by the Stockholm government was only too symptomatic for the behaviour of the small and medium-sized powers of Europe in the context of disarmament or arms control.[40] Sweden's line of argument thereby appeared characteristic for a much broader political disposition among the smaller powers.

As for the scheduled negotiations on arbitration at The Hague, Hammarskjöld was instructed to assume a similar, if somewhat more affirmative position.[41] Based on the results of the 1899 conference on international arbitration, including the establishment of the PCA, which Sweden had ratified in 1905, the country's delegation was expected to work for a 'limited, but in any case unconditionally and unambiguously stipulated, obligatory arbitration' and furthermore promote the 'expansion and unification of [the existing] arbitration conventions'. This correlated with Hammarskjöld's own assessment of the requirements and limitations

[37] His private papers not only feature the actual instructions of 4 June 1907 sent to him to Copenhagen by the Swedish foreign ministry [utrikesdepartementet, hereafter UD], but also an undated version in his own hand with a number of corrections, additions, and revisions, which appears to have provided the basis for the official line forwarded to him. Cf. Instruktionen för Sveriges ombud vid den andra fredkonferensen i Haag 1907, 4 June 1907, KB, Hammarskjölds arkiv: SE S-HS L175: 1: vol. 164–165: Internationella organ för fred och folkrätt: Fredskonferensen 1907, 1–2.

[38] The essence of the Tsar's programme arrived with Hammarskjöld in late April 1907, accompanied by comments of the UD. Cf. Foreign Office [signature illegible] to Hammarskjöld, 30 April 1907, KB, Hammarskjölds arkiv: SE S-HS L175: 1: vol. 164–165: Internationella organ för fred och folkrätt: Fredskonferensen 1907; Carnegie Endowment for International Peace and James Brown Scott (eds) *The Proceedings of the Hague Peace Conferences, vol. I: The Conference of 1907: Plenary Meetings of the Conference* (New York, NY: Oxford University Press, 1920) [transl. of the official French text, 1907], here: Program proposed by the Imperial Government of Russia, 3 April 1906, 1; Dülffer, *Regeln* (n 5) 283–4, on the genesis of the invitation; Abbenhuis, *Hague Conferences* (n 6) 145–68.

[39] Instruktionen för Sveriges ombud vid den andra fredkonferensen i Haag 1907, 4 June 1907, KB, Hammarskjölds arkiv: SE S-HS L175:1: vol. 164–165: Internationella organ för fred och folkrätt: Fredskonferensen 1907:2.

[40] Dülffer, *Regeln* (n 5) 194–5, with a number of examples, among them the Danish king Christian X, who stressed his country's status as the 'most disarmed on earth'.

[41] *Proceedings 1907* (n 38), Index Volume: Program proposed by the Imperial Government of Russia, March/April 1906, 2.

of future arbitration policies and institutions, as developed in his earlier work on international arbitration, especially his 1903 study 'Internationella skiljedoms-aftal'.[42] His room for manoeuvre was therefore greater than in the armaments' arena, especially as arbitration was less likely to touch directly on questions of immediate national security interests than on issues of military capacity, production, and spending. The final substantial point of the instructions was central for the government in Stockholm. It dealt with the neutral powers' rights and duties in a naval conflict. This aspect of the planned negotiations was closely related to the incessant debates on neutrality in a land war, but appeared in many ways even more complicated. Reinforcing the country's earlier commitments in this field, the government instructed Hammarskjöld to work in the interest of greater 'codification and qualification of the duties and burdens that would affect seafaring neutral nations and their vessels and subjects'. The geopolitical issue of the exposed Sound waterway necessitated more binding rules, guaranteeing the maintenance of the Sound as an 'open international waterway', especially in times of war. Finally, the government permitted, indeed suggested to its chief delegate that he should promote the future institutionalization of periodical intergovernmental peace conferences as vehicles for the existing 'international peace efforts'.[43] Even if these efforts seemed hijacked by the Russian government for the purpose of propaganda, Stockholm could not deny the necessity and function of a binding framework of international law that could usher in measures to enable the taming of war and the promotion of peace. Despite their inherent vagueness and ambivalence, and at times even their incongruity on the central issues of arbitration, neutrality, and the institutionalization of political-legal structures, Stockholm's catalogue of instructions formed a basis on which Hammarskjöld could work creatively and with a certain degree of cautious initiative. The same situation had been faced eight years earlier by Bildt, who had emerged as one of the most vocal actors of the first Peace Conference. For Maartje Abbenhuis, Bildt's 'impassioned plea' for a binding commitment to disarmament—distilled in the warning 'It is not enough!'—counts among the more iconic Hague interventions.[44] Hammarskjöld's predecessor appeared thereby to be both a colleague and advisor as well as a model of how to reconcile public expectation, the

[42] Hjalmar Hammarskjöld, 'Internationella skiljedoms-aftal', *Nordisk tidskrift* (1903), 561–77; separately published, Stockholm, 1904 (19 pp). The published work had been commissioned in 1902 by UD in order to clarify the Swedish position on The Hague's 1899 stipulations on arbitration. Åselius, '*Russian Menace*' (n 23) 174, interprets Hammarskjöld's realistic approach as primarily opportunistic, self-centred, and mostly in terms of international law as gesture politics, cf. as well 168–74, 324–7.

[43] Instruktionen för Sveriges ombud vid den andra fredkonferensen i Haag 1907, 4 June 1907, KB, Hammarskjölds arkiv: SE S-HS L175:1: vol. 164–165: Internationella organ för fred och folkrätt: Fredskonferensen 1907:3.

[44] Abbenhuis, *Hague Conferences* (n 6) 83–4; Agøy, 'Norway, Sweden and the Hague Peace Conference' (n 9) 198–202, largely limits his analysis to the 'Norwegian' element in the actual conference proceedings.

diplomatic dynamic of an enormous international conference, and the instructions of one's own government successfully.[45]

Hammarskjöld's capacity for initiative was boosted by the delegation that the Stockholm government had placed at his side. His right hand in the actual negotiations, the second delegate plenipotentiary Johannes Hellner, was a liberal jurist and aspiring politician of the left-of-centre forces in Swedish politics. Among the technical delegates, the senior military officer David Hedengren (1858–1946) also would have appeared to Hammarskjöld to be a promising choice. Offspring of an old military noble family, he commanded an artillery regiment, and had gathered substantial experience abroad as the Swedish military attaché to both Paris (1895–1897) and St Petersburg (1903–1905). Apart from his seniority and international profile, Hedengren seems to have been chosen because he was one of the country's foremost experts on artillery questions and military administration.[46] Like Hedengren, the technical delegate for maritime affairs, Commander Gustaf af Klint (1858–1927), had been born into one of the more prominent military-aristocratic families of the Swedish realm, in his case a distinguished family of navy officers and cartographers. Af Klint headed the communication department of the Swedish Fleet Naval Staff and rose to the rank of rear admiral.[47] Both Hedengren and af Klint were typical of the Swedish military elite at the turn of the century, dutiful military professionals with a certain international outlook, whilst also conservative and monarchist by ideological disposition.[48] Hammarskjöld's most essential addition on the staff was certainly the delegation's secretary, Carl Gotthard Bonde (1877–1937), a wealthy and well-connected, suave, and learned aristocrat who had chosen the diplomatic service as a temporary career before returning to his extensive landed estate south of Stockholm.[49] All in all, Hammarskjöld's delegation appears to have been well-equipped for the task, combining expertise in the essential fields of international law and legal discourse, politics, and diplomacy as well as military and strategic affairs. It was not only a delegation with which he could effectively work but also one that left his leadership as first delegate unquestioned.

[45] This appreciation is reflected in Hammarskjöld's initial letters to Bildt, Hammarskjöld to Bildt, 18 May and 8 July 1907 (both transcripts), KB, Hammarskjölds arkiv: SE S-HS L175:1: vol. 165.

[46] On Hedengren's background and career cf. Gunnar Carlquist (ed), *Svensk uppslagsbok*, vol. 12 (Malmö: Baltiska, 1932), 870; 'Hedengren, släkt', in *Svenskt biografiskt lexikon*, https://sok.riksarkivet.se/sbl/artikel/12710 (accessed 18 August 2020).

[47] For af Klint cf. Erik Wikland, 'Gustaf Klint, af', in *Svenskt biografiskt lexikon*, https://sok.riksarkivet.se/sbl/artikel/11633 (accessed 18 August 2020).

[48] Cf. Axel Odelberg, *Med kungen som verktyg: försvarsstriden, Borggårdstalet och Sven Hedin* (Stockholm: Norstedts, 2014), 40, for Hedengren's ideological position; on his period in St. Petersburg see Åselius, '*Russian Menace*' (n 23) 118–19.

[49] Bildt to Hammarskjöld, 22 May 1907, KB, Hammarskjölds arkiv: SE S-HS L175: 1: vol. 164. Bonde is today remembered as royal hunting master [*hovjägmästare*] and as an avid collector of coins and rare books; cf. Morten Axboe, 'En guldbrakteat från myntsamlingen på Ericsbergs slott', *Fornvännen: Journal of Swedish Antiquarian Research* 105, 2 (2010), 96–103, at 97, and the vivid memoirs of Amelie Posse, *Mellan Slagen* (Stockholm: Natur och kultur, 1944).

At The Hague: Arbitration, International Jurisdiction, and the 'Rights and Duties of Neutral Powers'

Hammarskjöld's prestige in the immediate context of the Hague proceedings was not only relevant in his interaction with the assembled international legal experts, but also with the informed public. Whilst he was celebrated by colleagues as 'the eminent jurist whom Sweden has sent us',[50] *Die Woche*, a German illustrated magazine, featured him as one of only two small-state representatives featured alongside the main delegates of the conference. The other was the head of the Norwegian delegation, Francis Hagerup, the country's foremost international legal expert and a long-standing member of the Institut de Droit International as well as a colleague of Hammarskjöld's at the PCA. A conservative party politician and twice-elected prime minister in Kristiania, Hagerup had himself been a sceptic of the Tsar's initiative in 1899 and anticipated the conference's failure.[51] Eight years later, he had emerged as one of the more forceful proponents of international arbitration and promoted the institutionalization of arbitration rules and practices at The Hague.[52] With Hammarskjöld, Hagerup shared a strong inclination for a rather positivist legalism, a similar conservative orientation in politics, and overlapping objectives, especially in the field of arbitration. What kept them apart, however, was the chasm that the dissolution of their countries' union in 1905 had left.

Whilst Hagerup's company is hence less likely to have pleased Hammarskjöld, the illustration, as distributed by *Die Woche*, otherwise places him in an extremely distinguished context, surrounded by the main figure of the international arbitration movement, France's chief delegate Léon Bourgeois, and the German foreign office's renowned, if 'personally rather unsympathetic' legal expert, Johannes Kriege.[53] In his informative, if at times highly opinionated letter from Rome of 22 May 1907, Bildt had warmly recommended the head of France's eminent delegation

[50] Italy's chief delegate Joseph Tornielli as president of the Third Commission, Sixth Meeting, 17 September 1907, in *Proceedings 1907* (n 38) vol. III: Meetings of the Second, Third and Fourth Commissions, 432, among a host of similar, if less explicit references.

[51] Agøy, 'Norway, Sweden and the Hague Peace Conference' (n 9) 192–3; on Hagerup's international engagement cf. C. L. Lange, 'Francis Hagerup som internasjonalist', *Tidsskrift for Retsvidenskab* 35 (1922), 59–97; for a re-appreciation of Hagerup's influence on both conservatism as a political force in Norway and international legal discourse cf. Sverre Blandhol and Dag Michalsen (eds), *Rettsforsker, politiker, internasjonalist: perspektiver på Francis Hagerup* (Oslo: Unipax, 2007), and especially Cecilie Schjatvet, 'Folkerett og småstatspolitikk—Francis Hagerup og opprettelsen av faste folkerettsdomstoler' in ibid., 161–92; furthermore Schjatvet, 'Internasjonal voldgift og unionsoppløsningen' (n 31) 49–78, and Lars Roar Langslet, 'Francis Hagerup', in Cecilie Schjatvet (ed.), *Konservatisme på norsk: Elleve historiske portretter* (Oslo: Pax, 2011), 167–87. The basic study on Norway's union and international policies as an international legal enterprise is Cecilie Schjatvet's PhD, *Fredssak og selvbestemmelse 1890–1909. Folkeretten under unionskonflikten* (Oslo: Akademisk publisering, 2012).

[52] Marta Stachurska-Kounta, 'Norway's legalistic approach to peace in the aftermath of the First World War', in Abbenhuis, Barber, and Higgins (eds), *War, Peace and International Order?* (n 6) 171–88, at 173–4, 182, who—based on Schjatvet's earlier work—distinguishes between Lange's internationalist political leanings and conceptions on the one hand and Hagerup's conservative legalism on the other.

[53] *Die Woche. Moderne illustrierte Zeitschrift* 22 (1907), 946. Cf. Dülffer, *Regeln* (n 5) 312.

as 'one of the most valuable and comfortable' colleagues one could have, 'an ideal leader' of any given commission or committee, capable of offering ways out of potential deadlock that reconciled the antagonising parties and allowed for the necessary compromise—in short: a natural ally of Hammarskjöld especially in the field in which he would invest most of his efforts, international arbitration. Both Swedes regarded the French delegation as among the most capable in the Hague context, followed by the Russian delegation around Hammarskjöld's and Bildt's colleague at the PCA, Friedrich Martens. Bildt was exceptionally unprejudiced in his assessment of the Russian presence at The Hague and even warned Hammarskjöld not to underestimate the Tsar's delegation, all the more as the Germans were doing their utmost to discredit the Russians in The Hague and beyond.[54]

As the organizing committee—as well as Hammarskjöld—swiftly noticed, nothing of the 1907 proceedings compared to the relative quiet of the first conference eight years earlier. In mid-June, the world had converged on The Hague and created a first truly international political arena.[55] This also translated into the delegates' everyday lives, with Hammarskjöld the recipient of numerous petitions, proposals, and letters, mostly developing the ideas debated at the conference.[56] Some of the more ambitious among them intended to enlist the Swedish delegate for peace and arbitration causes and were obviously aimed at the entirety of the 256 delegates, originating from 44 states throughout the whole world.[57] With the international public's attention focused on the conference, Hammarskjöld had to deal with the press too, which included the acclaimed Swedish writer and journalist Ida Bäckman. Bäckman, who had just returned from one of her trips through the periphery of imperial Russia and now reported officially for *Stockholms Dagblad* from The Hague, relied heavily on Hammarskjöld as a source of information.[58]

Considering the scope and variety of the proceedings and the need to be present at commission and subcommission level, the Swedish delegation pragmatically divided and prioritized its attention. Hammarskjöld and Hellner, as first and second delegate, opted for membership in the First Commission which dealt with the overhaul of the arbitration mechanism established in 1899. This decision is indicative for the weight attached to the issue, not only from the Swedish viewpoint but also generally. If significant movement was expected, the majority of contemporary observers thought, it would be on the question of arbitration and its

[54] Bildt to Hammarskjöld, 22 May 1907, KB, Hjalmar Hammarskjölds arkiv: SE S-HS L175:1: vol. 164, 3–4.

[55] Abbenhuis, *Hague Conferences* (n 6) 145–68, especially 157–8; Arthur Eyffinger, *The 1907 Hague Peace Conference. 'The Conscience of the Civilized World'* (Den Haag: Judicap, 2007), 82–95.

[56] KB, Hjalmar Hammarskjölds arkiv: SE S-HS L175:1: vol. 164.3 The letters reflect this in painstaking detail.

[57] Eyffinger, *1907 Hague Peace Conference* (n 55) 83–5; Abbenhuis, *Hague Conferences* (n 6) 155.

[58] KB, Hjalmar Hammarskjölds arkiv: SE S-HS L175:1: vol. 164: Bäckman to Hammarskjöld, 4 respectively 5 July 1907. For Bäckman's courageous early travel writing cf. *Farliga färder och roliga journalistiska ströftåg* (Stockholm: Norstedt, 1906–1910), especially vol. 3: Ryssland (1906); Per Erik Tell, 'Orädd reporter ständigt på väg', *Populär historia* 7 (2013), 44–7.

institutional structures and modalities. There were three issues related to arbitration that the conference's First Commission had to engage with: first, the establishment of an International Prize Court (IPC); second, the creation of a Permanent Court of Arbitral Justice (PCAJ), which was supposed to complement the work of the PCA; and, third and most sensitively, the so-called *obligatorium*, the question of obligatory arbitration in the international arena, as opposed to the earlier character of arbitral justice, which required parties to submit voluntarily to arbitration. Against this emphasis on arbitration, the other two commissions and their sub-commissions seemingly faded in importance. For Hammarskjöld and indeed most small-state representatives, however, the Second and Third Commissions possessed their own significance as they dealt with issues such as the neutrality stipulations on land and especially on sea. Consequently, he opted to become vice president of the Third Commission and featured rather prominently in most discussions on the relation between maritime warfare and neutrality, which were mostly contained in the Fourth Commission's work. Among them were the sensitive issues of regulating the presence of belligerent ships in neutral ports and the relationship of maritime warfare and merchant shipping, touching upon legal aspects of private property, contraband, and neutral prize as well as the constantly difficult question of naval blockade. Even if less prominent than the more general questions of arbitration and armaments, it is at this level that the legal umbrella and the different practices of neutrality could be defined. For this reason then, Hammarskjöld and the Swedish delegation's had a strong interest in influencing these aspects of the 1907 proceedings.[59]

In the First Commission's work, Hammarskjöld's participation appears to have been among the most pronounced and influential. One of the main enterprises in this field was undoubtedly the establishment of the IPC, as drawn up by the great powers and rather unceremoniously fed to the smaller and medium-sized states at The Hague. Throughout, this remained a sensitive, often controversialissue. The difficulty in which the smaller nations found themselves on international prize jurisdiction was aptly captured by Hagerup in the commission's second session. The Norwegian elegantly outlined his government's position, which in principle affirmed the establishment of the court but also elaborated existing misgivings. These reservations were echoed by the majority of smaller powers and shared by Hammarskjöld and the Swedish delegation. The problem apparently did not rest with the institution itself, and in Hagerup's and Hammarskjöld's case the opposite was true. Instead, what unsettled a coalition of smaller and medium-sized participants was the actual composition of the court upon which the great powers had agreed. According to the proposal in question, the appointment of judges—and hence the representation of states in the projected IPC—was to follow a system

[59] *Proceedings 1907* (n 38) vol. I: Plenary Meetings of the Conference, 17–34 (for the distribution and participation of the Swedish delegation).

based on four overall categories of states, drawn up largely on the basis of the size of an individual states' merchant marines. The logic behind this pattern of allocation was intended to favour those nations who were usually worst affected by confiscation and the capture of prize in war. For the great powers, however, this criterion was not to be applied, which left Hagerup and the Norwegian government, at least, bemused. In the most matter-of-fact manner he could muster, Hagerup pointed to the fact that, if it came down to the size of one's merchant marine as the sole criterion, Norway would easily outrank half of the great powers at the table. Because of the enormous scale of its merchant force on the seas, the country would undoubtedly suffer disproportionally more than others in the event of war—a prediction all too bloodily reinforced by the exorbitant death toll among Norwegian merchant sailors in the First World War.[60] Instead of vetoing the proposition, however, as the South American countries did, Hagerup—and the Norwegian government—were willing to put principle before state interest. In essence, Hagerup argued that accepting an imperfect system was better than having none—a position echoed by many, but eventually defeated.[61]

Hammarskjöld's point mirrored the understandably broader and more forceful statement of his colleague Hagerup. With an astute sense of diplomacy, he emphasized the change in Berlin's position, which had resisted any tendencies to more binding institutional commitments in 1899 and had now brought forward—along with British support—a concrete proposal for an international prize court.[62] In Hammarskjöld's view, Berlin's changed attitude allowed for a unanimous agreement at least on the principle and hence the institutionalisation of the projected court. The practical defects of the suggested great power-biased system would have to take a back seat for the moment, despite the undoubted 'importance of the objections', which Hammarskjöld, Hagerup, and the overwhelming majority of smaller state delegates and their governments shared.[63] Indeed, Hammarskjöld even tried to accommodate some of the objections, especially in terms of the sensitive issue of representation at the projected IPC. His compromise envisaged a rotation system

[60] Rolf Hobson, Tom Kristiansen, and Nils Arne Sørensen, 'Introduction. Scandinavia in the First World War', in Claes Ahlund (ed.), *Scandinavia in the First World War. Studies in the War Experiences of the Northern Neutrals* (Lund: Nordic Academic Press, 2012), 9–56, at 38–9; Olav Riste, *The Neutral Ally: Norway's Relations with Belligerent Powers in the First World War* (Oslo: Universitetsforlaget, 1965), 170–90; Patrick Salmon, *Scandinavia and the Great Powers 1890-1940* (London: Cambridge University Press, 1997), 129–45; Bjarne S. Bendtsen, 'Neutral Merchant Seamen at War. The Experiences of Scandinavian Seamen during the First World War', in Ahlund, *Scandinavia in the First World War*, 327–54; Johan Schreiner, *Norsk skipsfart under krig og høykonjunktur 1914–1920* (Oslo: Cappelen, 1963), 268–99; Jonas, *Scandinavia and the Great Powers* (n 10) 26–8.

[61] Protocol Second Meeting (First Commission), 10 September 1907, in *Proceedings 1907* (n 38) vol. II: First Commission, 15–17. Cf. as well Dülffer, *Regeln* (n 5) 304.

[62] Abbenhuis, *Hague Conferences* (n 6) 161; Dülffer, *Regeln* (n 5) 304–7.

[63] Protocol Second Meeting (First Commission), 10 September 1907, in *Proceedings 1907* (n 38) vol. II: First Commission, 17; Hammarskjöld, originally more forcefully, to the Second Subcommission, First Commission, Third Meeting, 11 July 1907, in *Proceedings 1907* (n 38) vol. II: Meetings of the First Commission, 799.

according to which the powers affected by war and prize taking would be automatically admitted in place of uninvolved powers. The relevant great powers—through Bourgeois, Fry, Choate, and Kriege—agreed and committed to a revision following his suggestion.[64] Against the backdrop of the smaller European states' willingness to compromise and hence work on principle rather than national interest, it appears almost tragic that the consensus on the necessity of the court did eventually not translate into anything practical. The Latin American states, primarily Brazil, rightly saw their sovereignty in international law infringed and continued to oppose the appointments system as developed by the great powers.[65] On closer inspection, however, the dichotomy between European and non-European small states appears artificial. Just as the great powers profoundly disagreed and at times coalesced in unexpected constellations, the smaller and medium-sized states floated rather freely throughout the proceedings, some of them—such as Norway—with a more pronounced, even 'progressive' international legal agenda, others with little more than the perpetuation of national interest in mind. This could even, as illustrated in the Swedish government's case, differ from issue to issue.

In addition to the difficulties in creating the institution of the IPC, there was only an ineffectually codified body of international maritime law available, on which the projected court could base its juridical deliberations. In order to avoid burdening the proceedings even further and to break the deadlock, British foreign minister Grey instructed his chief delegate at The Hague, Edward Fry, in mid-September to announce a conference on maritime affairs to take place in the immediate future. This permitted all present powers to agree formally to binding standards, if those could be revised, made relative, and neutered at a future conference—or simply not ratified, as happened with the London Declaration concerning the Laws of Naval War of 26 February 1909.[66] The First Commission's central achievement, Convention XII on the creation of an international prize court, nonetheless amounted to an impressive body of newly regulated international law. It formally established the IPC and defined the court's international legal status, its make-up, and procedural framework.[67] The eventual inconclusiveness of the whole process, including the London Naval Conference of 1908/9 and the conference's ineffectual declaration, could not be anticipated. The IPC was, after all, 'the world's first appellate court to which neutral merchants unhappy with the prize-taking decisions of a belligerent power could take their complaints'.[68] It was expected to form the

[64] Hammarskjöld to the Second Subcommission, First Commission, Examination Committee, First Meeting, 12 August 1907, in *Proceedings 1907* (n 38) vol. II: Meetings of the First Commission, 817 (with the responses).

[65] Primarily the Brazilian chief delegate Ruy Barbosa. In addition to the protocol, cf. Dülffer, *Regeln* (n 5) 306.

[66] Dülffer, *Regeln* (n 5) 307. On the context cf. Nicholas A. Lambert, *Planning Armageddon: British Economic Warfare and the First World War* (Cambridge, MA: Harvard University Press, 2012), 85–103.

[67] Convention (XII) Relative to the Creation of an International Prize Court, 18 Oct 1907, in *Proceedings 1907* (n 38) vol. I: Plenary Meetings of the Conference, 668–79.

[68] Abbenhuis, *Hague Conferences* (n 6) 161.

nucleus of an institutionalized juridical landscape and the beginning of the legal transformation of the international system.

While the outcome on prize jurisdiction appeared to many contemporary observers an unqualified success, the more ambitious matter of arbitration remained sensitive throughout the proceedings and eventually failed to be resolved. The revision, expansion, and implementation of the premises Hague I had set in motion, the Convention (I) for the Pacific Settlement of International Disputes, entailed addressing arbitration on two levels: first, the establishment of a PCAJ, which was not intended to replace but rather to complement the PCA. Whereas the PCA was political at heart, the projected PCAJ was intended to regulate arbitration. Second, once the institutions existed, the 1907 proceedings attempted to determine the extent to which and the areas in which international arbitration was supposed to be obligatory. For the potent arbitration movement and not least for Bourgeois, who headed the First Commission with verve, ambition, and seemingly inexhaustible optimism, this was the make-or-break issue of the entire conference.[69] Bourgeois' long-standing and vehement advocacy for international arbitration and his distinguished legal record in this field had prepared the ground for the discussions at The Hague. For weeks on end, the delegates deliberated on the two intertwined issues of the PCAJ and the *obligatorium*. In the end, the conference failed on both counts. The first programmatic premise, the establishment of the PCAJ, which Bourgeois had taken more or less for granted, did not materialize on similar grounds as the case of the IPC. A proposal for the actual make-up of the court, drawn up by the US chief legal adviser James Scott Brown and supported by the British and the German delegations, fell through in the face of vehement opposition offered by smaller and medium-sized states such as, again, Brazil. Ruy Barbosa, Brazil's first delegate, and with him quite a significant coalition of weaker states, rejected in particular the representation scheme prejudicing a future PCAJ in favour of great power interests.[70] The delegates eventually agreed to play down the controversy and postpone the project until further deliberations could be made, in essence for the envisaged Third Hague Peace Conference, which was planned for either 1915 or 1916 and was aborted with the beginning of the First World War.[71]

Hammarskjöld did his best to mediate between rather irreconcilable positions, both on the issue of the PCAJ, whose fate seemed to have been sealed by early September 1907, and on the question of obligatory arbitration. His government's

[69] Bourgeois also drew upon his 1899 experiences and the—admittedly frustrating, but not discouraging—interim. Cf., as an example, Bourgeois' summary of the results of the Tenth Meeting of Examination Committee A on 19 August 1907, in *Proceedings 1907* (n 38) vol. II: Meetings of the First Commission, 473; Abbenhuis, *Hague Conferences* (n 6) 123–4; Stanislas Jeannesson, 'Léon Bourgeois aux conférences de La Haye de 1899 et 1907: solidarisme et démocratisation des relations internationals', in *Histoire, économie & société* 33 (2014), 107–20.

[70] Payk, *Frieden durch Recht?* (n 6) 69–70; Dülffer, *Regeln* (n 5) 307–11. 'Weak states' according to Michael Handel, *Weak States in the International System* (London: Routledge, 1990), 30–47.

[71] In detail cf. Abbenhuis, *Hague Conferences* (n 6) 180–1.

instructions allowed for a sizable room for manoeuvre on arbitration, which he used eagerly and with an astute sense of realism. The overarching strategic goal of his initiatives in the First Commission was to push as much binding arbitration regulations through the proceedings as possible. As with the IPC, his position on the PCAJ was explicitly in favour of it, stressing the 'promise for the future' associated with an international court. In both fields, the PCAJ and obligatory arbitration, he opted for 'intermediate solutions' and placed himself firmly on the middle ground.[72] Noticing the reluctance of some parties and the general potential for disagreement, he submitted an alternative draft for the revision of the 1899 Convention (I). This proposal amounted to a classic compromise, on whose basis juridical arbitration could institutionally take off and prove itself viable. In turn, Hammarskjöld hoped the ensuing success of arbitral justice in the international arena would eventually allow for its gradual extension into other areas of war. In line with Stockholm's instructions and indeed Hammarskjöld's earlier assessments, the Swedish proposal emphasized the necessity for international arbitration by court not to 'involve the vital interests or independence of the parties in dispute'.[73] This would permit opting out of obligatory arbitration, if and where a given state assumed its national interests to be affected. However, in one arena of possible conflict, Hammarskjöld intended to make arbitration compulsory, whenever cases of 'pecuniary claims' arose. In his draft, those cases were, apparently deliberately, rather broadly defined. Existing bi- and multilateral treaties, especially those going further in terms of obligatory arbitration, would remain unaffected.[74]

Introducing his proposal at the commission's fifth meeting on 16 July 1907, Hammarskjöld espoused the virtues of the 1899 convention on arbitration and the subsequent 'tremendous progress' the 'idea of arbitration' had made throughout the world. Against this backdrop of an ever-growing arbitral internationalism, his government was 'wondering if the moment has not arrived to take still another step which would constitute a considerable progress in the path which it believes to be the path of the future': obligatory arbitration—as a means of establishing 'a stable regime of right and equity in international relations'.[75] In order to accommodate the opposition to the *obligatorium*, Hammarskjöld not only suggested a comprehensive limitation to property law but also called for a return to sober, realistic, and fact-based deliberations. 'Together with the false idealism which delights in sonorous phrases', these habitual deficiencies 'are the most dangerous enemies of a durable progress.' For him, 'the essential thing' was the mutually agreed

[72] Hammarskjöld to the Second Subcommission, First Commission, Second Meeting, 4 July 1907, in *Proceedings 1907* (n 38) vol. II: Meetings of the First Commission, 787.

[73] Annex 22: Proposition of the Swedish Delegation, in *Proceedings 1907* (n 38) vol. II: Meetings of the First Commission, 878–9, here: Article 16b, 878.

[74] Ibid., Articles 18 respectively 19, 878.

[75] Hammarskjöld's statement to the First Commission, Fifth Meeting, 16 July 1907, in *Proceedings 1907* (n 38) vol. II: Meetings of the First Commission, 238–40, at 238.

establishment of 'the principle of obligatory arbitration for certain cases of practical importance, even if such cases should at first be but few in number'.[76] The compromise Hammarskjöld developed was certainly among the more legally sophisticated suggestions to arrive at an internationally digestible solution on the question of obligatory arbitration. He could base his proposal on a substantial body of own research, particularly on his study 'Internationella skiljedoms-aftal', written in 1903 for the Swedish foreign ministry and then released through the influential *Nordisk tidskrift*. Here, he had illustrated the deficiencies of the existing regime(s) of international arbitration, first and foremost that—despite the impetus of Hague I in 1899—there simply was no unified synchronized body of arbitration norms and practices. Each and every one of the interested powers limited the effect of arbitration with conditional caveats such as exemptions in cases of national security or when questions of honour were raised. To Hammarskjöld, however, the proof of the pudding was in the eating, and as 'the practical results of the arbitration idea's implementation have so far been rather scant in comparison to the theoretical sympathy the idea has attracted', his study suggested a pragmatic solution to the existing dilemma. Through arbitrating compensation cases internationally and in a binding and unified fashion, the international legal community would—in Hammarskjöld's pragmatic approach—be able to breathe life into an international arbitration regime in general.[77]

To this pragmatism, he returned four years later at The Hague. Having been adopted as a member of the examination committee, he made his case compellingly, aligning the Swedish proposal with an almost identical plan brought forward by the Portuguese delegate Alberto d'Oliveira and supported by an alternative suggestion from the US delegation.[78] Their central argument was the formal introduction of the *obligatorium* into the revised convention on arbitration, even if conditionally limited to juridical cases. According to Hammarskjöld, such a practice was already established in more than twenty existing arbitration treaties. By explicitly committing to a limited and highly circumscribed form of obligatory arbitration, the future convention would normalize the practice in both international legal culture and the international system—a process on which both Hammarskjöld and d'Oliveira hoped one could build.[79]

The German delegation, however, made it clear that they would reject arbitral obligation. While, as opposed to its stance at the conference of 1899, Berlin

[76] Hammarskjöld's statement to the First Commission, Fifth Meeting, 16 July 1907, in *Proceedings 1907* (n 38) vol. II: Meetings of the First Commission, 238–9.

[77] Hammarskjöld, 'Internationella skiljedoms-aftal' (n 42) 573–7.

[78] President's (Bourgeois') concluding statement, Eighth Meeting, 27 July 1907, in *Proceedings 1907* (n 38) vol. II: Meetings of the First Commission, 311, 375 (n 1), 405. This, however, applied to all first delegates that had submitted proposals.

[79] Hammarskjöld's statement to the Examination Committee A, First Commission, Sixth Meeting, 6 August 1907, in *Proceedings 1907* (n 38) vol. II: Meetings of the First Commission, 416–17 (along with Alberto d'Oliveira's statement), 412–15 (for the concrete wording of the three proposals).

was prepared to accept the institutionalization of an international arbitral court, the German government would under no circumstances accept any obligation to submit to arbitration, no matter how limited.[80] In response to Hammarskjöld and d'Oliveira, Kriege pointed to the futility of an obligatory general clause in the revised convention, as obligation would not equally translate into the diverse constitutional bodies and legal traditions of the different parties. By creating these difficulties in implementation, a globally binding arbitration framework would hamper rather than support the actual and established practice of arbitration. Whilst allegedly not being 'pessimistic' about the eventual legal evolution of arbitration, the German delegation favoured the maintenance of the existing bilateral practices.[81] Germany, Kriege, and Marschall von Bieberstein stated in conclusion, 'cannot give its adhesion to anyone of the projects directed to the establishment of obligatory and world arbitration for all matters of a juridical nature, or relative to the interpretation of treaties'.[82] Had the German argument carried the day, the idea of an international body of binding arbitral law would have been buried entirely. Hammarskjöld consequently opposed Kriege's intervention as best as he could, pointing to both the 'practical value' of a general *obligatorium* and the importance of an explicit enumeration of the cases coming under obligatory arbitration, just as had been suggested by the Swedish proposal.[83] In this, he saw himself aligned with Martens, Bourgeois, and French legal advisor Louis Renault, who repeatedly insisted that the 'difficulty by which they are confronted, must not be regarded as an argument against obligatory arbitration'.[84] The British, in any case, considered the practical implications of revising the existing body of commercial and juridical commitments too vast and hence cautiously supported the German opposition tactically, if not in principle.[85]

Further interventions and a committee report on Hammarskjöld's part, along with the more forceful *obligatorium* defenders such as d'Oliveira, Renault, and Bourgeois, did not succeed in softening the existing opposition to obligatory arbitration.[86] Despite, as Bourgeois optimistically stated, 'the unanimous will of the

[80] On German (and British) motives see Dülffer, *Regeln* (n 5) 305–11.

[81] Marschall von Bieberstein's statement to the Examination Committee A, First Commission, Eighth Meeting, 18 September 1907, in *Proceedings 1907* (n 38) vol. II: Meetings of the First Commission, 469, 473 (cit. 'pessimism').

[82] Kriege's statement to the Examination Committee A, First Commission, Sixth Meeting, 6 August 1907, in *Proceedings 1907* (n 38) vol. II: Meetings of the First Commission, 418–20.

[83] Hammarskjöld's comment to the Examination Committee A, First Commission, Sixth Meeting, 6 August 1907, in *Proceedings 1907* (n 38) vol. II: Meetings of the First Commission, 421–2.

[84] Hammarskjöld's comment to the Examination Committee A, First Commission, Seventh Meeting, 10 August 1907, in *Proceedings 1907* (n 38) vol. II: Meetings of the First Commission, at 439, 435 (on Martens).

[85] Edward Fry's comment to the Examination Committee A, First Commission, Seventh Meeting, 10 August 1907, in *Proceedings 1907* (n 38) vol. II: Meetings of the First Commission, 434–435.

[86] Hammarskjöld's comments to the Examination Committee A, First Commission, Seventh, Ninth, Tenth respectively Eleventh Meeting, 10, 15, 19, respectively 23 August 1907, in *Proceedings 1907* (n 38) vol. II: Meetings of the First Commission, 434, 455, 465, 480. For Marschall's effectively unchanged position see ibid., 467–9, 480–1.

members of the committee of examination that obligatory arbitration should issue triumphant from the Peace Conference', no concrete solution to the actual and—in Hammarskjöld's and the majority perception of the delegates—occasionally imagined problems was found.[87] Marschall von Bieberstein and Kriege in particular became increasingly less flexible in their position and began searching for a veto coalition that would help to obscure the relative isolation in which Germany found itself. This fluid coalition involving Austria-Hungary and array of changing smaller and middle-sized states eventually emerged, propped up ironically by the US vote, which only echoed the frustration of Choate and Scott with the way in which the whole question of arbitration had been handled.[88] For Hammarskjöld, who had invested a lot of 'patient labour' in the proceedings on arbitration and especially on the *obligatorium*, the eventual collapse of his initiatives and the project at large certainly amounted to a defeat.[89] In late 1907, however, this feeling of disappointment was largely absent from The Hague, as the delegates—including the diligent Swede—were optimistically looking forward to a world increasingly governed by international law. Setbacks such as in the arbitration field were deemed to be temporary and could, in any case, be rectified again at a later date.

More progress was made in the other arena, the establishment and concretisation of a body of international law regulating the position of the neutral power in wars on land and at sea, which resulted in the 1907 Hague Conventions V on land war and XIII on maritime warfare.[90] Two facts spoke for a comparatively easy ride with regard to the conventions. First, there already existed a body of partly codified, partly uncodified neutrality law, which The Hague was supposed to collect, harmonize, and formalize. The need for this had been explicated by the 1899 conference—an expectation and programmatic objective pre-defining the 1907 proceedings.[91] Second, the thorough preparatory and accompanying work on the conventions had seemingly left few controversial aspects on which the conference's Second and Third Commissions could dwell. In particular, the secretaries and

[87] Bourgeois' concluding comments to the Examination Committee A, First Commission, Eleventh Meeting, 23 August 1907, in *Proceedings 1907* (n 38) vol. II: Meetings of the First Commission, 481–2 (see as well Tenth Meeting, 473–4).

[88] On the details cf. Dülffer, *Regeln* (n 5) 311–20.

[89] Bourgeois' comment to the Examination Committee A, First Commission, Eleventh Meeting, 23 August 1907, in *Proceedings 1907* (n 38) vol. II: Meetings of the First Commission, 481–2 (see as well Tenth Meeting, 473–4), especially the Sixteenth Meeting on 4 September 1907, ibid., 561–574, revolves largely around Hammarskjöld's suggestions and preparatory labours.

[90] James Brown Scott (ed.), *The Hague Conventions and Declarations of 1899 and 1907* (New York, NY: Oxford University Press, 1915), 'Rights and Duties of Neutral Powers and Persons in Case of War on Land (Hague V)', 18 October 1907, 133–9, respectively 'Rights and Duties of Neutral Powers in Naval War (Hague XIII)', 18 October 1907, 209–19 (ratified by Sweden, 27 November 1909).

[91] Fifth Plenary Meeting, 7 September 1907, in *Proceedings 1907* (n 38) vol. I: Plenary Meetings of the Conference, Annex D, 'Report to the Conference: Arrangement Concerning the Rights and Duties of Neutral States on Land', 136–7. Cf. the comprehensive account of Maartje Abbenhuis, *An Age of Neutrals: Great Power Politics, 1815–1914* (Cambridge: Cambridge University Press, 2014), especially 178–218.

reporters of the individual commissions, the Swiss military delegate Colonel Eugène Borel (land war) and Renault (war at sea), brought the deliberations into a legal form that allowed for the easy adoption of both conventions.[92] The discussions on some of the particularities were nonetheless extensive, primarily because some issues remained contentious, such as the treatment of neutral persons resident in belligerent countries, which was in the end effectively outsourced to bilateral arrangements among belligerents and their neutral counterparts.[93] The latter dispute was, strictly speaking, not part of the neutrality conventions, but it illustrates how related issues permeated into the legal realm of neutrality regulations and hence affected the status and behaviour of neutral states, no more so than in the area of maritime law.[94]

Among the most controversial of those was the sensitive question of laying automatic mines. The issue and its treatment in the proceedings epitomizes the cardinal problem of creating new international legislation. Against the unwillingness of the great powers of the nineteenth century 'directorate system' in international affairs, little could be achieved.[95] If both Great Britain and imperial Germany saw their interests violated or, as in this case, adopted irreconcilable positions, their refusal to concede hampered and often frustrated the negotiations. With both powers hesitant to submit to an institutionalized arbitral system and a comprehensively regulated legal order, new law could only be formed in areas of little controversy. For Britain, despite its willingness to make compromises on the general terms of legislation, the question of laying mines was not among these. Too much specification on mine-laying, if permitted by the international laws of war, would obviously limit the effectiveness of a blockade, one of the British Empire's primary means of exercising maritime hegemony in war. Against the British insistence to regulate the use of mines as much as possible, Marschall von Bieberstein and the German delegation argued for as little international legal restriction as possible, even vis-à-vis neutral powers and their rights to maritime access. A deadlock, then, quickly ensued between the 'positions of neutrals and of belligerents, of maritime and of continental States', so that Hammarskjöld felt inclined to put forward yet another

[92] Fifth Plenary Meeting, 7 September 1907, in *Proceedings 1907* (n 38) vol. I: Plenary Meetings of the Conference, 125, as well Annex D, 'Report to the Conference: Arrangement Concerning the Rights and Duties of Neutral States on Land', 136–48.

[93] Fifth Plenary Meeting, 7 September 1907, in *Proceedings 1907* (n 38) vol. I: Plenary Meetings of the Conference, 125, as well Annex F, 'Report to the Conference: Arrangement on Neutral Persons in the Territory of Belligerents', 150–9, respectively—for the draft of the new section added to the 1899 Regulations respecting the laws and customs of war on land—id., 160–1, and the definite proposal with hardly any definite implications in terms of international law, id., 177–8; for the complexity of the discussions cf. the different proposals for the 1899 regulations, in *Proceedings 1907* (n 38) vol. III: Meetings of the Second, Third and Fourth Commissions, at: 240–51, 272–81 (for a synoptic table).

[94] Abbenhuis, *Hague Conferences* (n 6) 163–4.

[95] Matthias Schulz, 'Vom Direktorialsystem zum Multilateralismus? Die Haager Friedenskonferenz von 1907 in der Entwicklung des internationalen Staatensystems bis zum Ersten Weltkrieg', *Die Friedens-Warte* 82 (2007), 31–50.

compromise.[96] This attempt, though eventually unsuccessful, seems most representative for the way in which he and indeed the Swedish delegation conducted themselves at The Hague.

Presented at the Third Commission's sixth meeting on 19 September 1907, his compromise recognized the stalemate reached and suggested, just as with his arbitration proposal, that absolutes were to be turned into conditional provisions. The proposed articles absolutely prohibiting anchored mine-laying in particular areas would have to be omitted, as no settlement was within reach. In order to preserve their intention, however, Hammarskjöld suggested what he termed a 'middle path' by 'laying down conditional and elastic rules on the subject'. The preamble preceding the minutiae of his proposal exempted cases of, as it read, 'imperious military necessity'. This deliberately vague phrasing cleverly accommodated the German opposition to restrictions, whilst sustaining the British and other parties' argument for maximum restriction on the new technology. His proposal was, as Hammarskjöld freely admitted, at best a 'modest advance'. Yet seen against the backdrop of increasingly frustrating and futile discussions in the Commission's different bodies from late June onwards, involving a total of 'three meetings of the first subcommissions, ten of the committee of examination and four of the plenary Commission', it was a step forward.[97]

Ernest Satow, the second plenipotentiary of the British delegation, jumped at the chance the Swedish proposal offered. Pointing to the public responsibility of the disagreeing parties not to separate without a deal, Satow and his delegation rallied to support Hammarskjöld's proposal. Despite British support, it was not to be, as the German position had become entrenched. Marschall von Bieberstein stated with almost brutal frankness that Germany would not 'admit any restriction either absolute or conditional' but left the actual hatchet job to his Hungarian colleague, Mérey von Kapos-Mére.[98] Politely but firmly, Mérey took apart the main pillar of Hammarskjöld's preamble, the alleged 'imperious military necessity', whose conceptual weakness the Swede had already anticipated in his own opening statement.[99] Against such upfront opposition, the centrepiece of Hammarskjöld's

[96] President of the Third Commission, Alexander Nelidov, to the Eighth Plenary Meeting, 9 October 1907, in *Proceedings 1907* (n 38) vol. I: Plenary Meetings of the Conference, 271 (cit. positions); Third Commission, Sixth Meeting, 19 September 1907, *Proceedings 1907* (n 38) vol. III: Meetings of the Second, Third, and Fourth Commissions, 435 (cit. compromise).

[97] Third Commission, Sixth Meeting, 19 September 1907, *Proceedings 1907* (n 38) vol. III: Meetings of the Second, Third and Fourth Commissions, 435–6 (previous citations). For the sub-commission's work cf. ibid., 521–54; cf. as well Eighth Plenary Meeting, 9 October 1907, in *Proceedings 1907* (n 38) vol. I: Plenary Meetings of the Conference, 272.

[98] Third Commission, Sixth Meeting, 19 September 1907, *Proceedings 1907* (n 38) vol. III: Meetings of the Second, Third and Fourth Commissions, 437; KB, Hjalmar Hammarskjölds arkiv: SE S-HS L175: 1: vol. 164: Bildt to Hammarskjöld, 22 May 1907, at 2 (cit. Austrian), describing Mérey furthermore as a mere stooge of Marschall.

[99] Third Commission, Sixth Meeting, 19 September 1907, *Proceedings 1907* (n 38) vol. III: Meetings of the Second, Third and Fourth Commissions, 437–8.

proposal, the preamble to the actual catalogue of regulations on the laying of automatic submarine mines, did not stand a chance. The immediate vote ended in unequivocal defeat, with thirteen nays, among them Germany, Austro-Hungary, and even the United States, sixteen abstentions, including the Danish vote, and only nine affirmative votes, with France, Britain, Italy, Japan, and the smaller European neutrals (Norway, the Netherlands, Portugal).[100] After Hammarskjöld's final attempt, the antagonism remained unresolved, with both sides explicitly claiming 'superior ... sentiments of humanity and civilization' for themselves, as Marschall von Bieberstein stated in the final plenary meeting on the issue against an intervention by Satow.[101] Abbenhuis has rightly noted that 'the language of 'civilization' had numerous applications and could underwrite ambitions for war and peace'.[102]

Even if representative for the underlying systemic flaws of the proceedings, Hammarskjöld's failure was certainly not symptomatic for his own role at the conference. This is particularly notable in the emergence of the convention of neutral powers in naval war (XIII), which addressed a host of intricate issues, whilst carefully trying to balance 'the rights of belligerents and the interests of the neutrals'.[103] Here, exorbitantly difficult questions were resolved and translated into an impressive body of international maritime law in war, among them agreements regulating the presence of belligerent ships in neutral ports and waters.[104] Hammarskjöld's participation in the debates was marked throughout, even if his job was not always easy. Besides dealing with a multitude of delegations at The Hague, he also had to consider his own government. Whilst he certainly enjoyed quite significant leeway, at times, the foreign ministry felt compelled to rein him in. One of these interventions took place in response to his effectively raising the issue of the Öresund, commonly known in English as the Sound. Based on an earlier interpretation of the Institut de Droit International, Hammarskjöld insisted existing proposals would have to make sure that '[s]traits which serve as a passage from one open sea to another can never be closed'.[105] This made sense against the backdrop of the discussions at hand and was certainly intended to allow for a greater degree of legal specificity. Stockholm, however, had become unwilling to follow him along this line. Whilst greatly satisfied with Hammarskjöld's conduct, the foreign ministry's state secretary, Albert Ehrensvärd, saw himself compelled to intervene. Just like Hammarskjöld, Ehrensvärd, the ministry's highest civil servant,

[100] Third Commission, Sixth Meeting, 19 September 1907, *Proceedings 1907* (n 38) vol. III: Meetings of the Second, Third, and Fourth Commissions, 438.

[101] Eighth Plenary Meeting, 9 October 1907, in *Proceedings 1907* (n 38) vol. I: Plenary Meetings of the Conference, 274–6.

[102] Abbenhuis, *Hague Conferences* (n 6) 163.

[103] Third Commission, Second Subcommission, Third Meeting, 27 July 1907, in *Proceedings 1907* (n 38) vol. III: Meetings of the Second, Third, and Fourth Commissions, 573.

[104] Rights and Duties of Neutral Powers in Naval War (Hague XIII), 18 October 1907, in Hague Conventions and Declarations of 1899 and 1907, 209–19.

[105] Third Commission, Second Subcommission, Fourth Meeting, 30 July 1907, in *Proceedings 1907* (n 38) vol. III: Meetings of the Second, Third, and Fourth Commissions, 590.

represented the internationalist legal wing within Swedish diplomacy. During his tenure between 1906 and 1908, he enhanced the international legal expertise of his ministry and followed the delegation's work at The Hague closely.[106] In his letter, Ehrensvärd intervened to revise Hammarskjöld's position on the Sound as an open international strait. This, he argued, would effectively undermine Swedish security interests, as Sweden—just as Denmark—would be unable to mine its own territorial waters and hence decimate its defence capabilities. Those would have indeed been the consequences of the stipulation suggested by Hammarskjöld. The suggestion, however, was not only fully in accordance with existing interpretations of international maritime law but also with his instructions, as Ehrensvärd readily admitted.[107] Stockholm, in any case, revised its position and informed Hammarskjöld accordingly, who in turn did not take up his proposal again. The passage in question, or indeed any other variant on international straits connecting seas, did not make it into the final text of the convention.

Despite the difficulties Hammarskjöld met, the overall sense and certainly his own outlook remained one of confidence and hope for the future. After all, the world had witnessed and participated in the genesis of a multilateral 'empire of international law', which promised to regulate and govern the world according to more objective principles than any previous global order had done.[108] Hammarskjöld himself could look back at the conference with a degree of satisfaction, both about its outcome and his individual performance. His standing as one of northern Europe's foremost international legal scholars and certainly Sweden's internationally most renowned jurist had been cemented. He had shown himself equally apt at legal argument and the search for juridical compromise, at conference diplomacy and consensus-building. In the following years, various Stockholm governments and the PCA commissioned him for manifold duties at The Hague and in various other international contexts.[109] He was seriously considered as foreign minister, despite his immediate career which saw him moving back into Swedish domestic politics as governor of the province of Uppsala. It was

[106] Bengt Hildebrand, 'Albert Ehrensvärd d. y.: anteckningar till hans arkiv', *Svensk tidskrift* 35 (1948), 622–39; Bengt Hildebrand and Folke Lindberg, 'Johan Jakob Albert Ehrensvärd', *Svenskt biografiskt lexikon* (1949) https://sok.riksarkivet.se/sbl/artikel/16741 (accessed 18 August 2020).

[107] Ehrensvärd to Hammarskjöld, 17 August 1907, KB, Hjalmar Hammarskjölds arkiv: SE S-HS L175:1: vol. 164; cf. as well ibid., vol. 164–165: Internationella organ för fred och folkrätt: Fredskonferensen 1907: Instruktionen för Sveriges ombud vid den andra fredkonferensen i Haag 1907, 4 June 1907, 3.

[108] Mazower, *Governing the World* (n 7) 65, situates this 'empire of law' in the last third of the long nineteenth century, with the Hague Peace Conferences as the movement's culmination point. For the term cf. Karen J. Alter, 'The Empire of International Law?' *AJIL* 113 (2019), 183–99.

[109] Among them arbitration responsibilities either within the PCA or in other international contexts, among them the multiple cases between Sweden and Norway (on the question of the Sami population's rights and on territorial issues) from 1908 onwards, between Germany and France on the Casablanca incident 1909, and as a delegate to the Swedish-Norwegian-Russian negotiations on Svalbard between 1910 and 1912. For further biographical details cf. Nils Herlitz, 'K Hjalmar L Hammarskjöld', in *Svenskt biografiskt lexikon*, https://sok.riksarkivet.se/sbl/artikel/12546 (accessed 18 August 2020).

once more his predecessor at The Hague, Bildt, who aptly captured the impression Hammarskjöld had made:

> Since I read of your nomination [as governor of Uppsala], I had the intention of writing to you, a little to congratulate you because, I assume, that you have received what you wanted to have, but mostly in order to express my regret about the loss our diplomacy suffers through your departure. I venture to flatter myself by hoping that the experiences you have had with diplomacy should powerfully sustain your interest in the field, and that we can probably count you among us again, if not as a colleague than as [our] boss.[110]

Conclusion: The 'Empire of Law' Unfolding

On returning from The Hague, not only Hammarskjöld but also the other Scandinavian delegations and with them their governments had grounds to look to the future with optimism. Despite pending legal and political ratifications, the position of the neutral small state had been significantly strengthened by the 1907 conventions on neutrality and the overhaul of the existing laws of war on land and at sea. Cumulating, formalizing, and institutionalizing the essential neutral tradition of the nineteenth century, Hague V on neutrality in a land war and XIII on neutral powers in naval war codified the rights and duties on which a neutral could fall back. If not entirely immunized against power politics and hegemonic intervention, the new international legal code at least considerably enhanced 'the value of legal argument' in international relations.[111] Their comparable experiences of the Hague process and their overlapping interests in the institutionalization and systematic codification of international law brought the Scandinavian countries closer to one another, so close indeed that Stockholm, Copenhagen, and Kristiania began negotiations on coordinating their neutrality policy. The ambitious, if somewhat unrealistic vision associated with these talks in late 1912 was the genesis of a neutral bloc in northern Europe, guaranteed by both existing international law and the great powers.[112] Considering the less than amical break-away of Norway from its previous union with Sweden just seven years earlier, this pragmatic recovery of bilateral relations is remarkable.

[110] Bildt to Hammarskjöld, 2 December 1907, KB, Hammarskjölds arkiv: SE S-HS L175: 1: vol. 164.

[111] Johan den Hertog, 'Dutch Neutrality and the Value of Legal Argumentation', in Johan den Hertog and Samuël Kruizinga (eds), *Caught in the Middle. Neutrals, Neutrality and the First World War* (Amsterdam: Aksant 2011), 15–34, at 15 (cit).

[112] Patrick Salmon, '"Between the Sea Power and the Land Power": Scandinavia and the Coming of the First World War', *Transactions of the Royal Historical Society*, 6th series, III (1993), 23–49; Maartje Abbenhuis, '"Too Good To Be True?" European Hopes For Neutrality Before 1914', in Herman Amersfoort and Wim Klinkert (eds), *Small Powers in the Age of Total War, 1900–1940* (Leiden: Brill, 2011), 27–55; Pertti Luntinen, 'Neutrality in Northern Europe Before the First World War', in Jukka Nevakivi (ed.), *Neutrality in History* (Helsinki: SHS, 1993), 107–14; Jonas, *Scandinavia and the Great Powers* (n 10) 19–34.

Within two years, however, Hammarskjöld's and the Scandinavian effort to consolidate results gained at The Hague would be made almost obsolete. The First World War aborted any dreams of an 'Empire of Law' and exposed neutral small states, like Sweden, to existential threats and their representatives, like Hammarskjöld, now prime minister, to incomprehension and ridicule.[113] This became most evident in the personal relations between Hammarskjöld and the British chief envoy in Stockholm, seasoned diplomat Esme Howard. More scholarly and matter-of-fact than his politically skilled foreign minister Knut Wallenberg, the prime minister felt compelled to clarify his and indeed his government's position on the war to Howard. Sweden's neutrality, as he saw it, functioned on the basis of the Hague conventions and should be evident to the world as a strict interpretation of those agreements, despite the country's continued and comparatively diverse economic relations to Germany. To Howard and the London government, Stockholm's position appeared to be pro-German in both intention and effect. In British eyes, Sweden was the archetype of the neutral profiteer, a *tertius gaudens*, a third party rejoicing at a world bursting asunder.[114]

The Swedish government's blatant hypocrisy and not least Hammarskjöld's disingenuousness, as Howard noted, left the diplomat increasingly bewildered. For him, the conservative and habitually condescending Swedish prime minister was an almost ideal representative of that 'true blue legalism' of the Hague tradition.[115] In his view, pro-German Swedes among the country's elites—like Hammarskjöld—concealed their actual political outlook behind spurious legal arguments and a deeply hypocritical application of international law. The Swedes, on the one hand, hypocritically raged against the British naval blockade of the North Sea, whilst, on the other hand, willingly excusing far greater abuses of international law when committed by Germany. Against that backdrop, Howard gleefully observed the emergence of a vocal liberal and social democratic opposition in parliament against the prime minister and his government. 'The campaign against Hammarskjöld', he reported in autumn 1916, 'has developed greatly.'[116] About half a year later, amidst a food crisis and mounting hostility between Hammarskjöld and his liberal and more pragmatic foreign minister Wallenberg, the prime minister, and his discredited government eventually resigned.

What seems to have alienated Howard and the Foreign Office from the chief policy-makers in Stockholm was not the generally legitimate Swedish abstention from the conflict but the country's endemic refusal to condemn what the British

[113] Mazower, *Governing the World* (n 7) 65.

[114] Howard, *Theatre of Life* (n 21) 229–30; on the context cf. Jonas, *Scandinavia and the Great Powers* (n 10) 19–34.

[115] Howard, *Theatre of Life* (n 21) 239.

[116] Howard to Foreign Office, 3 and 4 October 1916, TNA, FO 371/2754. On Hammarskjöld's resignation in the spring of 1917 cf. Wilhelm M. Carlgren, Minist*ären Hammarskjöld: Tillkomst—Söndring—Fall. Studier i svensk politik 1914–1917* (Stockholm: Almqvist&Wiksell, 1967), 194–253.

viewed as the excesses of an allegedly German way of war.[117] To the hardliners among British policy-makers and propagandists, and even to a highly nuanced observer like Howard, Sweden's purely legalistic interpretation of its neutrality, imbued with the older Hague premises, discredited the country morally. In this view, a mature Scandinavian polity built on Western liberal principles, and the alleged Teutonic propensity to atavistic barbarity and militarism were simply irreconcilable. The consequence of Sweden's 'unnatural' affinity with the German Empire was that the country was held morally accountable for a war it did not fight.[118] It was therefore not only in purely economic terms that neutrals were portrayed as war profiteers and hence morally discredited. In the politics and propaganda of moral recrimination, the self-reliant, probably slightly overconfident neutral state had effectively become an immoral pariah.[119]

In an age of transition from The Hague's legalist regime to the new age of Wilsonian liberal internationalism, Hammarskjöld's position was bound to appear increasingly anachronistic.[120] At the onset of the war, notions of neutrality had been based on an existing and internationally accepted legal code, that had just been enshrined in the 'Rights and Duties of a Neutral Power' of the Hague Convention of 1907. By the end of the war, neutrality as a purely legal conception had fallen into disrepute and was being reinvented along explicitly ideological, anti-legalist, and distinctly internationalist lines under the much larger umbrella of international and partly supranational cooperation and collective security.[121] Despite refusing to be part of this radical reinvention, Hammarskjöld, the tireless contributor to the Hague framework, certainly gave one of the more acute definitions of neutrality when insisting that being neutral 'is not saying yes to both sides, but saying no to both sides'.[122]

[117] Robert M. Citino, *The German Way of War. From the Thirty Years War to the Third Reich* (Lawrence, KS: University Press of Kansas, 2005), emphasises different strains of continuity. The argument has nonetheless not lost its appeal, cf. John Horne and Alan Kramer, *German Atrocities, 1914. A History of Denial* (New Haven, CT: Yale University Press, 2001), 161–74; Isabel V. Hull, *Absolute Destruction: Military Culture and the Practices of War in Imperial Germany* (Ithaca, NY: Cornell University Press, 2005).

[118] Most clearly, the episode recounted in Howard, *Theatre of Life* (n 21) 240–1.

[119] This pattern is discussed by Abbenhuis, *Age of Neutrals* (n 91) 10–12. Cf. Jonas, *Scandinavia and the Great Powers* (n 10) 67–86.

[120] Nils Ørvik, *The Decline of Neutrality 1914–1941: With Special Reference to the United States and the Northern Neutrals* (Oslo: Tanum, 1953, reprinted 1971).

[121] Similar in argument, though with differing assessments of the neutrals' discourse: Rebecka Lettevall, Geert Somsen, and Sven Widmalm (eds), *Neutrality in Twentieth-Century Europe: Intersections of Science, Culture, and Politics after the First World War* (London: Routledge, 2012); cf. as well Abbenhuis, *Age of Neutrals* (n 91) 10–11.

[122] Israel E. Levine, *Dag Hammarskjöld: Champion of World Peace* (Glasgow: Blackie, 1964), 61.

7
The Draughtsmen

International Lawyers and the Crafting of the Paris Peace Treaties, 1919–1920

Marcus M. Payk

Robert Lansing was, for once, satisfied. The US secretary of state, delegate to the Paris Peace Conference of 1919 and one of its most notorious critics, found the formal arrangements of the finished Treaty of Versailles much better than expected. Lansing had been critical of the disorganization of the proceedings in general, and of the high-minded attitude of US president Woodrow Wilson in particular, and had therefore been left out of much of the decision-making process. But the systematic composition and rationality of the treaty structure nonetheless met with his approval as a professional lawyer. Despite the negligence exhibited by the principal Allied leaders at the conference tables, Lansing found, much had been saved by the drafting committee, 'trained international jurists' who had taken the trouble to observe all the formalities and technicalities of treaty making: 'To their legal knowledge, carefulness, and industry are due the phraseology of the majority of the articles of the treaty and their orderly arrangement. One dreads to think what the document would have looked like if it had not passed through their experienced hands.'[1]

Yet it is astonishing that we know next to nothing about the drafting committee of the peace conference and how its members created one of the most contested peace treaties of all time. It is fair to say that this reflects the general tendency to underestimate formalities and technicalities in international politics. Too often it is supposed that the actual decision-making between states, governments, and diplomats is the only relevant part of the story, but this overlooks the work required between a substantive agreement of the parties and the final wording of a treaty. The practical drafting, the transformation of the political bargaining into

[1] Robert Lansing, *The Big Four and Others of the Peace Conference* (Boston, New York, NY: Houghton Mifflin, 1921), at 128f. On Lansing's relationship to Wilson see also Leonard V. Smith, 'The Wilsonian Challenge to International Law', *JHIL* 13, 1 (2011), 179–208; Ephraim Koch Smith, 'Robert Lansing and the Paris Peace Conference' (PhD diss., John Hopkins University Baltimore, 1972). For a more detailed look at the role of international law and lawyers during the Paris Peace Conference, cf. Marcus M. Payk, *Frieden durch Recht? Der Aufstieg des modernen Völkerrechts und der Friedensschluss nach dem Ersten Weltkrieg* (Munich: de Gruyter, 2018).

Marcus M. Payk, *The Draughtsmen* In: *Crafting the International Order*. Edited by: Marcus M. Payk and Kim Christian Priemel, Oxford University Press (2021). © The Several Contributors. DOI: 10.1093/oso/9780198863830.003.0007

legally binding rules and treaty provisions, is rarely examined. Moreover, we do not know very much about the people involved. Draughtsmen are mostly in-house lawyers of the foreign ministries involved, tasked with ensuring that any agreement both reflects the objectives of their government and conforms to the rules of international law. If counsellors to the kings and queens of pre-modern times were mostly shadowy figures, the legal advisors to modern governments are even more so. Their actions and accomplishments are usually shrouded in mystery. The professional role of these lawyers and their influence on international politics, a former governmental advisor remarked some years ago, still belong to the 'secret life of international law'.[2]

This chapter hopes to shed some light on this secrecy by taking a fresh look behind the scenes of the Paris Peace Conference of 1919. It aims to reconstruct the role of the drafting committee in making the Treaty of Versailles, to give contours to the lawyers involved, and to assess the general interplay between political decision-making and legal drafting. There is no shortage of literature devoted to the personalities and politics of the leading Allied statesmen in Paris, so we already have a fair picture of the main issues and problems of the peace conference.[3] And yet, little attention has been paid to what happened in the backrooms of the ornate Salle d'Horloge in the French ministry of Foreign Affairs—or, rather, on its first floor—after the notables had left the building. This chapter aims to explore those hidden proceedings and thus to contribute to the broader discussion on the impact of international law in the formulation of foreign policy: what exactly do international lawyers do in government service; and how do they entwine (or disentangle) law and politics, form and content?[4]

[2] Daniel Bethlehem, 'The Secret Life of International Law', *Cambridge Journal of International and Comparative Law* 1, 1 (2012), 23–36. See also Matthew Windsor, 'Consigliere or Conscience? The Role of the Government Legal Adviser', in Jean d'Aspremont, Tarcisio Gazzini, André Nollkaemper, et al. (eds), *International Law as a Profession* (Cambridge: Cambridge University Press, 2017), 355–88, at 358. For a less systematic treatment cf. A. W. B. Simpson, 'The Rule of Law in International Affairs: Maccabaean Lecture in Jurisprudence', *Proceedings of the British Academy* 125 (2003), 211–63; Robbie Sabel, 'The Role of the Legal Advisor in Diplomacy', *Diplomacy & Statecraft* 8, 1 (1997), 1–9.

[3] Jörn Leonhard, *Der überforderte Frieden. Versailles und die Welt 1918–1923* (Munich: Beck, 2018); Leonard V. Smith, *Sovereignty at the Paris Peace Conference of 1919* (Oxford: Oxford University Press, 2018); Margaret MacMillan, *Peacemakers: The Paris Conference of 1919 and its Attempt to End War* (London: Murray, 2001); Manfred F. Boemeke, Gerald D. Feldman, and Elisabeth Glaser (eds), *The Treaty of Versailles: A Reassessment after 75 Years* (New York, NY: Cambridge University Press, 1998).

[4] Mary L. Dudziak, 'Legal History as Foreign Relations History', in Frank Costigliola and Michael J. Hogan (eds), *Explaining the History of American Foreign Relations*, 3rd edn (New York, NY: Cambridge University Press, 2016), 135–50; Gerry J. Simpson, 'International Law in Diplomatic History', in James Crawford and Martti Koskenniemi (eds), *The Cambridge Companion to International Law* (Cambridge: Cambridge University Press, 2012), 25–46.

Installing a Drafting Committee at the Peace Conference

Ever since it has made sense to speak of modern diplomacy in international politics, secretaries have been recording the decisions of negotiations and turning them into legally binding agreements. Occasionally, this task was carried out by high-profile diplomats, such as Friedrich von Gentz, Metternich's counsellor in preparing the Final Act of the Vienna settlement in 1814/15. More often, however, the drafting was assigned to some advisor or subaltern clerk. It was not until the last third of the nineteenth century, following the professionalization of a diplomatic bureaucracy and the increasing complexity of modern relations between states, that Western nations began to create legal offices and treaty departments in their foreign ministries.[5] It was here that the persona of an in-house lawyer was created. There were various advantages to employing experts on drafting and treaty interpretation and to integrating them in the diplomatic process: to comply with the growing body of legal rules, of course, but also to (publicly) participate in the emergent academic field of international law, to strengthen negotiating positions vis-à-vis other nations, or to justify foreign policies through legal means.

These lines of activity matched broad trends of a 'juridification' of international relations around 1900.[6] They were also clearly visible in the preparations for peace negotiations after the First World War. A committee on drafting the treaties which would end the hostilities and mark the resumption of peaceful relations was among the first things considered by the French ministry of Foreign Affairs in November 1918. Its 'Note sur le Congrès de la Paix' provided for a six-person panel representing the major languages expected to be spoken at the conference: French, English, Italian, Portuguese, a Slavic language, and German.[7] This linguistic universalism should not be overrated. At the Quai d'Orsay, there was no doubt about the primacy of the French language in all matters of diplomacy and treaty making, an understanding that proved to be problematic later on as negotiations were often conducted in English and the Versailles Treaty even drawn up equally in English and French.[8] But the representation of other languages on this planned committee

[5] Stephen C. Neff, *Justice among Nations: A History of International Law* (Cambridge, MA: Harvard University Press, 2014), 305–8.

[6] Miloš Vec, 'From the Congress of Vienna to the Paris Peace Treaties of 1919', in Bardo Fassbender and Anne Peters (eds), *The Oxford Handbook of the History of International Law* (Oxford: Oxford University Press, 2012), 654–78, at 671–3.

[7] Note sur le Congrès de la Paix, n.d., AD, Papiers Tardieu, PA-AP 116/296, fol. 293–308 (301). See also: Plan of the Preliminary Conversations Between the Allied Ministers, Memorandum, 5 January 1919 in *Papers Relating to the Foreign Relations of the United States: The Paris Peace Conference, 1919*, 13 vols (Washington, DC: GPO, 1942–1947), vol. 1, 386–96 (396). For the French planning in general cf. Peter Jackson, *Beyond the Balance of Power: France and the Politics of National Security in the Era of the First World War* (Cambridge: Cambridge University Press, 2013), 224–34.

[8] Vincent Laniol, 'Langue et relations internationales: le monopole perdu de la langue français à la Conference de la Paix de 1919', in Denis Rolland and Jean-François Sirinelli, Collection International (eds), *Histoire culturelle des relations internationales: Carrefour méthodologique. XXe siècle* (Paris: L'Harmattan, 2004), 79–116.

stressed not only the importance of comprehending even slight variations of textual meaning during the drafting process, it also underscored the original idea of a universal peace congress. Early Allied planning for peace negotiations had anticipated a world congress to regulate international affairs among belligerents and neutrals alike; following this idea of a 'world treaty', the US delegates even argued for the inclusion of Spanish in the 'Committee on Style'.[9]

By early 1919, most of this Western-styled universalism had dissipated. Planning for the peace talks in December had been rocky. Direct negotiations with the defeated nations were soon postponed in favour of preliminary deliberations among the Allied and Associated Powers on the peace conditions to be imposed on the vanquished. High-level talks in early 1919 thus focused mostly on the difficult question of representation, with little to no interest in the technicalities of drafting. Translating political decisions into legal phraseology seemed a mere formality, at least in the eyes of the leading statesmen and diplomats. Rank and file delegates with experience in international negotiations were not so sure about this, however. James Brown Scott and David Hunter Miller, who jointly headed the legal division of the US peace commission, warned about neglecting the issue of drafting. In a memorandum discussing the French planning for peace talks, they drew attention to the experiences at the Hague Conferences in 1907—where Scott had played a prominent role—and argued for a close affiliation between the political discussion and the legal drafting. Direct access to the decision-makers was indispensable, the jurists wrote, as any 'changes in the wording of a text often affect form as well as substance, when only the former is intended'.[10]

This suggestion went unheeded. The formal 'Rules of the Conference', officially adopted at the first plenary assembly of the preliminary conference on 18 January, provided for a drafting committee walled off from any decision-making. Its five members were not supposed to be plenipotentiary delegates but should come from the ranks of the technical delegates of the Principal Allied and Associated Powers. Their task should be strictly limited to 'draw[ing] up the text of the decisions adopted'.[11] The committee itself was set up without any discussion about its members during the first plenary meeting. Only in the printed protocol would the delegates find the names of five lawyers: Henri Fromageot (France), who also served as informal chairman of the group, Cecil Hurst (British Empire), Nagaoka Harukazu

[9] David Hunter Miller, Memorandum Concerning the French Note, 22 November 1918, in David Hunter Miller, *My Diary at the Conference of Paris: With Documents*, 22 vols (New York, NY: Appeal Printing Comp., 1924), vol. 2, 28–42, at 42.

[10] David Hunter Miller and James Brown Scott, Observations, 12 January 1919, in *FRUS, PPC 1919* (n 7) vol. 1, 396–406, at 406. On Miller cf. John P. Posey, 'David Hunter Miller at the Paris Peace Conference. November, 1918–May, 1919' (PhD diss., University of Georgia, 1962), on Scott cf. Benjamin A. Coates, *Legalist Empire: International Law and American Foreign Relations in the Early Twentieth Century* (New York, NY: Oxford University Press, 2016); George A. Finch, *Adventures in Internationalism: A Biography of James Brown Scott*, with the assistance of William E. Butler (Clark, NJ: Lawbook Exchange, 2012). See also Benjamin Coates' chapter in this volume.

[11] Article XV, Rules of Conference, in *FRUS, PPC 1919* (n 7) vol. 3, 172–5, at 175.

(Japan), Arturo Ricci-Busatti (Italy), and, replacing David Hunter Miller at the last minute, James Brown Scott (United States).[12]

It is easy to see why these five men were selected. All were the principal lawyers of the respective peace delegation, with Fromageot, Hurst, and Ricci-Busatti also long-time legal advisors to the foreign ministries in Paris, London, and Rome.[13] Scott, originally a law professor, had been serving as solicitor in the State Department in Washington for a couple of years before he became head of the international law division of the Carnegie Endowment of International Peace in 1911; his influence as sponsor of many international law projects in the early twentieth century is hard to overstate.[14] Nagaoka had been attaché to the Japanese Embassy in Paris before the war, assigned to maintaining contacts with European international lawyers and jurists, following Tokyo's strategy to present Japan as a law-abiding and civilized nation.[15]

These men were well equipped for the task at hand and colleagues of long-standing, having met at a number of international conferences. All had been participants at the Hague Conference of 1907. Hurst and Scott had served as regular members of the drafting committee of 1907, whereas Fromageot had been the assistant to its chairmen, Louis Renault, then the first legal advisor at the Quai d'Orsay and internationally admired 'master of international law'.[16] Ricci-Busatti had been the legal advisor to the Italian delegation, Nagaoka the secretary of the Japanese deputation. Two years later, Renault, Fromageot, Hurst, and Ricci-Busatti had formed the drafting committee of the London Naval Conference of 1908/09.[17]

After the outbreak of the First World War, contacts had intensified along the front lines of the war. Connections with German counterparts such as Johannes Kriege from the Auswärtige Amt were rapidly lost, whereas ideas of Western and transatlantic unity fused with a sense of sober realism. Even though, among these legal advisors, only James Brown Scott might be called a true believer in a world built on international law, all the lawyers tried to grapple with the shock the war

[12] It was probably US secretary of state Robert Lansing, an old friend of Scott, who organized the replacement of David Hunter Miller by Scott, cf. Miller Diary, 18 January 1919. in Miller, *My Diary* (n 9) vol. 1, 83, Fn. e); Lansing Desk Diary, 18 January 1919, Library of Congress, Washington, DC (LoC), Robert Lansing Papers, Box 65.

[13] On Fromageot: June K. Burton, 'Fromageot, Henri-Auguste', in Warren F. Kuehl (ed.), *Biographical Dictionary of Internationalists* (Westport, CT: Greenwood Press, 1983), 277–8. On Hurst: Gerald Fitzmaurice, 'Sir Cecil Hurst (1870–1963)', *Annuaire de l'Institut de Droit International* 13, 2 (1963), 462–77; Arnold McNair, 'Sir Cecil James Barrington Hurst, GCMG, KCB, QC, LLD', *BYIL* 38 (1962), 400–6; also cf. Gabriela Frei's chapter in this volume. There seems to be no literature available on Ricci-Busatti.

[14] Coates, *Legalist Empire* (n 10) 96–8.

[15] Douglas Howland, *International Law and Japanese Sovereignty: The Emerging Global Order in the 19th Century* (New York, NY: Palgrave Macmillan, 2016), 104, 110f., 114. For Japanese approaches to international law see Andrew Cobbing's chapter in this volume.

[16] Elihu Root, 'The Codification of International Law', *AJIL* 19 (1925), 675–84, at 680. In a similar vein: James B. Scott, 'In Memoriam. Louis Renault', *AJIL* 12 (1918), 606–10.

[17] Verena Ritter-Döring, *Zwischen Normierung und Rüstungswettlauf. Die Entwicklung des Seekriegsrechts, 1856–1914* (Baden-Baden: Nomos, 2014), 277f.

meant to the authority and prospect of pre-war legal practice. Cecil Hurst wrote gloomily to Scott in June 1915:

> Are you sad at heart at seeing the lilies of the field of international law so ruthlessly trodden under foot on one side and so sadly left on one side on the other? When the diplomatic histories of the war come to be written, it will be a fertile mine for the student of the international law of the future. Certainly the rules were of but little services except to those who wished to pick holes in them. Fromageot made a remark to me the other day which I have thought about a good deal since. We were talking of the Declaration of London [and] he said [:] Never again must we attempt a codification of international law![18]

The meeting of these men in Paris in early 1919 was thus some sort of reunion, both professionally and personally. Fromageot had plenty of reasons to speak of the 'bonne amitié du comité'.[19] The members often invited each other to dinner along with their wives and families. Fromageot, Hurst, and Scott maintained especially close contact, occasionally taking automobile trips through Paris and nearby regions.[20] They were amicable towards the Italian and Japanese members of the committee, too, but it is hard to ignore the fact that the members of the three Western nations formed a firm nucleus and set the tone. 'They are to me, as to many a soul, three in one', wrote Scott to Hurst later, referring to the political and cultural affinities between France, Great Britain, and the United States.[21] It is hard to tell if the Italian and Japanese delegates even regularly participated in the meetings. There are only sparse traces of their presence to be found in the available sources; this could be due to their actual absence from the proceedings as much as to the ignorance of the Western majority on this committee. In addition, the group was often complemented by the second British legal advisor, William Malkin, who wrote to his wife in March:

> You understand that I am not really a member of the Committee (the American member is James Brown Scott, an old friend of Cecil's), but Cecil and I share things between us as is convenient, and even if as sometimes happens we both turn up it generally saves time in the long run.[22]

[18] Hurst to Scott, 25 June 1915, Georgetown University Library, Special Collections Research Center (GUL-SCRC), James Brown Scott Papers, Box 4/4. On the British-French agreement to abandon the Declaration of London cf. Isabel V. Hull, *A Scrap of Paper: Breaking and Making International Law During the Great War* (Ithaca, NY: Cornell University Press, 2014), 185–91.

[19] Fromageot to Scott, 25 June 1919, GUL-SCRC, Scott Papers, Box 3/9.

[20] Cf. Malkin to Margret Malkin, 20 March and 5 April 1919, Churchill Archives Centre (CAC), Malkin Papers, MALK 1/2.

[21] Scott to Hurst, 8 December 1923, GUL-SCRC, Scott Papers, Box 4/4.

[22] Malkin to Margret Malkin, 20 March 1919, CAC, Malkin Papers, MALK 1/2.

These personal acquaintances formed the basis for smooth operations. Sources are rare and sketchy, but it seems the lawyers sustained a relationship of mutual good will, collegiality, and trust throughout the deliberations. The US journalist Arthur Sweetser, after meeting the lawyers, spoke of the fortunate circumstance that

> three of the five on the drafting committee had performed an exactly similar task in those far off days of the Hague Conference. It is worthy of note that Scott, Fremegeot [sic!], and Hurst, fitted themselves for cooperation on this task by co-operation in what we are apt to think of as rather academic performance. Thus does internationalism develop from experience.[23]

One should not idealize the cooperative mood and team spirit among the lawyers, however. Even though Sweetser's anticipation of a nascent internationalism that would transcend national allegiances was widely shared among young Western elites at the peace conference, it needs be taken with a grain of salt. First and foremost, the legal advisors were representatives of their respective delegation, loyally committed to the political interests of their own side. Any other attitude would have disqualified them from serving as technical delegates. It was their unwavering loyalty and trustworthiness that had earned them the job in the first place, not their internationalist attitude or transnational networks. Admittedly, in some instances the drafting committee was used as an informal channel of communication and coordination between the delegations,[24] but for the most part their collegiality resulted from a shared understanding of their role. Each accepted that they were agents acting on the behalf of principals who expected them to accomplish the task at hand. And this daunting assignment the legal advisors took seriously. For many months, they met almost daily in a semi-private atmosphere in a separate room on the upper floor of the Quai d'Orsay. Things were usually talked out freely, with no formal minutes of the deliberations kept. The only sources on their meetings that have survived, scattered in various archives, are a plethora of galley proofs of various parts of the treaties, often with handwritten annotations, and a small number of files collecting the decisions of the Allied leaders as a basis for the drafting process.[25] During his visit, Arthur Sweetser was impressed how the lawyers would navigate between vast mountains of paper: 'All about was confusion, chairs, tables, piles of documents', he wrote after seeing the lawyers' workplace,

> There seemed to be no order in it, but Dr. Scott said that there was and that before me in the staking was the Treaty of Peace... We passed down the two tables, came to another series of papers on the redplushed seats of several chairs, then on

[23] Sweetser Diary, 12 May 1919, LoC, Arthur Sweetser Papers, Box 1.

[24] As an example: Protocol, 25 July 1919, in *FRUS, PPC 1919* (n 7) vol. 11, 468–70, at 469.

[25] See the papers in GUL-SCRC, Scott Papers, Box 24 to 27. A collection of the decisions of the Council of Four in The National Archives, Kew (TNA), FO 374/27 and FO 374/28; Archives Diplomatiques, La Courneuve (AD), Service Juridique, Fonds Fromageot, Box 4–6.

to more pages laid out on two sofas, around another side of the room to still more series of pages on chairs, and tables. Having thus made the grand tour of the walls of the room and picked up a copy of each article from its respective chair, table, or sofa, I had in my possession a complete copy of the Treaty.[26]

'The Wishes of the Political People'

But how exactly would the lawyers turn political deals and decisions into a coherent legal phraseology? As James Brown Scott dryly summed it up in July 1919, the duty of the drafting committee was and had been 'to put into shape the various proposals of the participating powers, adopted by the Conference in Plenary Session or by the Supreme Council'.[27] From an outside perspective, this job seemed easy enough. Most delegates did not regard the formal organization of the treaty as a special challenge, especially since the various commissions working on borders, reparations, disarmament, and the like had been instructed to prepare draft clauses with their final reports. All proposals submitted, a directive said upon the US suggestion, 'should be framed in such a legal form that no re-drafting would become necessary'.[28] After approval by the Supreme Council, these draft clauses would simply be stitched together to create the entire peace settlement. '[I]t may be said the treaty is built as we go along',[29] Sweetser wrote about this plan.

But efforts to streamline the making of the peace treaty soon ran into trouble. It was almost impossible for the commissions to keep within the schedule imposed by the Supreme Council. More importantly, the task of turning the flexible language of diplomatic negotiations into unambiguous clauses often proved to be a major stumbling block. Even the suggestion that in 'preparing such clauses, the members of the Commissions and Committees should consult their legal advisers',[30] did little to facilitate different opinions and to speed up the process. It is not entirely clear if and which advisors of the national delegations participated in the preparation of any draft articles at all, but what is obvious is that the drafting committee bore the brunt of the work. In the first weeks of March 1919, the five lawyers routinely, almost daily, paid visits to most commissions and assisted in the formulation of the relevant paragraphs. For example, on 15 March, Fromageot and his colleagues sat down for four hours with the Commission on Polish Affairs to consider how articles on the future borders of Poland or on aspects of nationality and citizenship could be drawn up in watertight legal terms. The task proved to be

[26] Sweetser Diary, 12 May 1919, LoC, Sweetser Papers, Box 1.
[27] Scott to Grew, 26 July 1919, Yale University Library, Manuscripts and Archives, New Haven (YULMA), Polk Papers, Box 22/99.
[28] Protocol, 6 March 1919, in *FRUS, PPC 1919* (n 7) vol. 4, 213–51, at 214.
[29] Sweetser Diary, 4 April 1919, LoC, Sweetser Papers, Box 1.
[30] Protocol, 6 March 1919, in *FRUS, PPC 1919* (n 7) vol. 4, 213–51, at 214.

contentious, however, so the drafting committee had to return on 17 and 18 March before there was sufficient agreement on the language of the disputed articles.[31] The commission's report of 19 March was thus complemented by an annex that translated the political compromises and recommendations in legal formulae as 'projet d'articles à insérer dans les préliminaires de paix'.[32]

Such an advisory role, which often implied mediating and refereeing between incompatible positions within the commissions, had no precursors at any international conference of the past. The work of the lawyers was therefore often met with great respect. After the legal advisors had sat with the Commission on Czech Affairs, British diplomat Harold Nicolson wrote in his diary: 'The Legal experts, Hurst and Fromageot are marvellous. Impassive and quick. Like electricians fixing a short-circuit'.[33] Robert Lansing praised James Brown Scott as one of 'greatest expert[s] in treaty drafting in the United States'.[34] On the other hand, the drafting committee also faced opposition and resistance. The opinion of the lawyers on what was legally possible and needed for a coherent treaty was by no means appreciated everywhere. It was not untypical when another British diplomat, James Headlam Morley, found that the legal advisors had overstepped their boundaries by talking back and by considering ifs and buts: 'My view is that it is the duty of the lawyers to draft treaties, however difficult, in accordance with the wishes of the political people'.[35] Headlam Morley was referring here to the disagreements in the Commission on Polish Affairs and how the lawyers dodged any attempt by the principal powers—namely the British delegation—to paper over differences with some vague provisions. Other delegates were worried too, especially since nobody really knew what became of the draft articles submitted by the commissions. French military leaders were so suspicious that they demanded to have their own representatives sitting with the lawyers during the discussion of all military clauses.[36]

There were good reasons for this scepticism, but it also showed a lack of understanding about how the peace treaties were actually constructed. Most commissions neither expected nor understood that their proposals could still be altered behind closed doors. In late April, the members of the Commission on the International Regime of Ports, Waterways, and Railways incidentally learnt

[31] Protocols, 15 to 18 March 1919, in Ministère des Affaires Étrangères (ed.), *Conférence de la Paix 1919–1920. Recueil des Actes de la Conférence*, 42 vols (Paris: Imprimerie nationale, 1922–1935), vol. IV–C–2, 42–53.

[32] Annex IV, Rapport No. 1, 19 March 1919, in *Recueil des Actes* (n 31) vol. IV–C–2, 54–73, at 67ff.

[33] Nicolson Diary, 18 March 1919, in Harold Nicolson, *Peacemaking 1919* (London: Constable, 1933), 285.

[34] Robert Lansing, The Services of Doctor James Brown Scott, 16 June 1919, LoC, Lansing Papers, Box 63.

[35] Headlam-Morley Diary, 20 March 1919, in James Headlam-Morley, *A Memoir of the Paris Peace Conference, 1919* (London: Methuen, 1972), 53.

[36] Frank S. Marston, *The Peace Conference of 1919. Organization and Procedure* (London: Oxford University Press, 1944), 185.

about several changes the drafting committee had made to their proposal. They were exasperated.[37] The commission's chairman, the Italian Silvio Crespi, wrote an angry letter to the president of the peace conference, French Premier Georges Clemenceau, complaining bitterly that the lawyers' modifications had distorted 'le sens et le fond des stipulations'.[38] On other occasions, the legal advisors scrapped the original terms almost completely. Following bitter debates about how to hold the German government and Kaiser Wilhelm II accountable for the outbreak of the war, the Commission on the Responsibility of the Authors of the War had settled for a compromise on how to set up a special tribunal for the Kaiser. The drafting committee, however, did not like the stipulations and felt, as Cecil Hurst put it, that 'more was required if the scheme was to be rendered workable'.[39] The lawyers convinced the Allied leaders that it made more sense to draft new clauses on this subject, 'filling in all the details which are not covered by the resolution'.[40] In the end, even though the meaning basically remained intact and some chunks of the original wording were used, an entirely new article on the prosecution of the Kaiser was created by the lawyers.[41]

This attitude of independence, self-confidence, and defiance by the drafting committee would, of course, not have been possible without the full backing of the Supreme Council and, after this body had proved to be inadequate for making decisions, of the Council of Four, consisting of the Georges Clemenceau, David Lloyd George, Vittorio Orlando, and Woodrow Wilson (the 'Big Four').[42] The leaders of the four principal Allied powers repeatedly stressed that the lawyers would only answer to them, eventually granting them the authority to reject any proposal or submission not formally authorized, that is initialled, by them.[43] The reason for the unwavering support is easy to see. The Council of Four understood how important it was to have draughtsmen at the epicentre of treaty making who were undoubtedly qualified as well as eminently loyal. A small group was best able to coordinate the response of dozens of commissions, to systemize terms and language used, and to consider gaps and overlaps in the treaties. If there were occasional conflicts between different provisions in the vast collection of several hundred articles, this was something the commissions and the Council of Four might well overlook; it

[37] Protocols, 22 to 24 April 1919, in *Recueil des Actes* (n 31), vol. IV–B–5, 246–87.

[38] Crespi to Clemenceau, 23 April 1919, AD, Service Juridique, Fonds Fromageot, Box 4.

[39] Hurst, Minute, 12 May 1919, TNA, FO 608/247/12, fol. 213.

[40] Hurst to Balfour, 14 April 1919, Parliamentary Archive, London (PA-UK), David Lloyd George Papers, F/147/8.

[41] The influence of the drafting committee is overlooked in most accounts, e.g. Mark Lewis, *The Birth of the New Justice: The Internationalization of Crime and Punishment, 1919–1950* (Oxford: Oxford University Press, 2014), 50. But cf. William Schabas, *The Trial of the Kaiser* (Oxford: Oxford University Press, 2018), 198f.

[42] Marston, *Peace Conference* (n 36) 165–76.

[43] Protocol, 2 May 1919, in *FRUS, PPC 1919* (n 7) vol. 5, 418–25, at 420.

was usually the lawyers who spotted them and sought clarification.[44] Thus, even though Wilson at that point still assumed that 'the work of drafting consists only of inserting completely finished clauses in the treaty',[45] he soon acquiesced to the indispensable role of the legal advisors.

In April and early May 1919, the drafting committee checked back with the Allied leaders on an almost daily basis, typically through Maurice Hankey as secretary to the Council of Four. Most enquiries asked for clarification of an unclear decision or to gain permission for some major modification. For example, on 29 April the drafting committee sent a note asking whether the harbour and fortifications of Heligoland were to be destroyed, as previous communications on this subject had remained unclear.[46] However, many textual dissonances and factual errors were straightened out by the lawyers themselves. Their discretionary handling of some issues later led some observers to chide the legal advisors as having 'gone further in interpretation than was perhaps intended'.[47] But to complete the draft treaty, no other way seemed possible. Only a few people knew about the actual work the drafting committee made on the instruction of the Council of Four (which in these crucial weeks was in fact a Council of Three due to the absence of Orlando). For those in the inner circle, however, the arduous workload of the lawyers could hardly be ignored, especially during the frantic last days before the peace conditions were presented to the German delegation on 7 May. The drafting committee was working exceedingly long hours, from early morning to late after midnight; according to Headlam Morley, the lawyers were almost 'worked to death'.[48] At one point, the Allied leaders even took the unusual step of not summoning the legal advisors to discuss a particular matter. In order not to distract them, and thereby to slow down the drafting of the treaty, the leading statesmen themselves paid a visit to their subaltern experts at the Quai d'Orsay.[49]

Nonetheless, the work of drafting committee should not be bestowed with a legalistic meaning or nourish the popular myth of non-political experts straightening out erratic and contingent deliberations. The legal advisors were by no means champions of a juridification of foreign affairs and, as far as one can tell, they would have preferred a more modest approach to peace-making. In other words, their strong standing was not entirely of their own making or connected to what they actually did. On a more fundamental level, the drafting committee was essential

[44] As an example: Protocol, 18 April 1919, in Paul Mantoux, *The Deliberations of the Council of Four: (March 24–June 28, 1919)*, 2 vols, Arthur Link (ed.) (Princeton, NJ: Princeton University Press, 1992), vol. I, 270.

[45] Ibid.

[46] Decision of 29 April 1919, in *Recueil des Actes* (n 31) vol. 1, 135.

[47] Harold W. V. Temperley (ed.), *A History of the Peace Conference of Paris*, 6 vols (London: Frowde [u.a.], 1920–1924), vol. 1, 266. See also: Marston, *Peace Conference* (n 36) 186f.

[48] Headlam-Morley Diary, n.d. [4 May 1919], in Headlam-Morley, *Memoir* (n 35) 116.

[49] Protocol, 2 May 1919, in Mantoux, *The Deliberations of the Council of Four*, vol. 1 (n 44) 448–55, at 451.

because it represented the idea that, at some point, negotiations had to stop and a final decision had to be made: in the domain of legal crafting, politics had to cease. This was a delusion, of course, but an indispensable one. The lawyers represented the overriding imperative that forced the Allied leaders to end the political quibbles and to acquiesce to the constraints of some formal agreement. The conference might well have collapsed and almost did after the Italians temporarily pulled out in the dispute over their Adriatic claims.[50] The Allied leaders could also have tried to manipulate the treaty drafting at almost any stage, or to disband the committee and recruit other draughtsmen. After all, the rules of the conference were of their own making and not imposed upon them. But precisely because there was no higher authority beyond the leading statesmen, the drafting committee is best understood as a pragmatic tool to maintain a distinction between the political and the legal side of the treaty making. Even if this distinction was a purely imaginary one, it created a set of self-imposed checks and balances to the unrestrained power of the Council of Four. The group of legal advisors operated as a kind of detached, semi-autonomous body. Even though each lawyer remained subject to the instructions and directives of his own national government as a matter of course, it was essential for the political decision-makers to treat them, at least in public, as exempt from all policy discussions and imbued with strict impartiality.

This pretence of an independent legal counsel beyond the immediate reach of politics was only possible if one assumed absolute loyalty and discretion on the part of the lawyers. Still, it was remarkably successful. The Allied leaders probably were surprised themselves at how difficult it proved to override their legal advisors, to reject their recommendations flatly, or to question their neutrality. It is revealing that the individual members of the Council of Four seldom attempted to exploit 'their' respective national representative for their own interest. A rare and glaring example happened in the final stages of finishing the treaty when Clemenceau tried to make a small modification behind the back of the other statesmen. He ordered Fromageot to change Article 22 of the Covenant of the League of Nations, with the purpose of softening the restrictions on military service in the mandated territories. Whereas the original wording stated that any 'military training of the natives for other than police purposes and the defence of territory' was forbidden, the words 'and of the territory of the mother country' were slipped into the article, thus making it possible for the mandatory power to raise forces from among the native population of a mandated territory. This had been a long-standing concern for the French army who sought to bolster their ranks by troops from the ex-German colonies, now to be ruled by France with a mandate from the League of Nations.[51]

[50] MacMillan, *Peacemakers* (n 3) 288–314.

[51] Susan Pedersen, *The Guardians: The League of Nations and the Crisis of Empire* (Oxford: Oxford University Press, 2015), 33f.; Paul Birdsall, *Versailles Twenty Years After. A Defense [1941]*, Reprint (Hamden: Archon Books, 1962), 77–82.

At first glance, it might seem astonishing that Clemenceau's clandestine demand for a modification without the consent of the other Allied leaders was brought to the attention of the Council of Four at the very next meeting. On the morning of 5 May, Hankey read a note by the drafting committee which indicated the latest changes in the covenant of the League of Nations. Most were of a purely formal and stylistic nature and would not have merited the communication. But the additional words in Article 22 were clearly relevant, so the lawyers, with all diplomatic tactfulness and restraint, acted as whistle-blowers on the French premier's attempted coup. As the French demand to recruit troops in the mandated territory had already been discussed and rejected by the Supreme Council in January, both Lloyd George and Wilson voiced their protest. Clemenceau immediately backed down, trying to put the blame on Fromageot. In the end, the original wording was unanimously reinstated and the debate moved on to other matters.[52]

What is remarkable about this episode is less the success or failure of the French machinations. It is the ability of the legal advisors to dodge such a political scheme and to project the impression of staying above the fray. The mandate to draw up the treaty text endowed them with a unique form of authority that was ultimately accepted by the Allied leaders for the sake of a legally sound and coherent agreement. Drafting the peace treaties thus implied a degree of freedom for the lawyers that nobody had anticipated but that was indispensable. Of course, this independence would exist only as long as the Allied leaders had confidence in the legal advisors and their work. But as long as there were no reasons to question the unconditional loyalty and political acumen of the lawyers, the drafting committee was able to create a remarkable autonomous, non-political sphere in a highly polarized and politically charged environment. In return for this autonomy, however, the lawyers did everything they could to translate the political agenda into legal provisions and to make their own opinions as invisible as they could.

Cooperation after Versailles

On the afternoon of 7 May, the Allied peace conditions were delivered to the German delegation in the Trianon Grand Hotel next to the palace of Versailles. In a short speech, Georges Clemenceau set out the procedure of the negotiations, declaring that any German observations on, or counter-proposals to, the Allied idea of a just peace as embodied in the treaty provisions were to be returned in writing. Following his speech, a 415-page tome, fresh out of the printing shop of the Imprimerie Nationale and bound in cream-white cloth, was handed to Ulrich von Brockdorff-Rantzau. The head of the German delegation responded with a defiant

[52] Protocol, 5 May 1919, in *FRUS, PPC 1919* (n 7) vol. 5, 463–73, at 463.

speech, rejecting most of the Allied premises—at least those that he believed to be included in the peace conditions. German knowledge of the peace settlement at this point had been mostly based on rumours, espionage, and the speculations in the Allied press.[53]

Most Allied delegates hardly knew more. The draft treaty was so voluminous, and the challenge of its timely completion had been so demanding, that even Maurice Hankey would later admit 'that, apart from the members of the Drafting Committee, no one in the Conference, not even the Council of Three nor their secretary, myself, had the slightest idea of its size, shape or total contents up to the eve of its presentation to the Germans'.[54] Seldom, if ever, had there been a peace treaty so long, complex, and comprehensive.[55] Brockdorff-Rantzau had good reason to tear the volume into several chunks immediately after returning to the delegation quarters in a nearby hotel. In order to gain an overview of all the Allied demands, it was imperative to produce a translation as quickly as possible. All delegates with a decent command in French or English (by now both the official languages of the treaty) were ordered to work on a cluster of clauses. By midnight on 7 May, the entire volume had been translated into German.[56]

While desperation and outrage about the peace conditions began to pile up in the German delegation in the following weeks, the drafting committee in Paris had other things to worry about. Even though the German treaty was far from complete, deliberations during the month of May turned to the peace settlement with the defeated Habsburg Empire. In consequence, the lawyers were coping with two sets of demands. First, they had to deal with a flood of suggestions hinting at misprints, typos, and substantive mistakes in the German draft. They began collecting an errata list which, in the end, went to over ten pages.[57] These points, as well as the minor concessions the German delegation were able to secure, were considered when the final treaty was drawn up in mid-June and signed in the Hall of Mirrors in Versailles on 28 June, 1919. Second, they were preparing the peace conditions for Austria, and there was still no indication of the timetable for the treaties with Hungary, Bulgaria, and the Ottoman Empire. Following a decision of the Council of Four in early April, it was clear that there would be five separate peace treaties of similar design and that the Versailles settlement should serve as a model for the other agreements. Yet, the preparation of what would become the Treaty of Saint-Germain-en-Laye with Austria soon exhibited a host of new problems, ranging, among others, from the name of the new Austrian republic to the borders of almost

53 MacMillan, *Peacemakers* (n 3) 473–6.

54 Maurice Hankey, *The Supreme Control at the Paris Peace Conference 1919: A Commentary* (London: Allen and Unwin, 1963), 134.

55 Jörg Fisch, *Krieg und Frieden im Friedensvertrag: Eine universalgeschichtliche Studie über Grundlagen und Formelemente des Friedensschlusses* (Stuttgart: Klett-Cotta, 1979), 612.

56 Victor Schiff, *So war es in Versailles*, 2nd rev. edn (Berlin: Dietz, 1929), 54.

57 Fromageot to the Council of Four, 25 June 1919, in *Recueil des Actes* (n 31) vol. I, 278.

all new nation-states in south-east Europe. Unsurprisingly, therefore, only days after delivering the German draft treaty, the back-and-forth of political decision-making and legal drafting was in full swing again.[58]

But neither the finalization of the German treaty nor the drafting of the other peace treaties proved to be as crucial for the legal advisors as the moment when the old Council of Four broke up. Soon after signing the Treaty of Versailles, Woodrow Wilson and David Lloyd George left Paris, as did Sidney Sonnino who had taken over the leadership of the Italian delegation after the fall of the Orlando government in Rome. Responsibility for the remaining peace treaties and for the execution of the Versailles settlement was transferred to the new Council of the Heads of Delegations, a body whose members, mostly seasoned diplomats, were much more dependent on directives and communications from their national governments.[59] As attention moved away from Paris and negotiations became more protracted after July 1919, the authority and influence of the drafting committee steadily grew. The expertise of the lawyers in all matters relating to the peace settlement was more in demand than ever. It was well understood that they were the persons with the most in-depth knowledge of the origins, reasons, and motives of all clauses and provisions, and moreover, they began advising the Council of the Heads of Delegations on a broad range of diplomatic affairs that had a legal aspect. In July, James Brown Scott stated 'that the Supreme Council as originally and as now organized submits for its [the drafting committee's] consideration and report many delicate and difficult questions of a legal nature'.[60]

There were several reasons the diplomats would seek the advice of the drafting committee. For one, it was imperative to understand the legal side of an international problem, but it was also a convenient way to avoid time-consuming consultations with the national governments on minor issues. Consulting the legal advisors also made it easier to push contested issues out of the spotlight, temporarily postponing any unwanted debate. The Council of Four had set precedents for this. In May, the Allied leaders had asked the lawyers for their opinion in a dispute on German submarine cables, and in June they had needed a legal assessment of the scuttling of the German fleet at Scapa Flow. During both discussions, however, it was hard to ignore that the statesmen were not so much interested in the 'long and learned report'[61] they eventually got as in using the involvement of the legal advisors to justify a certain course of action—or, rather, to rationalize the avoidance of any decision with unpredictable political consequences.[62]

[58] On the Austrian treaty see Isabella Ackerl and Rudolf Neck (eds), *Saint-Germain 1919: Protokoll des Symposiums am 29. und 30. Mai 1979 in Wien* (Munich: Oldenbourg, 1989); Nina Almond and Ralph H. Lutz (eds), *The Treaty of St. Germain: A Documentary History of its Territorial and Political Clauses* (Stanford, CA: University Press [u.a.], 1935).

[59] Marston, *Peace Conference* (n 36) 173–5.

[60] Scott to Grew, 26 July 1919, YULMA, Polk Papers, Box 22/99.

[61] Hankey, *Supreme Control* (n 54) 181.

[62] Protocol, 23 June 1919, in *FRUS, PPC 1919* (n 7) vol. 6, 641–4.

From the end of summer 1919, the drafting committee were routinely called upon by the Allied diplomats. In most cases, the lawyers would examine the issue and offer their opinion in a written statement, sometimes explained by Henri Fromageot in a subsequent meeting. Only in matters of great political importance, and when the differences of opinion were blatant, was the entire drafting committee invited to the discussion of the Allied representatives. The debate on the new German constitution is a good case in point. The Council of the Heads of Delegations believed Article 61 of the freshly enacted Weimar Republic's constitution to have violated the Treaty of Versailles as it suggested an eventual accession of German-speaking Austria: her representatives were permitted an advisory vote in the Reichstag until the formal integration of the Habsburg rump state into the Reich. In contrast, Article 80 of the peace treaty had stated the obligation of Germany to 'respect strictly the independence of Austria'. The French were adamant that they wanted to see this latter provision enforced and thus wanted to compel Germany formally to nullify Article 61 of the constitution. British and US delegates were more sceptical, however. The British member of the drafting committee, Cecil Hurst, noted during the discussion that the wording of the Weimar constitution abstained from all notions of coercion and simply took 'the form of an invitation to Austria to join Germany'.[63]

This incident provides an interesting illustration of how the legal advisors walked the tightrope between the collegiality of the drafting committee, their individual opinions, and their national commitments and loyalties. Since there had been no unanimous opinion among them, they had prepared a report which admitted that Article 61 of the German constitution was 'not consistent with the spirit of Article 80 of the German Treaty'. Yet, they avoided any specific political recommendations. Instead, the lawyers limited their advice to their specialist field and suggested a clarification in the relevant clause in the Austrian Treaty which was still in preparation. A provision should emphasize the sovereignty of the new Austrian republic, forbidding Vienna in strong words to 'compromise its independence directly or indirectly and by any means whatever'.[64]

Of course, no legal formula could solve the underlying political problem of how to prevent an eventual *Anschluss*. But it was all the lawyers could do and, in the end, they did not need to do more. At first, it might seem that Clemenceau had a point when he concluded the debate on 30 August with the statement that the Allied delegates were 'called upon to take a political and not a legal decision'.[65] But even though the French pressed for some decisive engagement, there were few opportunities for political action. The Allied nations remained divided on the issue and, in the end, followed the exact path laid out by the drafting committee: Article 88

[63] Hurst, Protocol, 30 August 1919, in *FRUS, PPC 1919* (n 7) vol. 8, 12–28, at 17.
[64] Report of the Drafting Committee, in ibid., 25f.
[65] Ibid., 18.

of the Treaty of Saint-Germain confirmed the independence of Austria, and the German side was formally required to declare that no provision of the German constitution was valid if it were found to be in conflict with the Versailles Treaty. Some days after the meeting with the Council, the legal advisors prepared a symbolic disavowal of Article 61 of the Weimar constitution. On 22 September, despite voicing strong protests about this interference in internal matters, the German delegation signed this declaration.[66]

It is somewhat ironic that the issue of the *Anschluss*, which had revealed the divided opinion of the legal advisors as well as the political weakness of the Council of the Heads of Delegations, would return to haunt Henri Fromageot and Cecil Hurst a decade later. In 1931, the German and Austrian governments announced their plan to form a customs union, presented as an economic necessity in the face of the Great Depression. Throughout Europe this proposal was seen as an attempted prelude to a political union, however, and strongly rejected by the former Allied nations, especially by the French. Financial and political pressures were not enough to stop the project, so the council of the League of Nations asked the Permanent Court of International Justice (PCIJ) to give an advisory opinion on the legal side of the matter. Among the judges who had to decide on this question in September 1931 were Fromageot and Hurst, who had both been sent to the bench in 1929 after years of service in the foreign ministries of Paris and London. Again, as in August 1919, both men differed in their legal evaluation of the problem: Fromageot led a narrow majority that pronounced the customs union as incompatible with Austria's international obligations according to Article 88 of the Treaty of Saint-Germain. Hurst, on the other hand, voted with the dissenting minority who found that the proposed economic regime would not impair Austria's independence.[67]

One should not overstate the differences between Fromageot and Hurst in the case of the *Anschluss*. Their divergence in substance would still go hand-in-hand with a general agreement on what international law meant to international politics. The two jurists shared a professional restraint vis-à-vis the utopian notion of an international legal order devoid of, or even opposed to, national interests. It was no surprise that their nomination as international judges to the PCIJ had been received with severe criticism; the German international lawyer and pacifist Hans Wehberg condemned the appointment of Fromageot as former 'Kronjuristen' in strong words (probably targeting the architects of the Versailles Treaty as well).[68]

[66] *Notes échangées entre le président de la Conférence de la paix et la délégation allemande au sujet de l'article 61 de la constitution allemande: Et déclaration relative à l'annulation de l'article 61 de la constitution allemande signée à Versailles le 22 septembre 1919* (Paris: Impr. Nat., 1919). For the German legal discussion see Rudolf Laun, *Deutschösterreich im Friedensvertrag von Versailles (Artikel 80 des Friedensvertrages), Kommentar nebst einschlägigen Noten*, Vorveröffentlichung aus dem Kommentar zum Friedensvertrage (Berlin: Vahlen, 1921).

[67] Ole Spiermann, *International Legal Argument in the Permanent Court of International Justice: The Rise of the International Judiciary* (Cambridge: Cambridge University Press, 2005), 316–24.

[68] Hans Wehberg, 'Zur Wahl des französischen Mitgliedes des Weltgerichtshofs', *Die Friedens-Warte* 29 (1929), 17.

As former governmental advisors, Fromageot and Hurst in fact agreed that the international order was not something self-evident or based on theoretical consideration but that it was dependent on the commitment of national governments and their willingness to project power to sustain it. Hurst was especially unwilling to see international law from an academic point of view, occasionally raging against the professors and theoreticians among his fellow judges at the PCIJ: 'Professors make bad judges. What is required is people who have had practical experience and not professorial experience.'[69]

In the years before they were appointed to the bench, Cecil Hurst and Henri Fromageot had kept close contact in their capacity as legal advisors to the British and French ministries of foreign affairs respectively. They met at countless conferences and committees in the years after 1920. A striking case in point was the preparation of the Locarno Conference of 1925, where Hurst and Fromageot hammered out all relevant details with their German counterpart from the Auswärtige Amt, Friedrich Gaus, before the first meetings of the statesmen took place.[70] Of course, Franco-British differences were often palpable in those years, as was German resentment towards the Versailles order.[71] But by invoking years of professional legal cooperation, a similar understanding of international politics, and personal trust, the two lawyers (or three, if one includes the like-minded Gaus) were able to create an allegedly non-political atmosphere for successful negotiations.

This collaboration behind the scenes of European diplomacy after 1920 was not the only outcome of the meetings in Paris. The drafting committee itself continued to exist. After the peace negotiations had come to an end in late 1919, with additional meetings until summer 1920 in London and San Remo to finalize the Hungarian and Turkish peace treaty, the Conference of Ambassadors had replaced the Council of the Heads of Delegations. This new inter-allied body consisted of the three ambassadors of Great Britain, Italy, and Japan accredited in Paris, and the French minister of foreign affairs; the ambassador of the United States remained an observer due to the refusal of the US Senate to ratify the Versailles Treaty. Since the main task of the Conference of Ambassadors was the enforcement of the peace settlement and the supervision of commissions created by it, the need for expertise on the legal architecture of the Paris peace treaties was obvious.[72]

In consequence, the drafting committee was not disbanded but transformed into an advisory body of the Conference of Ambassadors, albeit with a thorough

[69] Quoted in Spiermann, *International Legal Argument* (n 67) 308.

[70] Gerhard Stuby, *Vom 'Kronjuristen' zum 'Kronzeugen': Friedrich Wilhelm Gaus. Ein Leben im Auswärtigen Amt der Wilhelmstraße* (Hamburg: VSA-Verl., 2008), 160–73.

[71] William Laird Kleine-Ahlbrandt, *The Burden of Victory: France, Britain and the Enforcement of the Versailles Peace, 1919–1925* (Lanham, MD: University Press of America, 1995).

[72] Jürgen Heideking, *Areopag der Diplomaten: Die Pariser Botschafterkonferenz der alliierten Hauptmächte und die Probleme der europäischen Politik 1920–1931* (Husum: Matthiesen, 1979); Gerhard Paul Pink, *The Conference of Ambassadors (Paris 1920–1931)* (Geneva: Geneva Research Centre, 1942).

shake-up of its membership. James Brown Scott, the representative of the United States, had already returned to Washington in December 1919, rejecting an offer to stay in Paris as legal advisor to the US embassy.[73] In September 1919, Ricci-Busatti had been replaced by his younger colleague Massimo Pilotti, and William Malkin had temporarily stepped in for Cecil Hurst while the first British legal advisor had been on a mission to Egypt. Yet, from March 1920 the drafting committee displayed a remarkable stability in its composition, even though it was increasingly difficult for Fromageot to assemble the group's members in person at the Quai d'Orsay. Almost all legal advisors travelled frequently, often rotating between the foreign ministry in their home capital, diplomatic or inter-governmental meetings, and the new international institutions in Geneva, Paris, or The Hague. Against this background their productivity is even more remarkable. Between 1920 and 1927, they gave more than 100 opinions on various legal issues for the Conference of Ambassadors, leaving a lasting, if mostly hidden, mark on the course of European politics of the interwar years.[74]

Conclusion

'The Drafting Committee somewhat belied its modest title',[75] US-delegate (and assistant librarian) Preston Slosson found when looking back at the peace conference in 1920. There is more than a kernel of truth in this appraisal, as there is in Robert Lansing's eulogy on 'the speed and accuracy' of the drafting process 'unequalled in any other international conference'.[76] In theory, the peace treaties would be created by the various commissions, with the Allied leaders confirming or, in rare cases, modifying their recommendations. The drafting committee was thought merely to bring those decisions into an adequate legal form, building the treaty from written articles already at hand. In reality, this was a highly hypothetical procedure and never got anywhere. Each round of deliberations was fraught with uncertainties and irreconcilable interests, making it almost impossible to base the final treaty clauses on some straightforward and clear-cut political decision-making. The legal advisors had to step in at an early stage, helping the commissions to frame their recommendations—or sometimes even to make a decision. The Council of Four was no great help either. While the Allied leaders usually backed up the drafting committee against the lesser delegates and diplomats, their tendency to dismiss

[73] Scott to Wallace, 31 October 1919, GUL-SCRC, Scott Papers, Box 11.
[74] Heideking, *Areopag* (n 72) 39f.
[75] Preston Slosson, 'The Constitution of the Peace Conference', *Political Science Quarterly* 35, 3 (1920), 360–71, at 370.
[76] Robert Lansing, The Services of Doctor James Brown Scott, 16 June 1919, LoC, Lansing Papers, Box 63.

'tedious' details, to postpone decisions, or to prefer vague compromises is hard to ignore.

In the end, the effort to create a coherent structure and consistent phraseology of the treaties remained solely with the lawyers. There were good reasons the Council of Ambassadors continued to hold these reticent legal advisors in high esteem. Underestimated in most of the literature, they were workhorses, gatekeepers, and craftsmen at the same time, indispensable for transforming political decisions into legal form yet hardly champions of a legalistic stance. In other words, what the lawyers did was never a purely academic endeavour of non-political experts—but neither was it a simple charade or pretext for political machinations. Assuming a binary opposition between law and politics, or reiterating the established narrative about how politics ends when a decision becomes a legal rule or treaty provision, will only tell half the story. The work of the drafting committee at the Paris Peace Conference shows us how blurred the boundary between law and politics really was and, at the same time, how important it was to pretend that this boundary actually existed and mattered. It is this fundamental superposition of law and politics, form and content that reminds us, once again, that international law cannot be properly understood in supra-historical categories or vested with a predetermined meaning; it is the people, and their specific acts and experiences, practices and utterances, that create different meanings of international law at different times.

8

Legal Legwork

How Exiled Jurists Negotiated Recognition and Legitimacy in Wartime London, 1939–1945

Julia Eichenberg

> 'What does recognition mean? One can recognize a man as an Emperor or as a grocer. Recognition is meaningless without a defining formula.'[1]

Poignantly and provocatively phrased as ever, the British prime minister Winston Churchill wrote these words to US president Roosevelt in 1943, in the midst of a discussion of whether or not the United Kingdom, the United States, and the Union of Soviet Socialist Republics (USSR) should legally recognize the French Committee of National Liberation (FNCL), which at the time alternated between exile in London and Algiers. The FCNL was one of the exiled political representations of the European countries under German occupation, and the last to be recognized. Vichy continued to be the official French government.[2] Exiled political representatives of Belgium, Czechoslovakia, Greece, Luxembourg, the Netherlands, Norway, Poland, and Yugoslavia had all been recognized as official—and allied—governments in exile. France, despite having prominent representation in Charles de Gaulle, and despite having militarily importance in Northern Africa, had not yet been recognized, but acted as a National Committee.

Churchill's words point to a problem central to allied interaction during the Second World War: the legitimation of European allies. Germany had occupied most of the European continent; previous national governments were obliged to collaborate, were dismissed, or were even persecuted. Representatives of the occupied countries had fled the continent, mostly to Great Britain. These small,

[1] Winston Churchill in a telegram to US President Roosevelt on 21 July 1943, discussing the recognition of the French Committee of National Liberation (CFLN): Winston Churchill, *Closing the Ring, The Second World War* (Boston, MA: Houghton Mifflin, 1951), vol. 5, 179.

[2] Other representatives present in London were not recognized either; for example, oppositional forces representing Denmark, Austria, etc. However, their situation, more complicated than that of France, will not be considered in this chapter.

Julia Eichenberg, *Legal Legwork* In: *Crafting the International Order.* Edited by: Marcus M. Payk and Kim Christian Priemel, Oxford University Press (2021). © The Several Contributors. DOI: 10.1093/oso/9780198863830.003.0008

exiled groups had little contact with their respective populations and held limited or no military or executive power; they formed committees and cabinets without a people, without elections or parliaments. Under these conditions, what was a state and what was a legitimate government? Who defined legitimacy and how? What position and rights did these European representatives have to act on what they considered to be national interests? The situation put European politicians and heads of state in exile during the Second World War in a complex legal position. This chapter will describe the actors who lived within the exiled microcosm in London and engaged in a struggle to lobby both academically and politically for the recognition of their own governments to be legitimate. Throughout the war, they continually emphasized the subject of recognition and the legitimate representation of their statehood, even after a point at which the present-day reader might consider the matter settled in regard to legal concerns. During the war and occupation, it was necessary for some of the exiled governments legally to ensure their legitimacy, while others, as we are to find out, were in a more secure position with regard to international law. After the Munich Agreement and the breakup of Czechoslovakia, however, all exiled governments were intensely preoccupied with legitimacy and statehood as from then on it was never a given and never beyond doubt; it was a precarious limbo that needed to be negotiated on a daily basis.[3] The perception of impending threat to their state and nation influenced their legal discussions and political actions.[4] Thus, campaigning for the legitimacy of their government became a wartime occupation, even an obsession. In addition to political actors, this chapter argues that legal advisors and academics were also central to this lobbying. Using academic legal discourse to advance national interests, they functioned in a dual role as experts and political lobbyists, in a similar way to what Madsen describes as 'legal entrepreneurs' or 'legal diplomats' and what Keblus and Noldus call 'double agents' in describing the role of informality in political networks.[5]

Historiographies of law and legal debate during the Second World War have focused predominantly—and for good reason—either on the absence and trespassing of rights, or on the legal debates about war crimes and the origins of

[3] On the fragmentation of national legitimacy after Munich, see: Peter Romijn, Martin Conway, and Denis Peschanski, 'National Legitimacy—Ownership, Pretenders and Wars', in Martin Conway and Peter Romijn (eds), *The War for Legitimacy in Politics and Culture 1936–1941* (Oxford: Berg: 2008), 67–107.

[4] Arguing that even the reality of legal experts is a social construct, following Peter L. Berger and Thomas Luckmann, *The Social Construction of Reality. A Treatise in the Sociology of Knowledge* (New York, NY: Doubleday, 1966).

[5] See Mikael R. Madsen, 'Unpacking Legal Network Power: The Structural Construction of Transnational Legal Expert Networks', in Mar Fenwick, Steven Van Uytsel, and Stefan Wrbka (eds), *Networked Governance, Transnational Business and the Law* (Berlin: Springer, 2014), 39–56; Marika Keblusek and Badeloch Vera Noldus (eds), *Double Agents. Cultural and Political Brokerage in Early Modern Europe* (Leiden: Brill, 2011).

modern transitional justice.[6] However, the extraordinary situation created by the temporary residence of nine national representations in the British capital also provoked debates about legal issues of a different kind: negotiating legitimacy and statehood in exile was not only essential in laying the foundations for all further discussions about post-war justice and similar emerging legal concepts. In London, law was also an indispensably prerequisite for the allied governments to uphold statehood and legitimacy in exile. Maintaining a recognized government outside the occupied territory of the state amounted to maintaining the state, maintaining a voice, and maintaining power. Recognition was vital for a wide range of issues in connection with the war itself; it was required to uphold a belligerent status and to continue as an ally. It was also the prerequisite for access to foreign investments and—if they existed—colonial territories. Diplomatic recognition was a key to unlock all kinds of resources only a state would be able to access. Obtaining formal recognition thus was about more than just post-war planning. It was vital to the occupied nations. Their experience of being at war with a Nazi government that disregarded the rule of international law in warfare and in occupation had raised serious concerns and doubts about the protection international law could provide. This concern was increased by the memory of the Munich Agreement, in which the Western Allies had been willing to sacrifice the integrity of the Czechoslovak state as a pawn in the attempt to reach an agreement with Hitler. Accordingly, even when the law appeared to be in place to protect them, the exiled governments, deprived of usual state insignia like territory, population, and army, considered the work of legal discourse essential to uphold their national integrity and their agency as a state. Short of options, they were gathering legal arguments as means to defend themselves.

Exploring wartime legal exchange, several recent works have taken a biographical approach, focusing on single outstanding individuals.[7] While this has the advantage of following one person's actions and writings meticulously, it runs the risk of overestimating the input and impact by individual actors and of neglecting dynamics created by exchange and collaboration.[8] In contrast, this chapter displays

[6] This necessarily non-exhaustive list will guide you through the current state of the art: Annette Weinke, *Law, History, and Justice. Debating German State Crimes in the Long Twentieth Century* (New York, NY: Berghahn, 2018); Kim C. Priemel, *The Betrayal. The Nuremberg Trials and German Divergence* (Oxford: Oxford University Press, 2016); Guillaume Mouralis and Marie-Bénédicte Vincent (eds), *The Nuremberg Trials. New Perspectives on the Professions*, Special Issue *Comparativ* (2016/4).

[7] Some examples: Antoine Prost and Jay Winter, *René Cassin et les Droits de l'Homme: le Projet d'une Génération* (Paris: Fayard, 2011) ; Jochen von Bernstorff, *The Public International Law Theory of Hans Kelsen. Believing in Universal Law* (Cambridge: Cambridge University Press, 2010); Philippe Sands, *East West Street. On the Origins of Genocide and Crimes against Humanity* (London: Weidenfeld & Nicolson, 2016).

[8] A phenomenon Fleck describes in his work on thought collectives: Ludwik Fleck, *Entstehung und Entwicklung einer wissenschaftlichen Tatsache. Einführung in die Lehre vom Denkstil und Denkkollektiv* (Basel: Benno Schwabe, 1935). For an English translation see Ludwik Fleck, *Genesis and Development of a Scientific Fact*, translated by Fred Bradley, eds. Thaddeus J. Trenn and Robert K. Merton (Chicago, IL: Chicago University Press, 1979). (Chicago, IL: Chicago University Press, 1979).

strategies of a group of exiles to achieve and strengthen state legitimacy and the status of their governments' members in exile. Broadening the focus from individuals to discussions and networks makes way for the analysis of practices and strategies, restraints and agency of exile jurists amidst the international politics of the war.

The new setting in London created multiple legal challenges on an individual and a collective level: individually, the debate about legitimacy engages with the legal status of the European exiles, which not only defined their personal life but also shaped their political agency. Collectively, the legal status of the groups demanding recognition as national committees and exile governments and their legitimacy in legislative, judiciary, and executive functions had to be defined. This chapter thus explores a situation of legal challenges and the actions European exiles employed to improve it. At the heart of this, I argue, informal politics and informal diplomacy were at play. By outsourcing the debate about legitimacy from the official diplomatic sphere into academic circles and informal exchange, it was possible to formulate and negotiate demands in a safe place before reintroducing them into the formal political channels. In this way these demands could be justified, not in the context of allied decision-making but as conforming to established doctrines of international law. The geographic closeness of the London microcosm provided a catalyst for a renaissance of informality in European international relations in which legal experts flourished. This might seem like a paradox: on the one hand, international relations ever since the nineteenth century had been formalized and professionalized, in opposition to informal aristocratic practices of diplomacy. The legal profession and jurists had been central to this professionalization. However, during the 'London Moment', the European exiled legal experts took to this informal sphere their profession had sought to abolish.[9] Within this chapter, the focus will be on legal experts working in and with the governments in exile to advance recognition and to improve the status of the governments and their members. These men (and they were exclusively men) were the ministers of justice of the exiled governments, their staff, and some of the legal advisors working with them.

The In/Visible College of European Lawyers

Over the course of 1940 and 1941, London had become the last haven for refugees from all over Europe, a capital of free, allied Europe. Politicians and intellectuals from Belgium, Norway, Poland, Czechoslovakia, Luxembourg, Greece, Yugoslavia,

[9] Research on informal diplomacy has mostly centred on the early modern period: Barbara Stollberg-Rilinger, 'Die Frühe Neuzeit—eine Epoche der Formalisierung?', in Andreas Höfele, Jan-Dirk Müller, and Wulf Österreicher (eds), *Die Frühe Neuzeit: Revisionen einer Epoche* (Berlin: de Gruyter, 2013), 3–27. The concept is used in a broader sense here than in most political science research where it is mostly read as 'Track II diplomacy'.

and Free France found a new temporary home in Great Britain. Some of them were heads of states, monarchs, or the legitimate rulers even after their country's defeat. Others had a more difficult position in claiming to be the legitimate representation of their countries.[10]

The legal foundations for the claim to national representation and recognition under international law differed. In the cases of Norway, the Netherlands, and Luxembourg, monarchs had come to London together with their governments (some minor personal changes notwithstanding). Belgium's government came in defiance of their monarch, who had surrendered along with the Belgian troops. Czechoslovakia had ceased to exist as a state; members of the former government under Beneš tried to rebuild their administration as a recognized government in exile, first in Paris, then in London. In the Polish case, members of pre-war opposition groups had assembled to form a government representing the four biggest parties. The Greek and Yugoslav delegations were hybrids, accompanied by their monarchs. The agency of these exiled political representatives was restricted by their own precarious legal situation as well as by the lack of control over what had been understood as the pillars of statehood: they neither had control over state territory, people, and state power (Jellinek), nor did they hold a monopoly over the employ of physical force (Weber).[11] Lacking these proofs of statehood endangered their legitimacy and threatened a lower status within the allied hierarchy. Some legally educated European exiles thus actively lobbied to secure the individual legal situation of the exiled political elite as well as to institutionalize and consolidate legitimate representation of their respective nations within the borders of the United Kingdom. To do so, they had to develop new strategies: Traditionally, all communication would have to run via the Foreign Office and Home secretary on the British side and the respective national diplomatic channels on the other side. Conducted the official, diplomatic way, communication would have been rather administrative and slow, especially since the Foreign Office had more urgent concerns at hand in times of war. At the same time, there was great temptation to contact the people in charge directly, via informal channels. Adapting to these new conditions, the exiles often engaged in unofficial communication: networking, lobbying, and debate within the legal community served as a backdoor into the political discourse. All governments employed legal advisors or sought legal advice from experts. These experts—from all countries—participated not only in networking but they also published articles and essays in journals they knew would be acknowledged in the legal exiled community. Academic contributions by a legal

[10] For edited volumes providing an overview over the exiles in Great Britain, see Martin Conway and José Gotovitch (eds), *Europe in Exile. European Exile Communites in Britain 1940–45* (New York, NY: Berghahn, 2001); Vit Smetana and Kathleen Geaney (eds), *Exile in London. The Experience of Czechoslovaka and The Other Occupied Nations, 1939–1945* (Prague: Karolinum Press, 2017).

[11] Max Weber, *Wirtschaft und Gesellschaft. Grundriss der verstehenden Soziologie* (Tübingen: Mohr, 1922), §16; Georg Jellinek, *Allgemeine Staatslehre* (Berlin: Springer, 1929), 114ff.

advisor must accordingly also be read as a potential contribution to the political discourse about legitimacy.

Overall, the aims of the exiled political representations were twofold: one was official legal recognition (the right to form a government in exile), the second was a broader acknowledgement of legitimacy as a government (the right to have agency as government in exile), supported not only by the Foreign Office but by all ministries of His Majesty's Government and even beyond. The latter aim to have agency as a government in exile was linked to two challenges: first, the challenge of not only being regarded as an exiled figurehead but also accepted as a legitimate ally by the British Government; second, the challenge of being accepted as the legitimate representation of the nation by their own domestic population, where they were often faced with suspicion from the resistance movements within the countries. The latter challenge was in terms of identity (resistance versus exiles) as well as a legal problem. In some cases, such as the Netherlands, it was constitutionally disputed whether legislation could be introduced from beyond the Dutch territory.

To become and remain legitimate in order to achieve the goals of privileged status for government members, and to achieve recognition and support for legislative projects, exiled representatives needed broader public support, in Great Britain, on the continent, and internationally. Closely interlinked with the quest for legal recognition as a government was therefore a campaign to publicize the discourse about state legitimacy. This was needed as the nine European countries aimed to set up national representations in exile, which they hoped would eventually become recognized as governments or national committees.[12] All of these designated a prime minister and formed cabinets (or kept their existing ones, if the relevant personnel had made it over to London). Positions were filled according to the personnel at hand, usually prioritizing posts that were indispensable to their situation: in particular, the ministries of War or Defence and Foreign Affairs. The fact that all governments and national committees built cabinets indicates two decisive assumptions about their political task: first, they claimed the continuity of legitimate governance during the war, insisting that the reign of the German occupier was as illegitimate as that of collaborating regimes such as Vidkun Quisling's collaborationist government in Norway and those of his metaphorical namesakes elsewhere.[13] Second, they emphasized that their position in exile would be temporary, that the government would eventually return to their home country, and all decisions taken in exile should have validity for the post-war period.

[12] 'National' referring to the previously existing nation states, while of course many countries faced the additional challenge of uniting a multi-ethnic and multinational population, in particular Yugoslavia and Czechoslovakia, but this problem was well known to other states as well.

[13] Practices of German occupation in the context of international law are discussed in Jonathan Gumz, 'International Law and the Transformation of War, 1899–1949: The Case of Military Occupation', *Journal of Modern History* 90 (2018), 621–60.

In accordance with the social structure of European political and administrative elites during the twentieth century, jurists were highly represented within the ranks of the exile governments.[14] Many staff and ministers were lawyers and experts in international law, but even more had studied law at some point before focusing on politics or diplomacy. The governments in exile made an effort to include ministers and ministries of justice, and most employed legal advisors in addition to these. Facing a shortage of personnel and dealing with the political quandary of how to fill the few available seats and with what kind of people, governments in exile prioritized the appointment of Foreign ministers and staffing their ministries. The fact that even for these positions (of Foreign Affairs), legal experts were often considered or chosen—most prominently in the case of Norway's Trygve Lie—proves that law and legal questions were considered essential. In quick succession, the governments in exile created departments of Justice and appointed ministers, some with staff. In many cases, other ministries also included divisions that dealt with legal questions and thus employed legal experts. One of the best known and most influential of these subdivisions was, for example, the Belgian Commission for the Study of Post-War Problems CEPAG (Commission des Etudes pour les Problèmes d'Après-Guerre).[15]

The number, the situation, and the agency of these experts in London differed greatly between the different national cases. Some nations were represented by only a handful of people (as, for example, in the case of Luxembourg). Others alternated between London and representations in other countries, which promised different strategic advantages (again Luxembourg with a stronghold in northern America, Greece with a seat of exiled government in Cairo and, to a lesser degree, France, alternating between London and Algiers). Some of these ministries underwent repeated changes of personnel, especially in the less stable or politically contested governments (as, for example, Poland or Yugoslavia).

Three types of legal experts are relevant to this chapter. First, those who were appointed ministers of Justice, expected to represent a nation's commitment to the rule of law. While ministers are usually regarded as politicians rather than experts, I argue that ministers of Justice are both, as, unlike ministers for other departments, they possess professional training, expertise, and experience in the legal field. The second type of legal experts was the legally trained staff assisting the ministries of justice. The third type were legal experts in the orbit of the national representations.

[14] John Alexander Armstrong, *The European Administrative Elite* (Princeton, NJ: Princeton University Press,1973), 168–73; Hannes Siegrist, 'Public Office or Free Profession? German Attorneys in the Nineteenth and Early Twentieth Centuries', in Geoffrey Cocks and Konrad H. Jarausch (eds), *German Professions, 1800–1950* (Oxford: Berghahn, 1990), 46–65. Harold Perkin, *The Rise of Professional Society. England since 1880* (London: Routledge, 2002 (1989)).

[15] Staff were not shared. The Government Commission for the Study of Post-war problems listed two members of staff, among them Louis de Brouckère and later Paul van Zeeland, who turned out to be an influential legal expert working with the Belgian government. *The London Gazette* (LG), 26 August 1941, 4957–8; addition of van Zeeland on 29 August 1941, 5016.

They were engaged in an advisory role and were involved in the legal discourse concerning the situation of the exiled Europeans and, in some cases, put forward arguments in academic discourse on their behalf. The latter two groups will be described here as 'legal advisors'. In current research, the term 'legal advisor' is often used to describe an established occupational title for a government position,[16] while legal experts advising the ministries for Foreign affairs, are referred to by 'international legal advisors'.[17] In the case of the 'London Moment', however, the term 'advisor' is best used to describe official as well as informal experts—those who give counsel and advice, as will be shown here. While the British side kept to their traditional structures with officially appointed legal advisors in the Foreign Office, the European exiles worked with more fluidly attributed roles. Disruptions to staffing, due to political differences as well as to the war and the exiled situation itself, demanded more flexibility and led to increased fluidity of status.[18]

Together with the ministers of justice, the legal advisors formed a 'college' of international lawyers interacting in London at the intersection of their national interests and international legal discourse. Legal experts in the London microcosm fit well into Oscar Schachter's definition of an 'invisible college' in that in their biographies as well as in their professional actions the academic and the official intertwine, leading to a '*dedoublement fonctionnel*'.[19] Additionally, they correspond to his description of a 'European male community of international lawyers', in many cases sharing similar or even the same academic background and language, even those of a different national background.[20] However, contrary to Schachter's description of the college as 'invisible', the London microcosm allowed them a voice in national affairs and ensured their visibility to the exiled governments.[21] Thus, while overall corresponding to Schachter's definition of an invisible college in their backstage lobbying and their informal negotiations, their proximity to the exiled

[16] Andraž Zidar and Jean-Pierre Gauci (eds), *The Role of Legal Advisers in International Law*(Leiden: Brill Nijhoff, 2016), in particular the introduction, 1–10.

[17] Stephen Bouwhuis, 'The Role of an International Legal Advisor to Government', in *The International and Comparative Law Quarterly* 61, 4 (2012), 939–60.

[18] Even though the British example remained an influential example, as it had been before: Cf. Kate Jones, 'Marking Foreign Policy by Justice: The Legal Advisors to the Foreign Office, 1876–1953', in Robert McCorquodale and Jean-Pierre Gauci (eds), *British Influences on International Law, 1915–2015* (Brill: Leiden, 2016), 28–55. For a short history of the British Legal advisor see Marcus M. Payk, *Frieden durch Recht? Der Aufstieg des modernen Völkerrechts und der Friedensschluss nach dem Ersten Weltkrieg* (Berlin: de Gruyter, 2018), 48–51. See also the chapters by Marcus Payk and Gabriela Frei in this volume.

[19] In 1977, Oscar Schachter described international lawyers as an 'invisible college', a term to which many have referred. Oscar Schachter, 'Invisible College of International Lawyers', *North Western University Law Review* 72, 2 (1977–1978), 217–26, quotations 218, 225.

[20] An interview with Oscar Schachter, Mieke J. Clincy, and Oscar Schachter, *Proceedings of the Annual Meeting of the American Society of International Law* 95 (2001), 18–22, at 19.

[21] Andraž Zidar and Jean-Pierre Gauci, 'Introduction: Legal Advisors as the Visible College of International Lawyers', in Zidar and Gauci (eds), *Legal Advisers in International Law* (n 16) 1–10. David J. Bederman and Lucy Reed, 'The Visible College of International Law: An Introduction'. *Proceedings of the Annual Meeting of the American Society of International Law* 95 (2001), ix–xi.

governments also ensured, to a certain extent, a visible contribution, turning the London microcosm into an in/visible college of lawyers.

Ministers of justice in exile had a curious position. Compared to their fellow ministries of foreign affairs and war, the justice departments were often sidelined. Their offices were comparably small, starting out without any staff or just a handful, while the foreign ministry in many cases relied on the legwork of about twenty to thirty staff members.[22] Still, it had been considered essential to install ministers of Justice (as opposed to just combining the responsibilities under the ministry of Interior Affairs). After all, being in exile is a difficult position for a ministry whose main job description is to administer the national court and prison system—both far out of reach when residing in a foreign country. Establishing a ministry of Justice was, however, considered important in two ways: to uphold governance even in exile, and to further the legal concerns of the nation (in other words, legislative power, capacity to negotiate with other allies, impact on post-war order). Politics and law are closely intertwined systems, dependent on the other. Even if a legal system in exile could never resemble their predecessor, it was hoped that by establishing a ministry of Justice it could secure a voice for that country, which was relevant for legal and political affairs. Since the spheres of the political and the legal were even more intertwined in this exceptiional state of affairs, it can be argued that the legal basis was even more relevant in exile than before. Law produces more than law; it also produces agency, a feeling of at least temporary security, and the basis for further political opportunities. Legal lobbying in London was thus never just about changing the law but was aimed at changing the rules of the game where the players would at least gain a place at the table for when the time came for the cards to be dealt.

Despite a shortage of personnel, the large number of European jurists in exile ensured quality in the ranks. With the exemption of the interim French minister of justice Jules Abadie (who was, surprisingly, a surgeon), all ministers were qualified lawyers, mostly with a doctorate in law and relevant experience in court, in academia, or in national or international politics. If the position of the minister happened to be vacant, its tasks were usually temporarily covered by the prime minister (as in the case of the Dutch prime minister Gerbrandy, or the Polish prime minister Sikorski). While in later war years some groups of ministers (such as the *Comité des Ministres Etrangères* and the *Comité des Ministres de la Culture/de l'Éducation* consisting of European allied exile governments) were able to formalize an institutionalized exchange with their allied counterparts, ministers of Justice had to rely on their personal connections and networks. This increased the informal aspects of their work.

[22] Staff lists for all the ministries in exile were regularly published in *LG*, the UK's official public record.

Table 8.1 Ministers of Justice in Exile in London[a]

Country	1940	1941	1942	1943	1944	1945
Belgium	Albert De Vleeschauwer (Minister for the Colonies and Minister of Justice)		Hubert Pierlot	Antoine Delfosse	Maurice Verbaet	
Czechoslovakia	Juraj Slávik			Jaroslav Stranśky		
Free France	René Cassin			Jules Abadie	François de Menthon	
Greece	—			Stelio Dimitrakakis		
Luxembourg	Victor Bodson					
Netherlands	Pieter Gerbrandy		Johannes van Angeren		Gerrit Jan Van Heuven Goedhart	
Norway	Terje Wold					
Poland	Marian Seyda	L[b] P[c]	Wacław Komarnicki			Bronisław Kuśnierz
Yugoslavia		Slobodan Jovanović[d]	Milan Gavrilović	Nikola Mirošević –Sorgo	Vladeta Milićević	Drago Marušič

[a] Pierlot took over as interim minister of Justice from 19 February to 24 September 1942. *LG*, 4 December 1942, 5296; Czechoslovakia did not have a 'proper' ministry of Justice in 1941; for most of 1942, Juraj Slávik was minister of the Interior, Jaroslav Stranśky was minister of State without Portfolio, *LG*, 26 August 1941, 4958. Stranśky, who had been handling the ministry of Justice as minister of State since 1941, officially took over as minister of Justice on 12 November 1942; Cassin was first officially mentioned as Commissioner of Justice and Public Instruction in *LG*, 27 January 1942, 447, assisted by Jean Burhay, employed from 24 September 1941. *LG*, 24 July 1942, 3255; Dimitrakakis was appointed Greek minister of Justice on 25 September 1942. *LG*, 1942, 5296; Bodson was appointed minister of Justice on 30 August 1941, *LG*, 27 January 1942, 446; Johannes van Angeren is sometimes listed as minister of Justice in 1940. However, according to *LG*, Gerbrandy was prime minister and minister of Justice in 1940. *LG*, 26 August 1941, 4959; 3 February 1942, 559. Van Angeren was appointed minister on 25 February 1942. *LG*, 3 April 1942, 1508; based on information gathered from the *LG* (1941–1945), listing all members of government and official staff of the governments in exile who would fall under the Diplomatic Privileges (Extension) Act, 1941; and: Joel Cang (ed.), *The Who's Who of the Allied Governments, 4* vols (London: Allied Publications, 1941–1944). Cf. Julia Eichenberg, 'Macht auf der Flucht. Europäische Regierungen in London (1940–1944)', *Zeithistorische Forschungen 15* (2018), 452–73

[b] Herman Lieberman was minister of Justice from 22 August 1941 to 20 October 1941, his appointment and removal as minister was announced on the same day: *LG*, 27 January 1942, 446.

[c] Karol Popiel was minister of Justice from 20 October 1941 to 21 January 1942. *LG*, 3 March 1942, 1016.

[d] *LG*, 27 January 1942, 447. However, *The Who's Who* lists Marković. Either way, Gavrilović took over office on 11 January 1942, ibid.

The exiled ministers and members of government predominantly belonged to a generation who had been born between 1880 and 1900 (see Table 8.1). This was a generation who had lived through the First World War, who had been professionally and politically active in the interwar period and who had nearly all been involved with the League of Nation system. During the Second World War, they were between forty and sixty years old (some older), with an average of fifty-two years in 1940 and had already had experience in diplomatic and political affairs (see Table 8.2).

Confronted with the challenge of being granted international recognition, the challenge of securing legitimacy in acting as a government in exile, and the challenge of laying a legal foundation for a legislative process in exile, the governments in exile were in urgent need of the legwork of their legal counsels and advisors. While the most important negotiating partner, the United Kingdom, represented by the Foreign Office, could rely on their own legal advisers (at the time William Malkin and Eric Beckett), the exiled governments' advisors had more varied backgrounds.

Table 8.2 Dates of Birth, Ministers of Justice[a]

1870s (4)	1880s (11)	1890s (7)	1900s (4)
1870 Herman Lieberman (P)	1881 Władysław Sikorski (P)	1890 Juraj Slávik (CZ)	1900 François de Menthon (F)
1876 Jules Abadie (F)	1882 Milan Gavrilović (Y)	1891 Wacław Komarnicki (P)	1901 Gerrit Jan van Heuven Goedhart (NL)
1879 Marian Seyda (P)	1883 Hubert Pierlot (B) Maurice Verbaet (B) Bronisław Kuśnierz (P)	1894 Joannes (Jan) van Angeren (NL)	1902 Victor Bodson (Lux)
1874 Božidar S. Marković (Y)	1884 Jaroslav Stránský (CZ), Drago Marušič (Y)	1885 Antoine Delfosse (B)	1903 Stelios Dimitrakakis (GRE)
	1885 Pieter Gerbrand (NL), Nikola Mirošević-Sorgo (Y)	1897 Albert de Vleeschauwer (B)	
	1887 René Cassin (F), Karol Popiel (P)	1898 Vladeta Milićević (Y)	
		1899 Terje Wold (NOR)	

[a] Based on data provided in Cang (ed.), The Who's Who of the Allied Governments (n 23). Members of the exiled governments were exclusively male, as were the official legal advisors. There were, however, a handful of female jurists present in London who contributed to the discussions; for example, Wanda Grabińska and Margery Fry. See: Sara L. Kimble and Marion Röwekamp (eds), New Perspectives on European Women's Legal History (New York, NY: Routledge, 2016); Sara Weydner, Gendering Legal History: Women in the London Moment, https://exilegov.hypotheses.org/421 (accessed 18 August 2020).

Not all who had previously worked in such a capacity for their government were able to seek refuge in London. Shortage in qualified personnel, and the dire need for legal advice, thus opened the door for younger lawyers previously employed in the lower ranks of the diplomatic service, or even for well-connected outsiders.

When appointing a minister of Justice, the representations usually created the ministry of Justice and then appointed staff to fill it. However, as with all things in exile, this process was less straightforward than expected. Belgium was one of the first to build up their ministry in exile, and held a comparatively stable number of five (though changing) legal experts as staff, assisted by a further four staff members working under the joint supervision of the ministry with the ministry of Defence.[23] The Netherlands acted similarly: Gerbrandy, doubling as prime minister and minister of Justice in 1940, acted with a staff of four.[24] The Norwegian ministry of Justice started with one staff member in 1940, quickly rising to three in August.[25] The Polish representation started with four members of staff, cutting it temporarily to just one person, before building it up to almost its original size.[26] Exiled Czechoslovakia, later home of some of the most active voices in legal discussions in London, started out small. The first and only official staff member of the ministry of Justice—which began under the direction of Stranśky as minister of State, that is without a minister of Justice—was Václav Beneš, nephew to the president.[27] Greece, Luxembourg, and Yugoslavia, significantly smaller governments in exile, worked without any staff at the ministry of Justice.

Most of these staff members and legal advisors were younger than the European ministers of Justice in exile and the Foreign Office legal advisors. The majority of the men described in this chapter were born between 1904 and 1914, meaning they were between twenty-six and thirty-six years old in 1940 (thirty-one years on average[28]) (see Table 8.3). They had already gathered professional experience

[23] Members of staff under the direction of the Belgian minister of Justice included Charles Tschoffen, Herbert Speyer, Georges Waucomont, and Arthur Ducat; assisted by staff under the joint direction of the ministry of National Defence and the ministry of Justice: Marcel de Baer, Fernand Lepage, Jean Gerard, 'Frédéric Dumon, and Pierre Vermeylen', *LG*, 26 August 1941, 4957–4958. Delfosse's ministry had five official staff: Arthur Ducat, Maurice Heilporn, and Francois de Kinder, 'Ganshof van der Meersch, and Georges Waucomont', *LG*, 14 April 1944, 1719.

[24] Among them the later minister of Justice Johannes van Angeren, but also Petrus Kasteel, Frederik Snijders, Francois van't Sant et al., *LG*, 26 August 1941, 4959; 3 February 1942, 559.

[25] The first was Peter Stabell, but this soon rose to three on 29 August (Knut Thommessen, Aage Falkanger). At this point, however, the government was still small overall, the largest ministry sporting eight staff (Foreign Affairs), *LG*, 26 August 1941, 4960; additions on 29 August 1941, 5017.

[26] Stefan Glaser ('Glazer' in LG), Witold Legowski, Jerzy Karbowski, and Tadeusz Mincer. *LG*, 26 August 1941, 4961. With the exit of Lieberman, Glaser and Mincer were removed from the staff list. Under Popiel, staff was reduced to only one person: Eugeniusz Jarra. *LG*, 4 December 1942, 5301. Slowly, staff were augmented to three: Tadeusz Cyprian (1 January 1942), Jerzy Jaczynowski (1 January 1944), and Eugeniusz Jarra (1 September 1941). *LG*, 14 April 1944, 1723.

[27] *LG*, 26 August 1941, 4958, addition of Beneš on 28 December 1941, LG 3 March 1942, 1016.

[28] Although it is more difficult to calculate the average in this case as the number of legal advisors is more fluid than the numbers of ministers of Justice. The number varies (with time and from government to government), but we can probably speak of between one and four persons who would fill the position of a legal advisor per country, leading to a total estimation of between twenty and forty people.

Table 8.3 Dates of Birth, Legal Advisors (selected)[a]

1870s	1880s	1890s	1900s	1910s
			1900 Walter Jean Ganshof van der Meersch (B)	1910 Eduard Táborský (CZ), Vaclav Beneš (CZ)
1872 Herbert Speyer (B)	1881 Eugeniusz Jarra (P)	1895 Stefan Glaser (P)	1902 Aare Thor Falkanger (NOR)	1911 Knut Thomessen (NOR)
		1899 Egon Schwelb (CZ)	1905 John Lyng (NOR)	1914 Manfred Lachs (P)
			1908 Henri Fayat (B), Pater Stabell (NOR)	1913 Benjamin Payn (F)

[a] Biographies of staff are much harder to come by than biographies of ministers of Justice. Accordingly, this is not an exhaustive selection, but is based on data provided in Cang (ed.), *The Who's Who of the Allied Governments* (n 23).

in addition to their academic education, but they represented the next generation. They had experienced the First World War as children or adolescents; they became adults during the interwar period, and their professional experience began only in the latter half of it. Two age cohorts are represented: first, the older group, who had lived through the First World War and were part of the founding generation of the League of Nations. The second age cohort was professionally socialized under that international system and had gathered political experience both with regard to the internationalization of the League of Nations of the 1920s and the rising nationalism of the 1930s.

European legal advisors in exile were occupied with securing their national interests: recognition as a government, amelioration of the status of members of said government, and legitimation of the legislative (and executive) power of the government. While all countries sought legal advice, it seems that legal advisors gained influence with those governments whose status in at least one of these categories was precarious. Czechoslovak advisors, for example, were particularly active in London.[29] Since the focus of this chapter is to portray the legal exchange in London, the following short biographies shed light on some of the advisors who chose to further their national cause in the London microcosm by engaging in open international discussions.

[29] The Czechoslovak legal advisors, just like the whole of the Beneš government, were mostly of Czech origin. While all governments faced discussions about their ability to represent their country, the Czechoslovak government was particularly challenged in this regard—and often criticized for being more of a Czech than a Slovak government.

The exiled government of Czechoslovakia employed three very prominent and active legal advisors: Egon Schwelb,[30] Eduard Táborský,[31] and Vaclav Beneš. Only the latter was officially employed as a member of staff in the ministry of Justice.[32] The three men were born at the very end of the nineteenth century (1899, Schwelb), and in the early twentieth century (1910, Táborský, Beneš), meaning that at the outbreak of the First World War they were young boys (the latter two) or a young adolescent (the former, who was still serving in the Austro-Hungarian Army at the end of the war). Táborský and Schwelb were born in Prague, Beneš in Bohemia; all three were of Czech origin and all three had completed a doctoral degree in law at the Charles University in Prague (Schwelb in 1922, the other two in 1934). During the interwar years, all three took to politics with an outlook on international law and international relations rather than legal practice. After a short stint as a lawyer, Schwelb became actively engaged in local politics as a social democrat while still publishing academically on an international level. Táborský pursued a career in diplomacy as secretary of the minister of Foreign Affairs, preparing documents on international legal aspects of the Czechoslovak issue, and engaging in international networking. Beneš, fluent in English, French, and German, served in the ministry of Foreign Affairs in the Legal and League of Nations Departments and was a member of the Czech delegation to the League Assembly in 1938. None of them accompanied the Czechoslovak exiles to Paris. However, when the German Wehrmacht took Prague in March 1939, Táborský and Beneš (independently) decided to emigrate to London, realizing that Paris' days as a safe haven to Eastern European exiles were numbered. When, after the German attack on France, the national committee under Vaclav's uncle, Edvard Beneš, moved to London, they quickly joined the Czechoslovak inner circle. Schwelb, of Jewish origin and religion, was arrested by SS troops upon their arrival in Prague in March 1939. The British embassy intervened on his behalf, presumably due to his reputation as an expert of international law. After two months of imprisonment, Schwelb and his Jewish family were allowed to leave for Great Britain. Once in London, Táborský started working as Edvard Beneš' personal assistant and legal advisor shortly after the Czechoslovak exiles settled there. In 1942, Beneš appointed Schwelb as a legal advisor to the exiled government. Beneš' nephew Vaclav first joined the ministry of Foreign Affairs and then became the leading official in the ministry of Justice.[33]

[30] Egon Schwelb, 'Crimes Against Humanity', *BYIL* 23 (1946), 178–226, at 195. For biographical information cf. his Obituary: 'Egon Schwelb, Ex Aide of U.N. Rights Division', 22 March 1979, *New York Times*, New York edition, B13.

[31] Cf. Jožka Pejskar, *Poslední pocta. Památník na zemřelé československé exulanty v letech 1948–1981* (Zurich: Konfrontace, 1982), 182.

[32] Later, he served as the first post-war envoy of Czechoslovakia in Sweden, while also contributing to discussions about the new constitution. In June 1948, he resigned and remained in exile. From 1949 he worked at universities in the United States. His major publications include: Eduard Táborský, *Edvard Beneš between East and West 1938–1948* (Stanford: Hoover Institution Press, 1981).

[33] Some might include Bohuslav Ečer (born in 1893), who had a particular position working for the ministry of Justice while at the same time being named a 'minister extraordinary and plenipotentiary', a

The Polish government in exile was advised by Manfred Lachs and Stefan Glaser, among others.[34] Glaser and Lachs were both born in Austrian Galicia, though almost a generation apart (Glaser in Tarnów, today Poland, in 1895; Lachs in Stanislawów, today Ukraine, in 1914). Glaser spent the First World War studying law in Vienna but participated in the Polish-Russian war of 1919–1920. Both gained a doctorate in law, Glaser in 1918 at Lwów University (where he later became a professor), Lachs in 1937 at Cracow's Jagiellonian University. Lachs started working for the Consular Academy of Vienna and later joined the London School of Economics. Being a Polish national, he was drafted by the Polish army during the war and served as an advisor to the Polish government in exile throughout his military service.[35] Stefan Glaser worked for the Polish ministry of Justice in 1940/41. In 1942, however, he was transferred to a diplomatic position as minister to the governments of Belgium and Luxembourg. Glaser was a member of the Council of Catholic Action in Poland.[36] Listed as official staff and then as a member of the diplomatic corps, Glaser would later enjoy diplomatic privileges (see 'Negotiating Legitimacy' later in this chapter), while the non-listed Lachs was excluded from those benefits.

Hendrik Fayat, born in 1908, became internationally known as Henri Fayat. He worked as a legal advisor for the Belgian government in exile. He had studied law in Brussels, gaining a doctoral degree. After working as a lawyer in Brussels, he followed the Belgian government into exile in 1940—first to France, then to Great Britain. From 1942 on, he worked as a legal advisor in the ministry for Foreign Affairs before he was promoted to principal private secretary (Chef de cabinet) of the ministry of Interior of the Exile government.[37] His Norwegian colleague John Lyng was born in Trondheim in 1905 and studied law at the University of Kristiania (in today's Oslo). After the outbreak of the war, Lyng supported the resistance movement. In 1943, he sought refuge in Sweden, where he joined the Norwegian legal office in Stockholm in gathering information on Norwegian collaborators for post-war trials. From 1944 on, he continued this work from London,

high diplomatic rank. He was thus acting more as a representative than a legal advisor. Cf. Kerstin von Lingen, *'Crimes against Humanity': Eine Ideengeschichte der Zivilisierung von Kriegsgewalt 1864–1945* (Schöningh: Paderborn, 2018), 225.

[34] Other names listed in LG include Witold Legowski, Jerzy Karbowski, Dr Tadeusz Mincer, and Eugeniusz Jarra.

[35] For Lachs' later career with the UN and the International Court of Justice, see: Oscar Schachter, 'The UN Years: Lachs the Diplomat', *AJIL* 87, 3 (1993), 414–16; Edward MacWhinney (ed.), *Judge Manfred Lachs and Judicial Law-Making: Opinions on the International Court of Justice, 1967–1993* (The Hague: Nijhoff, 1995).

[36] Joel Cang, *The Who's Who of the Allied Governments in Great Britain. A Handy Reference Book with information about the Allied Governments, their Forces and Institutions* (London: Allied Publication Company, 1942), 99, cf. Marcin Cieślak, 'Stefan Glaser (1895–1984)', *Państwo i Prawo* 4 (1985), 104.

[37] After the war, he remained MP for the Socialist party and very much involved in European cooperation. Maria de Waele, 'Fayat, Hendrik', in: Reginald De Schryver, Bruno De Wever,Gaston Durnez, et al. (eds.), *Nieuwe Encyclopedie van de Vlaamse Beweging* (Tielt: Lannoo, 1998), 1113–15.

now based at the Norwegian ministry of Justice.[38] In his position, he was able to add to the existing expertise provided by Terje Wold, who had taken the responsibility of Foreign Affairs.

The British advisors, who counselled the Foreign Office on how to deal with the European demands, on the other hand, belonged to the elder generation: William Malkin, legal advisor of the Foreign Office (1929–1945), was born in 1883; Eric Beckett, second legal advisor and his eventual successor, was born in 1896.[39] They belonged to different, pre-war world. The British system still functioned as planned, their institutions were intact, everybody acted—more or less, given the state of war—according to their roles. At the same time, the European governments had been shaken and reshuffled by war, their representatives had been uprooted while fleeing their country, and, in many cases, there was political instability. The British legal advisors of the Foreign Office, a group with rather similar biographic and educational background thus faced a highly diverse group of agents, uprooted, mixed, and encompassing two different age cohorts. On the political chessboard, both sides played with a very different set of rules and figurines. Even the hierarchies and roles of ministerial staff and their legal advisor or informal counsellor are rather blurred in case of these exiled governments and were subject to chance.

The work of the legal advisors in London met Madsen's definition of 'legal diplomacy'. Lawyers and/or 'legal diplomats' had a significant impact on the discussions in London. Often, when talking about international lawyers, we are looking at a closed circle of elite legal experts, mostly closely linked to diplomacy and politics. As Madsen and Dezalay point out, 'this small cosmopolitan elite enjoyed the privilege of typically being members of not only a national higher class, but also an international cosmopolitan class'.[40] However, this was only partly true for the international lawyers present in London. It is difficult to describe the international exiled lawyers active as purely elitist, upper class, and privileged. Their interaction in London meant that 'the very distinction between the international and the national—traditionally based upon the legal dichotomy between inter-state and

[38] For Lyng's later career as public prosecutor, and pro-European minister of foreign affairs see: Norsk Biografisk Leksikon Bærum Joint Parish Council. *John (Johan) Daniel Fürstenberg Lyng;* prime minister, 28 August–25 September 1963. Minister of Foreign Affairs, 12 October 1965–22 May 1970; https://www.regjeringen.no/en/the-government/previous-governments/ministries-and-offices/offices/prime-minister-since-1814/john-lyng/id463397/ (accessed 18 August 2020); *New York Times* Obituary, 19 January 1978, 19.

[39] Cf. the entries in the various Foreign Office list and diplomatic and consular yearbooks (London: Harrison and Sons, 1939–1945), Foreign Office (Establishment in London), Legal Advisers.

[40] Mikael R. Madsen, 'Legal Diplomacy: Die europäische Menschenrechtskonvention und der Kalte Krieg', in Stefan-Ludwig Hoffmann (ed.), *Moralpolitik. Geschichte der Menschenrechte im 20. Jahrhundert* (Göttingen: Wallstein, 2010), 170–1; Yves Dezalay and Mikael R. Madsen, 'The Force of Law and Lawyers: Pierre Bourdieu and the Reflexive Sociology of Law', in *Annual Review of Law and Social Science*, vol. 8 (2012), 433–52, at 440. James Loeffler, *Rooted Cosmopolitans: Jews and Human Rights in the Twentieth Century* (New Haven, CT: Yale University Press, 2018). Cf. also Oona A. Hathaway and Scott J. Shapiro, *The Internationalists and Their Plan to Outlaw War* (London: Allen Lane, 2017).

domestic affairs—was itself challenged'.[41] Most of them had arrived in London as refugees, mostly for political reasons, some also because they, like Cassin and Schwelb, were of Jewish origin. Although they employed their social capital both nationally as internationally, they did not necessarily do so intentionally. Despite all being internationally educated and belonging to academic circles, one must also not forget certain restrictions and suspicions towards foreigners at the time. Even highly esteemed international lawyer Hersch Lauterpacht, himself a frequent visitor and reporter to the London International Assembly (an assembly of Allied nations present in London, declaring themselves as an heir to the League of Nations), was confronted with these prejudices when as late as 1955, British colleagues tried to veto his nomination to the International Court of Justice on the grounds of him not being British enough and, even more suspiciously, Jewish.[42]

Negotiating Legitimacy

The ministers of justice and the governments' legal advisors in exile had a significant impact on the legal discussions during wartime—on recognition, but also on topics beyond this article's scope, such as human rights, international criminal law, and the like—in so far as they advised on their government's political decisions while at the same time intervening on its behalf in international legal circles.[43] The latter was pursued by personal networking,[44] participation in academic and semi-political exchange on legal issues, and by taking part in transnational and international committees and meetings. This might partly be explained by a certain logic intrinsic to law and legal work, but this method was also utilized as a means to a political goal. Important platforms were the London International Assembly, the Royal Institute for International Affairs/Chatham House lecture series, and academic circles such as the Cambridge International Commission for Penal Reconstruction and Development,[45] but also smaller, more specialized academic legal circles such as the International Law Association.[46] The latter, after clearance

[41] Dezalay and Madsen, 'The Force of Law' (n 40) 440.

[42] Elihu Lauterpacht, *The Life of Hersch Lauterpacht* (Cambridge: Cambridge University Press, 2010), 376ff.

[43] Cf. the work of Annette Weinke, Daniel Marc Segesser, Kerstin von Lingen, Sara Weydner, and others.

[44] Thus relying on a 'community of government international legal advisors' as pointed out by Sir Michael Wood, 'Legal Advisors', in *Max Planck Encyclopedia of Public International Law* (MPEPIL), https://opil.ouplaw.com/view/10.1093/law:epil/9780199231690/law-9780199231690-e1064 (accessed 18 August 2020).

[45] As discussed by authors listed in n 43.

[46] René Cassin's private papers speak of these allied and legal circles in London: Archives Nationales, Paris (AN), Fond René Cassin, 382 AP 66 Associations internationales alliées, 1940–1945. Doss. 3: International Law Association 1940–1943.

with the British Foreign Office legal advisor William Malkin,[47] engaged with multiple legal challenges with regard to the Allied presence in London, recognition being a central point amongst others and took to organizing closer collaboration between exiled allied academics.[48] Malkin also became involved when not directly addressed, as other British ministries sought his council in questions that could be related back to the question of legitimacy of the exiled governments.[49]

A second way to strengthen their standpoint was by publishing on questions related to their government's situation in academic journals, in newspapers, and in monographs. Academic publication became the instrument of choice in influencing the public discourse nationally (meaning within the United Kingdom) and internationally (meaning within the Allied world, as far as accessible). In particular, contributions to the *Journal of Comparative Legislation and International Law* and to *Foreign Affairs* were important to reach an international audience, to inform fellow allies, and to lobby for their own cause on both sides of the Atlantic. The latter was a well-published journal that included shorter academic articles as well as broader essays, book reviews, and current affairs contributions aimed at a broader audience. The former had originally been considered for a mostly transatlantic academic audience, but over the course of the war it focused more and more on broader European questions, including Central and Eastern Europe.[50] Between 1941 and 1946, the *Journal of Comparative Legislation and International Law* even ran a series of contributions titled 'Legislation in Exile' to which legal advisors contributed articles discussing the specifics of their national government and the questions of legitimacy and legislation in exile.

Other possible platforms included the respective national publications (all exile communities published their own national newspapers and journals in the United Kingdom), but publications in English were considered more influential—to the extent that the journal formerly known as *Hlídka Mezinárodního Práv* was transformed into the *Czechoslovak Yearbook of International Law* in 1942 to cater to a broader, more international audience. Táborský and Vaclav Beneš co-edited the

[47] W. R. Bisschop to William Malkin, 11 October 1940, AN, Fond René Cassin, 382 AP 66; Doss. 3: International Law Association 1940–1943. Bisschop was the wartime Honorary General Secretary of the ILA, originally founded in 1873 in Brussels. On the ILA also see Katharina Rietzler's chapter in this volume.

[48] Minutes International Law Conference London 10–12 July 1943 incl. Resolutions 'How far can belligerent occupation create a valid title of acquisition of rights transferable outside the occupied country and the country of the occupant?' AN, Fond René Cassin, 382 AP 66; Doss. 3: International Law Association 1940–1943.

[49] As, for example, the question of whether France should be allowed to set up Prize courts in the United Kingdom. Malkin advised to deny this, one example where *de facto* recognition did not carry the same weight as the *de jure* recognition. Note by the Foreign Office. Status and Flag of Ships of the Free French Naval Forces. (Allied Forces (Official) Committee am 3.2. (n.d.), then Meeting FO on 26.3. chaired by Sir William Malkin, Legal Adviser of the FO. AN, Fonds René Cassin, 382 AP / 32 Finances D 69 "La Marine de Guerre et la Marine Marchande".

[50] *Journal of Comparative Legislation and International Law* (JCLIL), from 1958 onwards published by Cambridge University Press on behalf of the British Institute of International and Comparative Law.

Yearbook, and, alongside Schwelb, published several articles on Czechoslovak questions.[51] While not exclusively focusing on Czechoslovak questions, it offered the possibility to present these to other experts of international law. The 1942 issue contained several articles engaging with subjects related to the Czechoslovak cause but also broader issues of international law. It served both to broaden the platform for Czechoslovak interests and as a way to integrate international scholars in a Czechoslovak discourse. The issue was led by Edvard Beneš's article, 'The Rights of Man and International Law', which was to become influential far beyond its London context and set the tone for an internationalist and reformist agenda. Beneš wrote from his position as president of the Czechoslovakian government in exile but was himself a trained jurist who had obtained his doctorate in Law in France. It was followed by a contribution by James Leslie Brierly, holder of the Chichele-Professorship of Public International Law at All Souls College, Oxford, and author of the 1928 classic, 'The Law of Nations' ('Law, Justice and War'). Eduard Táborský himself contributed the article '"Munich", the Vienna Arbitration, and International Law' reflecting on the significance and consequences of the 1938 Munich agreement for current affairs. George W. Keeton (New Commonwealth Institute for Justice and Peace) discussed the 'Legal Guarantee of Peace'. His close collaborator and frequent co-author, Georg Schwarzenberger, a German-Jewish émigré lawyer who now lectured on International Law and Relations at the University of London, reflected on 'War Crimes and the Problem of an International Police Court'. Alfred Drucker (co-editor of the *Yearbook*, while at the same time a barrister-at-law of Lincoln's Inn) wrote 'The Legislation of the Allied Powers in the United Kingdom'. René Cassin, Commissary to Justice and Public Education in the French National Committee explored 'La Position Internationale de la Tchécoslovaquie' with regard to its history, in particular to the precedence of recognizing the Czechoslovak government abroad during the First World War. The circle was completed with a contribution by Schwelb on 'The Jurisdiction over the Allied Forces in Great Britain'.[52] By bringing together renowned experts in international law from different countries with prominent figures of the Czechoslovak legal discourse and even politics, by mixing broader topics of international law with those close to Czechoslovak interests, the editors, Táborský, Drucker, and Schwelb, had landed a coup: previously a niche publication, the journal now attracted international attention in academia and beyond.[53]

[51] *Czechoslovak Yearbook of International Law*, 1942, published under the auspices of the Czechoslovak Branch of the International Law Association.

[52] Other articles were authored by Adolf Procházka, Chairman of the Supreme Legal Advisory Council of the exiled Czechoslovak Government in London, on 'Czechoslovak Philosophy of Law'; Ilia Neustadt, Regional Understandings and Federalism; Jan Vojáček, on 'Post War Tasks and Patent Legislation'; Arthur Berriedale Keith, Regius Professor of Sanskrit and Lecturer in Constitutional History in the University of Edinburgh contributed an article on 'The Sanctity of Treaties'.

[53] As documented by the review in *JCLIL* 25, 3/4 (1943), 96

Inviting these international scholars to contribute to a formerly foreign (and rather insignificant) journal was made possible by many direct personal and transnational connections between European émigré lawyers. René Cassin and Edvard Beneš, for example, had met in Geneva while representing their countries at the League of Nations. Once in London, the two of them made a point of rekindling this connection and started exchanging letters right after both were settled in London, first primarily friendly informal letters of one acquaintance (and refugee) to another. After Beneš was once again recognized as president, the letters became more official and courteous, adjusting from personal letters to diplomatic conventions required in official correspondence. Beside their shared history, they also had clear political interests in keeping this contact alive: Cassin was particularly keen to find out how the Czechoslovaks had achieved diplomatic recognition as a government by the British, which was denied to the Free French until the fall of Vichy in 1944. Beneš, on the other hand, knew he could only profit from close contacts with the Free French who, despite lacking legal recognition, had a better political standing with the British than the Czechoslovaks.[54] Accordingly, an article by renowned legal expert Cassin about the legitimacy of the Czechoslovak government in this *Yearbook* served both agendas. In all cases, the legal experts (advisors, commissaries, and ministers) tried to use the scholarly legal discussion as a tool for political lobbying to ensure legitimacy and legal status.[55] During the first half of the war (until about 1943), this strategy proved quite successful. Despite all setbacks in international politics, lawyers in the service of the exiled European governments in London were able to employ international legal questions as a means to consolidate their legitimacy.

Recognition under international law, an amelioration of their individual legal status and simulating state functions helped to consolidate the governments in exile, legitimize their politics, and increase their agency.[56] During the first months (and sometimes years) in London, recognition and equal legal status thus became the focal point of almost all legal activities of the governments in exile and the legal experts connected with them. The European exiles sought to form exile governments and have them recognized in international law to maintain national representation throughout the time of Nazi occupation and to maintain agency in national political and legal matters. Recognition promised the indication of willingness to enter

[54] See correspondance and reports in AN, Fonds Réne Cassin 382 AP/65, D 129 Tchécoslovaquie (especially Memoire relatif à la Reconnaissance du Comité National Tchécoslovaque comme gouvernement provisoire); D 129 A and D 129 B (Position juridique et internationale de la Tchécoslovaquie, including Copies de lettres echangées entre les Membre du Comité National Tchécoslovaque et les Gouvernement Francais et Britannique, 13 November 1939 to July 1941).

[55] AN, Fonds René Cassin, 382 AP 65 ; D 129 Tchécoslovaquie B: La Position Internationale de la TS—livre de M. Taborsky. Contains Cassin's manuscript as well as a copy of the printed edition, accompanied by correspondence between Cassin and Taborsky about the introduction.

[56] Stefan Talmon, *Recognition of Governments in International Law, with particular reference to Governments-in-Exile* (Oxford: Oxford University Press, 1998); Hersch Lauterpacht, *Recognition in International Law* (Cambridge: Cambridge University Press, 2012 (1947)).

into official relations. It also manifested the British opinion on the legal status of the government in question. These two notions ideally coincided, but did not necessarily do so. [57] The process of legally establishing legitimate governments was not done via mere recognition. It entailed securing the situation of their members and ensuring legislation that would allow both for harmony with British laws as well as for frictionless transfer back home after the war. The European quest for recognition was backed by British scholars, amongst them Arnold McNair, professor of international law in Cambridge, who published his legal opinion on the matter in 1940/41, expressing his viewpoint that the 'dispossessed governments' on British soil did not even need to be recognized as the British government had never discontinued contacts with them in their native lands. Despite McNair's recommendations, the Foreign Office officially recognized the governments in exile. McNair's views on two other aspects of recognition were more crucial for the wartime interaction with the allied Europeans: constitutionality and property rights. The former was relevant to the legitimacy of the governments to pass legislation and acts from foreign territory (to which he had no objection), the second to ensure the opportunity to requisition merchant ships and other property for the allied cause. The latter he saw disputed, although he argued in favour. In his article, the intermixture of international law (recognition) with constitutional law (legitimacy of heads of state and legislation) and private law (property rights) becomes obvious.[58] While the Foreign Office, in this case Malkin, was generally in favour of accepting McNair's views, it was more critical of the legitimation of foreign decrees and even demanded his essay be amended in this regard.[59]

In all cases, a formal recognition of a government in exile was required to improve their agency. Depending on the particular country's situation, this was a process which could be more complicated in some cases than others. Considering the unprecedented situation of having so many different claims to European statehood in one city, the timeline of recognition ran comparatively smoothly, as the table indicates. Luxembourg, the Netherlands, and Norway were recognized upon arrival in Great Britain, as were Yugoslavia and Greece upon their arrivals in exile (Jerusalem and Cairo, respectively). In all these cases, it was precisely because they stood in a time-honoured tradition: the British King and the British government ('His Majesty's government' or HMG, as the primary sources emphasize) acknowledged the legitimacy of monarchs going into exile; that is, the right of a monarch

[57] Talmon, *Recognition of Governments* (n 56) chapter 1, esp. 23, 29, 33.

[58] The National Archives, Kew (TNA), FO 800/899 War Opinions. April 1940 to January 1945. File No. 77 (II); 40. Pamphlet by Arnold D. McNair. Municipal Effects of Belligerent Occupation. (Reprinted by permission from the Law Quarterly Review. January 1941).

[59] TNA, FO 800/899 War Opinions. April 1940 to January 1945. File No. 77 (II); 66. Correspondence between Dr A. D. McNair and Sir W. Malkin, 5 to 7 August 1942. Revision of Dr McNair's article on Effects of Belligerent Occupation: position of decrees of exiled Allied Govts.; 69. Correspondence between Dr A. D. McNair and Sir W. Malkin (also Mr Beckett and Mr Dean) 28 October to 12 November. Further revision of Dr McNair's article, with references chiefly to foreign decrees.

temporarily to take their seat outside of their respective territory.[60] With regard to Belgium, the capitulation of the King complicated this procedure. The Belgian government in exile became officially recognized when the existing cabinet sought refuge in France (20 May 1940), despite their monarch's surrender. Their legal status and constitutional rights, however, attracted close inspection and careful consideration within the Foreign Office. As late as 1942, well into the war years, the Foreign Office Advisors debated the political position and legitimacy of the already recognized Belgian government in regard of their absent King, who remained a prisoner of war in German hands. [61]

The recognition of the republics (Poland, Czechoslovakia, and France) caused more of a predicament. How was it possible to ensure that the men claiming to represent these countries had legitimation to do so? After all, the Polish representatives in London did not constitute an elected government. Czechoslovakia was, strictly speaking, not even a state anymore. Yet, Poland was able to ensure quick recognition. Czechoslovakia, on the other hand, had to struggle for more than three years from the time of the Munich Agreement to be recognized as a National Committee (not as a government) to a *de facto* recognition in 1940 before finally becoming officially recognized in the second half of 1941. The third republican case is especially surprising. Even though de Gaulle remains the very image of allied exiles in London to this day, Free France or Fighting France was only *de facto* recognized and did not receive *de jure* recognition until the liberation of France. This meant that despite being at war with Germany, the principal allies were unwilling to withdraw legal recognition from German satellite Vichy France and Pétain. Since it was not admissible in international law for any country to have two governments, de Gaulle's Frenchmen could not be recognized.

Britain entertained regular relations with the Free French committee, however. In fact, the relations between Free France and Great Britain are a perfect example of two governments entertaining relations without official recognition of the existence of a French allied government.[62] This, however, led to a precarious legal status of de Gaulle and his men, in particular with regard to military units and the navy, as well as the showing of flags and other aspects of representation. In daily political

[60] Torsten Riotte, *Der Monarch im Exil. Eine andere Geschichte von Staatswerdung und Legitimismus im 19. Jahrhundert* (Göttingen: Wallstein, 2018); Debora Gerstenberger, *Gouvernementalität im Zeichen der globalen Krise. Der Transfer des portugiesischen Königshofes nach Brasilien* (Köln: Böhlau, 2013); Philip Mansel and Torsten Riotte (eds), *Monarchy and Exile: The Politics of Legitimacy from Marie de Medicis to Wilhelm II.* (Basingstoke: Palgrave Macmillan, 2011).

[61] TNA, FO 371/30785: Political Departments: General Correspondence from 1906–1966: Central: Belgian and Luxemburg (file C 3662/402/4) From Foreign Research and Press Service SECRET, dated 10 March 1942, rec. in reg. 7 April 1942 C: Belgium and Luxemburg 'The position of King Leopold and of the Government in Exile'. Paper prepared by the Foreign Research and Press Service discussing the position of King Leopold and of the exiled Belgian Government. (Similar papers on Belgian Maritime courts, legislative powers in Congo, constitutional power, etc.)

[62] Contrary to the more common case of recognizing a government without entering official relations. Talmon, *Recognition of Governments* (n 56) 33ff.

Table 8.4 Timeline of the recognition of governments in exile[a]

1939	1940	1941	1942	1943	1944
Poland (17.9, in France) *Czechoslovak National Committee (13.11, in France)*	Luxembourg (10.5), Netherlands (13.5) Belgium (20.5) Norway (7.6) *Free France (de facto recognition, 28.6)* *Czechoslovakia (de facto recognition by UK 21.7)*	Yugoslavia (17.4, in Jerusalem) Greece (23.5, in Cairo, Sept in London) Czechoslovakia (18.7)			France (30.9)

[a] France was first to grant continued recognition to the Polish government in exile, followed by the United States, United Kingdom, and others in early October 1939. Recognition was later officially withdrawn from the London-based exile government when the cooperation with Soviet Russia led to recognition of the Soviet-backed Warsaw government. The Czechoslovak National Committee in Paris formed on 13 November 1939 had not been successful in gaining recognition as a government. Only after fleeing France for Great Britain and within the community of the other governments in exile, a Czechoslovakian government in exile became recognized. First to recognize it was Norway (12 October 1940), Canada (12 October 1940), Poland (27 November 1940), and Belgium (13 December 1940), while the United Kingdom as its host country only officially recognized it on 18 July 1941 (after the invasion of the Soviet Union), while the *de facto* recognition had taken place on 21 July 1940, shortly after its move to London in June 1940; Cf. Talmon, *Recognition of Governments* (n 62) 291–4.

and legal life in London, Free France was treated as almost equal to the European governments in exile. Diplomatic relations were set in place, even though not via official diplomatic posts, but rather as 'representatives' and 'attachés'; French ministers were integrated in meetings as equals and joint military actions were planned, and joint allied agreements, such as the Declaration of St James, were signed as equals.

The case studies of Belgium and the republics, in particular Britain's close ally France, show that recognition was a precious and delicate state of negotiations. Legal recognition was the basis on which to enter official diplomatic relations, to exercise state functions (to raise taxes from citizens, to draw up a budget, to exercise jurisdiction), and to pass effective laws. While the Montevideo Convention of 1933 stated that recognition of an entity does not in itself make a state, its definition of statehood was quite open: it listed the existence of a government and the maintenance of international relations along with the criteria of controlling a defined population and territory. While the exiled governments had neither access nor control over their territory, and very limited access (via propaganda), but no control over their population, their activities in exile, and their insistence on maintaining diplomatic relations enabled them to fulfil some of these criteria.[63]

[63] Inter-American Convention on Rights and Duties of States [Montevideo Convention] of 26 December 1933. For the text of the Convention, see *AJIL* 28 (1934), Suppl. 75–78.

In the case of the exiled governments, recognition *was* the way to ensure the capacity to govern, since it came with British and US financial guarantees and military cooperation. Some of these functions could be ensured by *de facto* recognition, meaning that while the government in question had not been officially and legally recognized by other governments, diplomatic relations were entertained and it was integrated into international (or at least bilateral) decision-making.[64] Even before the outbreak of the Second World War, the case of the Spanish Civil War had raised the question of recognition in British jurisprudence.[65]

The European legal advisors were not the only ones intrigued by the complex situation posed by the presence of so many governments in London. The Foreign Office legal advisors were equally concerned with these challenges, as were British international lawyers such as McNair, who discussed related concerns in a pamphlet upon request from the Foreign Office.[66] McNair was not only an authority frequently consulted in these matters, but also used the pages of the *Journal of Comparative Legislation and International Law* (*JCLIL*) to discuss legal questions and challenges created by these extraordinary circumstances. The European legal advisors felt the need to continuously justify and emphasize their governments' legitimacy. A series of articles published between 1942 and 1946 in the *JCLIL* assembled the different national legal advisors, arguing their case, only Greece and Yugoslavia were not represented, the articles included explanations and always referred to the legal element. Articles were even published on the legitimacy of the monarchies, which may have been easier to reason given the personal element.

The articles each referred to the national particularities, while at the same time drawing on general argumentative concepts. As a first common argument, the articles referred to the national historical constitutional background to explain how prepared their country had been in the case of invasion and how they had planned for the legal challenge of an exile government. Discussing the situation of Luxembourg, Ernst J. Cohn emphasized that it was, in particular, the experience of the First World War which had prepared his country for legitimacy in exile. The Luxembourg constitution specifically contained the option that the seat of government might be moved abroad (Article 109), thus laying the ground for a legitimate exile government.[67] While exile was not explicitly mentioned in the Dutch case, Zeeman argued that the Dutch constitution allowed for 'emergency

[64] On definitions of *de jure* and *de facto* recognition see Talmon, *Recognition of Governments* (n 56) 59–94.

[65] Hersch Lauterpacht, 'Recognition of Insurgents as a *de facto* Government', *The Modern Law Review* 3, 1 (1939), 1–20.

[66] TNA, FO 800 / 899, War Opinions. April 1940–January 1945. File No. 77 (II) 40. Pamphlet by Arnold D. McNair. 'Municipal Effects of Belligerent Occupation. (Reprinted by permission from the Law Quarterly Review'. January 1941. McNair also refers to 'G. Effects of Acts of a Dispossessed Government, Purporting to take Effect in the United Kingdom, in Neutral Territory, or in the Home territory', 67–73.

[67] Ernst J. Cohn, 'Legislation in Exile: Luxembourg', *JCLIL* 25, 3/4 (1943), 40–6.

circumstances, which render imperative the creation of emergency law'.[68] The contribution on Belgium, authored by Henri Fayat and published only after *de jure* recognition, explained the government's legitimacy in accordance with the Belgian constitution, enabling a government in exile to assume the 'King's assent' in his absence.[69] The article by Manfred Lachs on Poland, published in 1942, was a short statement on the constitutionality of the exiled government based on the fact that the former president Moscicki had transferred his power to Raczkiewicz. This step had been duly advertised in the Polish legal gazette, thus legitimizing the latter to form a government without additional elections.[70] Egon Schwelb, publishing his article on Czechoslovakian legislation in exile in 1942, took a different angle. Perhaps still haunted by the tedious process of the only recent *de jure* recognition, he began his article by stating that '[i]t is not within the scope of the present survey of Czechoslovak exile to deal with the constitutional problems confronting the democratic State when the legislative bodies are prevented from meeting'.[71] Declaring accordance with the pre-war constitution of their countries thus laid the ground for further argument of their current exile governments' legitimacy. On the one hand, the focus on constitutional law might seem surprising, given that their desire to convince a British and international audience (political, academic, and public) might be expected to focus on international law instead. However, since the campaign for recognition, legitimacy, and statehood was considered essential to the survival of their states and nations, as well as for the safe transfer of the governments to its home country, the goal required the mobilization of all means at hand. Law was not set in stone and since nobody knew for certain which arguments would still be valid at the end of the war, it seemed sensible to explore all available avenues. In addition, the European exiles sought to assist their own return (alive and in power) to their home countries. The publications were, thus, simultaneously aimed at a war-time and at a post-war audience.

The second discursive step was to show legislative action taken in response to the outbreak of the war. Arguing the case of Luxembourg, Cohn points out that in addition to the constitutional framework, significant privileges had been granted in 1938/39 to the government, ensuring legislative power even in absence of a parliament, while at the same time delegitimizing all legislation passed by a German occupier or a 'Quisling regime'.[72]

The article on Norway, published anonymously 'for security reasons' (although probably penned by Lyng), laid out that after the German attack, the Norwegian parliament had transferred legislative powers to king and cabinet to maintain

[68] J. H. Zeeman, 'Legislation in Exile: The Netherlands', *JCLIL* 26, 3/4 (1944), quotation 7.
[69] Henri Fayat, 'Legislation in Exile: Belgium', *JCLIL* 25, 3/4 (1943), 30–40, quotation 31.
[70] Manfred Lachs, 'Polish Legislation in Exile', *JCLIL* 24, 1 (1942), 57–60, quotation 58.
[71] Egon Schwelb, 'Legislation in Exile: Czechoslovakia', *JCLIL* 24, 2 (1942), 120–4, quotation 120.
[72] Cohn, 'Legislation in Exile' (n 67) 40–4, quotations 41 and 44.

legitimacy in case of exile.[73] Lacking a parliament, the Polish government in exile opted for a national council to legitimize their actions.[74] For the Czechoslovak case, Schwelb emphasized the legitimacy of the Czechoslovak representatives (sourcing it back to its recognition as a provisional government in 1940) and underlined that by recognizing it, the Allies were aware that this must entail modified legislation.[75]

Having thus quickly established the sources of legitimacy, the articles went on to detail the possible agency, including what kind of legislation may be passed in London. For the Netherlands, the Dutch exile government could pass a so-called emergency law, which was understood quite broadly. This interpretation should become, amongst other cases, essential when discussing post-war trials against collaborators as well as the question of requisitioning merchant ships in order to secure their value for the exiled government instead of letting them be used by the German occupiers.[76] With regard to Belgium, special attention was given to the close economic, diplomatic, and political relations with Luxembourg, as well as to the Belgian Congo and Belgian maritime courts acting in the United Kingdom. Military and maritime courts were of special importance to exiled governments, allowing them to settle internal conflicts independently, as long as they did not interfere with British law (and did not extend to the use of capital punishment).[77] In the French case, all measures of the national committee were redefined as governmental actions, while at the same time all measures taken by the Vichy government were delegitimized or at least questioned.[78] For Poland, Lachs emphasized that the exiled government might accordingly affect laws with regard to 'current problems and affairs' as well as 'the future problems of Poland, in particular questions which will arise after the invader is cleared from Polish soil'.[79]

Last but not least, the articles about legislation in exile served not only the national cause but aimed to contribute to the broader legal debate on legitimacy in international law. In his article on the Netherlands' case, J. H. Zeeman focused on the legitimacy of law-making in exile, a topic which would indeed prove to be a bone of contention in the Dutch case. Discussing whether or not Royal Decrees passed in exile had validity for the home country, he referred to McNair as well as to the other articles on allied legislation listed here.[80] Schwelb's article on Czechoslovakia makes many references to other allied governments, notably stressing the Czechoslovak case not as part of the rule but rather as an exemption to it.[81] Like Schwelb, Payn chose to emphasize early recognition, without focusing

[73] Anon., 'Legislation in Exile: Norway', *JCLIL* 24, 2 (1942).
[74] Lachs, 'Polish Legislation in Exile' (n 70) 58.
[75] Schwelb, 'Legislation in Exile' (n 71) 120.
[76] Zeeman, 'Legislation in Exile' (n 68) 7.
[77] Fayat, 'Legislation in Exile' (n 69) 31.
[78] Benjamin R. Payn, 'French Legislation in Exile', *JCLIL* 28, 3/4 (1946).
[79] Lachs, 'Polish Legislation in Exile' (n 70) 58.
[80] Zeeman, 'Legislation in Exile' (n 68) 7.
[81] Schwelb, 'Legislation in Exile' (n 71) 120.

on the exact definition of what exactly was recognized, thus stressing a continuous legitimacy of Free/Fighting France through the war.

Most of these articles were written by the official legal advisors of the European governments during the war, even though they were clearly also aimed at a post-war audience. Payn's article on France constitutes an exception amidst the others as first, it was published only after the war, in 1946.[82] Second, Payn was not a legal scholar. In fact, he was an economist engaging in international relations.[83] Ernst Cohn, on the other hand, was indeed a respected legal scholar, albeit without any closer connection to Luxemburg. Born in Breslau (today's Wrocław), he came to exile in London as a German-speaking Jewish refugee, serving in the British army during the Second World War.[84] J. H. Zeeman, acting deputy prosecutor at the Dutch Court in London from 1942, had been named secretary of the Netherlands War Crimes Commission (NWCC), the national sub-section of the United Nations War Crimes Commission (UNWCC), in 1944.[85]

The *JCIL* articles, interestingly published after the official procedure of legal recognition, show that first, recognition needed to be justified, promoted, and publicized both to a British and a continental academic and political audience. How important this support was became a bitter truth for the Polish government in exile in 1945, when Great Britain withdrew its recognition and installed the Interim Treasury Committee for Polish Affairs to take over their documents, making sure that papers, power, and buildings were handed over to the new Soviet-backed government. Second, legal advisors felt the need to spell out what recognition entailed with regard to legislative, judicial, and executive functions as well as with regard to chronological (will decisions continue to be valid after the war?) and geopolitical (will decisions affect the home territory, the colonies, etc?) issues.

On the British side, exactly how much recognition and agency should be granted was debated. Some, mostly international legal experts like Arnold McNair, had been forthcoming in their interpretation of the Europeans' status. Others, in particular politicians, had been more hesitant with their acceptance but were won over by constant lobbyism on behalf of the Europeans. To take the example of Alexander Cadogan, under-secretary for Foreign Affairs, who in his diaries in December 1940 still supported the idea to grant recognition to small European nations only under the premise that they should take the status of British dominions—a

82 Payn, 'French Legislation in Exile' (n 78).

83 Much in line with some of the other authors, though, he was born in Eastern Europe: in Swir, then Russia, today's Lithuania. 'Paid Notice: Payn, Benjamin Robert', *The New York Times*, 21 April 2004, B0009.

84 From 1944 onwards, he was responsible for the British Library of German Law. Cf. Werner Lorenz, 'Ernst J. Cohn (1904–1976)', in Jack Beatson and Reinhard Zimmermann (eds), *Jurists Uprooted: German-Speaking Émigré Lawyers in Twentieth-Century Britain* (Oxford: Oxford University Press, 2004), 325–44; Ronald Graveson, 'Ernst Joseph Cohn 1904–1976', in *Rabels Zeitschrift für ausländisches und internationales Privatrecht* 41, 2 (1977), 233–5.

85 Nederlandsche Commissie inzake Oorlogsmisdrijven (NCO) or Netherlands War Crimes Commission (NWCC).

proposition introduced, amongst others, by Trygve Lie.[86] Discussions over the following months were able to turn him into an ardent promoter of this cause, even supporting the recognition of the Czechoslovak state, the frailest composition in the London microcosm.[87] A constant flow of European visitors to his office, combined with regular invitations to embassy dinners and business lunches attested by his diaries (unfortunately, mostly vanished from the edited version), assumingly played their part in changing his mind.

Ensuring legitimate governance by diplomatic recognition was just the first step, all further details were up for legal interpretation—and thus negotiation. Recognition, formerly a diplomatic matter, had become highly susceptible to political considerations, turning it into a plaything of power politics and so ceasing to be a purely and objectively clear legal affair. Paradoxically, while this in the long term reduced the influence of legal advisors as opposed to politicians, it increased their influence in the short term. Facing uncertainty, legal advisors on all sides seized their opportunity to try and influence the game, to shift the scales towards their own agenda.

Conclusion

The transfer of nine Continental European governments to Great Britain (eight recognized governments in exile plus the Free French) created a legal anomaly. London became the seat of government of now ten European countries. The impact on the British capital was palpable, not only with regard to the cityscape and the people strolling through Hyde Park but also with regard to the legal situation. Immigration law had to be updated to receive allied refugees and, more specifically, members of government. Conventional diplomatic law (as well as diplomatic practices) was bent to accommodate heads of states, ministers, and their staff. Legal experts were at the centre of all these discussions. The legal advisors of the exiled European governments counselled their cabinets on the legal framework they were working in and lobbied on their behalf for further recognition and improvement of their legal status. Their regular addressees in this regard were the legal advisors of the Foreign Office. It is striking that while this situation was such an exemption to the political and legal 'normality', taking place during the turmoil of war, there was no attempt to treat it as an exceptional situation, to look for short-term solutions, or simply sit it out and tolerate the governments in London without officially recognizing them. Instead, situations were carefully assessed to estimate their legal

[86] Churchill Archives Centre (CAC)/ADAC/1/9, 16 December 1940: 'wrote a minute to H. about Lie's broadcast—which is on the right lines—recognition on the part of small European nations that they must be British dominions'.
[87] CAC/ADAC/1/10, 17 July 1941.

requirements. Within the London microcosm, legal experts and legal advisors took a special position: on the one hand, they provided legal knowledge to their governments, advising on their political decisions, and lobbying on behalf of their cause. On the other hand, many of these exiled legal experts quickly and increasingly became involved in personal and transnational exchange on legal issues. National legal discussions and their platforms were transferred onto a larger international—and English-speaking—stage. Laws were revised and adjusted. British laws were changed to accommodate the European exiles; the exiles changed national laws to secure continued war capability financially and militarily and to prepare for their post-war return. Positively speaking, the negotiation processes ensured the exiled governments' representation and legitimate agency. At the same time, these negotiation processes were problematic in the ways they sought to achieve legitimacy in at least two ways. First, boundaries between official and unofficial legal experts became blurred, national political interests and academic discourse were increasingly intertwined. Second, these negotiation processes were only partly democratic as none of the exiled governments could renew their democratic legitimacy during the war by holding elections or even simply consulting with a full functioning, properly elected parliament. Expertise and legal arguments took the place of democratic validation to ensure legitimacy, which would in all probability open up new problems once the exile governments prepared to return home.[88]

Recognition proved to be even more than Churchill had accounted for in his letter to Roosevelt. As we have seen, recognition largely depended on legal definitions as well as on the political will to acknowledge the importance of international law in troubled times. Via informal legal diplomacy, the exiled governments were able to, at least temporarily, negotiate a position of legitimized agency in exile. While they surely were not recognized as emperors—to come back to Churchill's quotation—the governments in exile and their legal advisors made an effort to be recognized as more than a grocer, and increasingly to improve their position in a continuous struggle for legitimacy.

[88] For a similar phenomenon cf. Antoine Vauchez, 'The Appeal of Independence: Exploring Europe's Way of Political Legitimacy'. Available at SSRN: https://ssrn.com/abstract=2881913 (accessed 18 August 2020), 3 or Antoine Vauchez, *Brokering Europe. Euro-lawyers and the Making of a Transnational Polity* (Cambridge: Cambridge University Press, 2015).

9

Changing Hats

Nuremberg's Visible College and the Politics of Internationalism, 1941–1949

Kim Christian Priemel

Oscar Schachter's famous notion of international lawyers forming an 'invisible college', bound together by a common epistemology as much as by a set of professional values and internationalist ethics, has long entered jurisprudential folklore.[1] Schachter, and many other jurists with him, appreciates that lawyers wear different hats at different times and that international law means many things to many people.[2] How many hats there are to wear and what lawyers actually think of international law, however, is a complicated issue and often lost in labels which conceal rather than reveal lines of division, shifting loyalties, and uncertain professional identities. Or, to stick to the hat metaphor, not only are there different types (or are the same style, yet are of different fabrics), they serve different purposes, they can be replaced, they come in different sizes, and some go out of fashion while others linger on.

A paradigmatic example in which the professional label obscures variety and differentiation is the blanket term of 'the Nuremberg lawyers' as a collective category for the several hundreds of jurists at work before, during, and after the proceedings of the International Military Tribunal (IMT) and the Nuernberg Military Tribunals (NMT) from 1945 to 1949.[3] Previous research, of course, has not claimed

[1] Oscar Schachter, 'The Invisible College of International Lawyers', *Northwestern University Law Review* 72 (1977), 217–25; see the specially themed *Proceedings of the Annual Meeting (American Society of International Law)*, 95 (2001), as well as Santiago Villapando, The 'Invisible College of International Lawyers' Forty Years Later, *ESIL Conference Paper Series* 3 (2013), 1–15. Cf. Peggy McGuinness, 'Jose Alvarez on the Internet, Blogging, and the Democratization of the "Invisible College" of International Lawyers', http://opiniojuris.org/2007/11/09/jose-alvarez-on-the-internet-blogging-and-the-democratization-of-the-invisible-college-of-international-lawyers/ (accessed 18 August 2020).

[2] See, for example, Carlo Focarelli, *International Law as Social Construct: The Struggle for Global Justice* (Oxford: Oxford University Press, 2012).

[3] With a variety of meanings, for example, Charles Strahan, 'Finale in Nuremberg', *The Central European Observer* 23 (1946), 297–8; Linda S. Bishai, 'Leaving Nuremberg: America's Love/Hate Relationship with International Law', *Review of International Studies* 34 (2008), 425–43, 440; Anton Weiss-Wendt, *The Soviet Union and the Gutting of the UN Genocide Convention* (Madison, WI: University of Wisconsin Press, 2017), 271; Jonathan A. Bush, 'Nuremberg and Beyond: Jacob Robinson. International Lawyer', *Loyola International and Comparative Law Review* 39 (2017), 259–86, 261. In his prosopographic study, *Le moment Nuremberg. Le procès international, les lawyers et la*

Kim Christian Priemel, *Changing Hats* In: *Crafting the International Order.* Edited by: Marcus M. Payk and Kim Christian Priemel, Oxford University Press (2021). © The Several Contributors. DOI: 10.1093/oso/9780198863830.003.0009

that all jurists belonged to one and the same Nuremberg college—incidentally, itself fairly visible—but has instead focused on individual biographies or groups along national lines: US prosecutors, French attorneys and judges, or German defence counsel.[4] These studies provide a helpful starting point for the following chapter on taxonomy which approaches the lawyers working or involved in Nuremberg from three perspectives. First, with an eye to the discord among and the varying intellectual and professional trajectories of lawyers who were, in a Bourdieuan sense, both the 'operators of international law' and 'the entrepreneurs building' the new legal field of international criminal justice.[5] Second, by inquiring into the presuppositions and premises these people brought to their jobs, their motivations, tenets, and self-perception. In short, by taking seriously 'the phenomenological lives of [law's] practitioners'[6] we may differentiate, perhaps even dissolve the umbrella term of 'Nuremberg lawyers' as well as those employed elsewhere. Rather than accepting the 'folk concept' of a profession as a clearly defined group with a common function within the social field of law the present chapter asks how and which groups were formed and reformed.[7] Thus, third, analysing the cast of lawyers in the Nuremberg courtrooms and behind the scenes also cautions us to historicize our own construction of Nuremberg's law(yers) as an object of academic study as well as to be mindful of how their conflicting views of 'Nuremberg' are reflected in our own understanding of its alleged legacies.[8]

While the term 'lawyer' obscures crucial differences and fault lines, equally common (and often binary) distinctions between 'practitioners' and 'theorists', 'politicians' and 'bureaucrats', or between nationalities offer neat categories which run the risk of failing to account for the in-between spaces in which many legal protagonists were moving. This chapter therefore sets out to identify and sort protagonists by the discrete and contingent contexts in which they were contributing

question raciale (Paris: Presses de Sciences Po, 2019), 21f., 215, Guillaume Mouralis arrives at a total of 3,000 people at all trials, of whom less than a third were trained lawyers.

[4] See, for example, Christoph Safferling and Philipp Graebke, 'Strafverteidigung im Nürnberger Hauptkriegsverbrecherprozess. Strategien und Wirkung', *Zeitschrift für die Gesamte Strafrechtswissenschaft* 123 (2011), 47–81; Jonathan A. Bush, 'New Dealer, Flüchtlinge und Radikale? Die Nürnberger Ankläger im Profil', in Kim C. Priemel and Alexa Stiller (eds), *NMT. Die Nürnberger Militärtribunale zwischen Geschichte, Gerechtigkeit und Rechtschöpfung* (Hamburg: Hamburger Edition, 2013), 547–85; Hubert Seliger, *Politische Anwälte? Die Verteidiger der Nürnberger Prozesse* (Baden-Baden: Nomos, 2016); Matthias Gemählich, *Frankreich und der Nürnberger Prozess gegen die Hauptkriegsverbrecher 1945/46* (Frankfurt: Lang, 2018), 105–60.

[5] Quotation from Yves Dezalay and Mikael Rask Madsen, 'The Force of Law and Lawyers: Pierre Bourdieu and the Reflexive Sociology of Law', *Annual Review of Law and Social Science* 8 (2012), 433–52, 444.

[6] Martti Koskenniemi, *The Gentle Civilizer of Nations: The Rise and Fall of International Law 1870–1960* (Cambridge: Cambridge University Press, 2002), 7.

[7] Pierre Bourdieu and Loïc J. D. Wacquant, *An Invitation to Reflexive Sociology* (Chicago, IL: University of Chicago Press, 1992), 242f.

[8] For a conceptualization of Bourdieu's rudimentary sociology of law see the excellent exposition by Dezalay and Madsen, 'Force of Law' (n 5) 433–52.

to the trials and by their ambition to rebuild international relations through the medium of law. Three major groups, each requiring further discrimination, can be distinguished. First come the institution builders, the lawyers who set down the rules and established the necessary organizations to run criminal trials under international law. They fell into three camps: (i) the jurisprudential establishment, united by its academic standing, yet divided along philosophical and practical lines; (ii) the newcomers to the study of international criminal law, often practitioners from outside the field; and (iii) the negotiators who created the actual tribunal(s). Second, there were the courtroom lawyers (and their respective aides) who conducted the actual proceedings and who were subdivided by their discrete judicial functions: (iv) the prosecutors who pursued goals beyond winning guilty verdicts, notably to establish precedent and to provide authoritative narratives; (v) the Allied judges who, on average, were less invested in the evolution of international law and whose priority was to preserve the trials' procedural integrity; and (vi) the defence counsel who had clients to serve yet who, for political reasons, were often eager to attack the tribunals' legality and legitimacy even if that made winning cases still more difficult. Third, Nuremberg's significance was determined by a heterogenous lot of 'peer reviewers': while the critics (vii), in particular a small but conspicuous cohort of jurists turned international relations scholars, conceived of the road to Nuremberg as a dead end, the legacy workers (viii) sought to stake their interpretative claims and place the trials on an evolutionary path towards international criminal justice.

Two caveats are in order. The above distinctions serve heuristic purposes but are far from rigid. Boundaries between one group and the other blur on closer inspection as different axes of categorization (status, judicial function, schools of thought) crossed specific contexts. Differences in training and professional experience, biographical and disciplinary background, normative inclinations, individual ambitions, and concrete jobs played out within all groups. And while the available prosopographic data on the Nuremberg personnel has increased enormously over the past years, more profound analyses of careers and convictions are still scarce. Accordingly, the following is, perhaps more than usual, preliminary and subject to revision.

The Institution Builders
Academic Establishment Lawyers

By the latter half of the Second World War, there was little doubt among international law scholars that their expertise would be requested sooner or later.[9]

[9] For the interrelation of scholarly, advisory, and political work see Benjamin Coates's chapter in this volume.

Speaking before the American Society of International Law in 1943, Charles Cheney Hyde, professor of law and diplomacy at Columbia University and author of a widely read international law handbook, told his colleagues that it 'whets the zeal for victory when among the main war aims is declared to be the punishment through channels of justice of those who have been guilty of war crimes'.[10] Hyde struck a much more hopeful note than his colleague Philip Jessup who, shortly after the onset of war, had lamented the League of Nations' failure to establish viable instruments of crisis management in general and to enforce the Kellogg–Briand Pact against aggressive war in particular. '[I]nternational law plods on its way', Jessup had written mournfully, 'followed automatically in routine affairs, invoked, flouted, codified, flouted again but yet again invoked.' His modest effort to retain some hope—'But can one say that the international law ... has no reality?'—sounded more like a dirge than a clarion call.[11] Jessup, of course, had written during the early triumphs of the German advance in Europe whereas Hyde spoke after the tide had turned, and he was not alone. Quincy Wright, who taught law and international relations at Chicago, now foresaw the opportunity to take up the thread of international criminal justice which had been abandoned in 1920 when the Entente powers had failed to prosecute the Kaiser, instead allowing the trials before the Imperial Court at Leipzig to develop into a farce.[12]

However, Hyde, Jessup, and Wright would soon part company when it came to how exactly justice should be dispensed by the victorious Allies, especially with an eye to the means and scope of prosecution. Hyde and Jessup, along with their British and French colleagues (and British Foreign Office and Quai d'Orsay advisers, respectively) William Malkin and Jules Basdevant, preferred to stick to those rules of *jus in bello* which had been enshrined in the Hague Conventions and related agreements,[13] which they viewed as providing an uncontroversial basis in positive law. In contrast, Wright deemed it both possible and inevitable to institutionalize international criminal law further. In his opus magnum, *A Study of War* (1942), he did the theoretical groundwork for a juridification of international politics and especially the illegalization of aggressive war. Building on earlier writings[14] Wright hoped that 'technological internationalism', that is, modernity's

[10] Charles Cheney Hyde, 'Punishment of War Criminals', *American Society of International Law Proceedings* 37 (1943), 39–58, at 45. Cf. Daniel Marc Segesser, *Recht statt Rache oder Rache durch Recht? Die Ahndung von Kriegsverbrechen in der internationalen wissenschaftlichen Debatte 1872–1945* (Paderborn: Schöningh, 2010), 335f.

[11] Philip C. Jessup, 'The Reality of International Law', *Foreign Affairs* 18 (1939–40), 244–53, at 253.

[12] Quincy Wright, 'War Criminals', *AJIL* 39 (1945), 257–85.

[13] Representing his government, Basdevant agreed to an international tribunal; on his position within French diplomacy, his methodical formalism, and his deep scepticism of transcending national sovereignty by means of international institution building, see Marcus M. Payk, *Frieden durch Recht? Der Aufstieg des modernen Völkerrechts und der Friedensschluss nach dem Ersten Weltkrieg* (Berlin: de Gruyter, 2018), 114, 134; cf. Koskenniemi, *Gentle Civilizer* (n 6) 312f.; Mouralis, *Moment* (n 3) 75f.; Gemählich, *Frankreich* (n 4) 51–5.

[14] Quincy Wright, 'The Outlawry of War', *AJIL* 19 (1925), 80–3.

manifold economic and technological cross-connections, would help overcome political nationalism. In this process, the role of the law was that of a mediator and tool which the Chicago professor, in the vernacular of nineteenth-century liberal legalism, described as 'the philosophy of human progress and human welfare'.[15]

Yet it would be misleading to think of Wright as naïve: his argument was an explicit appraisal of the disasters of the 1930s. For the very reason that the policy of appeasement had dramatically failed in Manchuria, Abyssinia, and Czechoslovakia, Wright explained, a much firmer policy toward aggressive governments was required. More comprehensive international jurisdiction therefore was but a part of the future international regime of which 'political legislation' was the other half. Importantly, Wright spoke of 'governments' and 'individuals' rather than of 'states', indicating that the ambition to let sanctions of concrete misconduct not be hindered by abstract categories.[16] Accordingly Wright welcomed efforts to abandon traditional defences rooted in the idea of national sovereignty such as superior orders, acts of state, and the immunity of heads of state.[17]

If such sweeping innovation made some of his colleagues at home uncomfortable, Wright could find comfort in the fact that across the Atlantic Hersch Lauterpacht, the Whewell Professor of International Law at Cambridge was thinking along similar lines and made pertinent changes to the sixth edition of *Oppenheim's International Law*, the pre-eminent international law handbook of its day.[18] Casting Lauterpacht in the role of the legal entrepreneur, a creative destroyer of old concepts, seems a little odd though. Conservative by inclination, Lauterpacht's thinking was steeped deeply in Victorian traditions of legal cosmopolitanism, and his forays into the war crimes debate were meant to reverse the retrogression caused by two world wars. Innovating international criminal law was not about disrupting established concepts, or about breaking away from well-tried interpretations. It was about continuing the progressive juridification of politics and war and adapting to changing circumstances, a path which he considered consistent with the Grotian tradition.[19] In a triad of ground-breaking articles whose language betrayed how urgent their author felt about these issues—'the individual human being . . . is the ultimate unit of law'—Lauterpacht laid the foundations for a

[15] Quincy Wright, *A Study of War*, vol. 2 (Chicago, IL: University of Chicago Press, 1942), 979, 1010, 1352.

[16] Ibid., 1314–46.

[17] Quincy Wright, 'Review of Glueck, War Criminals', *University of Chicago Law Review* 12 (1945), 296–9.

[18] Hersch Lauterpacht (r/ed.), *Oppenheim's International Law*, 2 vols., 6th edn (London: Longmans, 1944/1947); Lauterpacht revised the topical second volume on 'Disputes, War and Neutrality' first, then volume 1 on 'Peace'.

[19] Hersch Lauterpacht, 'International Law after the Covenant' (1936), in *International Law. Being the Collected Papers of Hersch Lauterpacht*, vol. 2 (Cambridge: Cambridge University Press, 1975), 145–58, and his 'The Grotian Tradition in International Law', *BYIL* 23 (1946), 1–54. The Grotian analogy was also drawn by Lord Phillimore, 'An International Criminal Court and the Resolutions of the Committee of Jurists', *BYIL* 3 (1922–23), 79–86; cf. Koskenniemi, *Gentle Civilizer* (n 6) 355f.

post-war international jurisdiction of war crimes and crimes against peace, as they would come to be called, and outlined general principles of 'the rights of man'.[20]

The nexus between theoretical and practical work was particularly intense in Lauterpacht's case. His work was instrumental in revising the British Army's Land Warfare Manual, eliminating superior orders as a valid defence of war crimes, and his 1944 article on the matter grew out of a memorandum, submitted two years earlier to the Commission for Penal Reconstruction and Development's committee for war crimes. The committee, along with the London International Assembly and the United Nations War Crimes Commission, served as a clearing house for jurists to discuss the state of international criminal law and conceptualize post-war measures of legal redress. These institutions also brought together established authorities including René Cassin and Arnold McNair with newcomers to the international arena such as Marcel de Baer (a judge at the Court of Appeal in Brussels), Bohuslav Ečer (a solicitor and municipal official from Brno), and André Gros (a French legal advisor who had previously taught in Brazil).[21]

That these men—women were all but absent—sat on the same commission did not mean that they were in agreement. Differences in terms of academic status and professional prestige were not only not transcended by a common endeavour to bring about justice, they were actively employed to score points, as a spat between the juridically conservative, former Cambridge don McNair and the Czech exile Ečer, intent on seeking out the opportunities of international law rather than its limitations, amply illustrated.[22] Yet, those very disagreements helped bridge gaps of knowledge and terminology between continental, British, North American, and even Soviet legal thinking. There, it was first and foremost Aron N. Trainin who engaged with and was engaged by his English and French-speaking colleagues. The closest there was to an official Soviet spokesman on international law, Trainin had been instrumental in replacing orthodox Leninist views of (international) law as a bourgeois tool of class warfare by a more pragmatic interpretation as a necessary medium for communication among states and orderly international relations. While his 1930s publications had gone largely unnoted abroad, the 1943 *Hitlerite Responsibility under Criminal Law* became a major influence on the debate on war

[20] See his 'Grotian Tradition', 'The Law of Nations, the Law of Nature and the Rights of Man', *Transactions of the Grotius Society* 29 (1943), 1–33, 31, and 'The Law of Nations and the Punishment of War Crimes', *BYIL* 21 (1944), 58–95, 58.

[21] See Segesser, *Recht* (n 10) 318–26; Arieh J. Kochavi, *Prelude to Nuremberg. Allied War Crimes Policy and the Question of Punishment* (Chapel Hill, NC: University of North Carolina Press, 1998), 92–138; Antonin Tisseron, *La France et le procès de Nuremberg. Inventer le droit international* (Paris: Prairies Ordinaires, 2014), 40–5, 114f.; Marie-Anne Weisers, *La justice belge, les bourreaux allemands et la Shoah* (Brussels: Editions de l'Université de Bruxelles, 2020), 54f., 71–4. Cf. Matthew Garrod, 'The British Influence on the Laws of War and the Punishment of War Criminals. From the Grotius Society to the United Nations War Crimes Commission', in Robert McCorquodale and Jean-Pierre Gauci (eds), *Contemporary Perspectives on British Influences on International Law* (Leiden: Brill, 2016), 317–65. See also Julia Eichenberg's chapter in this volume.

[22] Mouralis, *Moment* (n 3) 42–4; Segesser, *Recht* (n 10) 359f.

crimes. Translated into French and English, it was disseminated in London's war-time fora of international lawyers where European and US scholars found that there was much common ground with the Soviet side when it came to defining war crimes, atrocities committed against civilians, and even aggressive war.[23]

Several of the figures involved, notably Trainin and Lauterpacht, would become directly involved in the post-war trials. Lauterpacht would serve in a dual capacity: as an official member of the British War Crimes Executive (BWCE) at the IMT and as unofficial adviser to Robert H. Jackson, the Supreme Court judge made US chief prosecutor.[24] This connection with Jackson went back to 1940 when the British jurist had provided the then US Attorney General with legal expertise to back up claims that US Lend-Lease agreements were not flouting the rules of neutrality. He argued in effect that the 1925 Kellogg–Briand Pact provided a valid stipulation of the illegality of aggressive war whereby 'the historic foundation of the duty of impartiality' disappeared. His general point that '[t]here are obvious limits to the protection which the law grants to the lawbreaker' anticipated future German complaints about retroactive jurisdiction.[25]

In the summer of 1945, during the London Conference which drafted the IMT Charter, Jackson paid Lauterpacht a visit and brought back the notion of 'crimes against humanity'—itself a product of the multilateral talks at Cambridge and London during the war—to replace 'atrocities' as the legal term for crimes against civilians, including those against Jews.[26] The IMT constituted, in Lauterpacht's eyes, a 'contribution of enduring value to the cause of justice and of the authority of the law'. To his wife, the jurist confided his 'great satisfaction to watch the faces of the accused when Jackson was unfolding the story of the Jewish atrocities... It was an unforgettable experience to see, for the first time in history, a sovereign State in the dock.'[27]

[23] A. N. Trainin, *Hitlerite Responsibility under Criminal Law* (London: Hutchinson, 1945); Report made by Dr Ečer on Professor Trainin's Book at the Commission's Meeting of 31 October 1944, 11 November 1944, Harry S. Truman Presidential Library, Independence (HSTL), Samuel Rosenman Papers, Box 10, F. 'War Crimes File 2; cf. Francine Hirsch, *Soviet Judgment at Nuremberg. A New History of the International Military Tribunal after World War II* (Oxford: Oxford University Press, 2020), 35–8; Irina Schulmeister-André, *Internationale Strafgerichtsbarkeit unter sowjetischem Einfluss. Der Beitrag der UdSSR zum Nürnberger Hauptkriegsverbrecherprozess* (Berlin: Duncker & Humblot, 2016), 43–68, 210–12.

[24] See Elihu Lauterpacht, *The Life of Hersch Lauterpacht* (Cambridge: Cambridge University Press, 2010), 177f., 188f., 271–96; Mouralis, *Moment* (n 3) 32.

[25] Memorandum on Principles in International Law Involved in U.S. Measures against Germany between September 1940 and December 1941, Library of Congress, Washington, DC (LoC), Robert H. Jackson Papers, Box 29, F.6. See also Jackson's correspondence with Lauterpacht of 21 December 1941 and 5 January 1942: ibid., Box 15, F.7.

[26] Kim Christian Priemel, *The Betrayal. The Nuremberg Trials and German Divergence* (Oxford: Oxford University Press, 2018), 79 (fn. 87), 85f. On the intense and complex debate, see Kerstin von Lingen, *'Crimes against Humanity.' Eine Ideengeschichte der Zivilisierung von Kriegsgewalt 1864–1945* (Paderborn: Schöningh, 2018).

[27] Quoted from Lauterpacht, *Life* (n 24) 272, 277.

Lauterpacht's turn to the courtroom was mirrored by that of Hans Kelsen, his former Vienna teacher and now an expatriate at Berkeley. But the dean of positivism, best known for his *Reine Rechtslehre* (often misunderstood to be an apologia of apolitical jurisprudence, although it was anything but), was less sanguine when it came to applying new norms. Indeed, much of his writing in the 1940s was concerned with questions of international law[28] and the urgency of Kelsen's language articulated that this was far more than an academic matter to him.[29] To his programmatic *Peace Through Law*, Kelsen added an emotional preface which stipulated that there 'are truths which are so self-evident that they must be proclaimed again and again in order not to be doomed to oblivion. Such a truth is: that war is mass murder, the greatest disgrace of our culture, and that to secure world peace is our foremost political task.' Yet despite the book's simplistic title, Kelsen did not have much faith in a world parliament that would legislate away international conflict. On the contrary, he understood inter-allied agreements such as the 1943 Moscow Declaration as a more viable alternative. With no supranational government in sight, Kelsen argued, an international court would stand a better chance of succeeding, as the act of delegation did not imply any abrogation of sovereign rights.[30]

Promoting the punishment of war crimes and aggression was therefore both an ethical obligation and a legal necessity, and Kelsen's doctrinal services were drawn upon by the US Army's Judge Advocate General and the Nuremberg staff. Continuing his monistic view of international law, he was able to promote war crimes proceedings by pointing out there were no gaps between the national and the international sphere, only political shortcomings in stipulating positive law and sanctioning transgressions. In order to punish 'the authors of the second World War, the persons morally responsible for one of the greatest crimes in the history of mankind', Kelsen supported notions of individual liability under international law and was instrumental—through his much-contested condominium theory—in establishing Allied jurisdiction in Germany and over Germans. He even accommodated views that the Kellogg–Briand Pact had rendered aggressive war illegal.[31]

[28] Hans Kelsen, *Vergeltung und Kausalität. Eine soziologische Untersuchung* (The Hague: Stockum, 1941); 'Collective and Individual Responsibility in International Law with Particular Regard to the Punishment of War Criminals', *California Law Review* 31 (1943), 530–71; *Peace through Law* (Chapel Hill, NC: University of North Carolina Press, 1944); 'The Legal Status of Germany according to the Declaration of Berlin', *AJIL* 39 (1945), 518–26.

[29] See the Rooseveltian opening sentence of Kelsen's *Collective Security under International Law* (Washington, DC: GPO, 1957), 1: 'Security is the condition of being protected against, or not exposed to, a danger.'

[30] Kelsen, *Peace through Law* (n 28) vii–viii, 19f., 42–5. Cf. Jochen von Bernstorff, *The Public International Law Theory of Hans Kelsen. Believing in Universal Law* (Cambridge: Cambridge University Press, 2011), 191–224.

[31] Kelsen to Lippmann, 26 November 1945, Yale University Library, Manuscripts and Archives, New Haven (YULMA), Walter Lippmann Papers, Reel 71, Box 81, F.1199; The Rule Against Ex Post Facto Laws and the Prosecution of the Axis War Criminals, Cornell Law Library, Ithaca, NY (CLL), Donovan Nuremberg Trials Collection, XIX, 62.01.03; The Legal Status of Germany according to the Declaration

But as a positivist, Kelsen's flexibility went only so far. The Pact's statement of illegality was not the same as criminalizing wars of aggression, and there were also problems of municipal laws' potential priority and defences such as 'acts of state'. Unlike Wright and Lauterpacht, Kelsen struggled, evidently wanting to see those responsible for severe crimes stand trial but also looking for a basis in statutory or customary law. The result was a less than consistent argument: the ban on *ex post facto* laws, including the disregard for acts of state or superior orders, was valid unless a treaty stipulated the legal criminality of an act already regarded as ethically wrong, thereby 'transform[ing] moral into a legal responsibility'. Admittedly, no such agreement existed in the German case but as *de facto* sovereigns the Allies could proceed anyway, Kelsen concluded.[32]

Juridical Outsiders and International Newcomers

Kelsen's reasoning had an unmistakable smack of natural law, betraying a willingness to concede doctrinal points for the benefit of justice and to help the development of international law, showing him to be, *like* Lauterpacht and Wright, a proponent of an evolutionary, expansive international legal order.[33] Their words, and those of others such as Trainin, mattered: eminent, well-established scholars, they had been dealing with international law since before the war, and they would continue their reflections and reformist suggestions long after the Nuremberg trials had come to an end. Their basic research clarified first principles and provided the framework for the post-war trials.

No less essential were the contributions made by several new arrivals on the jurisprudential scene. Some were academics in their own right, others were practitioners who joined the project for a brief time only. Among the former was Sheldon Glueck, a criminologist who had earned his reputation by studying juvenile delinquency and now moved into the international law arena of his own accord.[34] Reading up on as well as teaching on the subject, Glueck became deeply involved in war crimes questions from at least 1941. Convinced that the 'silly performance' of Leipzig must not be repeated, he contacted various government departments to

of Berlin, undated, LoC, Jackson Papers, Box 104, F. 'Individual Responsibility'; cf. Bernstorff, *Public International Law* (n 30) 147f., 198.

[32] Kelsen, 'Collective and Individual Responsibility' (n 28) 538–58, 545; Kelsen, *Peace through Law* (n 28) 81–91.

[33] Jochen von Bernstorff, 'Kelsen und das Völkerrecht: Rekonstruktion einer völkerrechtlichen Berufsethik', in Robert Walter, Clemens Jabloner, and Klaus Zeleny (eds), *Hans Kelsen und das Völkerrecht* (Vienna: Manz, 2004), 143–67.

[34] John Hagan and Scott Greer, 'Making War Criminal', *Criminology* 40 (2002), 231–64, were first to analyse Glueck's role in the run-up to Nuremberg.

offer his newly acquired expertise and, from afar, joined the discussion circles in Cambridge and London.[35]

His first article which proposed an international tribunal appeared in the *Harvard Law Review* in 1943,[36] and in the following year his volume on *War Criminals. Their Prosecution & Punishment* was published prominently with Alfred A. Knopf. Glueck's emphatic stance was evident. Neither did he consider 'a victorious State ... legally bound to observe all the technical niceties of local peace-time administration of justice in dealing with a vanquished State and its nationals, who have themselves played havoc with every civilized concept of law and justice', nor did he subscribe to the idea 'that international law is a fully developed and highly exact science'. Instead he suggested a practical approach to cast the legal net as widely as possible, defined war criminals broadly enough to include politicians and businessmen, and called for drastic sentences. Glueck's priority was clearly to achieve justice, not least in respect to the destruction of the European Jews. That such a tribunal might provide the 'germ of the "international organization"' that so many publicists have called for' was a bonus.[37]

The newcomer's book and especially its disregard for procedural standards did not escape criticism—Quincy Wright wryly noted that 'Professor Glueck's detailed analysis is ... better than his statement of fundamental principles'[38]—but it would become a set text among the US prosecutors at Nuremberg. The fact that Glueck himself advertised the volume during his brief stint in Germany and had a number of copies shipped did not hurt either.[39] This impact was particularly notable in so far as his arguments sat ill with the US trial design in one respect: in 1944, Glueck could find no basis whatsoever for prosecuting crimes against peace. By the time the trial began, however, the professor had converted. While the move may have reflected Jackson's appointment as Chief of Counsel and his early emphasis on aggressive war, it also owed a lot to Glueck's exchange with another lawyer who had entered the fray, William C. Chanler.

A Harvard Law School graduate and a lawyer in La Guardia's New York City administration, Chanler had joined the Army in 1942 and served as the deputy director of Military Government at the end of the war. In this function the war crimes question came to his attention and what he found left him deeply dissatisfied. Any meaningful trial ought to prosecute the crime of aggression, and the 'wicked doctrine now espoused by most international lawyers that all wars are lawful; that it matters not how many treaties are violated or how many peaceful nations are

[35] Glueck to F. Frankfurter, 7 August 1942, Harvard Law Library, Cambridge, MA (HLL), Sheldon Glueck Papers, Box 111; Segesser, *Recht* (n 10) 318.

[36] Sheldon Glueck, 'By What Tribunal Shall War Offenders Be Tried?', *Harvard Law Review* 56 (1943), 1059–89.

[37] Sheldon Glueck, *War Criminals. Their Prosecution & Punishment* (New York, NY: Knopf, 1944), 12–16, 39f., 180.

[38] Wright, 'Review' (n 17) 297.

[39] Glueck to G. Dean, 14 July 1945, HLL, Glueck Papers, Box 73.

invaded or destroyed, provided only that the soldiers obey the "rules of chivalry" which form the basis of traditional war crimes', should be debunked once and for all. Chanler was particularly annoyed by the conservatism even of liberal jurists such as Jessup whom he held responsible for the 'moral and intellectual bankruptcy of present-day theories of inter-national law'. To Chanler they appeared no better than their antagonists abroad since 'old theory forms the backbone of the German and Japanese militaristic philosophy'.[40]

Such criticism was shared by Murray C. Bernays, then a little-known Wall Street lawyer and third-tier official in the US War Department but today frequently hailed (or derided) as the father of the IMT prosecution design. His design stressed aggressive war and, through the double-barrelled approach of conspiracy and group criminality, tried to target virtually all Axis perpetrators in one fell swoop.[41] Like Chanler, with whom he exchanged several memoranda, Bernays was not fussed about doctrine but how to deal with as many war criminals in as short a time as possible. His emphasis was clearly on meting out due punishment to these 'beasts', as he called them in private correspondence, and to seize 'the educational and therapeutic opportunity of our generation'. Academic lawyers and their craft appeared of little help to him in this endeavour as he considered them bound up in tradition and the search for precedent while insufficiently appreciative of international law's evolutionary character. '[T]imorous legalism' was not for Bernays who aspired to 'the moving verities of justice, or for statesmen to create, out of our own suffering history, beacon lights to guide us through our besetting problems'.[42]

Bernays' frustration, however, was nothing compared to that suffered by Raphael Lemkin. Today a seminal name in the history of international criminal law,[43] at the time, Lemkin was a marginal figure. A former Polish state attorney, he had been involved in the interwar debates on international penal law and, exiled to the United States, occasionally advised government agencies as so many émigrés did. Teaching at several prestigious east coast universities, he failed to secure a permanent position on account of his single-minded endeavour to incriminate Nazi criminality. This led to his 1944 book on German rule in occupied Europe, a heavy

[40] Chanler to Glueck, 19 December 1944 and 9 May 1945 (quotes); Glueck to Chanler, 17 May 1945, HLL, Glueck Papers, Box 111. Cf. Mouralis, *Moment* (n 3) 59–63, and Jonathan A. Bush, '"The Supreme … Crime" and Its Origins. The Lost Legislative History of the Crime of Aggressive War', *Columbia Law Review* 102 (2002), 2324–424, at 2359–65.

[41] On Bernays' key role see Bradley Smith, *Road to Nuremberg* (New York, NY: Basic Books, 1981); Kirsten Sellars, *Crimes against Peace and International Law* (Cambridge: Cambridge University Press, 2013), 64–75, 165f., and now Mouralis, *Moment* (n 3) 50–7.

[42] Still, Bernays needed Lauterpacht, Trainin, and Kelsen to explain Allied jurisdiction over Germany; [Untitled report], 10 June 1945, University of Wyoming, American Heritage Center, Laramie (UW-AHC), Murray C. Bernays Papers, Box 1, F. 'Letters 1945'; Bernays to Fite, 1 November 1945, HSTL, Katherine Fite Papers, Box 1, F. 'Letters to Katherine Fite'; for his nod to Kelsen, see 'The Man behind the Gavel', *The New Yorker*, 17 November 1945, 24.

[43] Among the many publications see, e.g. Philippe Sands, *East West Street. On the Origins of 'Genocide' and 'Crimes Against Humanity'* (London: Weidenfeld & Nicholson, 2016).

combination of legal analysis and collection of statutes, whose success owed everything to its key innovation, the term 'genocide', against the backdrop of the growing public awareness of the murder of the European Jews.[44]

It also brought Lemkin to the periphery of the Nuremberg project. He managed to have the term incorporated into the indictment, albeit in a very much abridged version. Neither was genocide defined as comprehensively as in *Axis Rule* nor was it made a stand-alone charge. And it was listed under war crimes rather than crimes against humanity, its principal competitor in conceptual terms.[45] Lemkin would continue lobbying for the adoption of his brainchild so as to establish a legal precedent but with limited success. While the British prosecution, with the support of Ečer, actively used the concept late in the trial, the judgment would not even name it. And despite their considerably broader agenda, the NMT mostly reduced 'genocide' to physical extermination of racially, nationally, or religiously defined groups, with more sophisticated usages remaining few and far between.[46]

The quartet—three of whom had family ties to occupied Europe—were crucial to Nuremberg's institution building; the IMT design, in particular, would have looked very different without their input. Yet of these four outsiders[47], only Lemkin would continue to work on matters of international law. Bernays left Nuremberg in frustration before the trial opened, worn out by the administrative responsibilities and disappointed by the lack of respect he felt. Glueck, too, was not entirely happy with his Nuremberg assignment, noting disapprovingly how lawyers half his age and, *quel horreur*, without so much as a doctorate, had a greater say in determining the further course of events. When Jackson, despite some lukewarm efforts to smooth the professor's ruffled feathers, did not hold him back, Glueck returned to the United States. There, he revised his stance on aggressive war, again published by the *Harvard Law Review*, which would—in a circular intellectual movement—inform the US attorneys' conceptions in the subsequent proceedings. That done, Glueck left international law for good, and returned to criminology, underscoring that his main ambition—to see the German and Japanese leaderships tried—had been fulfilled.[48]

[44] For Lemkin's intellectual upbringing in interwar Poland and the connection to Emil Rappaport, see Piotr Madajczyk, 'Raphael Lemkins Begriff des Völkermordes in den juristischen Diskussionen 1945–1949', in Enrico Heitzer, Günter Morsch, Robert Traba, et al. (eds), *Im Schatten von Nürnberg. Transnationale Ahndung von NS-Verbrechen* (Berlin: Metropol, 2019), 45–57.

[45] John Q. Barrett, 'Raphael Lemkin and "Genocide" at Nuremberg, 1945–46', in Christoph Safferling and Eckart Conze (eds), *The Genocide Convention Sixty Years after its Adoption* (The Hague: Asser, 2010), 35–54.

[46] See Hirsch, *Soviet Judgment* (n 23) 317f., 340; Alexa Stiller, 'Semantics of Extermination. The Use of the New Term of Genocide in the Nuremberg Trials and the Genesis of a Master Narrative', in Kim C. Priemel und Alexa Stiller (eds), *Reassessing the Nuremberg Military Tribunals. Transitional Justice, Trial Narratives, and Historiography* (New York, NY: Berghahn, 2012), 104–33.

[47] Mouralis, *Moment* (n 3) 46, 98, employs the same sobriquet.

[48] Sheldon Glueck, 'The Nuernberg Trial and Aggressive War', *Harvard Law Review* 59 (1946), 396–456; Sheldon Glueck, *The Nuremberg Trial and Aggressive War* (New York, NY: Knopf, 1946); cf. Hagan and Greer, 'Making' (n 34); Priemel, *Betrayal* (n 26) 70 (fn. 49), 85f.

The Negotiators

The quartet's exit in the course of the summer of 1945 was the direct result of a shift for which the London Conference marked the inflection point. The talks did not only bring together the four major powers'—very differently sized and equipped—delegations to carve out an agreement and the eventual tribunal's charter which, as Kelsen would later posit, established the true legal precedent, not the trial that followed.[49] The quadripartite negotiations also saw both the academic jurists and the newcomers, though still important, ceding ground to a new group who would first act as institution builders, before metamorphing into courtroom lawyers, either as future prosecutors or as judges.

The London conference witnessed intense debates on what international law had to offer and how it could be amended in order to try 'major Axis criminals'. Consensus both between and within the four delegations was often limited, especially where previously uncodified concepts such as crimes against humanity and crimes against peace were concerned. The conspiracy count, though, despite its very American lingua which was not entirely palatable to the French, could be translated into notions of complicity, as Kirsten Sellars has pointed out.[50] But discussions floundered frequently on issues of precision and scope as in the case of aggressive war. Evidently troublesome not only in regard to the Soviet-German Pact, but also the Anglo-French plans to pre-empt the German occupation of Norway, this issue caused major problems, both doctrinal and diplomatic. Among the French delegates—although now overseen by the Justice ministry rather than the more sceptical Quai d'Orsay lawyers such as Basdevant—André Gros rejected the notion of trying individuals for aggressive war out of hand because of its retroactivity and credited the idea tendered by Jackson and Trainin only with *de lege ferenda* validity. To the incredulous question put by his British counterpart and 'lawyer-statesman', David Maxwell Fyfe, if he did not consider it a crime to have caused the Second World War, Gros tersely replied that it was 'morally and politically desirable but . . . it is not international law'.[51]

Whereas Gros had done his reading and was aware of the US position in 1919[52] the US team remained unperturbed by such objections. Jackson cited his own, Lauterpachtian Havana speech as well as the recent edition of *Oppenheim's International Law*, in other words Lauterpacht again, to insist on making crimes against peace the trial's centrepiece. However, his intention to arrive at a

[49] 'Hans Kelsen, 'Will the Judgment in the Nuremberg Trial Constitute a Precedent in International Law?', *International Law Quarterly* 1 (1947), 153–71.

[50] Sellars, 'Crimes against Peace' (n 41).

[51] *Report of Robert H. Jackson, United States Representative, to the International Conference on Military Trials, London, 1946* (Washington, DC: GPO, 1949), 295–9, 297; Neil Duxbury, *Lord Kilmuir. A Vignette* (Oxford: Hart, 2015), 2–4; cf. Gemählich, *Frankreich* (n 4) 55–60, 67–9.

[52] See Payk, *Frieden* (n 13) 268–82, 500–4.

precise, binding definition, backed by Maxwell Fyfe who was anxious to avoid the Norwegian matter, met with stubborn Soviet resistance. Trainin and his associate Iona Nikitchenko—under strict orders and supervision from Moscow[53]—refused any such definition, arguing that critics would identify any inconsistency. To this Gros, who cut a dominant figure in the small French team, added that the London Charter should not anticipate too much 'of what will be adopted by the United Nations'. In the end, a compromise broadly defined aggressive war but limited the tribunal's jurisdiction to the Axis case, rendering it inoperative in all other contexts.[54] Such debates also pointed to the blurred boundaries between 'legal' and 'political' reasoning and the diplomatic travails required in sorting these out. While the Soviet side's reservations reflected the Kremlin's awareness of the potential incriminatory power—both in terms of past and future policy—these could not be formulated as political demands but had to be couched in legal categories. Yet by choosing this road, control over the trials' narratives was ceded to others, including the defence during the trial, as the Kremlin would soon learn.[55]

Yet the Soviet delegates had no monopoly on horse-trading, whether successful or not. If Jackson's insistence on a general definition was legally apposite it certainly was politically astute as any

> definition would sound pretty partial if we [the Allies] are defining an act as a crime only when it is carried out by the Axis powers... If it is a good rule of law, it should bind us all, and if not, we should not invoke it at this trial.

However, Jackson was enough of a politician to see the limits of what was possible; the notion of linking domestic anti-Jewish crimes to aggressive war resulted precisely from such reflections. Aware of the open flank of racial segregation at home, Jackson explained the so-called nexus requirement for crimes against humanity by pointing to 'some regrettable circumstances at times in our own country in which minorities are unfairly treated'.[56]

Such compromises and saving clauses indicated that the institution builders, in particular those in direct government service rather than filling external advisory positions, were acutely aware of the legal stakes of the first ever international criminal trial and of the pitfalls of precedent. Thus, very much like Gros, James Donovan, a legal counsel to the Office of Strategic Services (OSS) dispatched to Jackson's staff, warned that violations of the international laws of warfare were not necessarily criminal and that several of the accusations, including forced labour and spoliation, had been long regarded as morally reprehensible but not evidently

[53] See Hirsch, *Soviet Judgment* (n 23) 59–76.
[54] *Report of Robert H. Jackson* (n 51) 303–9, 315–18; Schulmeister-André, *Strafgerichtsbarkeit* (n 23) 238–47.
[55] See below and the detailed account in Hirsch, *Soviet Judgment* (n 23) 246–335.
[56] *Report of Robert H. Jackson* (n 51) 303–33 (quotation); cf. Mouralis, *Moment* (n 3) 135.

criminal. And crimes against peace as understood by Trainin and others introduced a novel concept to international criminal law, and '[t]he political implications of including such acts in the list of war crimes are quite considerable'.[57]

Courtroom Lawyers

Prosecutors

In the course of the IMT, the reservations Donovan and Gros articulated were usually overcome by invoking the evolutionary character of international law. Time and again, in court and behind the scenes, prosecution members would point out that international law could not be static but must grow, as the British chief prosecutor Hartley Shawcross put it in terms reminiscent of Kelsen, though borrowed from Cardozo, in 'a twilight existence during which it is hardly distinguishable from morality or justice, till at length the imprimatur of a Court attests its jural quality'.[58] The argument was stated in all clarity by Jackson in a pre-conference report to President Truman:

> International Law is not capable of development by legislation, for there is no continuously sitting international legislature... It grows, as did the Common-law, through decisions reached from time to time in adapting settled principles to new situations.[59]

In order to formulate these arguments precisely and succinctly for the benefit of the Tribunal, the scholars were once more called upon, and it fell to Lauterpacht to draft Shawcross's opening and, to a lesser degree, closing speeches; meanwhile Trainin worked on the Soviet side and law professor Suzanne Bastid-Basdevant co-authored the introduction delivered by François de Menthon.[60] Beyond opening and closing speeches, however, general arguments mattered ever less. In many instances, prosecutors—either out of their own inclination or because they understood the more conservative dispositions on the bench—suggested that rather than developing international criminal law further, they were merely applying well-tried rules and customs to their cases. The historical quality of their respective

[57] Legal problems to be encountered in the International Trial of War Criminals, n.d. [1945], Hoover Institution Archives, Stanford (HIA), James Donovan Papers, Box 35, F.35–31.

[58] For example, Walsh Diary, 23 July 1945, Georgetown University Library, Special Collections Research Center (GUL-SCRC), Edmund A. Walsh Papers, Box 2, F.126; F. Elwyn Jones, Broadcast: The American Trials at Nuremberg, 21 October 1947, National Library of Wales, Aberystwyth (NLW), Frederick Elwyn Jones Papers, C10; Bernard D. Meltzer, 'Comment. A Note on Some Aspects of the Nuremberg Debate', *University of Chicago Law Review* 14 (1947), 455–69, 456f.; quotation: Hartley Shawcross, 'Justice vs. Germany's War Crimes', *Prevent World War III* 38 (1951), 21f.

[59] *Report of Robert H. Jackson* (n 51) 52–3.

[60] See Lauterpacht, *Life* (n 24) 177f., 188f., 271–96; Mouralis, *Moment* (n 3) 32; Schulmeister-André, *Strafgerichtsbarkeit* (n 23) 397–408.

trials therefore resulted from the sanctioning of existing, not the creation of new law.[61] Maxwell Fyfe, the *de facto* leader of the BWCE and a man not known for his wild imagination, inferred customary law so as to declare that international common law rendered the charged Nazi actions criminal. Claiming a firm basis in tradition may have been 'beset by wishful thinking' but it also articulated the British politician's appreciation of the wider ramifications of the legal undertaking of which he was in charge.[62]

There were good reasons why many prosecutors at Nuremberg, especially in the lower echelons, had little use for the theories offered by academics, whether distinguished or of more recent fame. In their vast majority they entered the scene when the basic decisions had already been made and when the job to be done was to draw up a criminal case, collect evidence, formulate a trial narrative, and hone one's cross-examination skills to get the most out of witnesses and undermine defendants, as Jacques-Bernard Herzog did with Fritz Sauckel or Maxwell Fyfe with Konstantin von Neurath.[63] This focus also reflected their professional experiences: among the roughly 200 Allied prosecutors involved in the IMT and the NMT,[64] the practitioners dominated across the board, even if the four delegations all showed idiosyncratic features: the French delegation was nearly entirely made up of *magistrats*, career lawyers in state offices and often public prosecutors at that. If deputy chief Charles Dubost and his colleagues were also chosen for their anti-Vichy credentials their Soviet colleagues—both prosecutors and judges—had proved their mettle in the 1930s' infamous show trials. Practitioners such as chief prosecutor Roman Rudenko had no experience in international law; academic expertise was supplemented by jurists such as Trainin, Boris Mankovski, and Dmitry Karev. The British team was more variegated with lawyers drafted from different government offices, the military, and private practice, with an emphasis on experience in criminal litigation. And the US delegation at the IMT, easily the biggest contingent, recruited its personnel from public offices in the wartime administration as well as from private law firms; yet the composition would change from IMT

[61] This was the British argument, suggested by Lauterpacht, on the aggressive war count before the IMT, and would be reiterated repeatedly on the 'traditional' war crimes counts in the NMT, notably with an eye to spoliation, forced labour, and partisan warfare. See the echo in John J. Parker, 'The International Trial at Nuremberg: Giving Vitality to International Law', *American Bar Association Journal* 37 (1951), 493–6, 549–55.

[62] Duxbury, *Kilmuir* (n 51) 45f.

[63] Priemel, *Betrayal* (n 26) 125, 140; Gemählich; *Frankreich* (n 4) 248–54.

[64] Mouralis, *Moment* (n 3) 21–9, calculates that, all in all, some 450 qualified lawyers were involved at the IMT alone. These include judges, the secretariat, advisers, researchers, and analysists, many of whom held law degrees, but not the delegations dispatched by other signatories to the Charter who contributed information and evidence. The involvement of lawyers like Ečer and Manfred Lachs often went back to wartime commissions and publications; [Untitled list of foreign delegations], 13 May 1948, John F. Kennedy Presidential Library (JFKL), Drexel A. Sprecher Papers, Box 54, F. 'Historical File—Foreign Delegations'; Manfred Lachs, *War Crimes: An Attempt to Define the Issues* (London: Stevens & Sons, 1945).

to NMT, becoming more heterogenous, less elite, and indeed a little less male in the process.[65]

The practical mindset of the majority of prosecutors did not mean they no longer relied on outside experts, but their sources changed. Rather than legal theorists, archivists and victims' organizations now supplied information, evidence, and personnel. The *Service du recherche des crimes de guerre ennemis* loaned Aline Chalufour to the French prosecution, and the *Centre documentation juive contemporaine* dispatched documents and researchers to Nuremberg, significantly enhancing the slim evidence the so far available on deportation, forced labour, and mass extermination. At the same time, the US brief on the murder of the European Jews was improved by following the leads of Jacob Robinson, as prosecution lawyers Seymour Krieger and William Walsh appreciated. That Robinson, an emigré lawyer at the Institute of Jewish Affairs who had been affiliated to the OSS, was already well-versed in the terminology of 'conspiracy' made the cooperation all the easier for it. Such expertise and evidence would stand prosecutors in good stead, not least in light of the strong emphasis both IMT and NMT benches would place on these crimes in determining individual guilt.[66]

If evidence gathering and briefing (for an analyst such as Krieger), courtroom presentation (Walsh), and cross-examination (Herzog) characterized day-to-day operations, Nuremberg's work also continued to pose diplomatic demands. These were particularly critical at the IMT: inter-Allied cooperation meant that technical matters needed to be cleared and material consistency to be assured, while a 'taboo list; of subjects individual delegations wished to avoid was circulated on the top level. Yet such tiptoeing was made rather difficult by the 1939 Ribbentrop–Molotov Pact and was not helped by Moscow's insistence on adding the Katyń massacre to the list of German war crimes. While the Western prosecutors, eager to avoid embarrassment, were willing to support Soviet efforts to keep the Pact's secret protocol out of the courtroom, that goodwill only went so far; they would not lend a hand to falsifying the record on Katyń. And it did not help either that the Soviet lawyers failed to appreciate that, in contrast to their own situation, the other prosecutors were not on the same team as 'their' respective judges and thus had few possibilities for backstage arrangements.[67]

65 For the US team see Mouralis, *Moment* (n 3) and Bush, 'New Dealer' (n 4); for the French Tisseron, *France* (n 21) 7882, 135–41, and Gemählich, *Frankreich* (n 4) 106–46. On the Soviet delegation: Schulmeister-André, *Strafgerichtsbarkeit* (n 23) 375–81. There is no systematic study of the British team. Cf. Priemel, *Betrayal* (n 26) 71–8, 84–94, 158–61.

66 Krieger Diary, 20–24 November 1945, United States Holocaust Memorial Museum, Washington, DC (USHMM), Seymour Krieger Papers, Series 1, Box 1, F.4. Cf. Bush, 'Nuremberg' (n 3), 272f.; Mouralis, *Moment* (n 3) 87–97; Gemählich, *Frankreich* (n 4) 89–94. Cf. Priemel, *Betrayal* (n 26) 408.

67 Dubost to Champetier de Ribes, 10 June 1946, Archives du Centre historique de Sciences Po, Paris (AHC), Archives de Charles Dubost (CD) 5/3; Hirsch, *Soviet Judgment* (n 23) 66. While Nikitchenko usually backed Rudenko, there were notable dissents on procedure between Jackson and Biddle and between Charles Dubost and Vabres on sentencing; Gemählich, *Frankreich* (n 4) 264f., 277; Priemel, *Betrayal* (n 26) 78f., 104, 131–4.

Against the backdrop of these pressing tasks, abstract issues of international law were of secondary importance to most prosecutors. It was more sensible to start from the premise that individual responsibility *was* inscribed into international law and aggressive war *was* outlawed (but not criminal, as Herzog knew full well).[68] Efforts to go beyond the legal state of the art by introducing new concepts or broadening old ones remained fairly limited, as when Dubost advertised 'state criminality' as a distinct new offence.[69] On the other hand, discussions among the Nuremberg prosecutors whether or not to indict corporations never gained much momentum while the attempt to include 'Aryanization' among crimes against humanity was given short thrift by the tribunals.[70] Possibilities offered by Control Council Law 10, the NMT's legal basis, to charge a broader array of crimes, including sexual violence, remained unexploited as most defendants had been too high up the chain of command to commit them. Thus, the bold statement by Jackson's successor as Chief of Counsel, Telford Taylor, that '[a]lmost overnight, international penal law has become a living reality', may have been representative of the more ambitious prosecutors.[71] But overall the notion of bringing to justice those responsible for mass extermination, atrocities, forced labour, and the carnage of world war, outweighed whatever jurisprudential aspirations individual attorneys might have harboured. Beyond that, returning to civilian life and post-war careers was of primary importance.[72]

Judicious Judges

By comparison, the judges at Nuremberg—nearly all chosen because of their long experience on the bench—were even less keen on legal (r)evolution, at least not at what they perceived to be its breakneck speed. Still, John C. Young, the presiding judge in the 'High Command Case', later recalled that legal change was 'a slow process and . . . what we did in these trials will probably serve as a starting point in the future for the nations of the world to work out a system of law that is backed by sufficient international power to enforce the law'.[73]

[68] Facts and Figures no. 32, 25 October 1945, NLW, Elwyn Jones Papers, C10; Josif Marcu, The Roechling Trial, February/July 1948, Columbia Law School (CLS), Josif Marcu Papers, 2-B-9-9; Jacques-Bernard Herzog, *Nuremberg: un échec fructueux?* (Paris: Librairie générale de droit et de jurisprudence, 1975), 35.

[69] Gemählich, *Frankreich* (n 4) 262–4, 334–6.

[70] See Jonathan A. Bush, 'The Prehistory of Corporations and Conspiracy in International Criminal Law: What Nuremberg Really Said', *Columbia Law Review* 109 (2009), 1094–262.

[71] An Outline of the Research and Publication Possibilities of the War Crimes Trials, November 1948, LoC, Charles Fahy Papers, Box 14, F. 'Taylor, Telford'.

[72] See, for example, Krieger's rejection of Taylor's job offer: Krieger to R. Krieger, 3 January 1946, USHMM, Krieger Papers, Series 1, Box 1, F.4.

[73] Young to Sprecher, 16 November 1950, JFKL, Sprecher Papers, Box 62, F. 'Publications: English II, Aug. 1949-Dec.'50[1]'.

Young, a Colorado Supreme Court judge, was fairly typical for the NMT benches, although more self-deprecating in the appraisal of his own scope, hoping that 'I did the best I could in the place where I was with the things I had at my disposal'.[74] Among the thirty-two men who served as NMT judges the majority hailed from the US Midwest and the South, with a third recruited from state supreme courts and another ten from appeals courts. None of them had any experience in international law worth mentioning, including the sole scholar, Paul M. Hebert from Louisiana Law School.[75] Placed in unfamiliar surroundings, handling defendants and subjects they knew next to nothing about, and applying law in which they held little or no expertise, it was hardly surprising that most judges trod carefully, taking their cues from the IMT's findings. Virtually all tribunals decided to forego the opportunity of Control Council Law 10 to try defendants for pre-war, domestic crimes, and thus to go beyond the IMT's jurisdiction. In the Hostages Trial, the judges practically abandoned the new law altogether and took recourse to the Hague Conventions instead. The majority opinion's curt statement that 'it is not our province to write International Law as we would have it—we must apply it as we find it', duly expressed this self-restricting stance.[76]

On the other hand, what the judges chose to find was their own prerogative, and tribunals were free to base their reasoning on more progressive interpretations of contemporary jurisprudence. The judges in the Ministries Case quoted Quincy Wright extensively when they explained that 'aggressive wars and invasions have, since time immemorial, been a violation of international law, even though specific sanctions were not provided'.[77] Legal conservatism therefore should not be overstated. More than once, tribunals contemplated questions of *de lege ferenda*, prominently so in the Doctors' Trial whose opinion included the Nuremberg Code, a list of ethical principles for human experimentation. The often vilified tribunal in the Hostages Trial attempted something rather similar: realizing that the apparently firm ground of The Hague had been eroded by two world wars, the judges called for a major reform of the laws of war and suggested a catalogue of more than a dozen conditions which, if applied, would render the taking and execution of hostages more difficult, if not impractical.[78]

[74] Young to H. P. Burke, 5 August 1948, and Young to Gleaves, 4 March 1948, both HSTL, John C. Young Papers, Box 12, F. 'Chronological Corres. File 1948'.

[75] The missing knowhow was partly provided by the tribunals' legal adviser John Fried, see below.

[76] *Trials of War Criminals Before the Nuernberg Military Tribunals under Control Council Law No. 10*, 15 vols. (Washington, DC: GPO, 1949–53), XI, 1249.

[77] Ibid., XIV, 308–870, at 319.

[78] Ibid., XI, 1249f. In contrast to the Nuremberg Code, however, the 'Hostages Catalogue' fared much less well in the profession. It was immediately attacked by Lord Wright, chairman of the UNWCC, and by several other prominent lawyers. Recently, Kevin Jon Heller, *The Nuremberg Military Tribunals and the Origins of International Criminal Law* (Oxford: Oxford University Press, 2011), 210f., has noted that the list suffered from the absence of any specification how many and which criteria had to be met; cf. Priemel, *Betrayal* (n 26) 345f.

Maybe surprisingly, the IMT judges did not differ all that much from their NMT brethren. Donnedieu de Vabres was the only jurist with academic credentials in international law on the bench, and although he was intellectually at home—unlike his alternate Robert Falco who had come first to London, then to Nuremberg rather accidentally—he was hardly the radical vanguard.[79] Sharing the misgivings entertained by his fellow Frenchman, André Gros, he was unconvinced of the Charter's retroactive clauses, notably with an eye to crimes against humanity, opposed to the count of conspiracy, and wary of any moves which might turn judges into legislators. Still, unlike the even more cautious Basdevant, Vabres embraced the development both expressed and brought about by the IMT, considered its judgement a major contribution to establishing a universally accepted code of international criminal law as well as a testament to the legitimacy of international tribunals.[80]

Another advocate for more cautious steps was the US alternate, Judge John Parker, a Fourth Circuit judge from North Carolina with little expertise in international law and as little pretension. The latter set him apart from the voting US judge, former Attorney General Francis Biddle who clearly appreciated the opportunity to carve out his place in history. Essentially sharing Jackson's conviction (and hubris) that the IMT ought to gravitate around aggressive war he threw his weight behind outlawing crimes against peace. Yet both US judges agreed that Nuremberg had taken 'the romance out of aggressive war'.[81]

The British judges, prominent barristers and long-serving judges, did not display any great interest in matters of international legal theory but were more concerned with upholding procedural standards (Geoffrey Lawrence) and the quality of argument and presentation, as well as assuming a clear moral stance (Norman Birkett). To some extent their position was aptly summarized by James Rowe, a legal adviser to the tribunal. Commenting on the judgment's international law section, Rowe reminded Biddle that 'if the opinion is to have real strength in the future it seems to me it must be specific in its application to these actual wars and not confine itself to a lovely discussion of general principles à la Quincy Wright'.[82]

[79] On de Vabres see Ann-Sophie Schöpfel, 'La Voix des Juges Français dans les Procès de Nuremberg et de Tokyo. Défense d'une Idée de Justice Universelle', *Guerres mondiales et conflits contemporains* 249 (2013), 101–14. For Falco see his memoir *Juge à Nuremberg. Souvenirs inédits du procès des criminels nazis* (Nancy: Arbre bleu, 2012), 28f. Both Basdevant and Cassin had been canvassed; Menthon to Teitgen and Bidault, 14 September 1945, AHC, CD 3/2.

[80] *Trial of the Major War Criminals Before the International Military Tribunal, Nuremberg*, 42 vols. (Nuremberg: no publ., 1947–1949), VIII, 454; Note, n.d. [1946], CLS, Herbert Wechsler Papers, 2-C-6-11; cf. Henri Donnedieu de Vabres, 'Le Procès de Nuremberg', *Revue de Science Criminelle et de Droit Pénal Comparé* 2 (1947), 171–83. Cf. Mark Lewis, *The Birth of the New Justice. The Internationalization of Crime and Punishment, 1919–1950* (Oxford: Oxford University Press, 2014), 191–6. The judgement by Gemählich, *Frankreich* (n 4) 282–4, that Vabres was too much of a scholar to be a good judge seems overstated.

[81] Parker, 'Nuremberg' (n 61) 555; Biddle, Report to the President, 9 November 1946, HSTL, Truman Papers, PSF, Box 123, F.123–125. Cf. Letter from Elzie Wechsler to Ruth, n.d. [1945], CLS, Wechsler Papers, 2-C-6-9.

[82] Memorandum for Judge Biddle, 19 July 1946, Franklin Delano Roosevelt Presidential Library, Hyde Park, NY (FDRL), James Rowe Papers, Box 44, F. 'AssAttyGenl–Nuerenberg comments'.

As to the two Soviet judges, of whom Nikitchenko had worked on the Charter (as had Falco), we can only surmise if and what convictions they entertained since their peculiar position in the Soviet hierarchy provided precious little room for personal prerogatives.[83] Both promoted narratives of the antifascist coalition and the Great Patriotic War, sought to avoid political embarrassments in court but also contributed constructively to material and procedural questions, evidently intent to safeguard Allied unity and Nuremberg's prestige.[84]

The final text of the judgment would attest to this view. Very little was said concerning the degree of legal innovation accomplished by the IMT, suggesting that most, if not all members of the bench, had realized that there was no going back to before the Charter but no need to go beyond it either. From this vantage point, Kelsen's growing disappointment, discussed below, was that of an academic observer who failed to appreciate the judges' core task in the Nuremberg framework. Ironically, that placed him, of all people, in the company of his Weimar nemesis, Carl Schmitt, who deplored the fact that only Vabres had the scientific acumen to grapple with the complex issues of international law.[85]

On the Defence: German Lawyers

To expect the trials' German participants, including the defence counsel, to show enthusiasm for the opportunity to participate in the making of international law might have been asking too much. Any such hope would have also been ignorant of the larger trends in the German variety of jurisprudence. As Martti Koskenniemi has shown, German legal academia had taken a very different turn from the mainstream of international law studies, placing strong emphasis on the nation state as both the source and authoritative interpreter of law. Proponents of legal internationalism had been a minority in Germany (although widely respected outside) before 1914, and whatever credibility they had enjoyed had been largely lost in the aftermath of the Versailles Treaty which intertwined the tough, unpopular reparations and war guilt clauses with the ideas of a new global order as articulated by the League of Nations Covenant.[86] Ubiquitous absence of any belief in an international rule of law was compounded by the specific German take on the rules of war which

[83] According to Arkadi Poltorak, *Nürnberger Epilog* (East-Berlin: Deutscher Militärverlag, 1971), 176, Voltchov owed his assignment to his diplomatic and language skills which were in short supply in the Soviet delegation. For the very particular situation the Soviet lawyers found themselves in, see Hirsch, *Soviet Judgement* (n 23).

[84] Schulmeister-André, *Strafgerichtsbarkeit* (n 23) 212, 384–95, 530–9, and Hirsch, *Soviet Judgment* (n 23).

[85] Carl Schmitt, *Glossarium. Aufzeichnungen der Jahre 1947–1951* (Berlin: Duncker & Humblot, 1991), 256.

[86] Koskenniemi, *Gentle Civilizer* (n 6); on Versailles see Payk, *Frieden* (n 13).

had subordinated limitations to the *jus in bello* to military expediency.[87] The Third Reich's own view of international law had been dominated by *Großraumtheorie*, the notion of a post-Westphalian era of international relations between spatial entities transcending the traditional nation state, which was promoted by Schmitt from the late 1930s, adapting geopolitical categories to international law.[88]

These developments coalesced in Hermann Jahrreiß's career: a long-term opponent to the Versailles Treaty's treatment of Germany, the Cologne-based professor of law had joined the *Großraum* bandwagon during the war, and came to Nuremberg to dispute claims of illegal aggression and rampant transgression of international law.[89] Among the roughly 260 lawyers involved in the Nuremberg defence, academic jurists were a tiny minority, including two more specialists in international law: Jahrreiß's fellow *Großraum* proponent Ernst Wolgast and Herbert Kraus, a conservative professor who had been forced to vacate his chair in 1937. They were supplemented by criminal law professor Franz Exner and by Eduard Wahl who specialized in comparative private law. Behind the scenes, a number of university teachers, including Schmitt and his disciple, Ernst Rudolf Huber, but also Erich Kaufmann and Hermann Mosler, one a legal adviser to the *Auswärtige Amt*, the other the future doyen of West German international law scholars, contributed memoranda and briefs.[90]

The vast majority of defence attorneys, however, were trial lawyers of different backgrounds, varying legal abilities, and disparate political sympathies so that any sweeping categorization of their roles is bound to be too simplistic. Yet it is fair to say that virtually all of them interpreted their responsibility at Nuremberg to be as much in defence of their clients as of their countries, and at times priorities appeared to have been reversed.[91] In their effort to discredit Nuremberg, men like Alfred Seidl, Hans Laternser, or Otto Kranzbühler refuted the very foundation on which the international and the US tribunals rested as well as the validity of rulebooks they considered outdated in the age of total war. When it came it fundamental questions, the trial attorneys were fond of citing allied authorities and émigré scholars—viz., Laternser's endeavour to defeat the prosecution's

[87] That is the argument by Isabel Hull, *A Scrap of Paper. Breaking and Making International Law during the Great War* (Ithaca, NY: Cornell University Press, 2014), and Andreas Toppe, *Militär und Kriegsvölkerrecht. Rechtsnorm, Fachdiskurs und Kriegspraxis in Deutschland 1899–1940* (Munich: Oldenbourg, 2008).

[88] See Mathias Schmoeckel, *Die Großraumtheorie. Ein Beitrag zur Geschichte der Völkerrechtswissenschaft im Dritten Reich, insbesondere der Kriegszeit* (Berlin: Duncker & Humblot, 1994), 153, 178, 185, 198.

[89] Annette Weinke, *Gewalt, Geschichte, Gerechtigkeit. Transnationale Debatten über deutsche Staatsverbrechen im 20. Jahrhundert* (Göttingen: Wallstein, 2016), 144–58.

[90] Ibid., 144f.; Priemel, *Betrayal* (n 26) 262, 2379, 282, 324; Felix Lange, *Praxisorientierung und Gemeinschaftskonzeption. Hermann Mosler als Wegbereiter der westdeutschen Völkerrechtswissenschaft nach 1945* (Berlin: Springer, 2017), 150–66. A comprehensive picture is offered by Seliger, *Politische Anwälte* (n 4).

[91] See, for example, Gustav Steinbauer, *Ich war Verteidiger in Nürnberg. Ein Dokumentenbeitrag zum Kampf um Österreich* (Klagenfurt: Kaiser, 1950).

Lauterpachtian interpretation by invoking Lassa Oppenheim, or Jahrreiß's repeated nods to Kelsen,[92] or they brought in academic prestige such as Wahl's. In the IG Farben Trial, the Heidelberg professor submitted a full 113 pages in which he challenged the tribunal's international character, attacked the retroactive nature of crimes against peace, declared 'conspiracy' to be unviable in continental law, raised *tu quoque* objections when it came to spoliation and 'compulsory' (*not* forced or slave) labour, and held that private individuals were not liable under international criminal law and therefore could not be found guilty of crimes against humanity. Wahl's sweeping critique closed with strong procedural reproaches which essentially said the trials were unfair. In truth, he merely reiterated objections against Allied jurisdiction which had been formulated ever since the opening of the IMT, and which had been rejected just as often by various panels of judges. The fact that he still raised them was a reflection of his hope to impress the audience outside the court and to put the German point of view on record, lest it be said that even the defence had accepted Nuremberg's fundamental truths.[93]

Privately or in retrospect, though, more than a few lawyers conceded that the trials had been mostly—and perhaps surprisingly to them—fair, extolling the judges' even-handed decisions. In terms of material law, too, individual defence counsel found words of praise or at least appreciation for the trials. While disagreeing on concrete points, independent-minded men like Fritz Sauter, Theodor Klefisch, and, occasionally, Rudolf Dix agreed with the general thrust of Nuremberg in its effort to advance international law and criminalize aggressive war. Of course, such agreement could also be tactical, as it underscored the lawyers' self-serving argument that the educated classes in Germany had never subscribed to the Nazi perversion of justice but had continued to be in sync with liberal-legalist notions of the rule of law elsewhere.[94] Some academics agreed. Kraus, for one, had little reason to sympathize with the Third Reich anyway and was more willing than the likes of Jahrreiß to accept crimes against peace or the rejection of the superior orders defence. And to Mosler, whose memoranda displayed remarkably little of the nationalist polemics voiced by his colleagues, the allure of Nuremberg as a precedent must have been great, given that his own take on international law would henceforth be characterized by a determined turn away from theory in favour of the practicalities of conflict resolution.[95]

[92] Charge XV, n.d., Bundesarchiv Koblenz (BAK), AllProz 5/101; cf. Priemel, *Betrayal* (n 26) 324f.; Weinke, *Gewalt* (n 89) 153.

[93] Closing Brief on 'Fundamental Legal Issues' submitted on behalf of all defendants in Case No. 6, [1948], Smith College Special Collections, Northampton (SCSC), Mary Metlay Kaufman Papers, Box 3, F.3. Cf. Seliger, *Politische Anwälte* (n 4) 292.

[94] Seliger, *Politische Anwälte* (n 4) 276ff., 296–300; Priemel, *Betrayal* (n 26) 132, 227–9.

[95] Cf. Seliger, *Politische Anwälte* (n 4) 379–81; Lange, *Praxisorientierung* (n 90); Eva Schumann, 'Die Göttinger Rechts—und Staatswissenschaftliche Fakultät 1933–1955', in Eva Schumann (ed.), *Kontinuitäten und Zäsuren. Rechtswissenschaft und Justiz im 'Dritten Reich' und in der Nachkriegszeit* (Göttingen: Wallstein, 2008), 65–121.

Peer Reviewers
Critics

Such pragmatism also characterized the views of those Allied observers who were sceptical of the Nuremberg project. George A. Finch, a veteran of the Paris negotiations after the First World War, could not but decry the Charter's violation of *ex post facto* and its Lauterpachtian endorsement. But, as Finch added, now that a precedent had been set, it might as well be made use of and a permanent court—preferably the International Court of Justice—invested with pertinent jurisdiction.[96]

Yet it was precisely on the precedential qualities of Nuremberg that consensus among academics was missing. Other seasoned international lawyers who had been taken aback by the willingness of their colleagues, some of them not even considered peers, to shed established dogma and forge ahead, were unwilling to endorse the trials. For a formalist like Basdevant, Nuremberg never held much legitimacy (and whether or not the fact that his daughter contributed to the French case did anything to change this conception we do not know); he remained consistently aloof from what he considered to be a poorly reflected, badly managed, and legally contestable trial.[97] H. A. Smith was unwilling to accept a trial as precedent which, he felt, flouted key principles of the rule of law for the poor benefit of punishing a few 'wicked men'.[98]

But the criticism which proved most damaging to the Nuremberg trials' political standing did not come from the old guard. Pungent, and more problematic, was the cold reception with which the trials were met by a group of German émigré lawyers who had seemed likely supporters of the undertaking. These men were a motley crew indeed and included unorthodox Marxists like Ossip Flechtheim, Franz Neumann, and Otto Kirchheimer, as well as representatives of what would soon figure as 'realism', including Erich Hula, John Herz, and Hans Morgenthau. What they all had in common, though, was their legal training and the fact that their academic careers had come to a more or less abrupt end in exile. All of them would transform into political science and international relations scholars, some involuntarily and out of the sheer necessity of finding a job in a country whose legal system did not recognize their qualifications, others out of frustration with the law's powerlessness in the face of fascist and Soviet challenges.

[96] George A. Finch, 'The Nuremberg Trial and International Law', *AJIL* 41, 1 (1947), 20–37; George A. Finch, 'Review' *AJIL* 44 (1950), 784–6. On other matters, such as the superior orders defence, Finch had expressed progressive views in the aftermath of the First World War, see his 'Superior Orders and War Crimes', *AJIL* 15 (1921), 440–5. Cf. Payk, *Frieden* (n 13) 501f., and Segesser, *Recht* (n 10) 335.

[97] Tisseron, *France* (n 21) 94.

[98] H.A. Smith, 'The Nuremberg Trials', *Free Europe* 13, 162 (1946), 201–4.

The reasons for and the timing of their criticisms varied. Kirchheimer, for one, flatly refused to join Jackson's team in 1945 because he considered the conspiracy count 'sheer hypocrisy' and the whole undertaking flawed:

> as long as we all know that this was not the last of all wars, nobody has a right to convict the Germans for having started the war, and the legal basis for this count is more than shaky. To convict these people for having murdered millions of innocent Jews and Russians etc... seems justified although that seems to me the business of the respective eastern nations.[99]

Kirchheimer's rebuke articulated a fundamental distrust of liberal interventionism which echoed Schmitt who, continuing his reflections on just war, considered Nuremberg a paradigm shift which ushered international law into a new era.[100]

Kirchheimer's OSS colleagues Neumann and Herz tended to agree, however, expecting to exert some influence on the analysis of the Third Reich's workings and their reconstruction in the courtroom, they joined the US prosecution. The impact of Neumann's ideas was indeed significant but nevertheless he soon grew deeply dissatisfied with the selectivity of the trial lawyers' analyses. Not unlike students preparing for exams they only picked those bits and pieces which appeared helpful to their respective cases, and the result was a lack of complexity which the lawyer turned political scientist found hard to stomach. Herz felt similarly, and both men returned to the United States after a few months.[101]

Herz would remember the trials mostly for their inconsequentiality and switched to 'realist' thinking, entertaining little hope that law was able to play a meaningful role in international relations if not backed by effective state power.[102] *Idealism and Realism*, his major work, made him one of the founding fathers of academic 'realism'. When it was awarded the Woodrow Wilson Prize from the American Political Science Association in 1951, Herz asked his former mentor Kelsen—by then also teaching political science rather than law—to accept it on his behalf.[103] While the gesture reflected the two scholars' close relationship, it also illustrated Kelsen's oscillating views. The Austrian scholar had turned away from the IMT to dispute its very quality as a precedent. Neither did he accept the contention of the tribunal that crimes against peace found a basis in positive law prior to the London Charter, while the principle of group criminality to him seemed

[99] Kirchheimer to Vagts, 31 [October?] 1945, BAK, N 1269/2.

[100] Schmitt, *Glossarium* (n 85) 186.

[101] Priemel, *Betrayal* (n 26) 86, 369; Jana Puglierin, *John H. Herz. Leben und Denken zwischen Idealismus und Realismus, Deutschland und Amerika* (Berlin: Duncker & Humblot, 2011), 141–5.

[102] John H. Herz, *Vom Überleben. Wie ein Weltbild entstand. Autobiographie* (Düsseldorf: Droste, 1984), 142.

[103] Herz–Kelsen correspondence, 10 and 29 September 1951, University at Albany, Grenander Departments of Special Collections and Archives, Albany (UAA), John H. Herz Papers, Box 3, F.61.

incongruous with barely established individual liability. His strongest criticism, however, reflected disappointment in the ad hoc tribunal's restriction to Axis criminals. Explicitly foregoing universal application and reserving justice to the victors, Kelsen found, robbed Nuremberg of all general validity. This retreat from the project he had helped shape in its early stages would be echoed in his later, frequently critical comments on the UN system.[104]

Another former student of Kelsen's, Hans Morgenthau's professional and philosophical move away from law was much more determined and sharper. By 1945 a political science scholar at the University of Chicago, Morgenthau frontally attacked the Nuremberg trials as a 'dangerous precedent' which threatened to boomerang on US politics. Over the following years he would continue to take on legalist proponents such as Lauterpacht, displaying a deep distrust in what (international) law was able to achieve. But unlike fellow 'realists' such as Reinhold Niebuhr and George Kennan, Morgenthau was careful not to take sides with the Nuremberg defendants; after all, he had recommended summary execution as an alternative, not a general pardon. Morgenthau's intellectual brilliance, his poignant style, and his independent-mindedness—which, years later, would put him in opposition to the Vietnam War—gave his critical stance on Nuremberg in particular and the prospects of international law in general substance and weight.[105] This was all the more true when compared to the disinclination some former Nuremberg prosecutors, among them Maxwell Fyfe, Herzog, and Benjamin Ferencz, showed in disowning their governments' wars in Algeria, Suez, and Vietnam.[106]

Legacy Workers

Other Nuremberg veterans, of course, drew precisely these parallels, notably Taylor, who, through his teaching, public talks, and writings, became the living embodiment of 'Nuremberg'.[107] Indeed, if measured by publication points, the realists were hardly a match for the legacy workers. As early as March 1946, one IMT participant noted that 'everyone who comes back is writing a book', and that could not take into account the myriad journal articles, monographs, and memoirs which would be published over the following decades.[108] Yet the bulk of this literature

[104] Kelsen, 'Judgment' (n 49); *The Law of the United Nations. A Critical Analysis of Its Fundamental Problems* (London: Stevens & Sons, 1951), 48f., 738.

[105] Priemel, *Betrayal* (n 26) 368–70. For Morgenthau see Koskenniemi, *Gentle Civilizer* (n 6) 413–509, and Oliver Jütersonke, *Morgenthau, Law and Realism* (Cambridge: Cambridge University Press, 2010), 135–44, 179; cf. Herzog, *Nuremberg* (n 68) 115–17.

[106] Herzog, *Nuremberg* (n 68) 115–17; see Mouralis, *Moment* (n 3) 184–96, and Duxbury, *Kilmuir* (n 51) 46–62.

[107] Jonathan Bush, 'Telford Taylor: Bibliography', *Columbia Journal of Transnational Law* 37 (1999), 1015–48.

[108] Rosenbaum to Biddle, 8 March 1946, quoted in Priemel, *Betrayal* (n 26) 16. For an incomplete impression of the published output see the bibliography ibid.

was, besides being often self-congratulatory, distinctly archival in flavour, effectively consigning Nuremberg to history.

Illustrative of this shift was the failure of a large-scale research project several Nuremberg veterans such as Taylor, together with a number of Ivy League luminaries, tried to fund through the Carnegie Endowment at the end of the 1940s.[109] Intended to reinvigorate Nuremberg's role as the beginning of institutionalized international criminal justice, the main job would have fallen to John H. E. Fried, another émigré jurist (and, incidentally, Kelsen's nephew), who had come to Nuremberg as the International Labour Organization (ILO) specialist on forced labour. After a brief stint in the US prosecutor's office he had served as the NMT judges' principal legal adviser and on the editorial committee for the published proceedings. Preserving the trial's legacy, Fried contended, served a dual purpose: it would prevent a rerun of the war guilt controversy after 1918, and even more importantly, 'Nuremberg' deserved elaboration if 'the prospects for international legislation and international justice (which must precede world-government)' were to be kept alive.[110]

Fried's hopes seemed to be vindicated by the efforts of several protagonists to define the trials' legacy on the international stage and to see its innovations enshrined in international law. While Biddle urged the rapid drafting of an international code of criminal law,[111] several former Nurembergers reconvened in the run-up to the Genocide Convention. However, reflecting their different missions—Shawcross as a guarded British diplomat, Trainin as the Kremlin's leading theoretician, Vabres as the self-proclaimed 'champion of Nuremberg' in international jurisprudence, and Lemkin in his own lifelong pursuit—they were not necessarily on the same team. Against the backdrop of the escalating Cold War in which international law became one more arena for the two blocs to attack each other by instrumentalizing concepts such as genocide the Nuremberg coalition all but disintegrated. Efforts by the likes of Cassin, Vabres, and Trainin to campaign for an international criminal court were dead in the water.[112]

What followed was a fifty-year lull of international criminal justice in which Nuremberg was 'more a curiosity than a model'.[113] It would be saved only by the ad hoc tribunals for Yugoslavia and Rwanda and redeemed by the establishment of the International Criminal Court in 1998. That it would fall to Ferencz to represent the 'Committee of Former Nuremberg Prosecutors for a Permanent International

[109] Priemel, *Betrayal* (n 26) 397f.

[110] Fried to Lasswell, 13 April 1948, UAA, John Fried Papers, Series 2-3, Box 2, F.45. Cf. Priemel, *Betrayal* (n 26) 160, 192, 211.

[111] Biddle, Report to the President, 9 November 1946, HSTL, Harry S. Truman Papers, PSF, Box 123, F.123–125.

[112] Wechsler to Taylor, 16 June 1947, CLS, Wechser Papers, X–101–3; Lewis, *Birth* (n 80) 181–228; Weiss-Wendt, *Soviet Union* (n 3) 75–80, 101f., 109f.

[113] William Schabas, *Unimaginable Atrocities. Justice, Politics, and Rights at the War Crimes Tribunals* (Oxford: Oxford University Press, 2012), 2.

Criminal Court' combined poetic justice with irony, given Ferencz' untiring promotion of such a court as well as of his hazy position on Vietnam.[114] It also allowed drawing more or less straight lines from 'Nuremberg to The Hague', apparently vindicating the legacy workers while, at the same time the actual politics of the tribunals and especially the International Criminal Court, drove home 'realist' messages of power politics.[115]

Conclusion

There was very little rhetoric of 'the war to end all wars' kind heard in and around Nuremberg, but then again, this had not been a jurist's but a novelist's phrase, popularized by a historian turned politician. For sure, there were the high-strung formulas of Jackson's opening speech in which he professed his hope that the IMT would fulfil 'humanity's aspirations to do justice'.[116] These were not just mere soundbites, they expressed a genuine enthusiasm for the Nuremberg project. Jackson took great pride in the IMT's achievements and declared he would 'be willing to close my career on the record made here'.[117] If this betrayed a sense for the singular opportunity Nuremberg offered to crown an already distinguished career in law, Jackson was hardly alone. Other prosecutors, defence lawyers, and the odd judge appreciated that participation in the trials was likely to be their only claim to fame; advertising and preserving its achievements made biographical sense.[118]

At the same time key protagonists such as Maxwell Fyfe and Jackson were adroit politicians while Nikitchenko learned, if painfully, how to reconcile the orders from Moscow with the immediate expectations in Nuremberg. These men were certainly aware of the limitations of any trial. Advancing international criminal law and contributing to post-war institution building was fine, but compromises when it came to formulating counts and limitations as to establishing precedent were inevitable if Allied unity was to be upheld and unwelcome repercussions at home were to be avoided. They were also aware that the historical window of opportunity was rapidly closing.[119]

If these lawyers' strategies were strongly informed by their professional ambition and their politician personas, this did not rule out moral convictions. In this

[114] Circular, 28 May 1998, HLL, Belle Mayer Zeck Papers, Box 7, F.9.

[115] Ronen Steinke, *The Politics of International Criminal Justice. German Perspectives from Nuremberg to The Hague* (Oxford: Hart, 2012).

[116] *Trial of the Major War Criminals* (n 80) II, 101.

[117] Jackson to Frankfurter, 28 April 1946, LoC, Jackson Papers, Box 100, F. 'Correspondence Supreme Court'.

[118] Cf. Dirk Pöppmann, 'The Trials of Robert Kempner. From Stateless Immigrant to Prosecutor of the Foreign Office', and Hilary Earl, 'A Judge, a Prosecutor, and a Mass Murderer: Dynamics in the SS-Einsatzgruppen Trial', both in Priemel and Stiller, *Reassessing* (n 46) 23–46, 47–73.

[119] Jackson to Byrnes, 16 November 1946, YULMA, Lippmann Papers, Reel 70, Box 80, F.1135.

they resembled their rank and file who were mostly interested in staging successful trials, winning guilty verdicts and punishing defendants for whom they felt loathing and disgust more often than not. 'Justice' rather than 'internationalism' was the common denominator of prosecutors such as Jacques Herzog, Seymour Krieger, and, behind the barrage of antifascist rhetoric, Arkadi Poltorak; if both were feasible, all the better.[120] This sentiment was also shared by the majority of judges who understood their function to uphold legal standards by guaranteeing fair trials and sticking to well-trodden legal paths wherever possible. Still, the doctrinal conservatism displayed by many tribunals did not keep them from tendering suggestions of how to reform international law in the text of their opinions or in subsequent writings. Nuremberg's true critics did not sit on the bench but on its fences: the new cohort of 'realist' critics was fundamentally sceptical of law's systemic power to create a legally prescribed international community—even if this criticism misread what the institution builders were saying. Their point was not about inevitability but the lack of acceptable alternatives.

That it was perfectly possible to move from prosecution adviser to a realist-in-the-making, illustrates the mutability of juridical hats so typical of Nuremberg. Continued wartime pragmatism and the fluidity of juridical jobs promoted the transnational and transprofessional flow of ideas, often through productive conflict: novices to the academic discipline of international law turned into prosecution counsel, academic grandees into judges and judges into attorneys (and back again), and prosecutors took professorial gowns rather than silk. And even though for Germans, unless of the exiled variety, nationality was decisive in interpreting their role, personal ambitions and trivial but potent bread-and-butter concerns mattered too. At the end of the day, the defence played by the rules, confirming them in the process. A German lawyer's hat was not altogether different from that of his Allied peers.

But the common ground went only so far, and sharing a legal language did not always bridge gaps between different protagonists precisely because their vernaculars were deeply imbued with different traditions and beliefs. Returning to Oscar Schachter, there certainly was 'a *pénétration pacifique* of ideas from the nongovernmental into official channels'—even though it was not always all that peaceful—but 'dedicated to a common intellectual enterprise', the lawyers in and around Nuremberg were not. The making of 'Nuremberg' as a pivotal moment in international history was a prime example of the 'hidden turf battles' fought by lawyers over conflicting national goals, over legal substance and procedure, over career prospects and prestige.[121]

[120] Falco, *Juge* (n 79) 32, 75; Herzog, *Nuremberg* (n 68) xvi, xxi–xxii; Poltorak, *Epilog* (n 83) 160, 413, 623; Krieger to Rita Krieger, 2 & 15 December 1945, USHMM, Krieger Papers, Series 1, Box 1, F.1.

[121] Schachter, 'College' (n 1) 217; Yves Dezalay and Bryant G. Garth, 'Introduction: Constructing Transnational Justice', in Yves Dezalay and Bryant G. Garth (eds), *Lawyers and the Construction of Transnational Justice* (London: Routledge, 2012), 3–12, 5.

These were further complicated by the fact that the lawyers' varying activities in court, in governmental offices, in academic debate, and in the daily diplomacy that characterized London and Nuremberg, placed them near simultaneously in different social subsystems. That communicative codes changed if one ventured from politics to science to courts of law and back again, and that something might get lost in translation, few if any of the trials' protagonists were aware of. Yet it is precisely in identifying which hat which lawyer wore, at what stage of the trials, and with what degree of self-reflection, that we can explain both the dynamism of Nuremberg and its limitations.

10

Fluid Boundaries in the Divisible College

The International Law Association and the Indus Waters Dispute in the 1950s

Katharina Rietzler

The 1950s were a decade of considerable turmoil that transformed international law as a discipline and professional practice. The Second World War had undermined European pretences to posit Western culture as the moral core of the international legal community. Many Western jurists regarded with apprehension the admission of new sovereign states from the non-Western world to the international community. As non-Western traditions became sources for international law, some feared for its unity and coherence. Prominent European jurists such as the Austrian Alfred Verdross and the Belgian Charles De Visscher made this point in the early 1950s.[1] White European scholars who disagreed with this viewpoint, and who maintained that international law had never been solely of European origin, were rare. One such exception was C. H. Alexandrowicz, a Polish jurist who taught at the University of Madras in India.[2] Clearly, this was during a period when international legal universalism, often invoked after the mid-nineteenth century, was tested by the practical realities of decolonization and non-Western participation in the development of international legal doctrine.

At the same time, the professional bodies that had been founded in the nineteenth century, most importantly the International Law Association (ILA), clung to a self-image that has memorably been described as an 'invisible college'. Coined by Oscar Schachter in 1977, the term implies a unity of purpose among legal scholars but also recognizes the multiple allegiances of international lawyers, as representatives of governments, jurisconsultes, bearers of a specific national identity, or purportedly objective scholars. Schachter acknowledged that activities in the governmental sphere would have an impact on the scholarly sphere and vice versa. However, he also argued that structures and mechanisms within the international legal community balanced out particular interests and, via representative

[1] Arnulf Becker Lorca, *Mestizo International Law: A Global Intellectual History 1842–1933* (Cambridge: Cambridge University Press, 2014), 31.

[2] Ibid., 33–4. For a selection of Alexandrowicz' writings see C. H. Alexandrowicz contributions in David Armitage and Jennifer Pitts (eds), *The Law of Nations in Global History* (Oxford: Oxford University Press, 2017).

Katharina Rietzler, *Fluid Boundaries in the Divisible College* In: *Crafting the International Order.* Edited by: Marcus M. Payk and Kim Christian Priemel, Oxford University Press (2021).
DOI: 10.1093/oso/9780198863830.003.0010

bodies such as the ILA, produced authoritative statements on the contents of international law. In fact, Schachter claimed, it was essential for bodies such as the ILA to represent and amalgamate particular interests, so that they could make international law ever more responsive to the needs of states and their citizens: 'the individual jurists are likely to be affected by national or other particularistic factors linked to their origin and background. A more heterogeneous and representative body can be expected to balance out those particularistic influences.' Ideally, wrote Schachter, 'international juridical bodies should be representative of the world as a whole'.[3]

Yet, as scholars such as Anthea Roberts have argued more recently, there are real and multiple power differentials within the 'invisible college' Schachter described, and his idealized account masks the ways in which dominant approaches are made to appear as neutral. Thus, it would be more appropriate to speak of a 'divisible college'.[4] Representative scholarly bodies such as the ILA featured asymmetries of discursive power and intellectual resources. Historians have underlined how international law as an academic discipline and as a profession was structured by Eurocentric ideas about its Christian-European origins, and how an ostensible universalism rubbed against deeply ingrained hierarchies of power and influence.[5] Yet, differences between the 'West' and the Global South were not the only ones at play in the doctrinal disputes at the ILA. As Roberts rightly points out, there were multiple axes of difference that created multiple, overlapping communities under the broad umbrella of the international legal community.[6] The idea of discrete communities in the international legal profession is further complicated by the practice of legal advising across power-political, national, and cultural boundaries in the post-colonial era. Using a concrete case study, in which we see the ILA drawn into an international dispute between two post-colonial nations over water, an essential natural resource, I trace the complex interplay between these different forces. Legal disputes over international rivers such as the Helmand or the Jordan were rife in the decades after the Second World War. This was a specific moment in international law when decolonization drew up new international borders

[3] Oscar Schachter, 'The Invisible College of International Lawyers', *Northwestern University Law Review* 72, 2 (1977–1978), 217–26, at 223.

[4] Anthea Roberts, *Is International Law International?* (New York, NY: Oxford University Press, 2017), at 2; see also Peggy McGuinness, 'Jose Alvarez on the Internet, Blogging, and the Democratization of the "Invisible College" of International Lawyers', *Opinio Juris* blog, 9 November 2007, http://opiniojuris.org/2007/11/09/jose-alvarez-on-the-internet-blogging-and-the-democratization-of-the-invisible-college-of-international-lawyers/ (accessed 18 August 2020).

[5] Lauren Benton, *A Search for Sovereignty: Law and Geography in European Empires, 1400–1900* (New York, NY: Cambridge University Press, 2010); Antony Anghie, *Imperialism, Sovereignty and the Making of International Law* (Cambridge: Cambridge University Press, 2005); Martti Koskenniemi, *The Gentle Civilizer of Nations: The Rise and Fall of International Law, 1870–1960* (Cambridge: Cambridge University Press, 2000).

[6] Roberts, *International Law* (n 4)

across formerly politically integrated economic units and shifted meanings of 'the international'.

The case I focus on is the Indus waters dispute between India and Pakistan over the use of the waters of the Indus river system. The dispute was a direct outcome of the partition of South Asia in 1947. In the 1950s, it became a focal point for Cold War geopolitics as well as Western developmental ambitions. While the dispute was still ongoing and before it was settled by treaty in 1960, the ILA held a series of scholarly meetings and conferences and created a river law committee in 1954 that included the legal advisers of India and Pakistan. The ILA finally adopted the Helsinki Rules on the Uses of the Waters of International Rivers in 1966, which are still regarded as authoritative and have received more universal endorsement than similar UN conventions.[7] While the institutional structures of the ILA were important to the way the Indus waters dispute was resolved, the actions of individual jurists were also crucial because they mobilized their legal expertise within the ILA once the political negotiations had reached an impasse in the mid-1950s. Interestingly, Schachter himself held up the Helsinki rules as the ILA's key achievement in international legislation.[8]

I focus on four central figures: the German jurist and legal scholar, Friedrich Berber, advisor to the Indian government; the US lawyer and government official, John Laylin, who advised Pakistan; S. M. Sikri, the Advocate General of East Punjab and later Chief Justice of India; and Manzur Qadir, Senior Advocate at the Supreme Court of Pakistan and Foreign Minister from 1958. The governments of India and Pakistan regarded legal arguments over international river law as an important plank of their respective campaigns to win international support for their positions in the Indus waters dispute. In this context, I am interested both in the particular dynamics inherent in the way Western jurists advised non-Western governments, and the ways in which non-Western jurists sought to mobilize Western-dominated professional organizations such as the ILA for their purposes at a time when Eurocentric conceptions of international law were on the defensive. Moreover, this case highlights the ways in which multiple differences—with regard to language, training, power, and politics—resulted in shifting and overlapping communities within the ILA.[9]

Recent research has focused on the political, technological, and environmental history of the dispute, as well as the trilateral negotiations between India, Pakistan, and the World Bank in New York.[10] This chapter analyses the legal dimensions and

[7] Slavko Bogdanović (ed.), *International Law of Water Resources: Contribution of the International Law Association (1954–2000)* (The Hague: Kluwer, 2001), xiii.

[8] Schachter, 'Invisible College' (n 3) 224.

[9] On the role of Western expertise in South Asia see most recently David C. Engerman, *The Price of Aid: The Economic Cold War in India* (Cambridge, MA: Harvard University Press, 2018); Corinna Unger, *Entwicklungspfade in Indien: eine internationale Geschichte 1947–1980* (Göttingen: Wallstein, 20 15).

[10] Daniel Haines, *Rivers Divided: Indus Basin Waters in the Making of India and Pakistan* (New York, NY: Oxford University Press, 2017); David Gilmartin, *Blood and Water: The Indus River Basin in*

highlights the neglected role of the ILA.[11] Based on archival research, the essay moves the focus away from Karachi, New Delhi, and Washington, DC to the genteel conferences of the ILA, which were held in picturesque locations, covered by local and national press outlets, and featured ladies' programmes, banquets, and even the occasional castle, floodlit in honour of the distinguished jurists assembled.[12] This was where major arguments about what the law of international rivers was, and should be, were fought out. In this context, the ILA's 1954, 1956, and 1958 conferences were crucial, before the ILA finally adopted the Helsinki Rules in 1966. Of equal importance was the ILA's international Rivers Committee which met in between the main conferences. Of course, the ILA recognized that the participants in its conferences and members of its Rivers Committee were chiefly representing the views of governments 'who were concerned lest the outcome of the Committee's deliberations would prejudice their bargaining positions. This concern was reflected not only in the rapid increase in the size of the Committee but also in the individuals who became its members.'[13] But the ILA did not necessarily perceive such representation as undue influence, in keeping with the institutional logic of the 'invisible college' which predicted that in the end the spirit of disinterested inquiry would prevail.

In this chapter, I will first outline the differences in professional formation between the four jurists who became the main protagonists on the ILA international Rivers Committee in the context of the Indus waters dispute. I will then provide a short analysis of its main political, technological, and legal aspects before providing an analysis of the political and legal debates that took place under the auspices of the ILA from the mid-1950s. Here, Western legal advisers and jurists from the Indian subcontinent engaged in conflict resolution within the structures of a professional association with universalist ambitions. This interaction temporarily destabilized the consensus within the international legal community on the extent

Modern History (Berkeley, CA: University of California Press, 2015), chapters 6 and 7; Majed Akhter, 'The Geopolitics of Infrastructure: Development, Expertise, and Nation on the Indus Rivers' (PhD diss., University of Arizona, 2013); Undala Z. Alam, 'Water Rationality: Mediating the Indus Water Treaty' (PhD diss., Durham University, 1998); for an older but still authoritative study see Aloys Arthur Michel, *The Indus Rivers: A Study of the Effects of Partition* (New Haven, CT: Yale University Press, 1967); for a short summary see Miriam R. Lowi, *Water and Power* (Cambridge: Cambridge University Press, 1995), 61–7; and, from a legal perspective, though not based on archival research, Salman M. A. Salman and Kishor Uprety, *Conflict and Cooperation on South Asia's International Rivers: A Legal Perspective* (London: Kluwer Law International, 2002), 37–61.

[11] Studies on the dispute rarely mention the ILA's involvement in great detail. See, however, the reminiscences of an Indian official in the ministry of Works, Mines and Power, Niranjan D. Gulhati, *Indus Water Treaty: An Exercise in International Mediation* (Bombay: Allied Publishers, 1973), 328–9.

[12] ILA Edinburgh Conference programme, 8–14 August 1954, ILA/2/27, f.1, International Law Association Archive, IALS Archives, Institute of Advanced Legal Studies, London (hereafter ILA Archive).

[13] Charles Bourne, 'The International Law Association's Contributions to International Water Resources Law', in Slavko Bogdanović (ed.), *International Law of Water Resources: Contribution of the International Law Association (1954–2000)* (The Hague: Kluwer, 2001), 3–57, at 5.

to which international law could be regarded as settled in a postcolonial world. It was precisely because the ILA was a 'divisible' college that claims for the limits of international law's universality could be articulated and resolved.

Many Roads to the Divisible College

The ILA was founded in 1873 as the Association for the Reform and Codification of the Law of Nations, in the same year as its sister organization, the Institut de Droit International. Both devoted themselves to international law as a liberal reformist and cosmopolitan project and to advancing the interests of the international legal profession as an autonomous voice against, if need be, the interests of individual states. More Anglo-American and also more practitioner-oriented than the Institut de Droit international, the ILA was open to businessmen, politicians, and non-legal scholars. After the Second World War, it solidified its importance as an international non-governmental organization, achieving consultative status with several UN agencies, notably ECOSOC (United Nations Economic and Social Council). While its Executive Council was in London, most of the ILA's work took place in international committees and was debated at biannual conferences.[14] Although European and North American international lawyers dominated the ILA, its sessions welcomed members from the rest of the world from the decade of its foundation. In fact, the presence within the ILA of jurists from outside Europe and North America was essential for demonstrating the organization's universal character, thus affirming its legitimacy as a global institution.[15]

In the 1950s, the period under discussion, most ILA jurists from the non-Western world would have been steeped in Western legal traditions. The newly independent nations of the Indian subcontinent participated in international legal structures after the end of British colonialism, while jurists of that generation produced reams of scholarship which sought to prove ancient and medieval India's contribution to the evolution of the law of nations. In their training, jurists from the Indian subcontinent 'turned to the West to learn the language of international law'. But this did not mean that they wholeheartedly subscribed to a progressive narrative about international law as a universal force for good. The result, especially among Indian lawyers, was an ambivalent attitude which sought to resist the imperialism inherent in international law *and* to utilize international legal structures to improve the lot of India's population.[16]

[14] Ruth Frendo, 'The Archives of the International Law Association', *Legal Information Management* 17, 2 (2017), 97–102.

[15] Becker Lorca, *Mestizo International Law* (n 1) 1, 30; on the history of the ILA see also Maarten Bos (ed.), *The Present State of International Law and Other Essays: Written in Honour of the Centenary Celebration of the International Law Association 1873–1973* (The Hague: Kluwer, 1973).

[16] B. S. Chimni, 'International Law Scholarship in Post-colonial India: Coping with Dualism', *LJIL* 23 (2010), 23–51, at 24.

S. M. Sikri and Manzur Qadir, the jurists advising India and Pakistan in the Indus dispute, belonged to this generation. They began their legal careers in British India and became leaders in their profession. Both were first and foremost practitioners, and both acceded to high office in their country's political and legal system. Sarv Mittra Sikri (1908–1992) began his legal career in the 1930s as a practising lawyer at the Lahore High Court, after attending Cambridge University in England and being called to the bar at Lincoln's Inn. After the partition of British India, when Lahore became part of Pakistani territory, Sikri served first as Assistant Advocate General and then Advocate General of the Indian part of the Punjab. He continued in this role until 1964, when he was appointed as judge of the Supreme Court of India. In 1971, he ascended to the rank of Chief Justice. Sikri represented India at numerous international conferences and also served on the Executive Committee of the Indian Branch of the ILA. As a Supreme Court Justice and later Chief Justice, Sikri developed a reputation for fierce independence from political interference because he thwarted Indira Gandhi's attempts to push through amendments to the Indian Constitution.[17]

Sikri's Pakistani counterpart, Manzur Qadir (1913–1974), took a very different attitude when it came to questions of judicial independence from political power. Like Sikri, Qadir became one of his country's leading jurists following independence while working at the highest levels of policy-making and diplomacy. Trained in England (he was also called to the bar at Lincoln's Inn), Qadir had been serving as a senior advocate at the Supreme Court of Pakistan when he became involved in the Indus waters dispute. After the coup d'état of 1958, Pakistan's military dictator Ayub Khan made Qadir one of his closest advisers. Not only did Qadir serve as the country's Foreign Minister until 1962, he was also the architect of several policies that tightened Khan's grip on Pakistani culture and politics, such as the Basic Democracies Order of 1959. Qadir is also credited as the author of the country's 1962 Constitution, which did not allow for the judicial review of laws. In the same year, Qadir was appointed Chief Justice of the Lahore High Court, against the opposition of some Pakistani bar associations which claimed that Qadir had shown little respect for judicial independence.[18]

Laylin and Berber, the Western advisors involved in the Indus dispute, also acted at the interface of international law and politics for the entirety of their careers. John G. Laylin (1902–1979), a graduate of Harvard Law School, served in Franklin Delano Roosevelt's administration at the US Treasury before joining

[17] Supreme Court of India, 'Former Chief Justice and Judges', https://main.sci.gov.in/chief-justice-judges (accessed 18 August 2020); Kuldip Singh, 'Obituary: Justice Mittra Sikri', *Independent* [UK], 3 October 1992.

[18] Ralph Braibanti, 'Public Bureaucracy and Judiciary in Pakistan', in Joseph LaPalombara (ed.), *Bureaucracy and Political Development* (Princeton, NJ: Princeton University Press, 1967), 360–440, at 438–9; Saadia Toor, *The State of Islam: Culture and Cold War Politics in Pakistan* (London: Pluto Press, 2011), 86–92; Ayesha Jalal, *The Struggle for Pakistan* (Cambridge, Mass.: Harvard University Press, 2014), 105–6.

the prominent Washington, DC law firm Covington & Burling. As an attorney, Laylin began picking up contracts to provide legal advice to governments in the late 1930. After the Second World War, he became a sought-after legal consultant in interstate disputes over territory and natural resources, particularly in Asia.[19] Laylin's colleagues in the American Society of International Law, where he served on the Executive Council during the 1960s, would remember his 'keen sense of the interplay between law and politics'.[20] Such qualities were advantageous in Laylin's professional life. Important in the context of river law is his work for Iran, whom Laylin represented in the Azerbaijan case against the Soviet Union at the UN Security Council in 1946. Laylin continued to advise the Iranian government in the Helmand River dispute with Afghanistan, in which the United States was acting as a mediator. The dispute revolved around Afghan plans to divert, through dam and canal construction, the waters of the Helmand River which flows through Afghanistan before reaching eastern Iran.[21] Laylin thus acquired a considerable amount of knowledge on the geographical, political, and legal problems affecting river basins in a world region which was marked by British imperial retreat and a more assertive US presence. This put him in an ideal position to represent Pakistan in its dispute with India from 1949.

The interplay of law and politics also featured prominently in the life of Friedrich Berber (1898–1984). Berber, the son of a Methodist preacher, completed a doctorate on the legal relations between Britain and its Dominions. Fascinated with the intersection of law and politics in the early 1930s, Berber taught international relations and international law at the *Deutsche Hochschule für Politik* in Berlin and began to write polemics against liberal international law. After the Nazis assumed power in 1933, Berber decided to work with the regime and became a scholar-propagandist for the Nazi foreign policy elite. He headed foreign affairs institutes in Hamburg and Berlin, received a professorship, and was an advisor to Joachim von Ribbentrop, Hitler's foreign minister. After the Second World War, Berber worked as a legal adviser to the French military government in occupied Germany. His scholarly career, however, stalled due to his Nazi past and he was unable to assume another academic post. At this point Berber moved to India where he managed to secure the appointment as a legal adviser to the Nehru government in January 1951. His knowledge of legal problems affecting the British Empire was

[19] 'John Laylin, International Lawyer, Dies', *Washington Post*, 18 February 1979. In 1939, Laylin advised Colombia on servicing its foreign debt, Braden to US Secretary of State, Bogota, 18 July 1939, in *Foreign Relations of the United States, 1939, The American Republics*, vol. v, document 499, https://history.state.gov/historicaldocuments/frus1939v05/d499 (accessed 18 August 2020).

[20] Peter D. Trooboff, 'John G. Laylin (1902–1979)', *AJIL* 73, 3 (1979), 475.

[21] Some of John G. Laylin's personal papers have been made available digitally by Oregon State University. The Middle East Water Collection, 'Donor: John G. Laylin', https://oregondigital.org/sets/middle-east-water/page/laylin (accessed 18 August 2020); for a summary of the Helmand dispute see Glen Hearns, 'The Helmand River and the Afghan-Iranian Treaty of 1973', International Water Law Project blog, https://www.internationalwaterlaw.org/blog/2015/07/23/the-helmand-river-and-the-afghan-iranian-treaty-of-1973// (accessed 18 August 2020).

of advantage, as was a long-standing interest in Indian culture and politics. Berber advised New Delhi on the waters dispute with Pakistan and represented India in intergovernmental negotiations before moving back to Munich as a professor of international law in 1954. Although there was considerable opposition to his appointment, Berber benefited from the intercession on his behalf by the ambassador of the Federal Republic of Germany in India. After his return to Germany, Berber continued to act as a consultant for the Indian government, wrote several publications on international water law as well as international public law, and became a long-term member of the ILA's Rivers Committee, even rising to the rank of special rapporteur.[22] His experiences provided him with an acute sensibility for the ways in which international law could make a difference to the political ambitions of states, as was the case with Laylin.

The Origins of the Indus Waters Dispute

The Indus waters dispute had its origins in the partition of British India in 1947. The new international border between them, drawn up on the basis of religious demography, separated an integrated ecological and economic unit. The Indus river basin stretches from its delta in the south-west across an agricultural plain to a mountainous region in the north-east, where the six major rivers of the Indus system rise .

Under British rule the colonial state had entrenched its reach by controlling the basin's waters, the most critical natural resource in this dry region. Colonial authorities implemented large-scale irrigation projects (dams and canals) from the 1880s. These benefitted mostly the Western part of the province of Punjab, which, after partition, belonged to the territory of Muslim-majority Pakistan. The lands of the East Punjab, now on the Indian side of the border, possessed fewer canals for irrigation and were thus harder to farm. Apportioning water resources had already been contentious under British rule. A commission headed by Indian jurist Benegal Rau attempted to adjudicate a water dispute between Punjab and Sindh but the resulting agreement, drafted in 1942, was never ratified. Although the British Boundary Commission recognized at the time of Partition that dividing up an integrated canal system would only exacerbate disputes over water, it prioritized religious criteria over geography.[23] Once Pakistan and India achieved sovereign

[22] Friedrich Berber, *Die Rechtsbeziehungen der britischen Dominions zum Mutterlande* (Ansbach: Brügel, 1929); Friedrich Berber, *Sicherheit und Gerechtigkeit: Eine allgemeinverständliche Einführung in die Hauptprobleme der Völkerrechtspolitik* (Berlin: Carl Heymanns, 1934); On Berber's biography and intellectual formation see Katharina Rietzler, 'Counter-Imperial Orientalism: Friedrich Berber and the Politics of International Law in Germany and India, 1920s–1960s', *Journal of Global History* 11 (2016), 113–34.

[23] Haines, *Rivers Divided* (n 10) 28–30, 37–8, 42; on colonial water law in the Punjab see Gilmartin, *Blood and Water* (n 10) chapter 4.

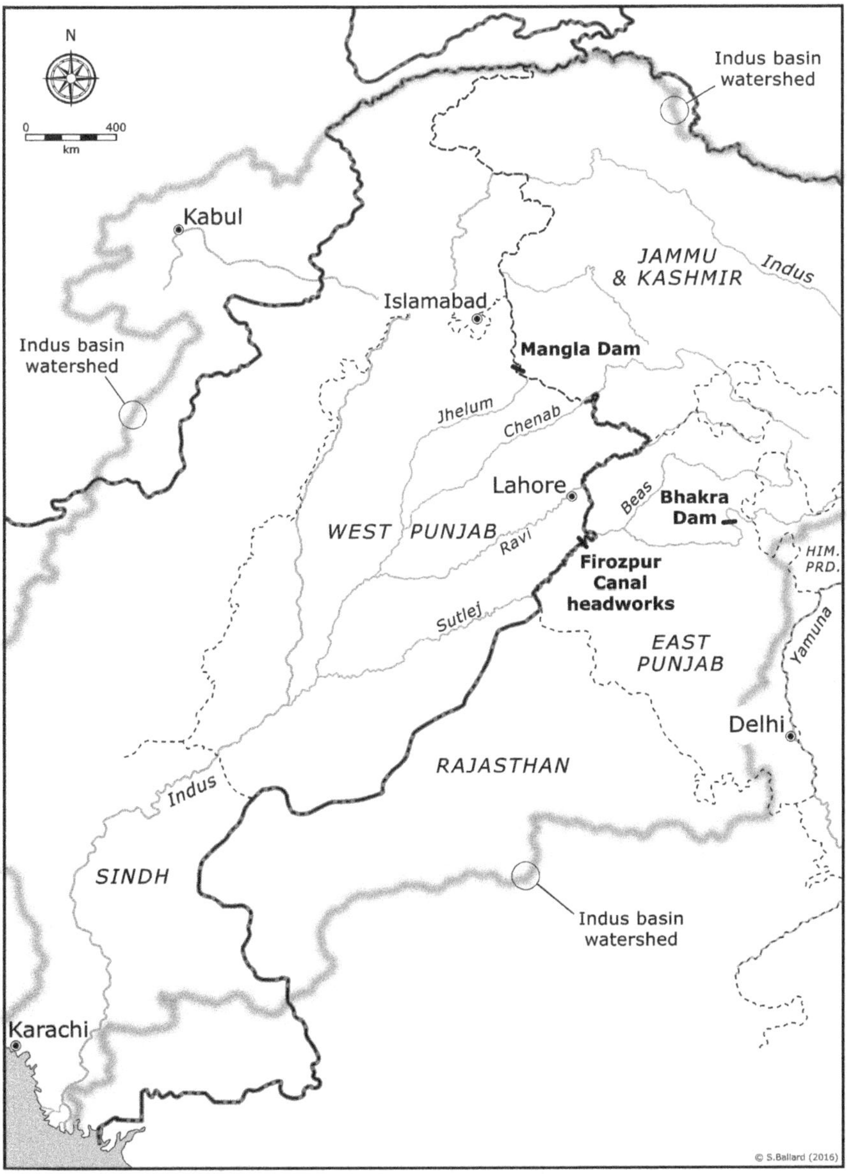

The Indus River Basin.

Reproduced from Daniel Haines, *Rivers Divided: Indus Basin Waters in the Making of India and Pakistan* (London: Hurst, 2017), with kind permission from C. Hurst & Co.

statehood, competing claims to the Indus basin's waters, which had thus far been put forward at the sub-state level, became the source of an international conflict that was intertwined with the nation-building projects of both countries.

Control over water was a powerful symbol of post-colonial sovereignty. As the historian Daniel Haines has argued, expanding the amount of tillable land through irrigation promised economic development and legitimized the authority of the post-colonial state. Leaders in both countries embraced development discourses as they formulated competing plans for their uses of Indus river waters. India, which had a large and restive refugee population in its north-western states, prioritized the irrigation of more land. This aim necessitated diverting canal waters that were flowing downstream into Pakistan. Indian engineers were physically able to re-route water flows as five of the six major Indus rivers rise on Indian territory. As the upstream nation, India also controlled important irrigation headworks. By 1948, there were over 100 water surface projects in planning or under construction in the (Indian) East Punjab.

Pakistani leaders also envisioned water resources development as a key plank of their nation's overall economic agenda, but this entailed maintaining colonial-era irrigation systems as well as developing new ones. As the downstream nation, Pakistan depended on Indian cooperation to fulfil its water needs.[24] Immediately after partition, a temporary agreement ensured continued water supply to Pakistan. However, when the agreement expired in March 1948, the state government of East Punjab temporarily stopped the water supply to West Punjab, threatening 1 million acres of agricultural land with drought. In May 1948, India and Pakistan signed the Inter-Dominion Agreement in which India agreed to release water to Pakistan against the payment of charges. This implied Pakistan's acceptance of India's legal right to dispose of river waters flowing through its territory. By the summer of 1950, Pakistan had discontinued the payments and declared the Inter-Dominion Agreement null and void.[25]

The Inter-Dominion Agreement crystallized the legal arguments on each side in the dispute. India argued that it possessed territorial sovereignty over the river waters. The claim was first formulated in 1948 by East Punjabi engineers who claimed that India had the right to divert river water for her own development needs and that Pakistan would have to pay if it wanted to benefit from upstream water resources. This position was an extreme one and only shared to some extent by India's central government. Prime minister Jawaharlal Nehru put pressure on the East Punjabi government after it shut off the flow of water to Pakistan in April 1948, and India's Attorney General recognized that a claim to absolute sovereignty over river waters was shaky. Yet, overall, Indian politicians consistently argued that an

[24] Haines, *Rivers Divided* (n 10) 3, 38–41, 43–4; Salman and Uprety, *Conflict and Cooperation* (n 10) 38–41.

[25] Haines, *Rivers Divided* (n 10) 43–5; Lowi, *Water and Power* (n 10) 64.

upstream riparian state had the right to dispose of water resources as it saw fit, even if such rights should be tempered by a general moral duty to share resources equitably. Crucially, the Indian position disputed the idea that West Punjab's historic use of the waters entitled it to future use, an argument termed 'prior appropriation'. Pakistani politicians, however, not only insisted that such historic use had to be protected but that it was also an essential element of Pakistan's own national sovereignty. In this view, India had no right to build new irrigation systems that could harm Pakistan's water supply in any way.[26] These two positions were irreconcilable. They also mapped onto a set of principles in the emerging law of international rivers.

By the mid-twentieth century, jurists began to recognize four possible principles in the law of international rivers as developed by legal argument and state practice. The principle of absolute territorial sovereignty, also known as the Harmon Doctrine, was the most controversial of these as it declared that states were free to dispose of water resources on their territory as they saw fit. There was no concern for the potential harm done to a downstream riparian state by an upstream one. However, the Harmon Doctrine had never been endorsed in practice. The second principle, absolute territorial integrity, was almost as inflexible, as it prioritized protecting the natural flow of water resources across borders. This meant a downstream riparian state could insist on its historical uses of water to remain undisturbed, thus depriving the upstream riparian state of any significant development of such resources on its own territory. Both principles in effect allowed states to disregard the interests of their neighbours and gave them a right of veto. The third principle combined limited territorial integrity with limited territorial sovereignty. All riparian states had to consider the interests of one another and establish a system under which they received the maximum benefit from shared water resources without doing harm to others. How they should do this was, however, unclear. The fourth principle built on the idea of international river systems as common economic units, to be administered collectively by a community of riparian states. In practice, however, such integrated economic development of rivers across state borders was hard to achieve.[27] (This was also the case in the Indus waters dispute which saw the eventual demise of a US proposal for the shared economic development of the basin.) Altogether, these principles did not add up to a universally accepted body of international law but rather possible lines of argument. The law of international rivers was far from settled.[28]

[26] Haines, *Rivers Divided* (n 10) 47–51.

[27] Salman and Uprety, *Conflict and Cooperation* (n 10) 11–16. See also Herbert Arthur Smith, *The Economic Uses of International Rivers* (London: P.S. King & Son, 1931), 144–53.

[28] However, legal regimes for international river systems date back to at least the nineteenth century. Joseph Chamberlain, *The Regime of the International Rivers: Danube and Rhine* (PhD thesis, Columbia University, 1923).

Nonetheless, as the downstream riparian state who had already been deprived of historic water flows once by its powerful neighbour, Pakistan could be seen to have the stronger case when it came to appealing to the international community on the grounds of universal justice. In the absence of a settled body of international law, there were routes available that would help establish legal principles. One of these was adjudication. In the aftermath of the Inter-Dominion Agreement, Pakistan attempted to push its claim for territorial integrity in several international fora. Such attempts picked up speed once the government of Pakistan hired John Laylin's law firm, Covington & Burling, in early 1949. In June of the same year, Pakistan proposed to submit the Indus waters dispute to the International Court of Justice, a suggestion that India rejected. US observers thought that Pakistan could win such a court case, even if it could not enforce a judgment in its favour.[29]

Pakistan then turned to codification. In October 1949, the government submitted a draft resolution to the Sixth Committee of the UN calling upon the UN's International Law Commission to include the subject of international rivers in its list of topics for codification. The Pakistani delegation at the UN argued that 'many rivers used for transportation and irrigation flowed through different countries and had consequently formed the object of international treaties and conventions, as well as of international disputes', in effect claiming that international law was more settled than publicists had previously stated. However, Pakistan failed to get international rivers on the International Law Commission's agenda. The Soviet representative on the Commission recommended that 'it would be more practical to settle [the dispute with India] directly' and urged Pakistan to withdraw the proposal, which it did after assurances from the US representative that the Commission would give due consideration to the question.[30] With codification stopped in its tracks, Pakistan was left to make 'a legal argument without recourse to the law'.[31]

Indian leaders understood that Pakistan was building a legal case to shore up its political position in the waters dispute. They mounted a two-pronged response. One element was to deny that international legal institutions or doctrine could make a meaningful contribution to the dispute's resolution. From the beginning of the dispute in 1947/48, Nehru repeatedly claimed that the issue at stake was not international law but human needs and development, creating a rhetorical opposition between two desirables that were not necessarily in opposition. Yet Nehru repeatedly emphasized that dry legal doctrines provided an unacceptably

[29] Gulhati, *Indus Water Treaty* (n 11) 73–4; Alam, 'Water Rationality' (n 10) 160–1, 322; Michel, *The Indus Rivers* (n 10) 219, 221.

[30] UN General Assembly, Sixth Committee, 166th meeting, 17 October 1949, A/C.6/SR.166, paragraphs 82, 100–5. In the 1930s, jurists had concluded that the law was 'not ripe for codification', Smith, *Economic Uses of International Rivers* (n 27) 158.

[31] Haines, *Rivers Divided* (n 10) 52.

narrow point of view on the conflict.[32] The Indian government was acutely aware of Pakistani efforts at the UN and briefed its foreign missions on how to counter Pakistan's invocations of international law.[33] At the same time, the Indian government built up its own legal expertise. In late 1949, it charged S. M. Sikri, then the Advocate General of East Punjab, with preparing an extensive study on the law of international rivers. Sikri, using the limited literature available in India, concluded that there were no international legal principles applicable to the Indus waters dispute.[34]

However, it seems that the Indian government felt the need to back up Sikri's assessment with the work of a foreign expert. In November 1950, three months after Pakistan declared the Inter-Dominion Agreement null and void, the governor-general of India asked a British Quaker contact to recommend a specialist 'in regard to waterways and also in private international law'.[35] This request resulted in Friedrich Berber's appointment in early 1951. One of Berber's first duties in Indian services was to collect legal source material in Western capitals (Berber was fluent in French and English) to establish whether there were accepted principles in the law of international rivers or whether the picture was too vague to assume the existence of any kind of customary law.[36] The research would lead to Berber's first substantial scholarly publication after the Second World War, a book on the sources of the international law of water resources. On his travels, Berber was accompanied by the Indian engineer Niranjan Gulhati, who subsequently published a book on irrigation methods.[37] In New Delhi, Berber advised the central government on the waters dispute but also on other international legal questions, for instance, on India's dealing with the UN's International Law Commission.[38]

Most importantly, Berber became a member of India's delegation to the World Bank in Washington, DC, where a potential resolution of the Indus waters dispute

[32] Jawaharlal Nehru, *Letters to Chief Ministers*, G. Parthasarathi (ed.) (New Delhi: Jawaharlal Nehru Memorial Fund, 1985–1989), vol. 1, 118; vol. 3, 606; see also Gulhati, *Indus Water Treaty* (n 11) 325.

[33] 'Directive on Canal Water Dispute between India and Pakistan—secret', National Archives of India, New Delhi (NAI), Ministry of External Affairs, Branch: External Publication, 6/1/7-XP(P)/49.

[34] Gulhati, *Indus Water Treaty* (n 11) 324.

[35] Horace Alexander to Bajpai, 28 December 1950 (copy), Library of the Society of Friends, London (LSF), Horace Alexander Papers, Temp. MSS 577/20.

[36] For more details on how the appointment came about see Rietzler, 'Friedrich Berber' (n 22) 130–1.

[37] Friedrich Berber, *Zwischen Macht und Gewissen: Lebenserinnerungen* (Munich: C.H. Beck, 1986), 190–1; Gulhati, *Indus Water Treaty* (n 11) 324; Alam, 'Water Rationality' (n 10) 189; Friedrich Berber, *Die Rechtsquellen des internationalen Wassernutzungsrechts* (Munich: Oldenbourg, 1955); revised edition in English: *Rivers in International Law*, transl. R. K. Batstone (London: Stevens & Sons, 1959); Niranjan D. Gulhati, *Irrigation in the World: A Global Review* (New Delhi: International Commission on Irrigation and Drainage, 1955).

[38] Canal waters dispute—Indo-Pakistan, Summary by Y. K. Puri, DS, NAI, External Affairs, Branch Pakistan—III, 6/1-Pak-III/51, on the proposal that India adhere to the convention of the International Court of Arbitration at The Hague. I am grateful to Daniel Haines for sharing this source; H.R. Krishnan, 'Comments on the Draft Convention on Arbitral Procedure', 20 October 1954, NAI, External Affairs, Branch UN II, 1611(100)-UNII.

was negotiated from 1952.[39] After David Lilienthal, a US New Dealer who chaired the Tennessee Valley Authority (TVA) in the 1940s, had published an alarmist article about the explosive potential of the Indus waters dispute in *Collier's* magazine in 1951, the World Bank offered its good offices to help Pakistan and India find a new arrangement over the canal waters. In the article, Lilienthal proposed developing the water resources of the Indus basin cooperatively, with India and Pakistan working together to irrigate more land than they could do on their own. This technocratic plan, envisioning complex engineering works for replacement canals that would allow India to use more water without reducing the overall supply to Pakistan, not only offered a seemingly neutral way out of a political impasse but was also tied in with US attempts to 'globalize' the New Deal in a Cold War context.[40] Promoting the TVA as a supposedly anti-totalitarian model for river development became an important plank of US foreign policy from the 1930s, not only in the Global South but also in Europe.[41] Lilienthal's suggestion to turn the Indus Valley into a new Tennessee Valley has to be seen in the context of developmental competition with the Soviet Union.

But the Lilienthal plan also embodied the legal ideal of a community of co-riparian states. Laylin, who had been given an advance copy of Lilienthal's article, strongly encouraged Pakistan to accept the World Bank offer. After 1950, there had been no real progress in resolving the dispute, and Lilienthal's proposal, which propelled engineers to prominence in the discussions, seemed to offer a way forward that would not force Pakistan to give up the legal rights it purported to have.[42] This did not mean that there were no attempts to exert political pressure. In June 1952, for instance, Laylin suggested to his contacts in the US diplomatic corps that India might be cowed into adopting a more conciliatory stance if threatened with the withholding of US security aid.[43] But overall, the negotiations at the World Bank proceeded on the understanding that the dispute could be resolved by the application of ingenious engineering solutions.

However, by early 1954, the negotiations at the World Bank stalled, and the opportunity to find a framework for the cooperative development of the Indus river basin had passed.[44] The discussions lingered on details, for instance the definition of what constituted Pakistan's 'existing uses' of water. There was also a considerable amount of technical complexity to be navigated as, in some cases, the cheapest

[39] American Embassy London to Berber, 29 February 1952, Archives of Ludwigs-Maximilians-University, Munich (ALMU), Friedrich Berber Papers.

[40] Haines, *Rivers Divided* (n 10) chapter 5; Akhter, 'Geopolitics of Infrastructure' (n 10).

[41] David Ekbladh, 'Meeting the Challenge from Totalitarianism: The Tennessee Valley Authority as a Global Model for Liberal Development, 1933–1945', *The International History Review*, 32, 1 (2010), 47–67; Vincent Lagendijk, 'Divided Development: Post-War Ideas on River Utilisation and their Influence on the Development of the Danube', *The International History Review*, 37, 1 (2015), 80–98.

[42] David Lilienthal, *The Journals of David E. Lilienthal* (New York: Harper & Row, 1966), vol. iii, 269.

[43] Gulhati, *Indus Water Treaty* (n 11) 110; Lilienthal, *Journals* (n 42) vol. iii, 323.

[44] Michel, *The Indus Rivers* (n 10) 233.

solution would have been to reroute water intended for Pakistan through Indian territory. Money was another sticking point. India was expected to contribute financially to improvement works on Pakistani soil, which meant that Indian engineering proposals tended to be frugal. Pakistan in turn wanted 'hydraulic independence', which was only achievable at great expense.[45]

There were wider political developments at play, too. One of these was the worsening relationship between India and the United States under the Eisenhower Administration. Eisenhower's secretary of state, John Foster Dulles, and Nehru differed over core elements of Indian foreign policy, such as India's championing of China's UN membership, which Dulles regarded as a hostile move. Nehru in turn did not appreciate US high-handedness towards nations which had just achieved sovereignty. As Ramachandra Guha has put it, 'America thought India soft on communism; India thought America soft on colonialism'. In the eyes of US foreign policy-makers, Pakistan was a more reliable ally in the fight against the Soviet Union and became more closely aligned to the United States by a military pact the two nations signed in 1954.[46]

These broader antagonisms ensured that the issue of national sovereignty became a dominant theme in the Indus waters dispute again. Fundamentally, both India and Pakistan equated sovereignty with sovereign ownership of water courses, and from 1954, the key principle of a future Indus settlement revolved around the allocation of whole rivers to either India or Pakistan.[47] With a cooperative technocratic solution increasingly unlikely, and a failure of the World Bank talks a real possibility, legal arguments over who owned the water became more relevant again because they could be invoked in an international court or arbitration tribunal. As before, Pakistan, encouraged by its US advisors, attempted to push the matter in international fora, most importantly the ILA.

The ILA Gets Involved

The formal involvement of the ILA in the Indus waters dispute began at one of its biannual conferences. By 1954, the trilateral discussions at the World Bank had become deadlocked. In the same year, Clyde Eagleton, a well-known US internationalist, professor at New York University, former adviser to the Nizam of Hyderabad (a princely state which had been occupied by and incorporated into India in the late 1940s), and president of the US branch of the ILA, convinced his colleagues on the ILA's executive committee that the ongoing disputes over international water

[45] Haines, *Rivers Divided* (n 10) 133–5.

[46] Ramachandra Guha, *India after Gandhi: the History of the World's Largest Democracy* (Basingstoke: Macmillan, 2007), 155–61, quotation at 161.

[47] Haines, *Rivers Divided* (n 10) 132.

rights across the world demonstrated the need for an authoritative legal statement on the issue. As a result, the ILA tabled a session on inland water rights at its next conference in Edinburgh.[48] At the end of the conference, the ILA established a new committee on water law, with Eagleton as its chairman.[49] This came to be known as the Rivers Committee and it remained in existence until 1966.

The way in which the committee was set up responded largely to US concerns about the dispute, framing it as a threat to geopolitical stability but solvable through apolitical technocratic arrangements as embodied in the Lilienthal plan. Articles in the press reported that the ILA committee was to issue 'practical recommendations for international arrangements', not abstract legal rules.[50] Eagleton himself underlined that the roots of the dispute lay in 'rival political desires' that would

> lead to bitter strife unless better solutions can be found. Such solutions can be found. Through integrated development of a river basin (the Tennessee Valley Authority as an example) all states upon it would stand to gain far more than would be possible through exclusive national control of their respective portions of the river.

Only the internationalization of the Indus basin would provide a solution: 'Development of rivers as a joint or international enterprise, encouraged and supported by the United Nations' for 'prosperity and happiness of all—and this with no danger to national sovereignty or security'.[51] This over-optimistic assessment utterly disregarded what was at stake for both Indian and Pakistani leaders, namely *asserting* post-colonial sovereignty.

South Asian voices were notably absent in Edinburgh. India had only sent two delegates to the ILA's conference that year, and Pakistan none at all. Reports in the press remarked that 'no attempt was made to discuss' ongoing disputes by ILA delegates from nations currently involved in water disputes, not only India and Pakistan but also Israel, which was locked in a contentious dispute with its Arab neighbours over the waters of the Jordan River.[52] Pakistan did not possess an ILA branch in 1954 but India did, and it had been remarkably active in the year previous

[48] Richard N. Swift, 'Eagleton, Clyde', in Warren Kuehl (ed.), *Biographical Dictionary of Internationalists* (Westport, CT: Greenwood Press, 1983), 231–2.

[49] For a chronological account of the Rivers Committee see Charles S. Bourne, 'The International Law Association's contribution to international water resources law', *National Resources Journal* 36, 2 (1996), 155–216.

[50] 'Plea for Abandoned Families', *Scotsman*, 13 August 1954, in ILA/2/27, folder 2, ILA Archive.

[51] 'International Law Association, Edinburgh Conference 1954: Diversion of Water in International Rivers: Inland Water Rights and Obligations Between States. Preliminary Study Outline by Professor Clyde Eagleton of New York University', ILA 2/27, folder 3, ILA Archive. (Also published in *International Law Association Reports of Conferences* 46 (1954), 324–32.)

[52] ILA Edinburgh Conference programme, 8–14 August 1954, ILA/2/27, folder 1; 'International Law Association, Edinburgh Conference', *Scots Law Times*, 25 September 1954, in ILA/2/27, folder 2, ILA Archive.

to this. Under the stewardship of its honorary vice-president Jawaharlal Nehru, the Indian ILA branch had held a major international legal conference in New Delhi. The matters under discussion included UN Charter review, the Indian constitution and nationality but nothing in relation to natural resources. The event had included representatives of the UN, the United Nations Educational, Scientific and Cultural Organization (UNESCO), and numerous foreign governments. The ILA touted it as 'the first of its kind to be held in an Asian country' and 'the first time when jurists from the East as well as from the West met together to discuss matters of vital interest to the world'.[53] While the ILA welcomed increased representation from the non-Western world, Indian leaders intended to put their country on the map in the professional world of international law. In the mid-1950s, Indian diplomats gave speeches in Europe in which they highlighted the important legal traditions of the Indian subcontinent and India's commitment to bringing the world under the rule of law.[54] Berber himself wrote articles in support of the notion that Hindu traditions entailed a deep belief in international legal structures.[55] However, while international law mattered to Indian statesmen, they did not want to rely on it in the context of the waters dispute. The new ILA committee was, from an Indian perspective that was generally supportive of international law, a wholly unwelcome development due to India's concrete political interests in the waters dispute. The creation of the committee coincided with Pakistan's request in late 1954 to broaden the negotiations at the World Bank beyond engineering questions, thus opening the door for another legal offensive.[56]

Once the ILA had established the Rivers Committee, it became a focus for Indian and Pakistani attempts to advance their claims in this influential scholarly body. These attempts were led by Laylin though Sikri and Qadir were also involved. In terms of the committee's membership, it is important to note that, from the beginning, it included Sikri, who had compiled the initial report for Nehru's government.[57] The committee did not meet in full until the next conference of the ILA in Dubrovnik in 1956.

The 1956 Dubrovnik Conference

From the beginning of the Indus waters dispute both the Indian and the Pakistani government had invested in expertise in the law of international rivers. With the

53 *International Law Association Reports of Conferences* 46 (1954), cxxxxiv.

54 'Indien und das Völkerrecht', speech by B. P. Adarkar, Indian chargé d'affaires, Grotius Society, Munich, 5 July 1954, NAI, EA, Europe-II, 1751/63, 1954.

55 F. J. Berber, 'Indien und das Völkerrecht', in H. O. Günther (ed.), *Indien und Deutschland* (Frankfurt a.M.: Europäische Verlagsanstalt, 1956), 228–35.

56 Haines, *Rivers Divided* (n 10) 134.

57 *International Law Association Reports of Conferences* 46 (1954), xxxviii. The legal advisor to the Foreign ministry of Israel, another state involved in a river dispute, was also a member.

World Bank negotiations hanging in the balance, debates on doctrine were likely to have tangible consequences for the resolution of the dispute. After the ILA formally put the law of international rivers on its agenda, both governments redoubled their efforts with a view to influencing the debate at Dubrovnik in late August 1956.

In 1955, Berber published his book on the sources of international river law, concluding that the law was not yet ripe for codification and that it differed widely across different world regions.[58] In the same year, and under Eagleton's leadership, the ILA's Rivers Committee published its first report which proposed eight principles on which to base future law on the use of international rivers. Overall, these principles were sympathetic to the Pakistani case, which portrayed Indian withdrawal of water as an existential threat. The report invoked the controversial legal principle of *sic utere tuo*, meaning that a state's sovereignty was circumscribed by the obligation not to cause harm on another state's territory, and also explicitly included 'pre-existent appropriation' as one of the factors that should be taken into consideration when weighing the benefit of one state against the harm done to another state caused by a change in water use.[59] Both Laylin and Sikri prepared detailed comments on the report and submitted them to the ILA in May 1956, Laylin under the auspices of the US branch of the ILA, and Sikri as a member of the Rivers Committee.

To briefly summarize both arguments, Laylin supported the eight tenets of the Rivers Committee's report. He argued that there was a set of accepted principles in the law of international rivers, most importantly that states were restrained in the use of waters even if they had jurisdiction and physical power over them. Laylin summarily dismissed the Harmon Doctrine and pointed to bilateral treaties and court decisions, principally those of the US Supreme Court, which, he stated, formed a body of law that would allow international courts to pronounce a judgment on a river dispute. India's willingness to enter into the World Bank negotiations was further proof of the general acceptance of the principle of limited sovereignty over waters and the duty of upstream riparian states to compensate downstream riparian states for any damage that resulted from the diversion of existing watercourses.[60] Unsurprisingly, Sikri disagreed vehemently, cited several publicists who had argued that the law of international rivers was not settled at all,

[58] Berber, *Rechtsquellen* (n 37).

[59] 'International Law Association, Dubrovnik Conference, 1956, The Uses of the Waters of International Rivers, First Committee Report' [28 October 1955, 5 pages], 3, 4, in 'Principles of Law Governing the Uses of International Rivers. Resolution Adopted by the International Law Association [August 1956, Dubrovnik], together with Reports and Commentaries Submitted to the Association', ILA/3/37/1, ILA Archive.

[60] John G. Laylin, 'Comments Submitted to Committee of American Branch of the ILA' [4 May 1956, 56 pages], esp. 2–3, 7–8, 18 in 'Principles of Law Governing the Uses of International Rivers. Resolution Adopted by the International Law Association [August 1956, Dubrovnik], together with Reports and Commentaries Submitted to the Association', ILA/3/37/1, ILA Archive.

and argued in favour of different regional water regimes in Europe, Africa, and the Americas instead of a universal body of water law.[61]

As the conference approached, Laylin worked on a comprehensive rebuttal of Sikri's observations, which he again submitted to the ILA. But he also sought support from his wider network. In a July 1956 letter to an Iranian politician, Laylin outlined his strategy. The letter is worth quoting at length as it underscores how acutely aware Laylin was of the sensitive issue of postcolonial sovereignty, and the way in which Indian jurists took advantage of it.

> Mr Sikri's strategy is to assume that international law is regional. He states that precedents from the principles come from regions other than Asia and he concludes that Europeans and Americans are not going to force on Asia their concept that an upper riparian must recognize and respect rights of existing uses in lower riparian states. This is clever and its unsoundness can be pointed out best by others than Europeans and Americans.

Laylin understood that in international law, it did not just matter what was said but who said it, precisely because bodies such as the ILA derived their authority from the principle of universal representation. Ergo, Laylin needed a non-Western voice arguing his case at Dubrovnik. In the same letter, he tried to recruit Iranian lawyers for this venture. 'I urged you to take up with your Government the desirability of having at the Dubrovnik conference the best available private attorneys from Iran with international experience. They should go as representatives of themselves not of the Government'. Laylin offered to brief personally any Iranian jurist planning to go to Dubrovnik. This could be done while Laylin was holidaying in Venice prior to the conference: 'I am meeting in Venice on August 24th certain Pakistani attorneys who are coming on a similar basis [before travelling on to Dubrovnik].'[62]

One of the Pakistani attorneys briefed by Laylin was Manzur Qadir, then Senior Advocate at the Supreme Court of Pakistan. Qadir submitted a note to the ILA on 27 August 1956, just before the conference, acknowledging help and documents he had received from Laylin's firm. In the note, Qadir addressed his 'friend and former colleague' Sikri in loaded language. Qadir argued that the ILA had a 'responsibility ... to distill legal principles from those practices that have come to be accepted as the hallmarks of civilized behavior'. In Qadir's view, there were many precedents governing water use. Importantly, he cited the (never implemented)

[61] S. M. Sikri, 'Comments on the First Report of the Committee' [22 May 1956, 19 pages], esp. 2–4, 10–14, in 'Principles of Law Governing the Uses of International Rivers. Resolution Adopted by the International Law Association [August 1956, Dubrovnik], together with Reports and Commentaries Submitted to the Association', ILA/3/37/1, ILA Archive.

[62] Laylin to Khossin Alam, 20 July 1956, Middle East Water Collection, Oregon State University, https://oregondigital.org/catalog/oregondigital:df70rq447#page/1/mode/1up (accessed 18 August 2020). As a downstream riparian state, Iran was in a similar position to Pakistan.

recommendations of the 1941/42 Rau commission and claimed they were sources for international law as British India also contained the quasi-sovereign princely states. This assertion went to the heart of the question of post-colonial sovereignty in South Asia, implying that independence in 1947 was no decisive break.[63] Qadir challenged the ILA to take seriously the duty to 'civilize' state behaviour and to pronounce on universal norms, in effect making, and not just stating, international law. Although Qadir had been drafted in by Laylin to speak from a non-Western point of view, he arguably defended the Eurocentric status quo in international law.

The discussion at Dubrovnik was chaotic. The delegates only received the four additional notes, two authored by Laylin, one by Sikri, and another by Qadir, at the beginning of the conference. Sikri, the first speaker, reminded his fellow ILA members that the Rivers Committee had never met in full. As a result, passing a resolution endorsing Eagleton's principles was premature. Sikri took particular exception to one of them, namely the duty to resort to arbitration if two riparian states could not come to an agreement. Sikri laid into Laylin's arguments, too, maintaining that most jurists agreed that there was no customary law of international rivers, that Laylin's use of US Supreme Court decisions wrongly introduced municipal law into international law, that the presumption of a restriction of sovereignty was wrong and that Laylin's use of *sic utere tuo* was highly dubious. Sikri then proceeded to dismiss Qadir's note as a regrettable political intervention: 'Mr. Qadir has in his paper attempted to bring the alleged facts of the Indo-Pakistan dispute into prominence here. These are entirely, I submit, irrelevant to our present discussion.'[64]

In the ensuing debate, ILA delegates almost unanimously rejected the reference to *sic utere tuo* as not meaningful in current international law. The Attorney General of Sudan, A. M. Atabani, expressed grave reservations about the inclusion of pre-existing apportionment in the principles endorsed by the committee report. This, Atabani explained, could systematically disadvantage post-colonial nations, as pre-existing arrangements might include 'rights acquired under harsh and unconscionable treaties imposed by a State upon another as well as rights acquired by usurpation'. Sudan had, of course, only become an independent state in 1956, and Atabani insisted that international law should not be used to perpetuate the 'gross injustice' of colonial regimes. Several delegates voiced their doubts as to whether the ILA had done enough work to pass a resolution on the principles of the law of international rivers, despite Laylin's attempts to conjure up an apocalyptic scenario if they delayed: 'There is not time to defer action ... statesmen [are] aware that time is running out and that we are living in an atomic age ... It is to us that they look

[63] 'Note by Manzur Qadir' [27 August 1956, 21 pages], 2, 3, 9, 15, in 'Principles of Law Governing the Uses of International Rivers. Resolution Adopted by the International Law Association [August 1956, Dubrovnik], together with Reports and Commentaries Submitted to the Association', ILA/3/37/1, ILA Archive.

[64] *International Law Association Reports of Conferences* 47 (1956), 218.

for guidance.' Laylin's US colleague Arnold Knauth adopted a similar tone, patronizing Sikri by calling him 'the gentleman from India' and admonishing him that '[h]e must govern his people so that the water is fairly managed. He must share it with his neighbours so that there is prosperous peace and not ruinous war.'[65]

When Sikri and the Israeli delegate tried to close the proceedings with a motion recommending that the Rivers Committee submit a fuller report at the next ILA conference, the move was scuppered by Laylin, who insisted on holding an additional meeting two days later. Subsequently, the Dubrovnik Resolution on the Uses of the Waters of International Rivers was passed, albeit with five abstentions. Sikri and M. C. Setalvad, the Attorney General of India, supported the motion but only after Eagleton had stated that the resolution did not intend to disadvantage upper riparian states.[66] From the Indian point of view, the resolution was highly problematic, though. Its existence alone suggested that there were indeed legal principles relevant to the Indus waters dispute. While *sic utere tuo* had been omitted, the resolution embraced the principle of restricted sovereignty, which put paid to the Harmon Doctrine, and it called for arbitration as a last resort should states not come to an agreement. Principle 5 specifically mentioned pre-existing arrangements as one of the factors that should be taken into account when apportioning waters to riparian states in an equitable manner.

The ILA's Dubrovnik conference was a set-back for Indian interests, and it came at a time when a negotiated settlement through the World Bank seemed more remote than ever. In October 1956, India and Pakistan submitted engineering plans to the World Bank that were wholly incompatible.[67] Two years later, though, Indian jurists were able to argue for a much more favourable resolution at the ILA's New York conference, which ultimately laid the groundwork for the Indus treaty of 1960. But the debates in New York did not only establish a compromise on the nature of the law of international rivers, they also brought forth a discussion about the principles and purposes of the ILA as an invisible college. US, Indian, and Pakistani jurists had deeply involved the ILA in an ongoing intergovernmental dispute, and this, along with the principles of water law, was scrutinized by the international legal community.

The 1958 New York Conference

The aftermath of the Dubrovnik conference witnessed a hardening of attitudes, both at the World Bank, which threatened India and Pakistan with shelving the talks altogether in July 1957, and in the legal sphere.[68] The Indian branch of the

65 Ibid., 218–33, 227, 229, 230.
66 Ibid., 233, 234, 241.
67 Haines, *Rivers Divided* (n 10) 135.
68 Ibid., 136.

ILA put together a scathing attack on the Dubrovnik Resolution which it regarded as essentially the fruit of Laylin's efforts. Eminent Indian jurists were adamant that the Dubrovnik principles could not become international law, given the 'errors and gaps and the inadequacy in general of the basis in international law, on which these principles are formulated'. The authors objected to the lack of distinction between *lex lata* and *lex ferenda*, and they cited Berber's book in support of their criticism of Laylin's use of municipal US law as a source for international law. Instead of abandoning the Harmon Doctrine, which had little support among international lawyers, they defended it on the tenuous grounds that while the United States had never endorsed Harmon domestically, US courts had not rejected it explicitly as international law.[69]

Meanwhile, Laylin mobilized semi-peripheral jurists in defence of his arguments. He submitted a seventy-page document to the 1957 conference of the Inter-American Bar Association in Buenos Aires. Here, he rehashed familiar arguments about limited sovereignty, India's participation in the World Bank negotiations and the need to protect existing uses first and foremost. Laylin singled out Berber and Sikri as defenders of the Harmon Doctrine and as the 'few writers even today who maintain that while a state should in a spirit of good neighborliness refrain from actions on an international river harmful beyond its borders, it has under existing international law the legal right to do as it chooses so'.[70] Laylin would submit a very similar document to the ILA's New York Conference.

Eagleton, the chairman of the ILA Rivers Committee, fed Laylin's team relevant information.[71] In 1957, Eagleton had secured a USD 67,000 grant for research on the legal aspects of the uses of waters of international rivers from the Ford Foundation. The Foundation was a major US player in South Asian development and also held significant investments in the World Bank.[72] Its International Legal Studies Program, under which the grant was made, intended to 'strengthen the legal profession as a strategic source of leadership in the conduct of international relations', assuming a coherence of the international legal community that arguably did not exist in light of the particularistic interests displayed at the ILA.[73] The Ford

[69] Indian Branch of the International Law Association, Branch Sub-committee on International Rivers, 'Consideration of the Question of Diversion of Waters in International Rivers by the International Law Association', n.d. [1957?], ILA/4/45/44, ILA Archive.

[70] John G. Laylin, 'Principles of Law Governing Use of International Rivers' [71 pages], 5, in *Principles of Law Governing the Uses of International Rivers, Resolution Adopted by the Inter-American Bar Association at its 10th Conference, November 1957, Buenos Aires* (Washington DC, 1958), ILA/3/37/1, ILA Archive. I borrow the term 'semi-peripheral' from Arnulf Becker Lorca.

[71] *Principles of Law and Recommendations on the Uses of International Rivers*, submitted to the International Committee of the ILA by the Committee on the Uses of Waters of International Rivers of the American Branch, Washington, DC, 1958, iii-iv, in ILA/3/37/1, ILA Archive.

[72] *Ford Foundation Annual Report 1957*, 87. On the foundation's development programmes in India see Unger, *Entwicklungspfade* (n 9).

[73] *Ford Foundation Annual Report 1958*, 78.

Foundation grant certainly strengthened Laylin's resolve to argue forcefully in favour of his client.

In this charged atmosphere, the Rivers Committee met, first in Geneva in October 1957, with Eagleton, Laylin, and Sikri present, and then in May 1958 at The Hague. Berber attended for the first time in 1958, his appointment suggested by his self-described 'friendly opponent' Laylin. There is no record of these meetings in the archives of the ILA but according to participants they consisted of hours of combative debate which resulted in only a bare minimum of agreed definitions, principles, and recommendations. External events may have contributed to a lack of unanimity. In January 1958, Eagleton, who was committed to the Dubrovnik Resolution, died suddenly, depriving the Rivers Committee of leadership. Three months later, India's Central Minister for Irrigation announced that from 1962, India would unilaterally draw more waters from the Indus Rivers, regardless of whether Pakistan had built replacement works.[74] In the end, Eagleton's successor, the US jurist Arnold Knauth, decided that the only way forward would consist of diluting the Dubrovnik principles in favour of much more general statements on the law of international rivers. Most importantly, principle 5 of the Dubrovnik Resolution was erased, a victory for the Indians who had long resented the priority it seemed to give to prior appropriation.

The resulting revised statement of principles, which was formally accepted at the ILA's conference in New York in early September 1958, was extremely basic. It merely stated that a river basin should be treated as an entity, that riparian states were entitled to a reasonable and equitable share of the waters (to be determined according to each particular case), and that co-riparian states had to respect each other's rights and induce those for whom they were responsible to do so, too. At New York, the ILA's secretary-general, Harvey Moore, announced that while Eagleton would not have agreed with all of the principles, he would have been happy with the fact that a minimum agreement had been reached at all.[75]

Many of the delegates at New York framed the passing of the new resolution as a victory for the invisible college. It is noticeable that these voices belonged mostly to jurists who represented states currently engaged in water disputes. Laylin praised Berber for acting 'as a scholar' (although he had no such accolades for either his Indian or Pakistani colleagues), while Sikri announced that he had reluctantly abandoned his defence of the Harmon doctrine because 'as a member of the ILA' he understood the requirement 'to make the relations of States more viable'. Qadir followed suit, solemnly stating that '[w]e meet here as lawyers, and not as negotiators sponsoring the separate and individual interests of the countries from which we come', while Berber rejoiced over the 'real progress over the

[74] *International Law Association Report of Conferences* 48 (1958), 37, 45, 64, 68; Haines, *Rivers Divided* (n 10) 137.

[75] *International Law Association Report of Conferences* 48 (1958), 38, 60.

so-called Dubrovnik principles' that New York represented: 'now we are on firm ground which is, perhaps, more modest but in any case safer'.[76] These remarks were largely performative. Of course, all four jurists had used the ILA as a forum for representing national interests, yet the institutional logic of the ILA required the performance of scholarly agreement and professional universalism once a compromise had been reached.

Other ILA members expressed their disappointment. A US jurist called the New York principles a 'retrogression from Dubrovnik', 'both blind and halt', and born of 'considerations of short-term expediency'. This was not the ethos that ILA members should endorse, that of 'a responsible citizen of the larger community of States addressing himself to other responsible citizens of the same community'. The Argentinian Guillermo J. Cano lamented that the Rivers Committee had lost 'sight of the fact that we are not here to defend the interests of governments, interests which are eminently respectable, but for the defence of which there are other and more suitable places than this'.[77] Nonetheless, the New York principles were adopted unanimously by the delegates, with the express support of the ILA leadership.

There are two different perspectives on the developments in New York. On a practical level that focused on power political realities, the New York compromise was simply a result of the recognition by the jurists representing governments in the Indus waters dispute that a pronouncement by the ILA on river law that would strongly favour one state over the other was bound to be disregarded. This had happened to previous legal guidelines on river law, notably one adopted by the Institut de Droit international in 1911.[78] The ILA had to represent particular interests if it wanted to achieve its universalistic and scholarly ambitions. In fact, what was required was representational work alongside the performance of scholarly detachment, a task that Laylin, Sikri, Berber, and Qadir accomplished. However, it was not only different national interests that divided the ILA community. If one returns to Anthea Roberts' question to what extent international law is international, the principles adopted at New York also temporarily made visible deep divergences between different communities within the idealized 'invisible college', along axes of difference that referenced culture and civilization. These divergences went beyond narrow state interests in the Indus waters dispute.

Perceived civilizational hierarchies and fractures within 'the West' also influenced the ways in which jurists at the conference in New York reflected on the workings of the international legal community. Such hierarchies were invoked but also challenged. In his introductory remarks, Knauth underlined the necessity for the ILA to develop international water law because of the, in his view, unruly behaviour of post-colonial nations. 'These new nations', he argued, 'do not have

[76] Ibid., 37, 38, 58, 60.
[77] Ibid., 41, 63.
[78] *Annuaire de l'Institut de Droit International* 24 (1911), 365–7.

the traditions of diplomacy developed over centuries in the older chancelleries of London, Paris, Vienna.' They were 'more apt to take unilateral action to assert their newly found sovereignty'. Knauth's Eurocentric reification of international law claimed for itself tradition and wise restraint, and implied that post-colonial nations were incapable of making a positive contribution to international law. Berber retorted by highlighting the pitfalls of Western thinking: 'In our Western civilization, in which every progress beyond what has ever been before is in itself regarded as a virtue, whilst caution, tradition, historical values are regarded as almost a vice, it is an easy task to plead ideal principles even if they lead us into a fool's paradise.' Citing Goethe, Bacon, and Montesquieu, Berber defended the cautious statements of the New York resolution and rebutted Knauth's claims to speak for a unified 'West'.[79] Other members of the Rivers Committee opposed Berber's attempt to destabilize the idea of international law's universality. Dante Caponera, the Italian delegate, presented a summary of different legal traditions of the world, ranging from that of the Soviet Union, Roman law, Islamic legislations, to Chinese and Hindu legal principles, all of which, he claimed, embraced the principle of limited sovereignty over water resources. Therefore, the ILA's ambitions to formulate universal legal rules were not just based on Western jurisprudence and thus legitimate.[80] The theme of Western nations imposing legal rules on post-colonial states was a powerful undercurrent in discussions within the ILA, and the ways in which European (but not Anglophone) jurists such as Berber and Caponera claimed to speak on behalf of non-Western legal traditions reinforced the sense that decolonization had irrevocably redefined the meaning of the international.

In the aftermath of the conference, the ILA leadership displayed a discernible exasperation with the topic. Secretary-general Harvey Moore admitted 'I fancy we may have said most of what we can usefully say on "Rivers" simpliciter'.[81] At the following conference in Hamburg in 1960, there was no significant debate on the topics that had been so contentious at Dubrovnik and New York, and the ILA only made a definitive pronouncement of international river law when it adopted the Helsinki Rules on the Uses of the Waters of International Rivers in 1966, several years after the Indus Treaty was signed.

The Indus Water Treaty and the 1966 Helsinki Rules

Historians have cited several factors for the resolution of the Indus waters dispute. Haines suggests that geopolitical changes in the period 1958–1960 were key. The military coup of October 1958, shortly after the New York ILA conference, ended

[79] *International Law Association Report of Conferences* 48 (1958), 30–1; 58–9.
[80] Ibid., 53–5.
[81] W. Harvey Moore, QC to John [Worsley?], 1 December 1959, ILA/2/28, folder 2, ILA Archive.

a period of political instability in Pakistan. The new prime minister, Ayub Khan, prioritized settling the dispute so that he could access technical and financial assistance for development projects. He also appointed Qadir as Pakistan's Minister of Foreign Affairs. With a militarily resurgent Pakistan, India was no longer the stronger party, and was further weakened by the failure of several economic projects, not least the second Five-Year Plan. US statesmen, rattled by the Sputnik shock of 1957 and intensified competition with the Soviet Union, became prepared to commit significant sums to development projects in the Third World. US willingness to underwrite costly engineering works for replacement canals enabled the World Bank to assemble the Indus Basin Development Fund in early 1959, with financial contributions from Australia, Canada, New Zealand, Britain, the United States, and the Federal Republic of Germany. The final settlement divided the tributary rivers of the basin between India and Pakistan with new canals giving both countries additional access to water. Pakistan received sovereign ownership of three western rivers (Indus, Jhelum, Chenab), India of three eastern rivers (Ravi, Beas, Sutlej). In addition, India paid financial compensation to Pakistan. The Indus Water Treaty was formally signed in September 1960.[82]

Did international law make a difference to the way in which the Indus waters dispute was settled? Historians have generally downplayed the importance of legal arguments and emphasized that engineering matters were at the forefront. Some have recognized that the 1956 Dubrovnik Resolution and the 1966 Helsinki Rules overall benefitted Pakistan because of the emphasis on territorial integrity. However, the fact that the New York conference, which came immediately before the significant steps that led to the Indus Treaty, represented a set-back for Pakistan and a victory for India, is generally not mentioned.[83] Yet international law clearly mattered to the governments involved. Indian jurists in particular must have recognized that the general trend was moving in a direction unfavourable to Indian interests. Thus, the period after the New York conference was a window of opportunity for signing a bilateral treaty with Pakistan while international river law was still vague.

This becomes plausible once the content of the 1966 Helsinki Rules is examined. Scholars have argued that the way in which the rules defined 'equitable' utilization protected 'the early developer from the ambitions of the late developer to utilize the water resources as well'. In the case of the Indus waters dispute, Pakistan was the 'early developer' as it had inherited most of the irrigation infrastructure that had been built under colonial rule. In some ways, the Helsinki rules represented a return to Dubrovnik. Principle 5 of the Dubrovnik Resolution was reintroduced in

[82] Haines, *Rivers Divided* (n 10) 140–50.

[83] Haines, *Rivers Divided* (n 10) 51–2, citing Cecil J. Olmstead, 'Introduction', in A. H. Garretson, R. D. Hayton, and C. J. Olmstead (eds), *The Law of International Drainage Basins* (Dobbs Ferry, NY: Oceana, 1967), 9.

an elaborated form. Although there was no obligation to maintain the status quo, prior appropriation was explicitly protected or alluded to in eight out of eleven factors that were cited as determining of what an equitable use of waters would consist.[84] The Helsinki rules were the first, and for three decades the only, codification of the law of international watercourses and came to be regarded as customary international law. However, they also explicitly stated that they would not affect existing agreements such as the Indus Water Treaty.[85]

Conclusion

As has often been acknowledged, international law perpetually oscillates between apology and utopia, and this was also the case in the juridical discussions that framed the Indus waters dispute.[86] Instrumentalization went hand in hand with attempts to 'improve' international law. Many of the actors involved made passionate cases for their doctrinal stance, which happened to align with either the interests of the nations of whom they were citizens, or the interests of the nations with whom they had contracts as legal advisors. Neither Sikri and Qadir nor Berber or Laylin were 'cause lawyers' but many lawyers around them appeared to act for more idealistic reasons, for instance Clyde Eagleton who fervently argued in favour of a settlement that would avoid a potentially devastating conflict in a region of the world that was stricken by all the ills that high modernity sought to banish: poverty, overpopulation, and low living standards.

Even among the four jurists, the boundaries between the juridic and non-juridic were fluid. Sikri's considerable intellectual investment and publication activity, as well as his later stance as a Supreme Court judge, indicate a stronger commitment to juridical autonomy as in the case of Qadir, who became part of the Pakistani military government in 1958. Berber and Laylin were paid advisers and chiefly tried to negotiate a settlement for their clients, irrespective of whether the eventual treaty would advance the law of international rivers. They developed and then mobilized scholarly expertise but their commitment to international law as an intellectual project varied. Berber, a professor, was more committed than Laylin, an attorney in private practice. Both were driven by other motivations. For Berber, his assignment with the Indian government represented a way back into the legal profession after he had compromised himself as a high-profile propagandist and legal

[84] Kai Wegerich and Oliver Olsson, 'Late Developers and the Inequity of "Equitable Utilization" and the Harm of "Do No Harm"', *Water International* 35, 6 (2010), 707–17, quotation at 710.

[85] Salman and Uprety, *Conflict and Cooperation* (n 10) 21–3; Salman M. A. Salman, 'The Helsinki Rules, the UN Watercourses Convention and the Berlin Rules: Perspectives on International Water Law', *International Journal of Water Resources Development* 23, 4 (2007), 625–40.

[86] Martti Koskenniemi, *From Apologia to Utopia: The Structure of International Legal Argument* (Cambridge: Cambridge University Press, 2006).

adviser in Nazi Germany. For Laylin, advising the Pakistani government was one of several lucrative contracts. There were occasions when he tried to make this work pay intellectual dividends in a similar case he had taken on for the government of Iran. Yet, Berber and Laylin's roles as legal advisers did not prevent them from participating in the scholarly discussions of the ILA. On the contrary, it qualified them for their roles.

Finally, the significant role of the ILA in the conclusion of the Indus waters dispute demonstrates the close entanglement of policy-oriented lawyering and scholarly-theoretical reflection on the content of international law within professional organizations. The Indus waters dispute was a political conflict in which both sides had a very clearly defined set of interests and deployed legal arguments that served these interests. Yet, hovering above this concrete dispute was a much more fundamental question which also touched upon the ILA's role as the organizational embodiment of the ideal of the 'invisible college'. Could the ILA agree on the extent to which changes in sovereignty over natural resources would change shared understandings of the nature of the international? The ILA thus became a forum for the debate on the impact of decolonization on the legitimacy of international law, making visible fractures not just within the global South but also within the West. To some extent, these fractures were repaired in 1966 with the Helsinki Rules. In the late 1950s, however, the ILA's actions contributed to shape an unsettled moment in international water law, an outcome that ran counter to its stated purpose as a unified professional body. And yet, because it was both an 'invisible' and a 'divisible college', the ILA could endure.

11

Agents of Constitutionalism

The Quest for a Constitutional Breakthrough in European Law, 1945–1964

*Morten Rasmussen**

In the first two decades following the Second World War, the popular and political support across Continental Europe for the establishment of a European federation based on a constitution was at its apogee. Two major attempts took place to bring about this vision, first in the context of the Council of Europe in 1949 and a few years later with the negotiations on a European Defence Community (EDC) and a European Political Community (EPC) from 1952 to 1954. As these projects failed, the governments of France, Italy, the Benelux countries, and the Federal Republic of Germany instead focused on economic integration in order to build Europe from the ground up. They first established the European Coal and Steel Community (ECSC) in 1952 and then in 1958 founded the European Economic Community (EEC) and EURATOM. The institutional setup and the legal basis for the three communities were far more modest than the federalist vision. All three communities included innovative supranational institutions, but with the establishment of the EEC and EURATOM the national government came collectively to play, in the Council of Ministers, the central role in running what would become the three European Communities (EC). Likewise, the failure of constitutional federalism also meant that all three communities were established on the basis of traditional international treaties.

This was the historical context within which European law first emerged.[1] Given the negative fortunes of European federalism, European law was shaped both by the fact that it derived from three international treaties but also by the intergovernmental approach to European integration that came to dominate the EC. This poses, then, an intricate puzzle for historians to solve as to why and how the EC experienced a breakthrough for a constitutional interpretation of European law as early as the mid-1960s. In two seminal judgments, *Van Gend en Loos* (1963)

* I would like to thank the members of the EU legal history network (http://europeanlaw.saxo.ku.dk, accessed 18 August 2020), who have all played such a big role in producing the research on which this chapter is based.

[1] 'European law' is the term commonly used to describe the law of the ECSC, the EEC, EURATOM, and eventually the European Union.

Morten Rasmussen, *Agents of Constitutionalism* In: *Crafting the International Order.* Edited by: Marcus M. Payk and Kim Christian Priemel, Oxford University Press (2021). © The Several Contributors.
DOI: 10.1093/oso/9780198863830.003.0011

and *Costa v E.N.E.L.* (1964),[2] the European Court of Justice (ECJ) established the proto-federal doctrines of direct effect and primacy of European law inside the national legal orders. By doing so the ECJ changed the institutional balance of the Treaties of Rome, in which the Council of Ministers had been supposed to introduce the legislative agenda outlined by the treaties (primary law) into the respective national legal orders by means of subordinate legislation. Moreover, the ECJ controversially sidestepped national constitutional doctrines on the reception of international law by defining how European law was to be received by national authorities and courts.[3]

Over the last decade, historians have begun to investigate this constitutional breakthrough.[4] This chapter will build upon recent research but will use a fresh approach. By telling the story about the breakthrough of European constitutionalism through five central actors, the aim is to illuminate the key themes of this book. A biographical approach is used to uncover the links between the life, professional experiences, and world views of central actors and their concrete actions in pursuing a constitutional understanding of European law. The story told will also offer the reader an overall explanation of the constitutional breakthrough in European law.

This chapter will first trace how a German law professor and diplomat, Walter Hallstein, kept the spark of European constitutionalism alive in the negotiations of the three international treaties that became the foundations of the EC by securing the establishment of an independent Court of Justice and a rudimentary legal order. It will also discuss how Hallstein, as the first president of the European Commission, helped to secure a constitutional breakthrough in European law as part of a wider effort to create a federal EC in the first half of the 1960s. The second section of the chapter will explain how the Dutch trade unionist, politician, federalist, and failed legal student, Petrus Serrarens, helped reform the way in which the Netherlands received international law. The Dutch constitutional reforms of the 1950s created the model for and the dynamic behind the two seminal judgments of the ECJ. The third section will then go behind the scenes of the European Commission to reveal how the then director of the legal service, French lawyer and civil servant Michel Gaudet, was intellectually and politically instrumental in bringing about the constitutional breakthrough in the case law of the ECJ. Ultimately, the chapter will close by exploring how two new appointee judges of the ECJ, the French politician and lawyer, Robert Lecourt, and the Italian law

[2] Case 26/62 NV Algemene Transport—en Expeditie Onderneming van Gend & Loos v. Netherlands Inland Revenue Administration, 5 February 1963 E.C.R. 1 and Case 6/64 Costa v. E.N.E.L., 15 July 1964 ECR 1141.

[3] Morten Rasmussen, 'Revolutionizing European Law: A history of the Van Gen den Loos judgment', *International Journal of Constitutional Law* 12, 1 (2014), 136–63.

[4] For a recent history of European law from 1950 to 2019 that specifically treats this topic. Morten Rasmussen and Dorte Sindbjerg Martinsen, 'EU Constitutionalisation Revisited: Redressing a Central Assumption in European Studies', *European Law Journal* 25 (2019), 251–72.

professor, Alberto Trabucchi, were decisive in swaying the Court in favour of the position of the European Commission. With the chapter, I aim to demonstrate that the agency of these five drivers of constitutionalism was decisive in securing a constitutional breakthrough in European law that went against the broader political and institutional trend of the EC. They did so out of a shared idealism that favoured close European cooperation and even federalization, but also out of a belief in law as a constitutive technique for building a new social and economic reality in Europe in shape of the common market. Their story also shows that jurists can influence international politics in myriad ways, from negotiating international treaties and working within international institutions and courts to realizing constitutional and parliamentary reforms that define how international law is received by the states. I would argue that, in this case, all these factors combined to produce the constitutional breakthrough in European law.

Walter Hallstein: From the Top Down—Shaping the Legal Dimension of European Integration

It was a unique moment in the career of Walter Hallstein. On 16–17 June 1965, he appeared as president of the Commission before the European Parliament in order to express his strong support for the constitutional interpretation of European law, signalled by the ECJ's new *Van Gend en Loos* and *Costa v E.N.E.L.* judgments. In passing these legal judgments, the Court had not only emphasized the autonomous nature of what it called 'a new legal order', it had also defined how the member states were to receive European law, thereby sidestepping their respective national constitutional clauses on the matter. The Treaties of Rome, the Court had argued, could, in certain cases, have direct effect inside the legal orders of the member states and internal primacy vis-à-vis national legislation, whether precedent or antecedent.[5]

Historians have, perhaps, understandably overlooked Hallstein's speech because it was overshadowed by the 'Empty Chair Crisis' that broke out two weeks later. This crisis saw the president of France Charles de Gaulle and French government boycott the Council of Ministers of the EC until early 1966. It was only solved when the so-called Luxembourg compromise between the member states introduced an informal national veto.[6] However, whereas the Luxembourg compromise and the informal right of veto would be abandoned by the EC from the mid-1980s

[5] Morten Rasmussen, 'Establishing a Constitutional Practice of European Law: The History of the Legal Service of the European Executive, 1952–65', *CEH* 21 (2012), 394–5 and Antoine Vauchez, *Brokering Europe. Euro-lawyers and the Making of a Transnational Polity* (Cambridge: Cambridge University Press, 2015), 129–39.

[6] Philip Bajon, *Europapolitik 'am Abgrund'. Die Krise des 'leeren Stuhls' 1965–66* (Stuttgart: Franz Steiner Verlag, 2012).

onwards, European constitutionalism had come to stay. Indeed, Hallstein's speech marked a high point in his continued efforts after 1950 to furnish European integration with a constitutional basis. As we shall see, Hallstein was the most important actor in the early history of European law, and one of the leading figures of European integration in general. As head of the German delegation negotiating the various treaties of European integration during the 1950s, he consistently offered a constitutional vision of European law and promoted the conception of the ECJ as a potential European supreme court. Moreover, in his capacity as president of the Commission of the EEC from 1958, he pushed for a constitutional interpretation of the Treaties of Rome. Much of the story told in this chapter deals with how Hallstein's political vision shaped his agency and we shall therefore begin by exploring how his life trajectory informed his views on European integration.

Born in Germany on 17 November 1901, Walter Hallstein grew up in Mainz, the son of Jakob Hallstein, a Protestant and the head of a planning department and building control office, and Anna Geibel. As a child, Hallstein was keenly interested in the life and exploits of Bismarck and nineteenth-century German unification. However, as a young man studying jurisprudence and political science in Bonn, Munich, and Berlin, he would soon come to favour the democratic ideals of the Weimar republic as well as develop a strong interest in international cooperation. Pursuing an academic career, he wrote a dissertation on the Versailles Peace Treaty,[7] before finally taking up a professorship at the University of Rostock in 1930 before the age of thirty. He never joined the National Socialist Party, but by keeping a low profile he was able to be appointed to a chair at Frankfurt's Johann-Wolfgang-Goethe University in 1940, before military service interrupted his academic exploits. From 1941, he served as an officer of the mounted artillery in occupied France until his capture at Cherbourg by Allied forces in June 1944.[8]

As a prisoner of war at Camp Como in Mississippi, the second phase of Hallstein's life began to take shape. He organized the library of the camp and helped set up lectures to teach his fellow prisoners. In 1945, he returned to Frankfurt and resumed his old position before being appointed as vice-chancellor of the University of Frankfurt in 1948. He now gradually became part of the new political elite in the American zone of occupation that would come to dominate the institutions of the Federal Republic of Germany. In 1948, as a visiting scholar at Georgetown University in Washington he familiarized himself with US constitutional law.[9] In the late 1940s and early 1950s, Hallstein continued his interest in international and European cooperation that had marked his formative years as an academic in the

[7] Walter Hallstein, *Der Lebensversicherungsvertrag im Versailler Vertrag* (Marburg: Verlag Elwer, 1926).

[8] Corrado Malandrino, *'Tut Etwas Tapferes' Compi un Atto di coraggio. L'Europa federale di Walter Hallstein (1948–1982)* (Bologna: Società Editrice Il Mulino 2005), 33–57.

[9] Bill Davies, 'Resistance to European Law and Constitutional Identity in Germany: Herbert Kraus and Solange in its Intellectual Context', *European Law Journal* 21 (2015), 434–59, at 444.

1920s. He participated at the Congress of The Hague in 1948, where politicians and public figures from across Europe met to discuss the future of European cooperation.[10] This was the first time he met the future chancellor of the Federal Republic, Konrad Adenauer. They were soon to meet again. Two years later, Adenauer had to find someone suitable to lead the German delegation in the upcoming negotiations on the Schuman Plan. He nominated Hallstein, who beyond his qualifications also had the advantage of never having been a member of the National Socialist Party. Adenauer wanted to integrate the Federal Republic into Western Europe, and Hallstein would be instrumental in shaping this policy of *Westbindung*, first during the negotiations on the Treaty of Paris and after that as undersecretary of the Ministry of Foreign Affairs until 1958.[11]

In Paris, Hallstein's first meeting with Jean Monnet, who had developed the Schuman plan and was now heading the French delegation, went very well on a personal level. Hallstein was struck by the atmosphere of close cooperation, even 'conspiracy', that developed among the negotiators who quickly came to share a common wish to help organize Europe. When it came to the negotiations over the institutional setup of the ECSC, however, differences quickly emerged between the French and West German delegations. The original French proposal had emphasized the key role of the supranational High Authority (HA), but Hallstein and the German delegation proposed to also include a European assembly and a permanent Court of Justice to provide the necessary checks and balances vis-à-vis the authority of the HA. Monnet was instinctively opposed to a permanent court in the new Community, which he saw as a dangerous limitation of the ability of the HA to act in a decisive and flexible manner. He was not convinced when Hallstein, in a meeting between the two in July 1950, attempted to explain the great potential a European supreme court could have in building a common European identity. Hallstein explicitly referred to the US experience in this field. However, under pressure from West Germany and the Benelux countries, Monnet ultimately had to accept that the extensive competences of the HA were to be checked and balanced by a Council, an Assembly, and a European Court of Justice.[12] To define the precise competences of the institutions required intense negotiations.

When explaining the institutional design of the ECSC at Georgetown University after the negotiations had ended in March 1952, Hallstein claimed that it was intentionally created in order to anticipate 'the future all-in Federation of Europe'.[13] This at least was the view Hallstein wanted to promote. During the negotiations he and his right-hand man, ministry of Foreign Affairs official Carl F. Ophüls, imagined the institutional and legal system of the ECSC as the embryo of a

[10] Jean-Michel Guieu and Christophee Le Dréau (eds), *Le 'Congrès de l'Europe' à La Haye (1948–2008)* (Brussels: P.I.E. Peter Lang, 2009).

[11] Hans-Peter Schwarz, *Adenauer* (Munich: dtv, 1994), 664–6.

[12] Anne Boerger, 'Negotiating the Foundations of European Law 1950–1957', *CEH* 21 (2012), 339–56.

[13] Cited from ibid., at 342.

future European federation. Consequently, they visualized the ECJ as becoming a European Supreme Court. The two men drew inspiration from mid-nineteenth century German liberal constitutionalism and the *Zollverein*, but were also inspired by the US constitutional experience.[14] Their views encountered fierce resistance amongst the German Advisory Group of legal experts drawn from across the nation. The Advisory Group was led by Herbert Kraus, a leading professor of public law, and included legal experts with very different and much more cautious views on the legal nature of the ECSC and how the court should be designed. However, Hallstein managed to sideline the committee, and Kraus resigned with an angry letter to Adenauer that cited differences with Hallstein as the cause.[15]

While successful in handling internal opposition, the impact of Hallstein's views on the negotiations concerning the legal dimension of the Treaty of Paris was more limited. The French delegation may have had to concede that the competences of the HA should be controlled by checks and balances. However, in the end it would be France that would greatly influence the ultimate design of the ECJ and the legal system. Hallstein and the German delegation had proposed a constitutional court that was accessible to private litigants, had jurisdiction over all Community institutions, and could decide conflicts between them. In addition, the court alone would handle disputes related to the interpretation and application of European law in the national legal orders. The Benelux countries supported the German demand for a permanent court, but conceived it as an international court with no access for private litigants.

Faced with such far-reaching plans for the court and the legal system, Monnet went on the counter-attack. Monnet wanted to limit the jurisdiction of the new Court to administrative questions. In order to do this, he appointed Maurice Lagrange, from the Conseil d'État, the French administrative court of last resort, to the group of legal experts, who negotiated the legal shape of the ECSC and the competences of the court. Lagrange quickly dominated the negotiations and under significant protests from the other delegations rejected much of the work already done. Instead, he modelled the ECJ on the Conseil d'État and turned the former into an adjudicatory body focused on controlling the legality of the actions of the HA. The German delegation insisted, however, on maintaining access of private enterprises and their associations to the Court, and this was finally conceded after a decision at the political level of the negotiations (Article 34 of the Treaty of Paris). The German delegation also managed to insert a general article on the purpose of the ECJ that in a discrete manner defined a European *Rechtsgemeinschaft* as the ultimate aim of the activities of the court (Article 31 of the Treaty of Paris). However,

[14] For three contemporary articles by Ophüls cf. C. F. Ophüls, 'Gerichtbarkeit und Rechtsprechung im Schumanplan', *Neue Juristische Wochenschrift* 4 (1951), 693 and C. F. Ophüls, 'Juristische Grundgedanken des Schumanplans', ibid., 25, and C. F. Ophüls, 'Europas partieller Bundesstaat', *Die Gegenwart* (1951), 14.

[15] Davies, 'Resistance to European Law' (n 9) 440–4.

any references to the constitutional nature of the Treaty of Paris were removed. In the end, Monnet and Lagrange felt that they had secured the liberty of action of the HA. Considering how West German negotiators had to tread very carefully in their negotiations due to recent past events, Hallstein was not too disappointed with the admittedly limited, but nevertheless concrete results, they had managed to secure.[16]

By the early 1950s, Hallstein had already come to a coherent set of beliefs about the nature of European integration and the role of European law that would guide him in the next two decades.[17] Given the failure of the attempt to turn the Council of Europe into a constituent assembly in order to formulate a federal constitution for Europe, the future of integration surely belonged to more modest schemes. Economic integration provided the European project with a purpose, Hallstein believed, but was at the same time only a means to a political end.[18] In order to establish a European federation, it was crucial that the European institutions created were independent and had exclusive competences in the new European policy fields. Moreover, the European institutions needed to be based on a democratic and constitutional basis.[19] The creation of a constitutional European legal order was thus a fundamental part of Hallstein's vision and strategy.[20] During negotiations on an EDC and, in particular, on the EPC from 1951 to 1954, Hallstein defined the German negotiating position along these lines. However, there was limited support among the other governments for an ambitious EPC that would sideline national governments in key policy fields such as defence. In the end, the French National Assembly rejected the EDC Treaty and consequently also the EPC in the summer of 1954. A majority of French parties found the establishment of a European Army dangerous and could not support the federal vision inherent in the EPC Treaty.[21]

This was a serious setback for Hallstein's federal vision of European integration. When the governments of the Benelux countries attempted to reignite the integration process at the Messina Summit in the summer of 1955, Hallstein and Adenauer were fairly convinced that the French government would block the new initiative. In the German government, the balance had also started to shift towards a more intergovernmental approach to European integration. The Minister

[16] Boerger, 'Negotiating the Foundations' (n 12) 343–7.

[17] For a retrospective analysis by Hallstein cf. Walter Hallstein, *Europe in the Making* (London: Allen & Urwin, 1973).

[18] Matthias Schönwald, Walter Hallstein et les institutions des Communautés européennes, in Marie-Thérèse Bitsch (ed.), *Le couple France-Allemagne et les institutions européennes. Une Postérité pour le plan Schuman* (Brussels: Bruylant, 2001), 151–70, 155.

[19] Frank Bärenbrinker, Hallstein's Conception of Europe before Assuming Office in the Commission, in Wilfried Loth, Willam Wallace, and Wolfgang Wessels (eds), *Walter Hallstein—The Forgotten European?* (London: Macmillan, 1998), 82–95, 85.

[20] Emile Noël, Walter Hallstein: a Personal Testimony, in Loth, et al., *Walter Hallstein* (n 19) 131–4, 133.

[21] Frank Bärenbrinker, Hallstein's Conception of Europe before Assuming Office in the Commission, in Loth, et al., *Walter Hallstein* (n 19) 82–95, 87–91.

of Economic Affairs, Ludwig Erhard, wanted a grand liberalization of all Western European trade and detested the supranationalism of the ECSC, which he equated with French *dirigisme* and economic planning. During the negotiations on the Treaties of Rome, he first tried to thwart them and when that failed, he attempted to limit the scope of the common institutions and their legal nature.[22] Adenauer would eventually support the negotiations of the Treaties of Rome all the way to their successful conclusion, but he was more focused on deepening European co-operation than securing any particular institutional or legal shape. The influence of Erhard and the ministry of Economic Affairs meant that Hallstein and the ministry of Foreign Affairs had to abandon their constitutional approach to the common institutions and the legal dimension of the new Communities.[23] This change also reflected the views of the majority of governments at the negotiations and addressed the concerns about how to obtain the ratification of the French National Assembly.

As a result, the institutional and legal design of the Treaties of Rome arguably constituted a step back on a federalist scale compared to the ECSC. The Council of Ministers would have, with very few exceptions, the legislative competence based on proposals from the Commission.[24] The treaties were designed in such a way that primary legal norms required legislative actions by the Council to take effect. The latter generally employed so-called directives, framework decisions to be filled in by national authorities, and to a limited extent, regulations that had direct applicability. National administrations were to implement Council decisions under the supervision of the Commission and national courts had exclusive competence to apply European law within their own national legal order. The French government blocked any attempt to enhance the status of the Assembly, direct elections required a new decision at a later point, and the new Court of Justice was to be modelled on the ECSC court. A few constitutional elements did enter the treaties, but they were relatively modest. How exactly they entered the treaties will be explored in the following section on Michel Gaudet. To conclude, the actual establishment of the new European Communities, based on the blueprint of the Treaties of Rome, depended on the collective political will of the member states. The treaties did not

[22] Mathieu L. L. Segers, *Deutschlands Ringen mit der 'Relance'. Die Europapolitik der BRD während der Beratungen und Verhandlungen über die Römischen Verträge* (Frankfurt: Peter Lang, 2008), 258ff.

[23] For evidence of the pressure which the Ministry of Economic Affairs put on the Ministry of Foreign Affairs in several meetings of November 1956, see Aufzeichnung. Betr.: Brüsseler Integrationskonferenz; hier: Institutionen, 10 November 1956; Aufzeichnung. Brüsseler Integrationskonferenz, Sitzung der Arbeitsgruppe Gemeiner Markt, 20/21 November 1956; Sitzung der Delegationsleiter, 23 November 1956, Politisches Archiv des Auswärtigen Amtes, Berlin (PAAA), Bestand 10, vol. 929.

[24] Competition was the main policy field where the Commission was to play a key administrative role. The heads of delegation nevertheless felt it necessary to publish a statement indicating that Article 85 of the EEC treaty had direct effect. Comité intérimaire pour le Marché Commun et l'EURATOM, *Relevé des déclarations interprétatives se rapportant à des dispositions du traité instituant la communauté économique européenne et de ses annexes, ou des protocoles, conventions et déclarations qui l'accompagnent*, Brussels, 6 May 1957, Archives du Service public fédéral Affaires étrangères (ASFAE), Brussels, Doc. no. 18.881/IV/4.

set out the legal foundations for a system of European public law.[25] Looking beyond the institutional and legal detail, however, the consequences of the Treaties of Rome, nevertheless, were potentially very far-reaching. If a common market was implemented it might over time completely transform the economic and social fabric of the member states with major political consequences.

When Hallstein on 21 March 1957 reported on the Treaties of Rome to the Bundestag during the debate on ratification, he chose an optimistic tone and emphasized the progress they represented for European integration. The treaties were not of an intergovernmental nature, he assured the representatives, but created a European Community with independent powers and 'special organizational elements'. He stressed 'the eminent political character of the process and the great political possibilities resting in it'. Reminding the members of the Bundestag that the treaties were the result of compromises, and that not everything could be achieved at once, he encouraged them to trust 'in the dynamic' of the Community and in its 'inherent powers' which would contribute to bringing about an 'ever more effective fusion of the whole'.[26]

When he was elected president of the Commission in late 1957, Hallstein had the opportunity to witness his own predictions come true. Under Hallstein's leadership the Commission would pursue a strategy to gradually federalize the EC.[27] The full implementation of the Treaties of Rome would constitute the first step to be followed by an increase in the powers of the Commission and the European Parliament. Moreover, European law would need to embark on the same journey from its roots in international law to become the constitutional law of a future European federation. The Community was, as Hallstein explained at a lecture at the University of Padua in March 1962, a system that created law, served as a source of law, and constituted a legal order. The creation of law was central, because it meant that, 'in the relations between the member states, violence and political pressure are replaced by the rule of law'.[28] When contrasting the legal features of the EC with an association of states under international law and a federation respectively, he concluded that it had much more in common with the latter model.[29] Hallstein's keen

[25] This was the view of one of the strongest supporters of a constitutional and federal Europe when he analysed the treaties in 1959. Pierre Pescatore, 'Les aspects fonctionnels de la Communauté Economique Européenne, Notamment les sources du droit', *Les aspects juridiques du marché commun* 51 (1958), 51–73.

[26] Verhandlungen des deutschen Bundestages. 2. Deutscher Bundestag—200. Sitzung vom 21. März 1957. Stenographische Berichte. eds. Deutscher Bundestag und Bundesrat. Bonn. 'Rede von Walter Hallstein', 11327–34, quotations from 11328–9.

[27] Michel Dumoulin (ed.), *The European Commission, 1958-72. History and Memories* (Brussels: European Commission, 2007), 56–7.

[28] Translated by the author from: 'in den Beziehungen zwischen den Mitgliedsstaaten werden Gewalt und politischer Druck durch die Herrschaft des Rechts ersetzt', taken from Die europäische Wirtschaftsgemeinschaft ist eine Rechtsgemeinschaft. Rede des Präsidenten der Kommission der Europäischen Wirtschaftsgemeinschaft. Professor Dr jur. Walter Hallstein vor der Universität in Padua am 12. März 1962, Bundesarchiv Koblenz (BAK), N 1266/1146.

[29] Address by the President of the European Economic Community Professor Dr Walter Hallstein to the 49th Congress of the International Law Association (Hamburg, 8 August 1960), BAK, N 1266/337.

interest in, and understanding of, the legal dimension of the integration process was not only unique in the Commission, it was also decisive because it allowed the director of the legal service of the Commission, Michel Gaudet, to push for a constitutional interpretation of European law. In the *Van Gend en Loos* case, Hallstein and the Commission Collegium supported the controversial position paper developed by Gaudet.[30] Hallstein would also publicly defend the new legal revolution in a pamphlet dealing with the topic in 1964 as well as before the European Parliament in 1965. However, within a year the Commission would suffer a devastating blow in the 'Empty Chair Crisis' in the autumn of 1965, exactly at the time when it was trying to force through institutional reform. As a result, Hallstein would step down as president in 1966. The new constitutional interpretation of European law would nevertheless survive and flourish in the coming decades.[31]

To conclude, the vision and agency of Walter Hallstein were decisive factors behind the survival and ultimate breakthrough of European constitutionalism. Hallstein's professional and personal experience very much shaped the vision he pursued with regard to European integration. He contributed decisively to the establishment of a European constitutionalism in three different ways. First, he played an important role in shaping the *Westpolitik* of the Federal Republic from 1950 to 1958. Even if his influence was waning during the negotiations on the Treaties of Rome, he ultimately overcame the opposition of Erhard and secured ratification. Second, as the West German chief negotiator of the Treaty of Paris and the Treaties of Rome, he was the leading proponent of the crucial role of law and a European court in the integration process. The result may have been modest at first, creating an ECJ that was not given a full constitutional role and an incoherent system of European law based on international treaties, but he nevertheless managed to keep European law's constitutional potential alive. Third, when he became president of the Commission, he finally had the power to secure a breakthrough for the constitutional interpretation of the treaties that he had so long promoted. He supported the legal service in its work to nurture this development and ultimately defended it publicly in the European Parliament. However, despite all the work done by Hallstein to further a constitutional understanding of European law, additional agency was needed to secure the breakthrough. One particular challenge, which we shall take a closer look at in the next section, concerned the fact that European law derived from three international treaties and not a European constitution.

[30] Note à M. Jean Rey. Président du Groupe Juridique et à M. Caron. Président du Groupe du Marché Intérieur. Objet: Observations de la Commission devant la Cour de Justice au sujet des demandes préjudicielles de la Tariffcommissie' néerlandaise, Historical Archives of the European Commission, Brussels Archives Commission (HAEC, BAC) 371/1991.620.

[31] For an explanation of this cf. Morten Rasmussen, 'From International Law to a Constitutional Dream? The History of European Law and the European Court of Justice, 1950 to 1993', in Ignacio de la Racilla Y del Moral and Jorge E. Vinuales (eds), *The Dream of International Courts—A History* (Cambridge: Cambridge University Press, 2019), 287–312, at 297–312.

Petrus J. S. Serrarens: From the Bottom Up—How to Prepare the Member States for a New European Legal Order

One of the key consequences of establishing the EC by international treaties, rather than a European constitution, was that the member states would receive European law differently according to their respective constitutional clauses defining the reception of international law.[32] Considering the stark differences between the ways in which the member states received international law, it was obvious that it would be almost impossible to develop a European legal order that would be interpreted and applied uniformly across member states. Italy and Germany, for example, subscribed to a dualist reception requiring national acts, mostly in the shape of ordinary statutes, to give European law effect in the national legal order. France had a monist constitutional approach, but lacked a tradition for judicial review, which made national courts reticent when it came to applying international laws that were considered to be in contradiction with national law. In those cases, French courts asked the ministry of Foreign Affairs for an authoritative interpretation. Finally, Belgium and Luxembourg lacked any precise constitutional provision to regulate their relationship with international law and had no tradition for judicial review, which national courts would exercise if international law were to be given primacy vis-à-vis national law. Solutions to this challenge were, in both cases, developed at the court level. In Luxembourg, the Cour supérieure de justice changed the doctrine in 1954 in order to allow national courts to apply international law,[33] whereas the Belgian Cour de Cassation, in the famous *Le Ski* case from 1971, introduced a monist conception of the reception of international and European law to the Belgian legal order.[34]

A European Constitution would have solved the problem of how the member states received European law by including a clause on how primary and secondary European law should be interpreted and applied within the national legal order. This was indeed what the West German delegation had unsuccessfully attempted during the Treaty of Paris negotiations when it had tried to give the ECJ jurisdiction to handle disputes over the application of European law in the member states. Likewise, during the negotiations on the Treaties of Rome, the legal committee, constrained by the rejection of national governments of a European constitution,

[32] Most member states enacted major constitutional reforms in the late 1940s and early 1950s, which included clauses allowing for the surrendering of competences to supranational and international organisations, but generally did not ensure the smooth reception of international law inside the national legal order. France had constitutional reforms in 1946 and 1958, Italy in 1947, Germany in 1949, Luxembourg in 1956, and finally Belgium in 1970. This section of the chapter will deal with the Dutch constitutional reform of 1953 and the technical revision of 1956.

[33] Monica Claes, *The National Court's Mandate in the European Constitution* (Oxford: Hart Publishing, 2006), 45–57.

[34] Morten Rasmussen, 'At the Vanguard? Belgium and European Law 1950 to 1993', in Bill Davies and Morten Rasmussen (eds), *The History of European Law, 1950–1993. The Battle over the Constitutional Practice*, forthcoming 2021.

had to accept that national constitutional rules would define how European law was received by member states.[35] However, as we shall see in this section a solution to the problem began to emerge in the Netherlands in the mid-1950s. Behind it was another key figure in the early history of European law, the Dutch trade unionist and politician, Petrus J. S. Serrarens.

Serrarens, the son of Petrus Franciscus Serrarens, administrator in the Dutch army, and Anna Maria Christina Janssen, was born in Dordrecht on 12 November 1888. After primary school, the young Serrarens wanted to study law, but he obliged the wishes of his parents and became a teacher instead. In 1915, he joined the Katholike Sociale Actie, a Catholic social movement, where he took the position as librarian at their Leiden headquarters while also studying law at the city's university. After a stint in the military in 1917, where he was mobilized as lieutenant, he finally gave up his ambitions to obtain a law degree, and accepted instead a position as general secretary of the RK-Vakbureau, a Catholic trade union. In the 1920s, he served as general secretary of the Confédération internationale des syndicats chrétiens (CISC) which brought together Catholic labour unions across Europe and became the Dutch representative in the International Labour Organization (ILO). In 1925, Serrarens finally embarked on a political career in the centre-right party Roomsch-Katholieke Staatspartij, serving as member of the Second Chamber of the Dutch Parliament from 1937.[36] When Germany occupied the Netherlands in 1940, Serrarens refused to liquidate the CISC and went into hiding until the end of the war.

After 1945, Serrarens continued to serve as secretary general of the CISC and a member of parliament. His commitment to international cooperation had, if anything, intensified, and he became a leading proponent for European integration in the Netherlands. By 1947, he was deeply involved in the so-called Geneva circle where leading Christian Democrats from Germany and Western Europe met to initiate reconciliation and plan the future of post-war Europe. The Geneva circle included notable figures of post-war Christian Democracy such as Adenauer, Robert Schumann, and Alcide de Gaspari.[37] Serrarens also joined a Christian democratic transnational network, *Nouvelles Equipes Internationales*, and the Dutch European Movement of which he would eventually become the leader. His European convictions were outspoken in the Dutch Parliament where he supported the creation of the Council of Europe. He did not shy away from joining socialist politicians when these presented pro-European motions in the Second Chamber, demanding

[35] For the key meetings of the legal committee see: Mühlenhöver, Aufzeichnung [...]. Hier: Gerichtshof, 17 December 1956, PAAA: Abteilung II, 225-30-04, 933.

[36] Vera Fritz, *Juges et avocats généraux de la Cour de Justice de l'Union européenne (1952–1972). Une approche biographique de l'histoire d'une révolution juridique* (Frankfurt: Klostermann, 2018), 310–17.

[37] Wolfram Kaiser, *Christian Democracy and the Origins of European Union* (Cambridge: Cambridge University Press, 2007).

that the Dutch government would support the various new initiatives towards European integration of the late 1940s and early 1950s.[38]

In late 1952, Serrarens was nominated as a judge of the ECJ of the ECSC, where he served until 1958. Yet ironically, it was not during his five years spell at the ECJ that Serrarens made his most important contribution to the breakthrough of the constitutional interpretation of European law. Indeed, the federalist inclined Serrarens found himself in the minority position in the ECJ. In a court formally headed by the elderly and infirm Italian president, Massimo Pilotti, it was the German judge, Otto Riese, a well-established professor of international law, who became the natural leader of the bench. He was flanked by the strong personalities of French neoliberal economist, Jacques Rueff, and former Dutch diplomat, Adrianus Van Kleffens. As a result, the ECJ did not favour a constitutional and federal interpretation of the European law before 1958 but rather focused on technical and economic issues based on comparative administrative law.[39]

Instead, Serrarens would leave his mark on the history of European law during the negotiations of the Second Chamber on constitutional reform in early 1952. A central part of the reform concerned the possible insertion of a clause that allowed for the delegation of competences to international organizations. This brought up the question of how international law would be received inside national legal orders. In two preparatory committees, legal experts recommended the insertion of the primacy of international law vis-à-vis national law in the constitution. This was argued to be the logical codification of the established doctrine. Only a small minority in the Van Schaik committee, including a young professor of constitutional law André Donner, opposed this view and believed it to be the role of the legislator to resolve conflicts between international and national law. If national courts were allowed to implement international law that contradicted national law, they would be exercising judicial review of which there was no constitutional tradition in the Netherlands. The government reacted reluctantly to the conclusions of the reports with regard to the question of primacy of international law. The prime minister, Willem Drees, a well-known sceptic of European integration, sympathized with the minority view and rejected the idea of giving national courts such sweeping powers. When the government presented its proposal for a constitutional reform to parliament, however, the pro-European members of the Catholic People's Party and the Dutch Labour Party criticized the absence of the provision in the constitutional proposal.

[38] Annemarie van Heerikhuizen, *Pioniers van én verenigd Europa* (Diss., University of Amsterdam, 1998).

[39] Werner Feld, *The Court of the European Communities. New Dimensions in International Adjudication*, (The Hague: Nijhoff, 1964), Nicole Condorelli Braun, *Commissaires et juges dans les Communautés européens* (Paris: Librairie Générale de Droit et de Jurisprudence, 1972) and interviews with Jean-Pierre Delahousse (attaché of Advocat General Maurice Lagrange) in January 2009 and Pierre Mathijsen (attaché of Adrianus Van Kleffens) in January 2009.

As president of the European movement and co-author of the earlier pro-European motions, Serrarens stepped in and proposed an amendment to the government bill that reintroduced the primacy provision. When defending the amendment in parliament, Serrarens explained how international cooperation had typically failed due to the lack of enforcement. It was crucial that the Dutch constitution enforced the decisions of international organizations in order to strengthen the latter. Serrarens emphasized that the courts in theory were neutral with regard to applying international law correctly, whereas national governments ultimately might defend national interest instead. In the end, his amendment was accepted with a slim majority of forty-six votes in favour and forty against. Although the Dutch government accepted the amendment and eventually defended it during the second vote on the constitutional form in the Senate, the minister of the Interior, L. J. M. Beel, argued that Dutch courts should only apply international law that was 'self-executing'. This implied that international law provisions that were vague or merely formulated indirect policy objectives were not to be applied. Beel also underlined that Dutch courts were obliged to continue the tradition of avoiding rulings that concerned political questions. This view was confirmed when, in 1956, the Dutch Parliament accepted that the primacy clause should be modified so it would only apply to international law that was self-executing.[40] Despite the new limitation to the original clause, the Dutch constitutional reform would be instrumental for the development of European law. The particular constitutional framework meant that Dutch courts were keenly interested in which parts of the Treaties of Rome might be considered self-executing, because these would claim primacy in the Dutch legal order. As we shall see below, for this reason Dutch courts would play a key role in developing European law in the first part of the 1960s. The Dutch constitutional reform led directly to the *Van Gend en Loos* and *Costa v. E.N.E.L.* judgments.

The road towards solving the challenge of how the member states would receive European law was long and complex. The Dutch constitutional reforms would prove decisive. They explicitly formulated a special version of the monist position that determined how Dutch courts would approach the legal effects of the Treaties of Rome. If European legal norms were self-executing they would also have primacy vis-à-vis national legislation under Dutch constitutional law. From a Dutch perspective, it was therefore crucial to clarify at the ECJ, which articles of the Treaties of Rome were self-executing. This led directly to the seminal *Van Gend en Loos* case that helped solve the overall challenge of how the member states were to receive European law at the European level. In this chain of events, Petrus Serrarens played a key role. His long-term interest in the legal aspect of international cooperation, his long interwar experience of the strengths and weaknesses of international

[40] Karin van Leeuwen, 'On Democratic Concerns and Legal Traditions: The Dutch 1953 and 1956 Constitutional Reforms "Towards Europe"', *CEH* 21 (2012), 367–72.

cooperation and his strong attachment to European federalism very much directed his political life in the late 1940s and the 1950s. It was in this sense quite natural that it was Serrarens who, out of his support for European integration, proposed to insert the primacy of international law directly into the Dutch constitution. With the seeds of constitutionalism sown both at the European and at national level, the remaining question was how to nurture its growth in the new European Communities. We will now turn to the European civil servant who did most of the work in sowing the seeds and tending the garden of constitutional change and finally, to the judges who picked the constitutional flower.

Michel Gaudet: The Architect of a 'New Legal Order of European Law'

It was only in January 1957, after the committee drafting the Treaties of Rome had been at work for several months, that the most prominent legal advisor of the HA, Michel Gaudet, joined the fray.[41] When Gaudet browsed through the paperwork of the committee, he was initially very disappointed by the first major outline of the institutional and legal design of the new Communities developed by the team surrounding the head of the intergovernmental conference, the Belgian minister of Foreign Affairs, Paul Henri Spaak. The core notion of the new Communities was that their future development would fully depend on the political will of the member states, since the powers of the supranational institutions were to be limited. This had obvious consequences for defining the kind of legal system that could be constructed to underpin the new communities. On the crucial question of how European laws were to be implemented and applied, for example, the decision had been made to leave this almost exclusively to the national administrations and courts.[42] This approach in Gaudet's view would make it difficult to establish a well-functioning common market. As he noted in the margin of the memorandum, in order to provide the crucial legal underpinning of the common market 'a *droit communautaire*—uniformly interpreted and applied' was required. Without it, European law would be interpreted in different ways and have different effects in the various member states, to the detriment of the social and commercial actors attempting to exploit the opportunities of the common market.[43]

[41] This section builds on a longer biographical study of Michel Gaudet. See Anne Boerger and Morten Rasmussen, 'The Making of European Law: Exploring the Life and Work of Michel Gaudet', *American Journal of Legal History* 57 (2017), 1–32.

[42] The Commission would only in certain fields cooperate with national administrations with regard to the implementation of European legislation, whereas national courts would have exclusively competence over the application of European law.

[43] Note du président sur le système institutionnel dans le Traité sur le marché commun européen, Brussels, 10 November 1956, Archive of the Legal Service of the European Commission (ALSEC), Brussels. Gaudet, Communauté Économique Européenne, 3. Handwritten comments by Michel Gaudet on MAE 524/56 (Ch. Del. 50).

Gaudet's thinking was the product of several years of professional experience in the ECSC. He had entered its legal service in 1952 and over time became one of the leading authorities on European law. Gaudet's life experience qualified him in many respects for his eventual position in the legal service. Born in Paris on Christmas' Eve 1915, he was the son of a bourgeois Catholic family. His father Maurice Gaudet was an advocate at the Cour de Cassation and the Conseil d'État, and Gaudet junior was raised to enter the upper ranks of French society. During his childhood his mother Suzanne hired an Irish nanny who taught him perfect English. After his school years, Gaudet studied public and private law at the Sorbonne and political science at the l'École libre de sciences politiques from 1933 to 1937. Enlisted in the army during the German invasion in 1940, he was wounded and captured in a battle outside Paris. After his return from captivity in late 1941, he took his entry exams to the Conseil d'État, and began his service there in January 1942. Although Gaudet avoided any compromising political commitments during the difficult years under Vichy rule, he did become friends with Maurice Lagrange. The latter cut a highly controversial figure at the Conseil d'État because he had been in charge of reforming the office of the French civil service, and his proposals had excluded French Jews.[44] After the war, Gaudet obtained a position as legal advisor in the French protectorate of Morocco and would spend the next three years there. This proved a formative period for the young lawyer. In Morocco, in contrast to Algeria, France did not transfer its mechanisms of governance; instead Moroccan law incorporated elements of French law while also respecting Islamic law. Moreover, the French protectorate exercised some oversight over the International Zone of Tangier, which was simultaneously regulated by the Mixed Court of Tangier. This gave Gaudet a crucial international experience in legal pluralism and accustomed him to work in an environment of several cultures.[45]

Back in Paris in September 1948, he was promoted to *maître de requêtes* at the Conseil d'État before he finally entered the legal service of the HA of the ECSC in 1952. It was Lagrange, who had been the legal advisor to Monnet in the negotiations on the Treaty of Paris and was to become Advocate General at the ECJ, who recommended Gaudet. In Luxembourg, Gaudet quickly acclimatized to the new multinational environment. With his solid French legal training, his experience in Morocco, and proficiency in English, he was well suited to adapt and make the most of his new position. Gaudet had not been a supporter of European federalism before meeting Monnet, who interviewed him personally for the job. However, Monnet made such an impression on the young French lawyer that he soon converted and would spend a long European career fighting for those very ideas.[46]

[44] Boerger and Rasmussen, 'The Making of European Law' (n 41).

[45] Michel Epelding, *International Law and the European Court of Justice. The Politics of Avoiding History*, Paper at the Conference: Politics and the Histories of International Law, 4–5 February 2019, Max Planck Institute for Comparative Public Law and International Law, Heidelberg.

[46] Francoise Gaudet Diary (on file with the Gaudet family). See also Francois Duchéne, Interview with Michel Gaudet, Paris, 15 April 1988, Historical archives of the European Union (HAEU), INT 500.

By the time the ECJ began to receive cases in late 1953 and pronounce its first judgments in early 1954, Gaudet had already developed his own approach to the Treaty of Paris. He found that the treaty had to be interpreted in a teleological manner in order to ensure that each article was interpreted in light of the treaty's objective. This objective was, in his view, the gradual establishment of a European federation.[47] This would allow the ECJ to interpret single treaty articles that could consolidate the competences of the HA in the various policy fields, and not under classical international legal doctrine in a manner that would tend towards preserving the sovereignty of the member states. The ECSC experience was frustrating to Gaudet in so far as the ECJ generally shied away from more general conclusions on the nature of European law.[48] In addition, it proved difficult for Gaudet and the legal service to convince the most prominent professors of international law as well as national legal elites that the Treaty of Paris was of a federal character. At a conference celebrating the achievements of the ECSC in Stresa in 1957, a committee of eminent professors of international law led by Belgian jurist Paul de Visscher, concluded that European law was just a peculiar case of international law and did not constitute a new and autonomous legal order. This sparked a heated debate with members of the audience, where a number of younger scholars, who came predominately from a background in comparative law, argued that European law was autonomous and thus of a constitutional nature.[49] Gaudet would afterwards describe the debate as a battle between internationalists and federalists[50] and despite the negative report he found the debate encouraging, because a new generation of legal scholars were seemingly ready to embrace his views.[51]

To Gaudet, the negotiations on the Treaties of Rome once again showed how difficult it was to promote European federalism when confronted with the conservatism and cautiousness of national governments. However, even if the end result was not fully to Gaudet's satisfaction because the treaties did not establish the foundations for a genuine European public law, Gaudet had helped to insert several legal elements into the treaties that started the ball rolling in a constitutional direction. In the committee, he teamed up with the Italian representative, Nicola Catalano, whom he knew from their years working together in the legal service, in order to push the committee towards more constitutional solutions. A few key contributions were successfully inserted. The nature of the decision-making system,

[47] Robert Eisenberg to Eric Stein, 18 April 1955, University of Michigan, Bentley Historical Library, Ann Arbor (UM-BHL), Eric Stein Papers, Box 18.

[48] Donald Swatland to Michel Gaudet, 29 December 1957 and Letter from Michel Gaudet to Donald Swartland, 31 December 1957, Fondation Jean Monnet, Lausanne (FJM), Archive of Jean Monnet, AMK 30/3 Michel Gaudet.

[49] Julie Bailleux, *Penser l'Europe par le droit. L'Invention du droit communautaire en France* (Paris : Dalloz, 2014), 155–221.

[50] Gaudet to Stein, 18 March 1958, UM-BHL, Stein Papers, box 6.

[51] Note à Messieurs les membres de la Haute Autorité. Objet: Débat juridique au Congrès de Stresa. 3 juillet 1957, HAEC, BAC.1030.

for example, went beyond standard international law by turning the Council into a quasi-legislative organ that could rely on both regulations with direct applicability and directives to develop European public policies.[52] Perhaps, the most important contribution was the preliminary reference mechanism of Article 177 of the Treaty of the EEC proposed by Catalano. The mechanism was originally intended to facilitate the uniform interpretation of European law through references sent from national courts to the ECJ, but it also had the potential to shape how member state courts applied European law (even if that was strictly within the exclusive competence of the latter).[53] In combination with the Dutch constitutional reform, this clause would become the key driving force for producing important cases to the ECJ. Yet despite these achievements, he wrote to his American friend, the legal scholar Eric Stein, saying it had been a major challenge to convince the member states' legal elites, as well as the professors of international law, that there was something federal in the Treaties of Rome.[54]

It was not an easy task to adapt the federal interpretation of the Treaty of Paris to the new European Communities. However, as Gaudet made clear in a speech in September 1958 at the Luxembourg Faculté internationale de droit comparé, he still believed that the new Communities constituted a step towards a united Europe and should be interpreted accordingly. Moreover, the most important objective of the EC, the common market, required a solid legal order to function.[55] It was the Dutch constitutional context that really made the difference. From 1958 to 1962, the Dutch academy and courts discussed and began to explore the extent to which the treaty articles on competition policy had direct effect. This gave rise to the first preliminary reference under article 177 of the EEC Treaty, the so-called Borsch case, sent from a Dutch court in 1961. In May 1962, the Dutch supreme court, the Hoge Raad, ruled that the ECJ had the exclusive competences to interpret which European legal norms took direct effect.[56] As a result, Dutch courts fully availed

[52] Morten Rasmussen, 'Constructing and Deconstructing European Constitutional Law. Some Reflections on How to Study the History of European law', in H. K. Koch, U. Haltern Hagel-Sørensen, and J. H. H. Weiler (eds), *Europe. The New Legal Realism* (Århus: DJØF Publishing, 2010), 639–60 and Boerger, 'Negotiating the Foundations' (n 12).

[53] Catalano was well aware of this potential for Article 177. See his contemporary analysis: Nicola Catalano, *La Comunità Economica Europea e l'Euratom* (Milano: Giuffré, 1957), 37. Gaudet was probably also aware of the potential. See his positive assessment from the negotiations in: Handwritten note on MAE 838/56, Groupe de rédaction. Projet de rédaction d'articles relatifs à la Communauté pour le marché commun, Brussels, 27 December 1956, 14. LSA, Gaudet, Communauté Économique Européenne, 3 and also his analysis from 1959 in Michel Gaudet, 'Les problèmes juridiques', in *La Comunità Economica Europea* (Milano: Giuffré, 1960), 293.

[54] Michel Gaudet to Eric Stein, 18 March 1958, UM-BHL, Stein Papers, Box 6/Gaudet.

[55] Conférences. Michel Gaudet, La structure juridique de la C.E.C.A. (Faculté Internationale de Doitr Comparé, 17 September 1958, FJM, Archive of Michel Gaudet.

[56] Hoge Rad 18 May 1962, Robert Bosch GmbH et al V. De Geus and Uitenbogerd. Nederlandse Jurisprudentie 1965, no. 114–15, 437–45. See also the archival dossier on the case that reveals that three members of the court were members of the Dutch association of European law, including the judge that drafted the judgment G. Wirda, Nationaal Archief, Den Haag (NADH), Hoge Raad Archive 2.09.65, Inventory no. 180.

themselves of the preliminary reference mechanism to clarify which clauses of European primary law had direct effect and gave the preliminary reference mechanism a crucial first boost (thirteen out of the first fifteen cases were sent from Dutch courts). The second case sent was the famous *Van Gend en Loos* lawsuit, in which the Dutch Tariffcommissie, a customs court of last resort, asked whether Article 12 of the EEC Treaty that demanded a tariff standstill of the member states during the transitional period of establishing the customs union had direct effect.[57]

In the *Borsch* case in 1961, the legal service formulated for the first time its general view on the nature of European law. The Treaties of Rome were not considered traditional agreements under international law in the position submitted before the ECJ, because they had a much more far-reaching objective and included important elements of constitutional law. Consequently, the treaties had a presumption in favour of being self-executing.[58] However, the ECJ did not follow the legal service's lead on this occasion. After this defeat, Gaudet went back to the drawing board. In a memorandum, he argued that at the most abstract level all European legal norms held the same legal force because they emanated from the same legal order and the same institutions. The key objective was therefore to get the ECJ to recognize that the primary legal norms of the treaties had direct effect and primacy inside the member states.[59]

The next opportunity to put this controversial position back on the table arrived with the *Van Gend en Loos* case in August 1962. Gaudet now developed a position paper that was as ambitious as the one submitted to the Borsch proceedings but left out the constitutional language. The key message was to leave international law behind, just like Hallstein had proposed in his speeches in the early 1960s, and thus sidestep the problem related to the various ways the member states received international law. Gaudet argued that European primary law could have, depending on the decision of the ECJ, direct effect and primacy inside national legal orders if it constituted a proper 'règle de droit'. Private litigants could then ask national courts to apply such legal norms inside national legal orders or if the status of a primary legal norm had not yet been decided, ask the national court to send a preliminary reference to the ECJ. The revolutionary feature of this argument was that the ECJ would decide how European law entered the national legal orders (through direct effect and primacy). In addition, private litigants would be empowered to police the enforcement of European law before national courts. With the support of Hallstein and the Commission collegium, Gaudet was able to present his position to the ECJ, which not only endorsed the direct effect of Article 12, but also the more general constitutional interpretation of what the ECJ shrewdly chose to call 'a

57 Rasmussen, 'Revolutionizing European Law' (n 3).

58 Mémoire. October 1961, HAEC, BAC.371/1991.577–578.

59 Michel Gaudet, Applicabilité du droit communautaire dans les États members. I. L'objectif à atteindre, FJM, Archive of Michel Gaudet, Chronos 1962.

new legal order of international law' in its *Van Gend en Loos* judgment that adopted the doctrine of direct effect. A year later in the *Costa v. E.N.E.L.* judgment, the ECJ also endorsed the primacy of European legal norms with direct effect and now defined European law as constituting a 'new legal order', quasi-incidentally losing the word international.[60] In this judgment, the Court followed the argument outlined by Gaudet the year before as opposed to the position of the Advocate General, Lagrange, who instead had argued in favour of the view that the member states needed to adapt their constitutional rules to accept the primacy of European law. Given the political difficulty associated with major constitutional reforms, it was exactly this position that Gaudet's argument had so elegantly sidestepped.[61]

The contribution of Gaudet to the constitutional breakthrough in European law was a decisive one. His contribution in the legal committee during the negotiations on the Treaties of Rome helped ensure that certain elements of constitutionalism did enter the texts of the treaties, despite the political choice in favour of a more intergovernmental approach to European integration. Moreover, as director of the legal service, he did the innovative intellectual groundwork for the legal doctrines of direct effect and primacy that the ECJ would adopt. These doctrines solved the key challenge posed by the different constitutional receptions of international law of the member states and offered a solid ground on which the *droit communautaire* could build upon and which Gaudet, as early as January 1957, had believed to be essential for the construction of the common market. His professional experience and expertise, in particular his years in the legal service of the ECSC, combined with his strong political convictions, provided him with a firm background from which to promote the daring and revolutionary positions pursued in the *Borsch*, *Van Gend en Loos*, and *Costa v. E.N.E.L.* cases. As an official employed in the Commission, it is also clear, however, that his contribution was conditioned by the broader policy of Hallstein and the Commission collegium. As important as Gaudet was as the architect of the 'new legal order of European law', the ECJ still had to favour his contribution before a constitutional breakthrough could be achieved.

[60] Privately Gaudet had expressed his regret about the reference to international law in the Van Gend judgment to Pierre Pescatore. FJM, Archive of Michel Gaudet, Chronos 1963. Letter to Pescatore, May 16 1963.

[61] For a new historical analysis of the *Costa v. E.N.E.L.* case cf. Amedeo Arena, 'From an Unpaid Electricity Bill to the Primacy of EU Law: Gian Galeazzo Stendardi and the Making of Costa v. ENEL', *EJIL* 30 (2019), 1017–37.

Robert Lecourt and Alberto Trabucchi: Tipping the Balance of the ECJ

February 1963 was a turning point in the history of European law. It was time for the judges of the ECJ to finally decide the *Van Gend en Loos* case, which turned out to be one of the most divisive and dramatic judgments of the Court.[62] During the public proceedings of the case, the Belgian, Dutch, and German governments presented their opinions. They unanimously concluded that Article 12 of EEC Treaty, which obliged all member states to a tariff standstill during the transitional period until a customs union had been established, did not have direct effect because it, as in public international law, was directed to the states and not the citizens.[63] The Advocate General, Karl Römer, followed the lead of his own government. The core of his argument was that Article 12 could not take direct effect because it belonged to a number of articles in the EEC treaty, dealing with the complex field of tariffs, which were clearly addressed to the states. Moreover, it would have the most serious constitutional ramifications to grant Article 12 direct effect because not all member states handled the question of primacy of international law in a similar way. The direct effect of Article 12 would thus create legal uncertainty in the complex field of tariff harmonization, which was mostly regulated by national authorities.[64] At the Court, the judge rapporteur from Luxembourg, Leon Hammers, put forward a similar position emphasizing the contractual nature of the Treaties of Rome under public international law. When two of the most prominent members of the Court, Riese and the new young Dutch president, André Donner, supported his position, it looked likely like Hammers would sway the majority of the seven judges in his favour. Donner had been part of the minority position in the Van Schaik committee that opposed the primacy of international law during the preparations of the Dutch constitutional reform of 1952.[65] Donner, moreover, opposed a constitutional and federal interpretation of European law, which he considered to misrepresent the concrete political and social facts of the EC where state power played a central role at every level of integration.[66]

For the two newcomers at the Court, Italian judge Alberto Trabucchi and the French judge Robert Lecourt, this outcome was less than satisfactory. During the

[62] The analysis of deliberé of the Court below builds when no other references are made in an interview with Paolo Gori (April 2008, together with Antoine Vauchez) and the precious memorandum of Alberto Trabucchi published in Marco Azzalini and Claudia Sandei (eds), *La formazione del diritto europeo: Gionata di studio per Alberto Trabucchi nel centenario della nascita* (Milan: Casa Editrice Dott. Antonio Milani, 2008), 71–83.

[63] Stellungnahme der Regierung der Bundesrepublik Deutschland. E 2—Jan. 11, 1998, Mémoire du Gouvernement du Royaume des Pays-Bas, Case 26/62, at n. 71; Mémoire de l'État belge. Doc. No. D.123/E.L./N.126/S.F.1, HAEC, BAC.371/1991.2,1.

[64] Conclusions de M. l'avocat général Karl Roemer dans l'affaire 26/62, HAEC, BAC.371/1991.621.

[65] van Leeuwen, 'On Democratic Concerns and Legal Traditions' (n 40).

[66] André M. Donner, *The Role of the Lawyer in the European Communities* (Evanston, IL: Northwestern University Press, 1968), 1–27.

previous six months working together at the Court, they had formed a strong personal bond, and now jointly prepared two memoranda to counter the position of Hammers. Trabucchi, who was a professor of private law from the Università degli studi di Padova, was judge rapporteur in two related preliminary references that also involved the question of direct effect of Article 12, and had developed a clear view on the matter.[67] What concerned Trabucchi was the question of how to secure individual rights in the future common market. International law did not offer sufficient legal protection in his view, despite the fact that he considered Article 12 to be self-executing under international law. Instead, he argued that the autonomous legal order that he believed to be inherent in the Treaties of Rome had to be made explicit in order to safeguard individual rights. He also advised that the primacy doctrine which the legal service had pushed for should be put on hold for the time being, due to the constitutional problems it would pose in Italy and West Germany.[68] Lecourt backed Trabucchi. In a memorandum now lost, Lecourt is said to have underlined the EC's constitutional nature by highlighting the autonomous nature of the European legal order.[69] During the délibéré of the Court, Trabucchi managed to convince his co-national, Judge Rino Rossi, to support their alternative position,[70] and Lecourt could draw on his old Christian Democratic networks to bring the Belgian judge Louis Delvaux on board as well. In the end, four judges against three supported the *Van Gend en Loos* judgment. The *Costa v. E.N.E.L.* judgment the following year completed the legal revolution by introducing the doctrine of primacy; here Lecourt was judge rapporteur.

The sources on which the analysis of the *Van Gend en Loos* case is based do not allow us to disentangle entirely the intellectual contributions of Trabucchi and Lecourt. Let us consider in some more detail how both judges' lives and professional experiences influenced their actions. Lecourt was the politician. He was born on 19 September 1908 at Pavilly to Léon Lecourt and Angèle Lepron. After having finished high school, he was enrolled at the Faculté de droit de Caen, where he earned a law degree. In 1931, he completed a dissertation on the litigation in disputes over real estate. The lofty conclusion of the dissertation was very much in vogue with contemporary legal writing in focused on how law substituted violence, first in private law, but ultimately also between nations (the Kellogg–Briand Pact to outlaw war had been signed three years earlier in 1928).[71] Despite his

[67] Joined cases 28–30/62 Da Costa en Schaake NV and Others/Nederlandse Belastingadministratie.

[68] The memorandum is reproduced in Azzalini and Sandei (eds), *La formazione del diritto europeo* (n 62) 71–83.

[69] Interview with Paolo Gori (April 2008, together with Antoine Vauchez).

[70] Trabucchi replaced Nicola Catalano at the ECJ, who as an ardent federalist, would also have supported the judgment. However, allegedly Catalano and Rossi were at odds and it was consequently decisive for the breakthrough that Trabucchi had entered the Court and befriended Rossi. Gori, Paolo, Quindici anni insieme ad Alberto Trabucchi alla Corte de Guistizia delle CE, in Azzalini and Sandei (eds), *La formazione del diritto europeo* (n 62) 71–83, at 77.

[71] William Phelan, 'The Revolutionary doctrines of European law and the legal philosophy of Robert Lecourt', *EJIL* 28 (2017), 935–57.

academic degree, Lecourt would turn his attention towards the political world. In the 1930s, he joined the Parti Démocrate Populaire (PDP), a centre-right party in interwar France and became general secretary and later president of the Fédération des Jeunesses du PDP. During the war, he entered the resistance movement. His membership of the committee of directors of the *Résistance* catapulted him into the new provisory assembly by the end of the war. As member of the new party Le Mouvement Républicain Populaire (MRP), he would serve as member of the National assembly from 1945 to 1962 and as minister of Justice in three governments from 1947 to 1958. During this time, he became an ardent supporter of European federalism. He participated in the *Nouvelles Équipes Internationales* and joined the Action Committee for a United States of Europe organized by Jean Monnet in 1955. When Charles de Gaulle took over power in France in 1958 after the collapse of the Fourth Republic, Lecourt was once again elected to parliament and served as minister from 1959 to 1961 in various capacities in the government led by Michel Debré. Lecourt eventually resigned in August 1961, probably due to his views on European integration, which differed from the Gaullist mainstream.[72] Surprisingly, given his positive views on European integration, de Gaulle nominated him to be a judge at the ECJ in 1962, presumably because the general had little regard and understanding of the distant Court in Luxembourg. The consequences of Lecourt's nomination to the European law establishment, as we saw above, were immediate and quite the opposite of what the Gaullist establishment would have liked.[73]

Lecourt's legal thinking is difficult to trace because as a politician, he did not publish regularly on legal matters. His key publication, the famous monograph *L'Europe de juges*, only came out at the end of his stint at the ECJ in 1976. As a retrospective analysis of the achievements of the Court, it therefore carries little weight as a source to reveal his legal thinking in the first half of the 1960s.[74] What we know is that his dissertation from 1931 trumpeted the emergence of an international rule of law that would replace unilateral actions of the states.[75] In the 1950s, he had, moreover, worked incessantly to further a move towards a federal Europe. It is indeed Lecourt's efforts to imagine and promote an international legal system, or indeed a European federal system, forcing states to accept common rules and solutions, that seems to have been the central theme in his legal thinking. This is confirmed if we take a closer look at two contemporary ECJ cases, where he functioned as judge *rapporteur*, which were bookends to the famous two judgments of

[72] Fritz, *Juges et avocats généraux* (n 36) 241–9.

[73] Michel Debré to Charles de Gaulle, 1 December 1961, and Michel Debré to Robert Lecourt, 1 March 1962, Dossiers de personnes: Lecourt 1961–1962, Archives du Centre historique de Sciences Po, Paris (AHC), Archive of Michel Debré, 2 DE 11.

[74] Robert Lecourt, *L'Europe des juges* (Brussels: Bruylant, 1976).

[75] See William Phelan, 'The Revolutionary Doctrines of European Law and the Legal Philosophy of Robert Lecourt', *EJIL* 28 (2017), 935–57.

the legal revolution, namely the *Gingerbread* case[76] from December 1962 and the *Dairy* case[77] from November 1964. In the *Gingerbread* case, Lecourt by all accounts had a decisive hand in introducing the notion that the Treaties of Rome rested on an implicit 'general scheme'.[78] The nature of the underlying 'general scheme' was of course made explicit in the *Van Gend en Loos* judgment a few months later. Thus, in November 1964, when the judgment of the *Dairy* case had to be formulated, the Court, and most certainly also Lecourt as judge rapporteur, could draw upon the full consequences of the legal revolution.[79] The European legal order was not based on reciprocal rights (as in international public law), the ECJ argued, but constituted a new legal order, the rules, powers, rights, and obligations of which could not be broken unilaterally by the member states. The economy of the treaty, therefore, did not allow the member states to take justice into their own hands.[80] Hand in hand with a constitutional approach to European law also went the rights and obligations of individuals. As Lecourt argued in an article in *Le Monde* immediately following the *Van Gend en Loos* judgment, the Common Market could now be built from the ground up through litigation in a situation where Gaullist France blocked the political development of the EC.[81]

Individual rights constitute the link to Trabucchi's legal thinking. Born in Verona in 1907, the son of advocate Marco Trabucchi and Maria Zamboni, he studied law at the University of Padua. By 1928, he had become doctor of law and one of the disciples of Francesco Carnelutti, an expert on civil and criminal law. Moving from Ferrara to Venice and then to Cagliari in pursuit of academic positions, he finally returned to the University of Padua as professor in civil law in 1942. In 1948, he published a manual on civil law that would go on to become the great classic on the topic in post-war Italy. During the 1950s, a former student of his, Giulio Pasetti had joined the legal service of the HA of the ECSC, and Trabucchi was called on several occasions to represent the latter before the ECJ. Pasetti and Trabucchi would

[76] Judgment of the Court of 14 December 1962. *Commission of the European Economic Community v Grand Duchy of Luxembourg and Kingdom of Belgium*. Joined cases 2/62 and 3/62.

[77] Judgment of the Court of 13 November 1964. *Commission of the European Economic Community v Grand Duchy of Luxembourg and Kingdom of Belgium*. Joined cases 90/63 and 91/63. ERC 01217.

[78] Pierre Pescatore has argued that this case preceded the Van Gend en Loos judgment and that the linguistic style proves it was Lecourt who had authored this key contribution. Pescatore worked alongside Lecourt in the Court from 1967 to 1976. See Pierre Pescatore, 'Information Communication. Culturee, Audiovisuel', in *49 ans des Traités de Rome—colloque universitaire organisé à la mémoire d'Emile Noël—Actes du colloque de Rome 26–27 mars 1997* (Brussels: Bruylant, 1997), at 72–76 and 108–9, and Pierre Pescatore, 'Robert Lecourt (1908–2004)—Eloge funèbre par Pierre Pescatore ancient Juge de la Cour, à l'audience solennelle du 7 mars 2005', *Revue trimestrielle de droit européen* 3 (2005), 589–796.

[79] Analysing the judgment immediately afterwards in an internal memorandum, Gaudet believed the Court 'drew the consequences' of the Costa decision and the fact that European law constituted 'a new legal order'. HAEC, BAC.371.1991. Affaire 90–92/63. Note à l'attention de messieurs les membres de la commission, 27 November 1964.

[80] Judgment of the Court of 13 November 1964. *Commission of the European Economic Community v Grand Duchy of Luxembourg and Kingdom of Belgium*. Joined cases 90/63 and 91/63. ERC 01217.

[81] Robert Lecourt, 'L'Europe dans le prétoire', *Le Monde*, 23 February 1963.

also jointly publish a Codice della Comunità europea in 1962.[82] His nomination as judge to the ECJ was nevertheless highly controversial. According to the treaty rules the new Italian judge, Nicola Catalano, who had taken office in 1958, was supposed to serve until 1964. His term was cut short, however, when the Italian government asked him to resign in order to nominate Trabucchi. The latter not only had the support of the Italian foreign minister, Antonio Segni, but also of his own brother Giuseppe Trabucchi, who was minister of Finance. His nomination was very ill received in Luxembourg, where Catalano enjoyed great respect from his colleagues. Besides the textbook on European law and his limited experience as lawyer, Trabucchi had no qualification to serve at the ECJ.[83] However, as the *Van Gend en Loos* case would demonstrate, Trabucchi was able to translate his academic knowledge into good use when developing the doctrines of European law. Trabucchi's work on civil and family law, and his inspiration from traditions of roman and catholic law, led him to emphasize the inalienability of basic human rights and focus on the relation between the state and the individual.[84] It was this theme which Trabucchi focused on in the *Van Gend en Loos* case.

To conclude, the combined careers and experiences of these two figures enabled a carefully calibrated judgment which did not hasten to establish a 'full federal form', as Donner would note in his commentary on the judgment.[85] There is no doubt that the judgment went beyond simple legal analysis. The choice to interpret the underlying legal system of the Treaties of Rome as constitutional in order to introduce the direct effect of European primary law (and later its primacy) had important institutional and political consequences. The exploration of the biographies of Lecourt and Trabucchi demonstrates how closely intertwined the legal and political views and arguments were that shaped the *Van Gend en Loos* judgment. In a circular argument, the notion that an autonomous (i.e. constitutional) legal order was inherent in the Treaties of Rome and the effort to protect the individual rights of national citizens justified each other. As a result, the ECJ could introduce the twin doctrines of direct effect and primacy for European primary law in two steps and thus install a new constitutional legal order with a proto-federal structure.

[82] Giulio Pasetti and Alberto Trabucchi, *Codice delle Communità europee* (Milan: Giuffrè, 1962).

[83] Fritz, *Juges et avocats généraux* (n 36) 325–9.

[84] Paolo Mengozzi, Il rapporto tra stato e individui nella giurisprudenza comunitaria, in Azzalini and Sandei (eds), *La formazione del diritto europeo* (n 62) 111–12 and P. Grossi, in ibid., 52–3.

[85] André Donner, 'National Law and the Case Law of the Court of Justice of the European Communities', *Common Market Law Review* 1 (1963), 8–16, at 14.

Conclusion

The core narrative of this chapter reconstructs the role of five agents of constitutionalism and demonstrates how they, in different ways, were instrumental in producing a breakthrough for a constitutional interpretation of European law. Remarkably, they did so in a period from 1950 to the mid-1960s when the political and institutional development of European integration was moving in the opposite direction. Ambitious visions of establishing a European federation on a constitutional basis had to give way to a more pragmatic approach. In practice, this meant constructing a united Europe from the ground up through economic integration based on international treaties and intergovernmental cooperation with an innovative, but also modest, dose of supranationalism. Despite this political trend, the agents of constitutionalism were able to shape the development of European law in such a way that their preferred interpretation ultimately won the day. The chapter demonstrates that Hallstein was crucial in securing the inclusion of an ECJ and the development of a rudimentary legal order in the EC; as president of the EEC Commission he supported a breakthrough for a constitutional interpretation of European law. Serrarens helped develop a solution, through the Dutch constitutional reforms of the 1950s, as to how a European legal order could be interpreted and applied uniformly, despite that fact that it was based on international treaties. Gaudet influenced the design of the Treaties of Rome and would later, as director of the legal service of the EEC Commission, develop the core constitutional doctrines of the new legal order of European law. Finally, the two new judges of the ECJ, Lecourt and Trabucchi, changed the balance of the bench in favour of the new interpretation.

The chapter also revealed the deeper motives of the five men through the biographical approach that linked life experiences, world views, and legal and political practices. The interwar period and, in particular, the disaster of the Second World War shaped their outlook and political vision and led them to conclude that European integration and a European federation was the key to solving Europe's predicament. In a situation where the member states of the ECSC could not agree to take a decisive step towards establishing a European federation based on a constitution, the five actors described here found in law the tool for political change, and the technique to promote a gradual federalization of the European construction. The chapter thus highlights how European law and legal techniques could be and indeed were used by convinced federalists to promote political ends with success.

The story told here shows the multiple ways law and lawyers could influence the integration process of the 1950s and 1960s. They played an important role in the different intergovernmental negotiations by promoting the role of law and the ECJ in the integration process. National constitutional reform would indirectly contribute to the building of a coherent European legal order. The role of lawyers in the European Commission both at the presidential level and in the shape of the legal service left an important mark on the integration process. And finally, the establishment of an independent ECJ with a mandate to interpret European law created a semi-autonomous room for judges and lawyers to promote a European constitutional law still in the making. All in all, the supranational institutions of the EC were very much shaped by law and lawyers. It is not too much to say that the political battle over the institutional nature of the European construction was partly fought in the domain of law, over legal questions such as the definition of the competences of the institutions, the nature of European law, or the definition of the EC (that quickly gained a legal form in the concept of the acquis communautaire). It is thus high time that we begin to incorporate legal history into the broader historiographical narratives on European integration.

Index

For the benefit of digital users, indexed terms that span two pages (e.g., 52–53) may, on occasion, appear on only one of those pages.

Footnotes are indicated by n. and tables by an italic *t*.